P9-EJU-238

THE FREELANCER'S BIBLE

SARA HOROWITZ,
FOUNDER AND EXECUTIVE DIRECTOR, FREELANCERS UNION

WITH TONI SCIARRA POYNTER

WORKMAN PUBLISHING, NEW YORK

FOR BERNICE

LIBRARY OF CONGRESS CATALOGING-IN-PUBLICATION DATA IS AVAILABLE.

ISBN 978-0-7611-6488-3

COVER DESIGN BY RAQUEL JARAMILLO
INTERIOR DESIGN & ILLUSTRATION BY JEAN-MARC TROADEC

Names and certain identifying characteristics of individuals quoted in this book have been changed.

Workman books are available at special discounts when purchased in bulk for premiums and sales promotions as well as for fund-raising or educational use. Special editions or book excerpts can also be created to specification. For details, contact the Special Sales Director at the address below, or send an email to specialmarkets@workman.com.

WORKMAN PUBLISHING COMPANY, INC.
225 Varick Street
New York, NY 10014-4381
workman.com

WORKMAN is a registered trademark of Workman Publishing Co., Inc.

Printed in the United States of America
First printing October 2012

10 9 8 7 6 5 4 3 2 1

CONTENTS

ACKNOWLEDGMENTS

I would like to thank Peter and Rachel—who make my life so full.

To Sidney Hillman, Bayard Rustin, FDR and Eleanor, and to my Grandfather Israel and Aunt Esther, whose lives have taught me so much and who act as my northern star.

To my sister Anne and to Ron and Natalie—I love you so much—and for my nieces Josie, Sage, Paulotta, and Tessa: the next generation. To Michele Molotsky, my dearest friend.

To Toni Sciarra Poynter, who is divinely inspired in taking all forms of intuitive knowledge or ideas and expertly turning them into thoughtful, understandable, logical prose. You made this book journey a pleasure and I know that meant crazy extra amounts of work for you. Your ideas are genius and you are a good friend to boot.

To my agent, Heather Schroder, who had lunch with me for ten years before I could finally birth a book. I love your toughness and charm.

To Mary Ellen O'Neill, who added extra zing here and there and made the book leaner.

To Savannah Ashour for reaching out and gently persuading me to make this book happen.

To the team at Workman—many thanks for working your magic. And to Peter Workman, who is such an entrepreneur and steward that his publishing company flourishes amid much ruin.

To the Board of Freelancers Union—Joe Caserto, Trisala Chandaria, Ohad Folman, Andrew Kassoy, and especially to Charles Heckscher, Hanan Kolko, and Stephanie Buchanan, whose wisdom and kindness know no bounds.

To the staff at Freelancers Union, who have spirit, resolve, and dedication to independent workers. I would especially like to thank Althea Erickson, Caitlin Pearce, Dan Lavoie, Gabrielle Wuolo, Kaitlyn Newman, Gillian Sewake, Hollis Calhoun, and Jen Stern for all their great help on this book. Thanks also to Dina Sena, Diallo Powell, and Ann Boger for being great leaders and friends. And to Bob Belfort, whose legal brilliance is matched only by his wit and tolerance of my grumpiness (on rare occasion).

To those funders and friends who want to catalyze resources for great change, including Janice Nittoli, Nancy Barrand, Mara Manus, and Maria Gotsch. And to the Ford Foundation for getting Freelancers Union started and moving us forward.

To Bill Drayton at Ashoka, who shares with me a love for Bayard Rustin and for realizing that a life of persistence toward something good is truly a life well lived.

To Cheryl Dorsey and Echoing Green for setting me on the course of social entrepreneurship and catalyzing much support along the way.

To Nick Salvatore and the late Clete Daniel for giving me a deep love of labor history and for constantly reminding me that unionism is part of a social movement for all workers.

To Richard Winsten and New York State Assembly Speaker Sheldon Silver, who have made New York the most freelance-friendly state in the country. To Shelly Korman, a true legal warrior, and Jean Tom, an expert navigator through all storms.

My deep thanks to the following accomplished professionals who agreed to be interviewed for this book and who generously gave of their time and expertise—with a special thanks to Howard J. Samuels, CPA, MST, and Galia Gichon for their time and effort in reviewing portions of the manuscript:

Ilise Benun, cofounder of Marketing Mentor (marketing-mentor
.com) and author of numerous books, including *The Creative
Professional's Guide to Money.*

Erica Ecker, owner of The Spacialist (thespacialist.com).

Galia Gichon, founder of Down-to-Earth Finance
(downtoearthfinance.com) and author of *My Money Matters,*
a boxed set of affirmations, tips, and workbooks.

Evelyn Hecht, PT, ATC, president of EMH Physical Therapy
(emhphysicaltherapy.com).

John Indalecio, OTR/L, CHT.

Peggy Post, etiquette expert, a director of The Emily Post
Institute (emilypost.com), and coauthor with Peter Post of
The Etiquette Advantage in Business, among others.

Barbara Safani, owner of Career Solvers (careersolvers.com).

Howard J. Samuels, CPA, MST, KDMS LLC Certified Public
Accountants (Howard@KDMSCPA.COM).

Jennifer Shaheen, The Technology Therapist® and president
of the Technology Therapy® Group (technologytherapy.com),
creator of Tech Therapy TV (techtherapy.tv).

Brigitte Thompson, president of Datamaster Accounting
Services, LLC (datamasteraccounting.com), author of
Bookkeeping Basics for Freelance Writers.

Colleen Wainwright, a.k.a. "the communicatrix"
(www.communicatrix.com).

My sincere thanks to the freelancers who offered their personal
stories, experiences, and insights. You helped bring alive the ideas in
this book.

Finally, thanks to freelancers and independent workers everywhere, who every day find their own solutions while some still believe that they're slacker dudes wearing jammies at their computers. Little do those people know that freelancers are quietly designing the next safety net, powering the economy, and often creating pretty groovy lives for themselves.

—Sara Horowitz

Working with Sara Horowitz has been a gift. Through our many conversations and through my experiences with Freelancers Union, she has raised my consciousness about what freelancers need as professionals and as people. She has grown my faith in the capacity of human beings to create solutions where none previously existed. She has given me a close-up view of how one continues to press forward toward goals that seem very large and far away. Thanks to her and our work together, I'm a better freelancer, and maybe a better person, too.

Thanks to the wonderful team at Freelancers Union who were welcoming and helpful at every turn, especially Judy Osteller, Caitlin Pearce, Jennifer Stern, and Gabrielle Wuolo.

I would also like to thank:

Ann Bramson for recommending me; Savannah Ashour for offering me the opportunity to work with Sara; Mary Ellen O'Neill for her clear editorial insights and for her careful shepherding of this project; Dona Munker for listening, listening, and listening; Neil Felshman and Josleen Wilson for their living room couch in July, and Jos for her wisdom about "the wall"; Fern Sanford for her editorial expertise; my sister and my mother for listening raptly when our phone calls became monologues on advocacy issues for freelancers; and my husband, Donald, who, after I accomplish anything, always says, "Of course, I'm not at all surprised."

—Toni Sciarra Poynter

> "What do I like most about freelancing? The first four letters."

WELCOME!

Hello, freelancer—or future freelancer. I'm writing this book so we can talk about the rules of the road I've learned from being the head of Freelancers Union for fifteen years and meeting thousands of freelancers. I've listened as they've shared the tricks of the trade they've picked up and perfected to get ahead. I want to teach you the strategies that work.

I've also heard about freelancers' challenges and what they've done to meet them. I want to help you meet these challenges and grow. Most of all, I want to share the models for success that I've seen and provide tools you can use to make the living you need.

FREELANCERS: A BREED APART

When you ask freelancers about their work, they're likely to tell you about not just one thing, but five or six: accountant by day, singer by night, professional office organizer on weekends, accounting firm part-timer during tax season, bookkeeper for their local professional group—oh, and last year they started selling their special handmade jewelry on Etsy "just for fun"!

A freelancer is a different kind of worker from the "Organization Man" of the 1950s or the current cubicle crowd. In the cubicle world, you get an assignment, complete it, and pick up your next assignment. As a freelancer, you can and often do perform multiple kinds of paid work. You network and market to find the work, complete the work, and then bill for it (and, too often, fight to collect payment).

Once you're paid, you switch gears and become an HR specialist, apportioning every dollar into accounts to cover regular expenses and pay taxes and benefits. You also need to know how to buy health insurance, plan for retirement, implement financial planning, and structure business ventures and deals.

Freelancing is a fluid work medium that rewards nimbleness and flexibility. When it's working well, there's no better feeling. *The Freelancer's Bible* will help you find that feeling as you start, grow, and thrive in your freelance career. I'll demystify the process and help you sort through advice that often conflicts from source to source or overwhelms with detail. Given that freelancers have to do so many different tasks to do their work well, this book, curated by someone who has done the sorting and vetting beforehand, will put the essential information you need at your fingertips.

We'll talk about best practices for things every freelancer needs to know, from getting started to setting prices; from dealing with clients to dealing with taxes, health insurance, and retirement saving. I've also addressed lifestyle issues such as taking time for yourself, handling workload and work habits, and keeping connected with others.

If you're new to freelancing, this book will help you learn the ropes. If you've been freelancing for a while, it'll help you grow and expand.

I'll also introduce you to the world of freelancing—a world where you can build a community that's far more than a professional network. It's what I call your "love" network: a family of fellow freelancers that shares knowledge, resources, encouragement, and the naked truth about what's going on. Freelancing may be officially defined as working alone, but the super-successful freelancers know they're not alone. Keeping connected is key to their success.

The most accomplished businessperson you know probably has a lot in common with the stickiest website. Mainly they're helpful—with lots of connections, links, interaction, and information. They give. They build a following and enormous loyalty. You will be a freelancer with lots of links and great advice so people will come to you with ideas, help, and lots of work they need done.

A PROFESSION ON THE RISE

Freelancers are at the center of a huge shift in the workforce that has finally reached critical mass—and that's great news for freelancers:

As many as one-third of workers in the United States work independently.

How'd we hit that big number? In business days of yore, companies couldn't accurately predict workflow, so they kept workers on staff, ready for when they'd need all hands on deck. As technology helped companies better predict workflow, they adopted a "just-in-time" hiring model, cutting full-time staff (reaping colossal savings in salary, benefits, and real estate) and hiring additional workers only when necessary. Those just-in-time workers are freelancers.

As a freelancer, you face challenges staff workers don't. You're not eligible for unemployment insurance between gigs. And while companies get slammed with penalties if they don't make their payroll, no such protections safeguard freelancers from deadbeat clients. Freelancers also have to buy their own health insurance and fund their own retirement. We'll talk about how to meet these challenges.

Since the just-in-time workforce first evolved mainly in media and entertainment (and later, technology), freelancing was associated with creative work and seen as a "lifestyle choice." That euphemism conveniently allowed business and government to view freelancers' challenges as "not our problem." But the freelance wave kept growing: Between 1995 and 2005, the number of independent workers grew by 27 percent. In New York City alone, two-thirds of the job growth between 1975 and 2007 was attributed to self-employment.

Then in 2008 came the Great Recession, an economic game-changer as none since the Great Depression. Layoffs and company closings spurred huge growth in the freelance community. According to one study, in the Great Recession the number of Americans starting their own businesses reached a fifteen-year high—and most were sole proprietors.

Today, freelancing's gone mainstream. Employers rely more and more on independent workers to sustain and grow their businesses. Freelancers exist in all kinds of professions: the media, entertainment, manufacturing, health care, finance, real estate, nonprofit, and many more. They're computer programmers and nannies, opera singers and anesthesiologists. They're all ages, freelancing for all kinds of reasons:

- New grads freelance to start their careers.
- Full-time workers freelance to earn more for their kids' education, save more for retirement, or transition to a new career.

- Laid-off workers freelance while job-hunting or go solo as their next act.
- Workers leave full-time jobs to freelance for greater work-life satisfaction or more flexible hours for school or training.
- Parents who want a flexible schedule to take care of kids and/or aging parents will freelance.
- People turn their hobbies into profitable freelance ventures, making money doing what they love.
- Seniors freelance to supplement their incomes and stay active.

Freelancers are everywhere in the new workforce, finally in a position to participate as major players as our country looks for ways to prosper in a changing world economy, and to drive the changes needed to build a new social safety net that will include them.

With all this growth, you'd think there'd be an official definition of a freelancer. It turns out there are many. And that's actually a problem for your day-to-day freelance life.

JUST ANOTHER DAY AT THE OFFICE . . .

Sam Prescott loves his job as a senior VP and the team he works with at X Corp. This morning starts like most others: He buys his coffee and toasted muffin in the company cafeteria and talks sports with Ted, the guy behind the counter.

In his office, Sam's executive assistant, Tina, briefs him on messages and his calendar for the day. Then he meets with IT specialist Gordon, who has been doing troubleshooting around the company's fulfillment system. Gordon recaps feedback from customer satisfaction surveys, analyzes financial losses from shipping delays, and makes recommendations for system updates.

After lunch, there's an afternoon-long conference with Angie, who's been working for the past eighteen months on a marketing campaign for a new product, now in the countdown to launch. Angie presents her team's plan and press kit, which Sam puts in his briefcase to look over at home.

In all, a good day's work. Now, here's the catch: Only one person in this dramatization is getting a salary and benefits from X Corp. Everyone else is a freelancer. I'm sure you can guess the exception: Sam!

Let's meet the others who are making Sam's work life so successful:

Ted, a contract worker whose services are leased to X Corp. by another company.

Tina, a temporary worker hired through an agency to fill in for Sam's assistant, who's on maternity leave.

Gordon, a former full-time employee who decided six months ago to work part-time to care for an ailing parent.

Angie, an independent consultant or "permalancer," previously a full-time X Corp. employee, retained by Sam after being laid off (by Sam!) in a company downsizing.

Angie's team, a group of independent marketing consultants, copywriters, and designers to whom she's subcontracted components of the product launch.

All of these workers are skilled professionals, all helping Sam reach X Corp.'s goals (and Sam's goal of getting a juicy bonus if the product launch succeeds).

The list below, adapted from the Freelancers Union website, gives you an idea of the many faces of freelancing:

Independent contractor (aka freelancer, consultant, sole proprietor): You obtain clients on your own and provide them with a product or service.

Temp employee (via a temp agency): You work for a temp agency that assigns you to work at a client's site.

As you flip through this book, you'll notice boxes marked by various icons. The Advocacy Alerts provide often-surprising facts about freelancing and build solidarity among freelancers by clueing you in to key issues about indie life that could use improvement.

Building solidarity is tricky when there are so many different types of freelance work that even the government messes up the count! For example: The General Accounting Office (GAO) has *eight different categories* of "contingent" workers, but the Current Population Survey only tracks part-time and self-employed workers. And the Bureau of Labor Statistics, whose assessments are fundamental in policymaking, doesn't even include independent workers in most reports.

While this apparently makes sense to bureaucrats, to anyone else, it's obviously nuts to exclude one-third of the workforce from national decisions about wage payment, unemployment benefits, taxes, health insurance coverage, retirement saving, and other pressing quality-of-life issues for workers. And traditional workers are much better served in these areas than freelancers.

Thus the Advocacy Alerts. If freelancers don't stand up together to be counted, they may not be counted at all.

Temp employee (direct hire): You work in a temporary position at a company but are not assigned through an agency.

On-call or per-diem employee: You're called to work on an as-needed basis, usually to fill in for an absent employee or to help handle a heavy workload.

Part-time employee: You work as a permanent employee for less than thirty-five hours per week.

Leased employee: You work as a permanent employee for a client but are paid by another company handling payroll and benefits.

Contract employee: You work for a company that serves other firms under a contract. You work for one client at a time, usually on-site.

Day laborer: You gather with other workers in your industry and wait for an employer to pick you up to work that day.

WHENCE FREELANCE?

The word *freelance* has been part of our language for so long that we don't stop to question what *"free"* and *"lance"* have to do with working for yourself. Where does it come from, anyway? Like the flowing-tressed women languishing in the castle towers of Pre-Raphaelite art, it's an invention. *Free lance* was coined during the Industrial Revolution of late eighteenth- and nineteenth-century England when factories and machines were changing how people lived and worked. The Victorians reacted against these dramatic shifts by longing for a simpler time and creating a romantic vision of the medieval past. Sir Walter Scott originated the term in his 1820 novel *Ivanhoe,* set during the Crusades, writing: "I offered (King) Richard the services of my Free Lances" to describe knights not owing allegiance to a particular feudal lord who would offer their services for payment. The term obviously struck a chord and fit a need, because it has endured and expanded beyond a reference in a popular novel to define the resolutely self-employed, from artists to zoologists.

(STILL) WORKING WITHOUT A NET

When I started getting involved with freelance issues, I learned freelancers have long lacked the safety net enjoyed by other workers, and that differences between worker and government have been around at least since biblical times, when Pharoah refused to allow the Israelites days off for worship and stopped supplying the straw they needed to make bricks—while still (no surprise to any freelancer) expecting them to make their quota and deadline.

Even the multiname thing has deep roots. Freelancing has had many names over the generations: cottage industry, piecework, moonlighting, sideline, gig, kitchen-table business, home-based business, and paid hobby. More recently, we've added consultant, independent worker, self-employed worker, independent contractor, temp, permatemp, solopreneur, sole proprietor, contingent worker, flexible or alternative staffing, crowd sourcing, and even "Gigonomics."

All proof that the workforce has always been more varied than the economy formally recognizes. But the numbers are greater now, and the economic stakes higher. As our Freelancers Union 2011 survey of more than 2,500 independent workers found:

- 79 percent of independent workers surveyed didn't have enough work in the last year (2010).
- 44 percent had trouble getting paid their owed wages in the last year.
- 83 percent say that paying for health insurance is a challenge.

COMPARE? DON'T GO THERE!

When you start freelancing, the roller-coaster ride of freelance cash flow can be scary and stressful. It's important to realize that freelancing is its own animal, entirely different from regular paid work, with its own mindset and methods. We'll talk in later chapters about strategies that can help even out the peaks and valleys, as this freelancer learned:

Four months into freelancing, I had as much work as I could do and was so excited! But contracts took months to finalize, and payments were tied to approvals on deliverables that also took months. My cash flow was dismal. I thought these big income fluctuations meant I wasn't working hard enough—but I was going flat out. Finally, my husband, a lifelong freelancer, gave me some great advice: "You can't keep comparing your work and income to people who have salaries. If you do, you'll never feel good about yourself." It made me realize that freelancing is a business model all its own. Freelancers have to deal with cash flow fluctuations as part of the job.

I've learned that everything takes longer than I think—from landing the gig to doing the gig to getting paid for it. So I never stop networking. I start prospecting for new gigs much earlier as others wind down. I pad my deadlines if possible. I assume getting paid will take longer than anyone says—so I keep close track of my expenditures against my income. And I ask other freelancers how they negotiate to get the best deals for themselves they can.

THE FOUR OPPORTUNITIES

From listening to thousands of freelancers share their stories over the years, I've learned that while freelancers definitely face challenges staff workers don't, the changes I've described also offer big opportunities, which we'll explore in this book:

1 **The opportunity of security:** Leaner companies means more work for freelancers, more people being able to succeed as freelancers, and the potential to form a larger and more supportive community to share information and strategies.

2 **The opportunity of sustainability:** The timing is perfect for freelance life to take off. Technology can literally put your office in the palm of your hand, so you can stay productive wherever you are, use online tools to streamline your work, and market yourself around the world. Add this to the many other rewards freelancers love: the chance to choose your clients, no long commute, no corporate meetings or politics, flextime for what's

really important to you, and savings on clothes and meals, to name just a few.

3 The opportunity of leverage: The freelance surge gives freelancers clout in national decisions about taxes, wages, and benefits. When freelancers withdraw their value from the workplace, it hurts. When they withdraw their votes, that hurts, too.

4 The opportunity of community ("a hive that thrives"): With the leverage of numbers, a more stable income, and a fulfilling lifestyle, there's the opportunity for what I like to call "the love." This is the camaraderie independent workers have long extended to each other to inform, support, engage in healthy and ethical competition, and foster a climate where freelancers succeed. At Freelancers Union, we call it "a hive that thrives." This unity, I believe, is the foundation for building long-term sustainability for freelancers as individuals and as an organized, recognized group.

A PUSH, A JUMP . . . WHO CARES?

Whether you found freelancing or it found you; whether you left a job or were let go; whether you fled to freelancing or fell into it—the freelance life can be the life for you. Millions have done it, millions are doing it, millions more will. You can be one of them. Setting yourself up for success is what this book—and Freelancers Union—is all about.

FASCINATED BY FREELANCERS: MY STORY

It was a combination of father/daughter insomnia, a smart mom, an activist granddad, Quaker schools, peeling potatoes and breaking dishes, living on a kibbutz, law school, and being misclassified as an independent worker that made me so passionate about freelancers.

When I was a kid, my father and I loved to stay up late talking politics (we really were insomniacs). Having spent his life in and around the labor movement as a labor lawyer, he was fascinated by all things pertaining to work—history, policy, and people—and so was I. And because of his age (he was born in 1918), he brought alive the social movements from the 1930s through the 1960s—the pivotal decades of the New Deal and the civil rights movements.

To that, my mother added what I think a child needs most: a hug and a push. An independent spirit who left home at a young age to live and work on her own, she was scrappy. She let me know in the most loving way that a) I had things to do in life, and b) she expected me to do them. From her example, I developed a mantra that keeps me going through tough times at work even today: "Take a deep breath, get a glass of water, and put one foot in front of the other."

Although he died before I was born, my grandfather, Israel Horowitz, lived on in the family lore for his longtime activism as vice president of the International Ladies Garment Workers Union (ILGWU)—and for his fondness of another phrase every dedicated worker can relate to: "Excuse me, but I'm allergic to bullshit."

I attended Quaker schools, where there was a pervasive idea that global change through individual effort was not only possible, but necessary. I went on to study labor issues at the School of Industrial and Labor Relations at Cornell, where I became involved in labor and union work. There I learned the fundamentals of organizing and mobilizing groups (my first assignment involved unionizing the kitchen staff at a nursing home—long story involving lots of potato peeling capped by a dessert-tray crash of biblical proportions—I was a far better organizer than kitchen aide).

Then I lived for a time on a kibbutz, where I saw, essentially, a model of the hive: individuals working according to their strengths for the betterment of the whole. What struck me most was the beautiful fluidity and seamlessness of it: The parents saw their children a lot more, taking meals and breaks with them. I also noticed the sense of well-being from a life lived doing work you love: I've never seen seniors happier, healthier, or more engaged. It was so different from the segmented model most of us grew up with: Go to school, get a job, maybe take a break to have kids, retire.

All this reached critical mass when, after law school, I got a job in a small law firm that misclassified me, with some others, as an independent contractor! As you'll learn in Chapter 6, companies that misclassify workers as independent workers when they're doing the work of full-time employees gain huge tax savings. For the worker, however, it means no health benefits, no unemployment insurance, no retirement plan, no wage protection. When it happened to me, I was livid. We dubbed ourselves the Transient Workers Union. We even made up mock letterhead—and my fellow members named me president.

I wanted to know why things like this could still happen. Why are so many workers in the new economy underrecognized in so many ways? How can we set up systems that answer the needs of the new, fluid workforce, help nontraditional workers help themselves, and prevent their exploitation? I went to Harvard's John F. Kennedy School of Government on an intellectual sabbatical of sorts. By the time I emerged, I had the beginnings of the structure that would become Freelancers Union.

When I founded Freelancers Union in 1995, freelancing was viewed as either a euphemism for being unemployed or for being a slacker dude hanging out at a café with a laptop. But times have changed. As mentioned, one-third of the workforce is now independent. As this book is published, membership in Freelancers Union, a nonprofit organization dedicated to serving and advocating for independent workers, stands at nearly 200,000 nationwide. The numbers are there for a true movement.

We define Freelancers Union as "a federation of the unaffiliated" because we seek to combine the independent spirit and diversity of freelancers with the community that freelancers savor and, we believe, need in order to flourish. We also aim to develop and implement programs to help freelancers enjoy a more stable life as they pursue work they love.

To that end, in 2001, Freelancers Union started offering health insurance to freelancers, and in 2008 we launched Freelancers Insurance Company, providing health insurance in New York state. Freelancers Union has also been selected to sponsor nonprofit health insurance companies called CO-OPs in New York, New Jersey, and Oregon in 2014. The Freelancers Retirement Plan, the first 401(k) plan for freelancers, was launched in 2009.

Freelancers can't rely on companies for training. They have to be self-starters and mentor themselves and one another. So we offer seminars on everything from taxes to marketing. Freelancers connect, collaborate, and share info via our job board and discussion groups. Our Client Scorecard lets members rate clients and alert unsuspecting fellow freelancers to potential problems, and our member-sourced Contract Creator helps freelancers negotiate an agreement that's fair to them.

On the advocacy side, the leverage of our growing membership helps us lobby for fair treatment for independent workers, from cracking down on misclassification to pushing for tough punishments for deadbeat clients.

Our symbol, the beehive, reflects the ideal we hold for the freelancer's world: a community of individuals where the well-being of all and the well-being of each are one. Helping freelancers achieve well-being, singly and collectively, is my mission in writing this book.

THE FREELANCE LIFE

Much has been written about employees navigating the demands of work and home. It's a pretty artificial distinction these days, as people bring work home on weekends, check in with the babysitter from the office, and make phone calls to boss, clients, mate, and kids during their commute. Many will tell you that feeling pulled between the domains of work and home is a big stressor.

Those domains don't exist in the freelance life, where your home may be your office, your family may be your staff, friends may become clients, clients may become friends, and fellow freelancers may become coworkers.

It turns out when that artificial work/home boundary is dismantled, as happens for freelancers, life can get a lot richer and more satisfying.

The Freelancer's Bible is structured to reflect the full spectrum of the freelance life:

When you look at them in the graphic below, you might see that you move back and forth on this spectrum a lot during a typical freelance workday.

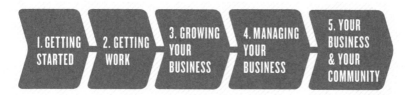

Here's a possible example: You spend the morning working on a project (Getting Work). Then you head out to a doctor's appointment, where you answer emails while you wait, and run some personal errands on the way home (Your Business and Your Community; Managing Your Business). At home, you finish and send out your monthly email newsletter (Growing Your Business) and call a few freelancer friends for negotiating advice on a contract (Getting Work). Then you pick up your child from school and make a run to the grocery to pick up supplies for a cookout, where you talk with several parents in your neighborhood about setting up a babysitting co-op to trade off after-school and weekend child care (Your Business and Your Community).

Sound familiar? Some days it might feel like you're scrambling to keep up. But on the good days, it's invigorating, liberating, and fun. And you wouldn't trade your freelance life for anything.

My goal in writing *The Freelancer's Bible* is to help you have many, many good days.

TALK TO US!

Almost everything I've learned about freelancing has come from freelancers themselves. We want to hear from you—your experiences and opinions about the freelance life, your questions, your problems, and how Freelancers Union can help. Here's how to reach us:

sara@freelancersbible.com

Freelancers Union
20 Jay Street, Suite 700
Brooklyn, NY 11201
Tel: 718-532-1515
Fax: 718-222-4440
freelancersunion.org

A NOTE ABOUT CHANGE

The freelance world is constantly changing. While I've made every effort to provide current information as of this writing, the story of freelancing is fast evolving. To find the latest news and information, please visit the Freelancers Union website (freelancersunion.org), as well as contacting the other organizations and resources listed in this book, as we continue to advocate for the recognition and positive change that freelancers deserve.

PART 1: GETTING STARTED

Chapter 1

SEVEN START-UP STEPS

Fire, ready, aim. That's the phrase I often think of when freelancers tell me how they got started. There's nothing sweeter than landing that first gig. You, rainmaker. *Yesssss*.

But you don't want to spin your wheels. Wasted motion, for freelancers, is money lost. This chapter will help you launch a calmer, more successful, more satisfying freelance life.

Maybe you've heard or read that you can't make it as a freelancer unless you work and network 24/7, thrive on risk and rejection, are a fierce negotiator, and can do your own IT.

Ridiculous.

I've known freelancers who work around the clock and freelancers who shut down at close of business . . . freelancers who love to network and freelancers who've learned to network . . . tough-hided freelancers and tender-hearted ones . . . computer geeks and technophobes. They're all freelancers. They all make it work.

So forget the myth of the Perfect Freelancer. There are no perfect freelancers. But there are smart ones. That's what the questions below are about.

STEP 1: KNOW WHY YOU'RE FREELANCING

WHAT ARE YOUR GOALS?

Do you want to make significant money, or supplement the family income? Do you want to grow your career, or taper down? Do you want to freelance on a limited basis (i.e., be a part-time freelancer) in order to have more family time? If so, can you still make the income you need, or will you need to change your lifestyle?

Being clear about what you want from freelancing will help you embrace it: "I'd always wanted to be a freelancer—I loathed attending meeting after meeting in sunless offices. As soon as I could, I ditched the corporate digs to work from home. I loved that I could focus on putting in exactly as much time as a project required and then go for a walk, run errands, or even take a nap."

If you need courage to take the leap, knowing your objectives can help: "I'd been working in corporate America for as long as I could remember and was mentally and physically exhausted. I'm also a single parent and felt it was essential that I be present during my child's middle-school years. The only way I could find to do that was to take a flying leap into the unknown and start my own business."

Finally, your goals will be your baseline for all the major freelance career decisions we'll talk about in this book: what kinds of projects you pursue, your rates, your work pace, and your marketing strategy.

DO YOUR DREAMS AND REALITY MATCH?

Now think about your ultimate life aspirations. As a freelancer, how'll you get there from here? "Look at your industry realities squarely against your dream lifestyle," one freelancer advised. "I moved out of the city, and for people in my profession, moving far away is a problem. Can you really live in that fantasy cabin in the woods and still make the same good living, even in these days of virtual everything? I couldn't. My revenue was cut in half within a very few years."

On the other hand, freelancing's inherent flexibility may offer unprecedented freedom to live life on your own terms: to pursue multiple work interests rather than being locked into a single career path; to hit the road without having to ask the boss for time off; to pick up and move in order to live closer to family . . . or in the climate you prefer . . . or where your favorite sports or activities are plentiful . . . or where taxes are lower or health insurance more affordable. With research and planning, you may find an exciting new life is within reach.

ARE YOU BURNED OUT OR COMING OFF A LAYOFF?

Take some time to sort things out. Working at a company can be killer stressful. Bad bosses, tight budgets, lack of flexible time, and other dissatisfactions have eroded workers' confidence and sense of pride and reward in their careers. That's a draining place to be.

Unless you've been building an exit strategy, you may have no idea what your goals are, or whether you can get there as a freelancer. People will ask what's next—sometimes because they're nosy, but often because they want to help. Test the waters: Tell them you're "looking at a lot of options, including working on my own." You might find gigs faster than you think: "I told a literary agent, 'I'm open to another corporate job, but I'm looking at going out on my own, too. I'm a very hands-on editor, and I also write. I've written a relationships book—' 'You have?' he interrupted. 'I'm looking for a writer for a relationships book.' That's how I got my first gig."

FREELANCERS SPEAK **Burned Out, Walked Out ... Worked Out!**

For a lot of people, the leap from unstable, unsatisfying company job to freelancing isn't as crazy-scary as it used to be:

"The company where I worked wasn't doing well. People were getting fired, and the environment had become toxic. I applied for a job in another division, but then thought: *Do I really have what it takes to give 150 percent to a new job right now?* I wanted to have kids, and I realized it made more sense to build a freelance business than devote myself to another in-house job. I withdrew my application, quit, and went freelance. One day, as a freelancer, I was sitting on my couch at home in the sun reading some really interesting research, and I thought, *I can't believe I get paid to do this!* "

"My employment ended abruptly after a public blowup with the boss's pet. Turned out my departure coincided with a travel promo where for $600 you could fly as often as you wanted for a month. I visited friends all over the United States. I met with someone who became a core freelance client, plus an old friend who became one of my editors at a popular magazine. It was one of the coolest things I've ever done."

STEP 2: FIGURE OUT YOUR KEY STRENGTHS

Technology can make the world your client. A click sends a project from your crib in Kokomo to a glass tower in Tokyo. Of course, it works in reverse, too: Companies have their pick of the indie talent pool. How will you stand out?

HOW SHARP ARE YOUR SKILLS?

We aren't all excellent, and we aren't all excellent all the time. Do you need to get up to speed, get training, retool, recertify, add credits? The greater your skills, the higher you can set your prices. If you're working full time, carve out some time and money for some skill upgrades while you still have the security of the regular paycheck. If you're already freelance, you might have to take midlevel gigs while you save for that workshop, class, or certification. Talk to some successful freelancers about what kind of training or retooling they recommend.

ARE YOU NEW TO WHAT YOU DO?

If you're new to your work or coming back after a hiatus, you may need to set your rates lower at first to get clients and experience: "I figured out what to charge for copywriting from a friend who's a copywriter. I lowered his rate by about thirty percent, since he's a career communications guy, and I was transitioning back into copywriting after nearly a decade."

Consider working part time to stabilize your income while you grow. Could be clerical work, waitstaff work, retail sales during holidays or tourist season, filling in for employees on vacation or maternity leave, or temping at companies going through a hiring freeze. "I waited tables at night and took my portfolio around in the daytime. Gradually, I built my freelance design work, getting one assignment in, then three, then ten. Having that part-time job allowed me to build the funds to promote myself and buy equipment. It was also a good lesson in managing with just the basics and getting creative about becoming visible in the industry."

MAKE A LIST, CHECK IT TWICE.

Make a two-sided list. One one side are the skills you love to use and could happily exercise daily. On the other side are skills you don't enjoy as much, but they're in your bag of tricks.

Include *all* your skills, from *all* the parts of your life, that you can legitimately offer for a fee. Freelancing lets you bring the whole you into making a living. All sorts of abilities can pay—including stuff you've never thought of charging for (helping kids with their math homework . . . fixing things around the house . . . figuring out frozen computer screens) or stuff you love doing (knitting, cooking, coaching, improv, making playlists for your friends, or taking the best pictures at parties). In fact, the whole you may turn out to be hugely important to your freelance success. There are two sample lists on the next two pages:

Your Key Skills List will help you see different ways to market yourself and find the project mix likely to be most satisfying. Is there work you love that others find not-so-fun? Congrats—you might have just discovered a high-paying niche.

Sometimes the best-paying skills aren't ones you like the most. In lean times, you might tap your "Other Skills" column more. But ideally you shouldn't "live" there for too long: "I was a book packager for about a year. I hated every minute of it. I was an agent for six months but was terrified to negotiate. Eventually, I realized that if the main aspect of my work was making me unhappy, I had to change it because I wouldn't relish it."

Hey—if you want to be unhappy with your job description, go work for a company!

WHAT ARE YOUR TOP-RATED SKILLS?

Competence doesn't make clients want you. You want to be irresistibly valuable. Think of someone you know who is an amazing professional. There are probably one or two things they do that they're absolutely the best at—the things you mention when you rave about them to others.

What are those top-rated skills for you?

Recall a work achievement or obstacle you've overcome. Pull out the value results:

- Did you do it faster or more efficiently?
- Was it safer . . . more beautiful . . . more ingenious . . . more "out there"?
- Did it save money . . . make money . . . gain customers?

SAMPLE KEY SKILLS LIST 1

PREFERRED SKILLS	OTHER SKILLS
Editing books and articles	Editing brochures, ad copy, press releases
Writing books and articles	Writing Web content
Project development	Project management/production
Teaching editing/writing/publishing	Fact-checking; research
Proofreading	Transcribing
TV/film script doctor	TV/film script reading
Character actor/understudy	Theater usher
[et cetera]	[et cetera]

SAMPLE KEY SKILLS LIST 2

PREFERRED SKILLS	OTHER SKILLS
Financial analysis and accounting, corporate	Compliance assessment
Financial analysis and accounting, small business/start-ups	Bookkeeping
Nonprofit accounting	Tax preparation
Business plan consulting	Data entry
Math teacher/tutor	Teaching accounting/bookkeeping
[et cetera]	[et cetera]

- Did it find a new market . . . win votes . . . win awards?
- Was it an against-all-odds on-time delivery?
- Did it produce a perfect result from a mess of mistakes?
- . . . or what?

Your top skills create your reputation—which drive your marketing message, your negotiating leverage, and your pricing. Employees can hide their mediocrity inside the bureaucracy. You, freelancer, are out there. Clients learn fast who's excellent and who's phoning it in. If you want them to return and bring their friends, provide value.

KNOW YOUR METRICS.

We live in a data-obsessed world. The more measureable your work successes, the better.

- How much did sales increase?

- How much traffic did your campaign drive to the website?
- How much time was saved?
- How much money was made?
- By what percentage were losses reduced?
- How many bestsellers have you worked on?
- How many design awards have you won?
- How much grant money have you raised?

Ask clients (or coworkers, if you're transitioning from a staff job) if there are sales figures, financials, or other measurable results from your work that you can use in self-marketing.

CAN YOU SPECIALIZE?

Specialization heightens reputation. Is there a very specific product or service you know customers want? You want that well-paid specialist to be you.

Really get into brainstorming this. Maybe you perfect a gourmet mini-cupcake recipe that's the surprise hit at the parties you cater. Voilà! You're the go-to chef for luscious finger-food desserts. Or you wed your training as a videographer to your love for music and make music videos for new bands. Or you specialize in physical therapy for the elderly, with a subspecialty in PT following hip surgery. If training or certifications would help, budget for them (see Chapter 15 for info on taxes and professional education).

The best specialties are where your skills and passions intersect. "I know a dancer who's also a writer," one freelancer told me. "He writes dance reviews, blogs on dance, designs related websites, and is starting to teach dance. It's so cool to watch him build his career by combining these things he loves."

You can—and should—have multiple specialties. It'll tide you over through dry time and make you a rainmaker year-round. The mini-foods chef might be snowed under with holiday catering gigs. Come summer, she morphs from chef to teacher, teaming up with a kitchenware store to lead classes on grilling and fancy picnics. She can also handle computer emergencies and tutor the inexperienced. Most of us have disparate abilities like this. Tapping them all is one of the great joys of freelancing. Stumped for a specialty? Not sure if yours is marketable? Check freelance job boards and employment listings for posts relevant to your skills and interests.

CAN YOUR SKILLS TRANSFER?

Work drying up in your biz? Let others wring their hands. Be nimble. Jump to a different pool. If you're an architect struggling in a housing slump, maybe you help homeowners save money and improve their property value by making their homes more energy- and space-efficient. If you're a real estate agent in the same market, maybe you and the architect team up to do community seminars and you share your contacts list to find those homeowners, taking a percentage of the fee.

Others may miss these connections. But you, nimble freelancer working outside the box, are more likely to discover income opportunities hidden in plain sight.

WHAT PERSONAL TRAITS ENHANCE YOUR SKILLS?

Communicating well, being able to lead and follow, to problem-solve, be curious, and keep your cool—all these are part of your freelance identity, too. They improve with experience and are often what clients remember best about you. They're the basis of your reputation and are what will ultimately distinguish you from other, equally talented workers. Sometimes you can boast measureable results: You drive a monster project to the finish line and it becomes the company's holiday bestseller. Other times you'll get glowing references and testimonials. Build these traits by spending time with people who embody them. Read up on qualities of leadership, teamwork, and social and emotional intelligence. Consider taking some personality assessment tests to help identify your particular strengths.

STEP 3: FIGURE OUT YOUR CUSTOMER'S NEEDS

Don't you hate people who are always selling? Or the nice but clueless who drone on about their work? We pitch their cards when we get home.

This, of course, will not happen to you. Because *you* know:

THE THREE ESSENTIALS OF GETTING CLIENTS

The best freelancers hit this trifecta:

1 They're empathetic in their analysis of what their clients need.

2 They've matched their skills to those needs.

3 They've distilled it into a pitch of utter simplicity.

Go back and match your skills, your metrics, and your specialty ideas to what your market needs—not what you think they *should* need, but what they *actually need.* If your specialty is "I'm the most detail-oriented freelance animator in town," but your customer's need is "We need it fast, not perfect," you'll quickly become the most detail-oriented unemployed freelancer in town.

What's important to them, and in what order? Speed? Efficiency? Accuracy? Beauty? Durability? Luxury? Affordability? Simplicity? Health? Security? Reliability? Profitability? For hints, look at:

• Feedback on your work
• What others say when recommending or complimenting you
• Why prospects decline your services
• How people in your field describe others they see as excellent or inferior

If your customer isn't happy, it won't matter that you beat out fifty other freelancers for the job. Besides, your fellow freelancers are a community that could be helping you. More on that later.

NOW, SAY IT FAST!

Now that you know your freelance identity/ies, come up with one succinct sentence that says what you do. Sometimes it's called an elevator speech. Or think of it as a "tweet." Here are some to get you started:

"I help people prepare to publish."

"I design costumes, restore textiles, and lecture on fashion history."

"I develop websites, with a special focus on helping small businesses move their online presence to the next level."

WHAT'S IN A NAME?

If you want to give your business a name besides your own, to avoid brand confusion and possible legal hassles, make sure it isn't already in use and that it's not trademark or service mark protected. Check local listings and online sources such as Switchboard (switchboard.com) and The New Ultimates (newultimates.com). Your state's website may have the secretary of state's database of reserved corporate names. Log onto the U.S. Patent and Trademark Office (USPTO) website (uspto.gov) for a free trademark search. Consider paid searches of databases such as Trademarks, Etc. (trademarksetc.com). For best assurance, consult a patents and trademarks lawyer. For an overview of the issues, check out the Small Business Administration's article "How to Name a Business" (sba.gov).

STEP 4: KNOW WHAT YOU'LL CHARGE (MORE OR LESS)

"How I set my prices in the beginning was simple. I guessed."

Sound familiar? Your goal isn't just to pay your bills, but to be paid what you're worth. We'll get you started here, but it's something you'll continue to evaluate throughout your career. In Chapter 5, we'll talk tactics for discussing money with prospects and in negotiations. And in Chapter 17, you'll learn about taking freelance finances an important step further: making money today *and* saving money for tomorrow.

You've already taken the first step in pricing: knowing your skills and your value. Also, look at the norms in your profession. Fee structures and norms vary widely, but here's a rundown of common fee structures and their pros and cons:

COMMON FEE STRUCTURES AT A GLANCE

Type: Hourly

Pros: Accommodates variable job scope. Less stressful to negotiate, since the rate is fixed. A rush rate can be established for time-sensitive jobs.

Cons: Penalizes skill and speed: The faster you finish the job, the less you're paid. No rate flexibility for a challenging project or client. It can be hard to predict your income. Clients may dislike open-endedness. And you may reach a market ceiling that doesn't reflect your abilities.

Type: Unit- or quantity-based (per word, per foot, per dozen).

Pros: Once calculated, easy to negotiate.

Cons: Penalizes you on jobs that are small in size, yet complex or time-consuming. Not flexible for rush schedules unless you set a rush rate. No flexibility for a challenging project or client.

PRICELESS ADVICE One reason finding out about pricing is so difficult is because laws restrict activities that could result in overcontrol of an industry or restraint of free trade. For example, the Sherman Antitrust Act prohibits industries or groups from engaging in price fixing. The only exceptions are unions, and it was a hard-fought political gain to demonstrate that workers uniting to agree on pay scale doesn't restrain trade.

One of Freelancers Union's goals is finding ways to establish some reasonable pricing practices or standards so freelancers aren't operating so much in the dark, and so they have some leverage against market forces that tend to push prices as low as possible. Otherwise, pricing becomes a race to the bottom—and the bottom could be an income that puts freelancers' standard of living at modern-day Dickensian levels.

Sharing info with other freelancers about pricing and deal making is priceless not just because it helps you get paid what you're worth, but because it helps *all* freelancers be paid what they deserve: "If we don't talk about money, we're at the mercy of low-balling clients who drive down the value of our work. We've divided and conquered ourselves."

Here's what other freelancers had to say:

"Soon after I became a freelancer, I joined a small networking group. In one meeting, one member stated what she charged per hour. There was this short silence. Then conversation resumed. And a member whispered to me, 'I'd *never* charge that much!' We were all doing similar work and had similar levels of experience. So, why *wouldn't* she charge as much—and why weren't we all talking about it?"

"It was hard to set fees because I had no frame of reference. Luckily, friends who'd been freelancing awhile helped me figure it out. But there's definitely been some trial and error. I undercharged for one project—I won't do that again. Ask as many freelance friends as possible for advice on what to charge."

Type: Project fee

Pros: Can be tailored to job scope and client. Enables you to predict your income. Adjustable, depending on personal financial requirements, available time, market changes.

Cons: Can be difficult to calculate. Must renegotiate if job scope changes, unless ranges or provisions are built in to handle "scope creep" (incremental or sudden increases in project specs or requirements).

Type: Pricing package(s). *Example:* X amount will buy X/Y/Z service(s)

Pros: Can be posted publicly. Streamlines negotiating, since many clients can select the package or choose from a menu of services. Less time is wasted negotiating with tire kickers. May be efficient with a long-term client you know well.

Cons: No flexibility for challenging project or client.

"I worry if my fee's too high, people won't hire me. If it's too low, they won't think I know what I'm doing."

Type: Minimum amount

Pros: No need to negotiate. Useful for a small project that wouldn't be cost-effective otherwise. *Example:* a carpenter going to the client's house to put up a single shelf.

Cons: Little recourse in a dispute over project scope or duration.

Type: Day rate

Pros: See Minimum amount, above. Efficient if your work is specialized (i.e., the projects have similar scope) and if you've correctly calculated your costs, overhead, and project requirements. Can be broken into time increments spaced over a longer period. *Example:* a day rate of $1,000 for an eight-hour day can be broken into four hours a week worked over two weeks.

Cons: You may be underpaid if the job scope outpaces your rate, or if you've miscalculated your costs or overhead. Can be difficult to raise once word gets around about what it is.

Type: Percentage of profits

Pros: Potential for ongoing income after project is complete.

Cons: Risk of no income, unless a recoupable amount is paid up-front.

FREELANCERS SPEAK **Pricing with Pride and Purpose** Think of all the nail-biting employees do around negotiating their salary. Now multiply that by every gig for freelancers.

Undercharging hurts you and other freelancers in your profession by dragging down what your skills are worth in the marketplace and conditioning buyers to expect lower prices. Help hold the line in what the market will bear: Price yourself right! It's not only a matter of calculating what you're worth, but *accepting* it:

"I love the work, and I hate talking about the money. But I've realized that I deserve to earn a decent living, and that it's important to be forthright about money."

"Be fearless about charging high. Other people are already charging more than you are."

"After several years of barely beating insolvency as a freelancer, I discovered I'd adopted a very constrained earning ideology: To win, I only had to 'make ends meet.' If I needed another $1,500 to make my monthly expenses, I'd seek $1,500 and, in many cases, get it, nothing more, sometimes less.

"But what if I started quoting my jobs not to meet just my financial obligations, but to meet my financial desires? What if I wanted to make $80,000 a year, and the only way to make that amount was to actually *charge it*? Plus expenses! The first quote I generated using this philosophy was $5,000 to help a company name a new product and assist with their concept art. The job would take an estimated three weeks, or roughly 6 percent of my work year, so the quote was easy. I had my floor and displayed confidence in it—and it paid off, leading to a nine-month contract at $5,000 per month plus expenses!"

FIGURING OUT FEES

Whatever rate structure you choose, it should take into account the following:

Billable time: I can't emphasize enough how important it is to know how long specific tasks take, whether or not you actually quote an hourly rate: "I based my prices on an hourly rate, even though I didn't necessarily relay that to the client. It was a baseline."

Purchases connected with the project: Unless the client agrees to buy them, these could include supplies, ingredients, ad space, domain names, photo research and procurement, or any other expenditure you have to lay out to complete the project. If you bring especially strong knowledge or skill to the task, such as photo research, your price might reflect that.

Overhead: This is a percentage of the proverbial "what it costs to keep the lights on." It includes everything that enables you to live and be in business, from your mortgage or rent to your Internet bill to your insurance to your accounting costs, equipment, marketing costs, and more.

Your profit: This added percentage reflects your value: your experience, your specialty, or that certain something that distinguishes you. It may grow as you grow: "I do a lot of writing projects for my main client that only take thirty to ninety minutes. I've realized that I'm adding more value than I'm being paid for. The changes don't take much time, but it's clear that they're pivotal to the way the material and messaging are understood."

How much you charge for profit also depends on industry norms, your region, your level of excellence and expertise, what you want your annual income to be, and what percentage of your annual earning time this project is likely to take.

Market considerations: You can be the best on the planet but be sitting idle if there's no demand for your kind of work, your industry's in a slump, or the same work can be had for much less. The larger economy affects demand for what you do, as does the type of client: "I learned when the economy was good, it was good to set my prices high. When companies were paying as opposed to individuals, I charged more. My hourly rate now is a hundred dollars less than it was in 1983 because when I started I had very little competition."

Having a specialty can help stabilize your income against market changes because it's perceived as having higher value. Value-adds such as degrees, certifications, training, and awards help, too.

CALCULATE YOUR RATE

Below are some guidelines and resources you might find helpful in getting a handle on your rates. But this is definitely an art, not a science. Run your numbers, talk to your peers, trust your gut, and learn from experience. Everyone else does. If there were set formulas for pricing, it would be illegal and called price fixing.

The Freelance Switch Hourly Rate Calculator is an online tool that helps you get a great start on calculating your hourly rate. Developed by Freelance Switch and Errumm Web Consulting, the tool walks you through plugging in your annual business costs, personal costs, the number of hours you'll work (allowing for vacation, holidays, and personal or sick days), and your desired level of profit or savings. Then it does its calculating magic and gives you a break-even and an "ideal" hourly rate. From there, you can fine-tune the results using your knowledge about your profession and the marketplace. Type into your browser: freelanceswitch.com/rates.

In their book *The Designer's Guide to Marketing and Pricing,* Ilise Benun and Peleg Top provide a clear step-by-step process for calculating a basic hourly rate derived from your desired salary, your business overhead, billable hours, and desired profit—which you then adjust based on other factors in play (the nature of the gig and the client, how fast they need it, et cetera).

You really need to personalize this for yourself, but a very general equation to keep in mind is:

(annual salary + annual expenses + annual profit) ÷ annual billable work hours = your basic hourly rate

---

Annual Salary: How much would you like to make?

Annual Expenses: Your rate must cover your business overhead. Remember to include taxes and health insurance. What about living expenses? For ways to figure a reasonable estimate for taxes and your monthly living expenses, see Finances for Freelancers in Chapter 17.

Annual Profit: Benun and Top point out that profit isn't the same as salary. Consider your salary a business expense (paid out to you as your own boss). Profit is charged over and above your expenses. Benun and Top suggest 10 to 20 percent as the norm.

Annual Billable Work Hours: Allow for vacation, sick time (including the kids'), and weekends off. And "billable work hours" means project work time, not time you spend doing administrative or other non-billable work—so figure a percentage of total hours.

Basic Hourly Rate: This is for you to know, not your client (unless you're comfortable sharing). You might use it as a guide for coming up with a project fee. And you can adjust it based on any number of factors: your experience; how fast they need the job done; how high-maintenance the client will be; how this project would advance your career, et cetera.

Are you wondering how high to set your rates—and how to raise them with clients you've worked with in the past? If you're new to your field, right out of school, need someone to take a chance on you, or are trying to break into a higher level of client, you'd likely be in the low-to-middle range, increasing with experience.

If your fees are high or super-high, you'd better be excellent.

It's cool to be a middle-of-the-pack worker if you're OK with a middle-to-lower pay range. Since you'll be in a larger pool of free-lancers looking for gigs, you'll be more vulnerable to market slumps, when there are fewer projects to go around. If you need to make more money, your choices are either to increase your project volume or raise your value (skills, experience) so you can raise your prices.

It can be tough to raise rates with existing clients. If the client's a steady income source, it may not be worth jeopardizing your relationship for an incremental rate increase of, say, 10 percent. Instead, prospect for new clients and quote higher for them. Maybe you'll find a new steady. Then you can negotiate with the lower-paying client from a more secure place financially.

FIVE FEE-SETTING STRATEGIES

1 **Track your time.** Task by task. You can track it pencil-to-paper or use an online tool (try searching under "personal time tracking," "free time tracking software," or "time tracking freeware").

2 **Avoid feast or famine pricing and know your rock bottom.** Find the zone that reflects your value, but leaves room to negotiate. This means doing market research and getting a sense of job scope and, if possible, budget from the client before you crunch numbers (we'll talk about talking money in Chapter 5). Going too low or too high causes stress and costs time. "When I've undercharged, I feel taken advantage of, even though I know it's my fault." Or: "I once spent days pricing out a project. When l laid it out on the phone to

the prospect, there was dead silence. Then he said, 'Wow. We're way far apart.' The call ended fast, with disappointment on both sides."

Also know your lowest number—the one you won't go below, no matter how great the gig is.

3 Do your homework. Learn the benchmarks for rates in your industry. Some professional organizations post info on their websites (for example, the Editorial Freelancers Association: the-efa .org/res/rates.php) or have a legal/contracts arm that can offer negotiating help. Check industry discussion boards and professional networking sites where people swap stories and strategies, and magazines and books, too: "When I started freelancing, I often referred to various industry standard books, like the *Graphic Artists Guild Handbook of Pricing and Ethical Guidelines.*"

You can even talk to trusted pros who use services like yours: "I had breakfast with an agent who's also a friend, and asked her if my rates were OK. I was relieved to learn I was in the upper third of what she usually gets for her clients—and really glad I'd raised my rates from where I'd begun."

4 Educate the client about what you're worth. Calculating and communicating your value to your clients is your job: "I see it as a service to my client to be clear about what I'm worth and why. It's not their job to know what I do. A really good freelancer makes it look effortless. So I make sure my clients know something of the skill and thought that go into my work. It shows my chops and shows that I care."

5 Don't fear fluctuation. In some industries, it's pretty much "one price fits all" for a given task. But if there's a price spectrum, quote 'em as you see 'em. Do you see hours of meetings and revisions in your future? Think of the cost to you of serving that client—the time you won't have for other projects, plus the aggro factor. And if it's your busy season or you're cramming this

BUILDING A FREELANCE MIDDLE CLASS For employees, performance reviews and promotions serve as built-ins for improving economic security. Freelancers have to build their own economic sustainability, client by client, year by year. A single big job, underpaid—or worse, unpaid-for—can wreck the most careful budgeting. That, plus an industry or economic downturn, or a personal or medical crisis, can spell financial disaster. That's why it's essential to have a community of freelancers around you to help you gauge whether you're undershooting on pricing, and why we must advocate for government policies that support greater economic security for freelancers.

gig onto a full plate, that can be another reason to raise prices.

On the other hand, will this gig boost your career, add visibility, or give you a new skill? Do you believe in the project and want to help it happen? Do you need work? All are valid reasons to allow a discount.

STEP 5: WORK OUT YOUR BUDGET AND DO ANY NECESSARY PAPERWORK

Why didn't I make this the first step? Because I didn't want it to stop you from envisioning your future as a freelancer. Now that you've done due diligence about your skills and your value, you're in a better position to look at the fit between freelancing and your finances.

WHAT'S YOUR PERSONAL BUDGET?

First, pour yourself a drink. Then get your checkbook, your credit card and bank statements, and any other financial records from the last twelve months.

If you want to make a detailed budget right now, check out the My Budget chart in Chapter 17, and the instructions for filling it out. To download a customizable family budget form, check out BizFilings's Business Owner's Toolkit's "Personal Monthly Budget Worksheet" (toolkit.com/tools) or look for other examples online. What follows are some basic strategies for measuring freelancing against your finances.

Use your records to make a list of your family's expenses month by month, from mortgage or rent to vacations and medical bills (if there's an unanticipated expense in a given month, such as a big vet bill thanks to your beagle taking on the neighborhood Weimaraner, exclude that as a one-time cost). You'll quickly see how much you need to earn per month to cover your expenses at home—including months where you'll need extra cash for tuition or other large sums that are due. Obviously, you should be looking for places to cut costs if necessary.

If you're employed right now, write down your income (and your partner's, if you have one) and break it out month by month.

Now, revise the income numbers to reflect freelance income. Suppose you'll be freelancing full time while your partner works. Subtract out your employment income and you'll quickly see the shortfall each month. That's what your freelance work needs to bring in to meet expenses.

But freelance work doesn't always bring in the same amount each month. That's why you need to be saving to pay expenses, plus for taxes and retirement. You'll learn more about all this later in the book, but for now, know that each check that comes in from a client, you'll want to apportion into these buckets (you'll learn how in Chapter 17):

- For emergencies
- Retirement
- Estimated taxes
- Expenses

"Have a pla Have significan savings. Have some clients lined up."

WHAT'S YOUR BUSINESS BUDGET?

Now let's look at what it'll cost to start your freelance career.

List any necessary start-up costs, from "one-time" costs such as equipment to "ongoing" costs such as supplies. Some will be unvarying "fixed" costs such as insurance; some will be "variable" such as shipping costs. To find free start-up calculators online, search under "start-up costs calculator."

GET SET FOR TAXES

We'll talk bookkeeping and taxes in Chapters 14 and 15, but during your start-up, whether you're doing your own taxes or hiring an accountant, attend to the following:

"I made a mess of my finances. I'd suggest checking out an adult education program about handling money. I did."

Show you mean business. The IRS wants to make sure you're not dabbling at a hobby and deducting it as a business, so one assessment it applies is whether you report a net profit in a minimum of three out of five years. Since that can be a tall order for a start-up, there are also standards to assess whether you're putting in time and effort to make this a profit-making endeavor. Keep a business diary of all your appointments, client sessions, and project deadlines; have business cards, promotional materials, website, or other items showing you're going after business, and:

Start right with record keeping and accounting. From the get-go, keep careful records and receipts of every business-related expense. You'll need them as documentation if you itemize business-related tax deductions.

Separate your business and personal accounts. This will put all your work-related income and expenditures at your fingertips for financial planning, your accountant, and just in case you're audited.

Home in on your home office. The IRS has specific requirements for deducting expenses pertaining to business use of your home. For starters, your home office needs to meet IRS rules of exclusive and regular use as your principal place of business. So the dining room table or den where you also watch TV won't cut it. For more specifics, see Chapter 2. And if you're game for some scintillating reading, see the IRS's "Tax Topics: Topic 509: Business Use of Home" and IRS Publication 587, *Business Use of Your Home* (irs .gov), which even has a handy flowchart.

PERMITS, LICENSES, AND REGISTRATIONS— NEED 'EM?

As part of your prelaunch due diligence, make sure you have the official paperwork you need. For example:

Business structure: Generally freelancers start as sole proprietors and later decide whether it makes sense to structure themselves as an LLC (limited liability company) or incorporate (see Chapter 10). The other options involve legal paperwork and specific duties and paperwork going forward. If you have any questions about which structure's right for you, consult a knowledgeable lawyer or accountant. The best way to find one is by asking a couple of established freelancers. Also check out the guidelines in Chapters 5 and 15.

Business permits, licenses, and registrations: It's very possible you'll need one or more of these. Make sure. Look it up using the "Search for Business Licenses and Permits" tool from the US Small Business Administration (SBA) (sba.gov). Requirements vary by industry and location. Also check state licensing requirements at CareerOneStop under "Licensed Occupations" (careerinfonet .org), sponsored by the US Department of Labor, Employment and Training Administration.

Sales tax and seller's permit: You may need to collect, report, and pay county, city, or state sales tax (or in some states, a sales-type tax) on your product or service. If so, you'll also need a seller's permit (also called a resale license or certificate of authority) so you don't have to pay sales tax if buying items from wholesalers for resale.

STEP 6: GATHER YOUR BRAIN TRUST

Find the trusted inner circle who can help you as you launch and grow, offering advice and ideas, referring prospects, problem-solving, and cheering you on. It could be fellow freelancers, company buddies, relatives. They should be people you feel you can be totally honest with. Your Brain Trust has your back and you've got theirs: "When I started freelancing, a former coworker-turned-freelancer took me to lunch and was incredibly encouraging—and forthcoming about pricing. Another advised, 'Give it a good six months to get rolling' and told me where to order great-looking business cards online. Another spent forty-five minutes coaching me through a big negotiation, even though she was on a deadline. Now I answer questions from a guy who calls me his 'freelance mentor.' It's like there's this chain of people helping one another, opening up to let newcomers in. I'm so moved by how generous these freelancers have been. And it makes me want to be that way myself."

"One thing I loved about working in a company was being surrounded by people whose brains I could tap into. Now I have to provide that for myself."

STEP 7: MAKE YOUR GAME PLAN FOR GOING PUBLIC

When I started Freelancers Union, it was pretty much just this crazy idea hatched from my years of studying labor, history, and politics. When I told people what I wanted to do, I'd get this blank look, like, *Whaaaat?* I learned that I had to put some friendly distance between certain people and what I was doing. We still stayed in touch; I just didn't bring them into the discussion about what was going on in that part of my life.

With indie workers comprising one-third of the workforce, the time's long past for viewing freelancing as a euphemism for slacker dudes or the unemployed. Surround yourself with people who are practical and positive about freelancing. There'll be some who say the wrong thing for the right reasons: They care about you and want everything to be great. For others, though, it might be a case of envy. Questions like: "How can you afford it?" "What about health insurance?" or "Isn't it lonely?" might seem undermining or depressing. But often people who ask them are secretly wondering how someone might actually make freelancing work. So talk about it. Not like you have to defend yourself, but like any businessperson having a serious business discussion: what's great about it, what's challenging about it, how you're going about it. Who knows, you might be giving them the information and the courage they need to take the leap.

TELLING FAMILY, FRIENDS, AND COLLEAGUES

You'll share the news a little differently with cousins than with work colleagues. But here are the common denominators:

1 **Tell everyone.** The first law of freelance life: Everything is a marketing opportunity. Don't be shy about saying you're building

your network and looking for work: "Here's what I'm doing/here's my card/here's the link to my website, if you know anybody who needs this kind of work." People will want to help. Give them what they need to spread the word.

2 Don't be pushy. Watch out for the glaze-over that says they've heard enough. They're people first, prospects second.

3 Make it professional. Start strong. Have your one-line or short pitch polished. A great first impression takes seconds and lasts years.

IT'S IN THE CARDS

Your business card is your stand-in, reminding people of how you can help them. Between make-your-own templates and online ordering options that let you choose from a bewildering array of colors, fonts, and decorative motifs, getting your business cards may be your first serious foray into the fine art of freelance procrastination. Your card can be simple or info-packed. To figure out what's right for you, remember what a business card is for. It's meant to explain and remind others about:

- Who you are
- What you do
- Your unique value
- How to contact you

Consider what contact info to include. Real estate agents pretty much live on the phone, but a writer may decide a phone number isn't essential and just include an email address. Consider privacy, too: "Most of my business is done by email. Pretty much the only reason clients need my address is for mailing a check—so I put that on my invoice."

Here are some other options:

Lure them with links. If you have a website, professional blog, are active on social media for business reasons or are listed on a professional networking website, include the links. Watch out for using too many. Two or three is a good number; more than that and people don't bother looking up any. If you have your own website, that's the one they'll look up and all you need to include.

See both sides. With two-sided printing, you can put your contact information on one side and a tagline, bullet points, or distilled elevator speech on the other.

A picture's worth . . . If your image is part of your professional identity, a profile picture could work. It's a good idea to use the same image in all your media. If a photo is not part of your work, then it may look odd or unprofessional to include it.

Quick Response (QR) Codes on cards. These two-dimensional codes can contain hundreds of times the data of a conventional bar code. Contacts with the appropriate app on their smartphone can scan the code and get your contact info—or links to your website, images, videos, or music—so people who meet you can immediately save your data or take a deeper dive into what you do. Generating the QR code itself is generally free; putting it on a print item such as your business card or other promo piece would be part of your printing costs.

Go digital. A virtual business card eliminates the chances of your business card ending up in someone's garbage can, because the data goes digitally directly from your device to the recipient's. While it's fast and green, not everyone networks this way, so carry physical cards for contacts who prefer those. To find apps and services online, search under "virtual business cards."

And here you are, ready to go. Trust yourself. Have confidence in what you know as a pro. Whatever else you need to learn, you'll learn. Welcome to the ranks!

"My husband and I are both freelancers, working at home. Our house has a pool and we spend all year looking forward to enjoying our pool and our backyard. During the summer, he'll walk down the hall and poke his head in my office, at six o'clock or five o'clock or sometimes even four, and say, 'Are you ready for a dip?' And I can say yes. Because I'm a freelancer."

Chapter 2

YOUR OFFICE SETUP

For years, independent workers camouflaged their freelance status, paying to join plug-and-play offices with impressive mailing addresses and executive-style meeting spaces. That's when freelancing had second-class status, compared to having a "real" job. Now we know freelancing *is* a real job. And no one cares anymore whether you work in an office, at home, in a car, or in a café. It's not about where you work, but how well.

With these shifts has come an explosion of new ways to work, from communal workplaces to worker-friendly office products and designs, making independent work way more productive, comfortable, and fun. In this chapter, we'll cruise the options, wherever you call your freelance home.

QUIZ: WORK AT HOME, OR NOT?

It depends on what you can afford and how you work best. Some questions to consider:

1 Can you afford to rent space or cowork?

2 If you meet clients in your office, how will they (and you, and your family) feel about being in your home?

3 If your profession has workspace standards, can you meet them, working from home?

4 Do you have special requirements, such as having noisy equipment, needing 24-hour package reception, et cetera?

5 Will kids or family responsibilities pull you off-task at home?

6 Do you tend to get distracted by chores, hobbies, and stuff to do?

7 Do you get cabin fever if you don't get out of the house?

8 Are you more productive when you're with others?

9 Do you need total quiet for work?

10 Do you have a network of colleagues and friends to connect with?

Some people love working at home. When they want to meet people, they make a date to do so. Otherwise, they just focus on work.

Others find it isolating and prefer the energy that comes from having other working bodies nearby. If this is you, try these low-cost alternatives:

• Create a schedule that takes you regularly to the library, a favorite café or public space, or even a park bench.

• Build your Brain Trust and network so you can call people for input or just to talk.

• Join a coworking space.

• Rent office space with another indie.

• Work a part-time job until you can afford a rental.

THE HOME OFFICE, ACCORDING TO THE IRS

If you work from home, you might be able to deduct your home office on your taxes as a business expense if it meets the IRS's definition. If so, a proportion of your home costs, such as mortgage interest, rent, and more, can be deducted as business expenses. That lowers your business income—which lowers your self-employment taxes.

THE BIG IRS HOME OFFICE RULE: EXCLUSIVE AND REGULAR USE

In order for a home office to be deductible, the IRS requires the space be used for your business on an exclusive and regular basis (exceptions: storing inventory or using part of your home as a day-care facility). "Exclusive" means that the space, whether a full room or a designated area of one, isn't used for any other purpose. As for what "regular" means, think about it. You don't use this space sometimes. It's where you work.

You need to be able to answer "yes" to one of the following:

• You do most or all of your work there. If you work elsewhere, you need to be able to prove that your most important work's done in your home office.

• You meet clients there regularly.

• There's a separate structure on your property that you use only for business.

• You're using your home regularly to store product samples or inventory. (This is allowable only if you don't have a workplace or outside office you go to.)

• You operate an at-home day care center for children, adults aged sixty-five and older, or people who can't take care of themselves. This has to be a regular, though not exclusive, use.

In the end, the home office deduction and everything that comes with it shouldn't be guessed at. Check with your accountant to make sure you're eligible.

DO YOU MEASURE UP?

Make sure you know the size of your home office in relation to the size of your house, since this affects the proportion of home expenses you can deduct.

Below are two calculation methods often used. Try both to determine which gives you the greater deduction:

1 Rooms:

---

number of rooms used for your work ÷ total number of rooms in your house (excluding closets, other storage, and bathrooms) = percentage of household expenses you can deduct

---

2 Square footage (assuming the rooms in your house are approximately the same size):

---

square footage of your work area ÷ your home's total square footage (entryways, halls, stairs, garages, and attics can be excluded) = percentage of household expenses you can deduct

---

HOME OFFICE TIPS FOR TAXES

If possible, have one room just for your freelance work, so you've got the exclusive use rule totally handled. If you have to carve out space in a larger room, strategically located bookcases, files, sofas, or screens can help cordon off workspace from living space.

Once your office is set up, shoot some pix. You can also make a basic floor plan of your home, highlighting your office area. These can help support your claim (and your math) if questioned.

Keep great records showing that you seriously pursued your business (i.e., it's not a hobby) from this space; for example, dates and times of client meetings, business cards, invoices, client proposals, and correspondence on letterhead showing your home office address as your official business mailing address. Keep receipts and bills for any household expenses you'll be claiming as deductions (for details on bookkeeping and taxes, see Chapters 14 and 15).

Check out the IRS's explanatory publication on the home office: IRS Publication 587, *Business Use of Your Home*. For IRS information for child care providers, see Child Care Tax Center (irs.gov/businesses/small/industries).

Like any business, you have two zones to protect: your physical office space and your virtual one. For the home-based freelancer, that means taking extra steps to secure the place where you live.

Increase insurance. Find out what your homeowners or renters insurance covers for your home office. You may want to get coverage especially designed for a home-based business. Losing a business on top of a home is a real risk for a home-based freelancer, so think about what you need in the way of coverage.

Shore up safety. Protect against fire and water damage. Some examples: smoke alarms, fire extinguishers (including in your office), water sensors.

Strengthen security. Consider upgrading your door and window locks or investing in a burglar alarm system. Even just adding a lock on your office door boosts security. Ground-floor office? All this goes double.

Defend your data. Get a quality shredder that shreds paper and disks. Get good antimalware protection and keep it up-to-date. Passwords can protect your network router and block access to your computer and to specific files (you can keep passwords in an unmarked address book or journal, or in some other hard-copy form, hidden in a place only you and another trusted person know). If necessary, consult a security-smart IT person about file encryption, software that can shred data, and other protections. Be sure your equipment is UL-listed (meets Underwriters Laboratories' safety requirements)—important for insurance reasons, among others.

Have a disaster plan. If you had to pick up and leave fast, do you have important papers, licenses, permits, and certificates, passwords, backup files, and your laptop case ready to go? Think what you'd need to be up and running quickly, and what documents you need to keep on file or in a secure place off-site.

RENTING SPACE

Here are some questions to ask:

Can I afford it? Cost it out; talk to your accountant or financial adviser. Can you bring in the income every month to pay the projected new cost?

How about sharing? Talk to a potential office mate or two. You might even formally team up: She's the career coach; you're the résumé whiz. Whatever you do, have a written agreement with a termination clause so no one is left with a lease they can't afford alone.

Where's best? Someone displaying merchandise needs a different setup (good foot traffic? window space?) than a therapist who sees clients (private and quiet? safe, easy parking?). Make a must-have list.

Can I work here at night and/or on weekends? Is the building open? Secure? Heat or air-conditioning on?

Are there any zoning restrictions or ordinances that could restrict my business?

What services does the lease include? For example: security, cleaning, telecommunications, and utilities? If utilities aren't included, ask the utility company for usage and billing history. Ask if you'll need to pay a security deposit on utilities.

How are mail and other deliveries handled?

What are local insurance rates?

What's the minimum deposit?

If I don't want to continue the lease, how far in advance must I notify the landlord?

Can this space grow with me?

WHAT ABOUT COWORKING?

Coworking—communal office spaces where indie workers can drop in, hold meetings, hang out, or hunker down—is a worldwide phenomenon. In a world where small is not just beautiful but powerful, coworking provides the right-size space to get you out of your own little silo. You can hatch big ideas without the financial drag of renting space yourself—a good move in an economy merciless toward those who grow too fast.

> "My favorite workplaces have been shared studio spaces. So much time is spent alone as a freelancer; it's nice to have that human and professional connection."

Since coworking is about community, different spaces have different characters, policies, and pricing. Some focus on a specific profession or group. Some host events—screenings, parties, meet-ups. Some offer tech support and local discounts or access to equipment or communications.

Designs range from workstations to family-style tables. Some are sleek and modern; others are laid-back with a video game setup and sofas for dreaming up your next big idea. Think of it as a freelance village. Who do you want your neighbors to be? For more info, see the Appendix.

MAKING YOUR WORKSPACE WORK

Most freelancers are so busy that their office kind of grows up around their projects. If you're peering over piles of stuff, you know this doesn't work once things get rolling.

A few key workspace decisions can boost your efficiency and comfort big-time. They don't have to cost a lot. And they can work whether your desk is a door slung over sawhorses or a teak heirloom; your files are stackable crates or sleek laterals; or your computer is a battered laptop or a triple-screen, Starship Enterprise setup.

For more info on office setup and management, see Chapter 14.

MAKE IT REFLECT YOU

Not for you standard-issue office-drab. Will your workspace be country or chrome? Cool or hot colors? Zen-calm or cozy? Browse furniture and office stores to get a sense of your style. Comb thrift shops for affordable vintage pieces, or look on Craigslist and eBay.

SIZE COUNTS

Most people underestimate how much space, surface area, and storage they need. Piles are a major source of inefficiency. Give yourself room to grow—because you will. Order two instead of one; large instead of small.

If space is limited, think vertical: shelves, lateral and stackable files, cubbies, bins, or slatwall for mounting the tools of your trade within reach.

To keep your work surface uncluttered, find auxiliary space nearby to stow things you don't need daily, but use often enough that they shouldn't be far away—such as reference books, printer and desk supplies, stationery, or art supplies. You might recruit nonoffice furniture for this—a bureau, a vintage medical cabinet, or an armoire.

"I work on my computer," you say. "I don't need much desk space." What about writing checks? Opening mail? Sorting photos? Assembling a presentation? Typing from a document? Untangling a medical billing issue? Paradoxical but true: Having space to make a mess can help organize your thinking and your work.

So, what about a desk with a return or a work surface at a right angle so you can do tasks on the side, set them aside, or move your computer aside? How about a work surface, drawers, shelves, or files directly behind you?

Or save your pennies and have something made: "After years of trying to combine desks and tables in a satisfactory way, I finally special-ordered a ten-foot parson's table. Best piece of furniture ever for a writer or editor. Other than that, the less said about my office, the better."

WHAT'S YOUR 24/7/360?

What goes on your work surface? Only items you use daily (24/7), in arm's reach all around you (360 degrees). If you're an accountant, you'll want your calculator there. A writer may only need a calculator to invoice or bid on a job. Drawers were invented for things you need on hand, but not in sight. Be firm: If you don't use it all the time, it doesn't make the cut.

ASK SARA

Q Dear Sara, I know my workspace should have "good ergonomics," but what does that mean, exactly?

A Good ergonomics helps you work well and feel great doing it.

Ergonomics relates to the safe and efficient interaction between people and things they use—in this case, you and your workspace.

Your body notices every change in its environment: "When I varied from my usual sitting spots for a few weeks last month, I ended up with lower back pain from a chair that was wrong for my work needs."

A bad ergonomic situation, uncorrected, can lead to debilitating physical problems. Your workspace should accommodate you, not the other way around. And since you're the center of the action, do yourself the favor of sitting correctly, working correctly, and taking breaks. It's important to get up and move every hour or so. You can set an alarm to help you remember.

THE KEY COMPONENTS OF YOUR WORKSPACE

There's no one workspace arrangement that's right for everybody, but what follows are ergonomic principles to keep in mind. Check out "Computer Workstations" on the U.S. Department of Labor Occupational Safety and Health Administration's website (osha.gov).

SURFACE DISCUSSION

Kitchen tables or folding tables are for noshes, not eight-hour workdays. Here are some guidelines for work surfaces.

"My workspace is a long library-style table where I can spread out. I have a big, flat computer screen that makes me feel like I'm in command central."

• If your desk height's adjustable (including for standing), that's great. You should be able to move your legs comfortably and scoot in close enough to easily reach your keyboard. Your desk should be deep enough to fit your computer keyboard and monitor (if not, investigate a computer tray) and so your monitor can be at least 20 inches away from your eyes. Generally, that's about 30 inches total. It shouldn't be so deep that you overreach to grab your phone, pens, or anything else you use a lot.

• If your computer's your main weapon, keyboard, monitor, and mouse should be in front of you. When you're seated, feet flat on the floor, your desk surface should be at about elbow height.

BE SEATED

Kitchen or dining-room chairs and folding chairs aren't body-friendly for hours of work. Make sure the small of your back (lumbar spine) is supported and in a neutral position, whether by adjusting the chair back so it follows the lumbar curve or buying a lumbar cushion: "I had back pain, so I bought a lumbar pillow for my chair. Best thing I could do for my workspace." Even a pillow or rolled-up towel can work. Some ideals to aspire to:

• The chair back should follow the curve of your lower back and shouldn't interfere with your arm movements.

• For the seat: Figure approximately 16 inches high, 15 to 17 inches long, with contoured, rounded edges, especially on the front edge, so there's no impeding of circulation. You shouldn't have to slide forward to put your feet flat on the ground, since that makes it harder for your spine to keep its curve (try a footrest).

• Ideally, all parts are adjustable, it swivels 360 degrees, and it travels smoothly on casters. A five-legged base gives good stability.

• The best armrests are padded, removable, and adjustable for distance and height.

• Avoid chairs with radical, fixed shapes that limit how you can sit.

You don't need to break the bank when buying a chair—but your chair shouldn't break you. It's best to shop for it in person. Bring something to read. Sit in the chair for 15 minutes or so, ideally in front of a table or desk in the store. Adjust whatever is adjustable—height, arms, back. Adjust the armrests for a 90-degree angle at the elbow; check that you can position your arms and hands properly for typing or whatever work you do. Swivel and scoot. Can you work in this chair? Will it help reduce your body's fatigue? Do you want to take this chair home?

CHOOSING YOUR PHONE

Whether you use a cell phone or a land line, there are logistical and tax reasons for separating your business and personal calls: You won't be fighting your family for phone time, family members won't be picking up business calls, and you won't be interrupted by personal calls.

A dedicated business cell phone or phone line also makes it tons easier to document your professional phone costs for tax deduction. You have better things to do than untangle personal calls from business calls on every bill.

"I'm incredibly lucky to have the second bedroom as an office. It's dedicated completely to my work and my style and features a lot of items that express who I am."

If you go the cell phone route, the smarter your cell phone, the more mobile your office can be, letting you make calls, check email, and use productivity-boosting apps.

If you're super-busy or travel a lot, services can cover your calls, forward calls to a designated number, deliver messages, book appointments, and more. They're called remote receptionists or virtual receptionists and are easily found online.

Whatever phone you use, you'll be using it a lot. So I'd like to add a "Be Kind to Your Trapezius Day" to the national calendar. On that day, people wouldn't clench their phones between neck and shoulder.

Your upper trapezius is that big, sloping muscle running from the back of your neck to your shoulder joint. Shrug, sling on a backpack, burp the baby, or just balance your head on your shoulders and you're using it. The trapezius can do a lot of things well. Holding a phone isn't one of them. Phone clenching contracts neck area muscles involved in breathing—you need those for breathing deep and thinking fast on a tough phone call. It even causes headaches and jaw pain. Does any of this sound good to you?

If you're on the phone a lot, a hands-free headset lets you type, review documents, tie your running shoes, or stir the soup while you're talking: "I slipped a disk in my neck and the orthopedist told me to get a hands-free headset. What a difference! I had no idea how tense I was from clamping the phone against my shoulder."

ILLUMINATING IDEAS

General lighting should be diffused so you can easily read your computer screen, and not flickering. Window lighting should be at right angles to your monitor.

Task lighting can save energy and money. At the computer, use limited task lighting, positioned to avoid screen glare. A screen glare filter can help.

For task lighting on print, go for larger-area, bright lighting, directly on the documents, on the left if you're right-handed and vice versa. Ideally, brightness and angle are adjustable.

TECH TALK

Your technology decisions will depend on the kind of work you do, but here are some general points.

Know who you'll call for troubleshooting. "I'm not terribly tech-savvy, so I find computer problems challenging. I often call designers I used to work with for help with layout issues." Chances are, someone in your Brain Trust can help or can recommend a computer geek. Maybe as a group you could retain someone, or have him or her give some tutorials. Also, post tech questions on professional or product discussion boards.

Shop for the best Internet service deal you can get, at the speed you need. Generally, faster is better, but website developers' needs are different from writers', for example.

Go wireless. It gives you flexibility in your office design: computer, printer, keyboard, et cetera, don't have to live right next to one another.

Find a multifunctional printer. Some people need professionally printed stationery, but many freelancers prefer to print their own. If your printer doubles as a scanner, you can scan your receipts for tax documentation. Many models copy and fax, too.

See how software stacks up. Make a list of your current and future work needs—Accounting? Writing? Mailings? Blogging? Talk to others in your field about what they use, what they like, and why. Many software programs offer free versions. Try before you buy.

Splurge a little. For fun, or to work smarter or more stress-free. Maybe you want great speakers for music while you work, or headphones to screen out noise: "I splurged on high-quality headphones because I like to work in cafés and libraries but I transcribe a lot of interviews and need to hear perfectly. Now I can work anywhere I want." For the cost-conscious, check places like eBay and Craigslist.

MONITOR PROGRESS: YOUR SCREEN

Your monitor should be in front of you, 20 to 40 inches away, with the top of the screen at about eyebrow height. Adjust contrast, brightness, or font size to keep from constantly leaning forward or squinting.

A laptop stand with a wireless keyboard (see Just Your Type) is a great way to put a laptop monitor at the right height. It also helps air circulate around the computer and can be moved to clear the work surface for other projects. Need more room for the right monitor distance? Try pulling your desk away from the wall, putting your keyboard on an adjustable tray and pulling it toward you, or a flat monitor.

Working mainly from printed material? Put it in front of you and move your monitor slightly to one side.

Using a document holder? Find one adjustable for angle and height. It should match your monitor in height and distance, so you don't have to refocus or move your head much looking from one to the other.

ON-SITE QUICK FIXES If you're working at an office that isn't your own, here are some simple things you can do to make the workspace fit you. Ask if you can have a swivel chair. Put a delivery box under your feet if they don't rest flat on the floor. Bring your own lumbar support pillow or antiglare screen. See if you can move the computer monitor in front of you. Ask if they have an adjustable tray for the keyboard and mouse, or a hands-free headset for the phone. There's nothing wrong with asking for things that'll help you work better.

We've all had that zombie stare from too much screen time. Every fifteen minutes or so, look away from the screen, blink to moisten your eyes, focus on something 20 feet or so away or just gently close them, take a full breath or two, and then return to work. Or spend a few minutes doing another task—a phone call, some filing, or something that gets you up and moving.

JUST YOUR TYPE

Place the fingertips of one hand against the outside of your opposite forearm, just below the elbow. Now wiggle your free fingers as if typing. Feel those muscles and tendons rippling? Typing has far-reaching effects.

When you type, your elbows should be by your sides, forearms at about a right angle to your upper arm, and wrists—this is really, really important—straight, or neutral when positioned over the keyboard. Type with your fingertips, not flat-fingered, and keep your hands parallel.

Anything that breaks that right angle takes your wrists out of neutral, forcing the tendons of your fingers to bend around your wrist bones in ways they shouldn't. Do that for hours, days, months, years, and you'll find it really hurts.

Bring the keyboard to you, versus reaching toward it. Keyboards with adjustable feet on front and back might help. If you use a wrist rest, it's usually best to have it separate from the keyboard, not built in. Take out the pencil drawer on a traditional desk if it helps you adjust your seat height for correct keyboard posture.

Or try a keyboard tray: a sliding tray attached under the desk surface that can be tilted, raised, or lowered. Make sure you can still scoot in close to your desk.

With laptops, if the keyboard's in the right position, the monitor's too low; if the monitor's at proper eye level, the keyboard's too high. Also, the laptop's smaller keyboard forces poor wrist positions for some. The answer is a wireless keyboard and laptop stand. They're affordable, neat (no trailing wires), and can change positions with you while you work.

THE MOUSE AND MORE

A mouse (or trackball or other device) can cause wrist stress injuries, depending on its location, size, and how much you use it. Even just moving your thumb repeatedly on a trackball can cause chronic problems over time.

Your mouse and your keyboard should be at the same level. Try a) a mouse that fits your hand size and contour and puts your wrist in a neutral position, b) a computer tray to hold keyboard and mouse at the correct level, c) learning to mouse with the nondominant hand, or d) a keyboard that lets you connect the mouse on either side. Also:

- Look for a mouse that fits either hand and can be adjusted for sensitivity.

- Don't use a trackball requiring you to use your thumb.

- Reduce mouse use: Use keyboard shortcuts.

- Use your arm to mouse, not your wrist. The heel of your palm shouldn't rest on the desk surface or mouse pad, but should slide along the surface as you mouse.

ANATOMY OF AN INJURY (AND TIPS FOR PREVENTION)

Good ergonomic habits are your best defense against work-related musculoskeletal disorders (MSDs) or repetitive stress injuries (RSIs), which can sap your productivity, cause pain and stress, and drive up your medical bills. Working in nonneutral or awkward positions tires your muscles, pulls tendons, nerves, and blood vessels over ligaments and bones, and can pinch, restrict, or even fray them. Swelling occurs, pressing on nerves and blood vessels—especially in compact areas like your wrists and fingers. What starts as stiffness, tenderness, or soreness can become tingling, numbness, pain, and a chronic, disabling problem. The tissues lose their well-oiled-machine smoothness and efficiency—and you feel it.

Anyone who does repetitive work—computer work, hefting skillets, wielding a paint roller, bowing a violin, working at a drawing table, et cetera—can develop RSIs. If you have any pain or discomfort, consult your physician. Below are some strategies that can help, and some warning signs.

YOUR SITTING POSTURE

When you think of the correct posture for sitting, think of leading with your heart. The sternum (that bony area in the center of your chest), should be gently lifted upward. Result: Your shoulders settle down and back, your lower back rests in its S-shape, and your chin tucks slightly inward. And all of this should happen with your lower back in contact with the back of your chair.

Sure, you'll move around—bending to finish a detail on a drawing or to read the fine print in a contract. But you always come back to your heart-lifted posture—which, P.S., is also optimal for blood flow and breathing—two useful recruits for clear thinking.

Below the waist you should have two feet flat on the floor. If you can't reach the floor, a couple of phone books, a delivery box, or a step stool will help. Slightly elevating the thighs destresses the lower spine. Crossing legs is bad for circulation and the desire to do so is often the body's request for better support.

PRACTICE PRODUCTIVE FIDGETING, TAKE BREAKS, CHECK YOUR FORM

Rotate tasks to mix in movement. Sit for a while, then make a phone call and stand or walk while you talk (moving around can sharpen thinking).

Don't twist and shout—do a miniworkout. Instead of straining to reach for something out of range or rolling your chair over, get up, take a few steps over to that low shelf or file, squat down, get what you need, push back up again. Work those abs and quads.

Reboot your body. Every thirty to sixty minutes or so, give your body a few minutes' break. Change positions. Focus on something in the distance, close your eyes, breathe deeply, get up and do some stretches, refill your water glass. "I set a timer for sixty minutes and then do something physical. I wash or put away dishes, take out the trash, vacuum a room, dust a little. I feel better, and my house gets clean!"

Take a real lunch break. Give yourself a full-hour, official lunchtime away from desk, email, and phone. Have a sandwich, take a walk, run an errand, exercise, or take a nap.

Watch your posture. Most of us have no idea we're slouching, straining to read on-screen, or tensing our shoulders while working. Hang a mirror in your workspace and do microchecks of your posture, just like at the gym.

WARNING SIGNS AND RED FLAGS

If you get achy or uncomfortable while working, feel little "zings" of pain, intermittent tingling or pain, or can't sit for fifteen minutes or so without pain starting, don't ignore it. Addressing symptoms early is key in preventing more serious problems. Some warning signs connected with computer use include:

- Joint stiffness or swelling
- Aches, tingling, cramps, or weakness
- Less range of motion in back, neck, or shoulders
- Pain in back, neck, elbows, forearms, or wrists
- Numbness, burning sensation, or a change in grip strength
- Double or blurred vision, or sore, dry, or itchy eyes

If any of these happens to you, evaluate your workspace design and your work position and consult a qualified health professional. Have someone take a photo of you working at your desk. Showing it to your doctor and/or physical therapist can help them evaluate your workspace ergonomics and posture. Tell them: Where you hurt. When. For how long. Whether it goes away when you stop working. Contact your physician if you experience any of the following:

- sharp, shooting pain
- sudden weakness
- inability to hold things or dropping things
- pain that doesn't ease or change with movement
- pain with no apparent injury that persists for a week to ten days
- pain that wakes you up at night
- pain that shoots down your arm when you cough or sneeze
- nausea, diarrhea, dizziness, blurred vision, ringing in the ears, numbness, tingling, or weakness in your arms or legs

THE GREEN OFFICE

You can green your office by buying energy-efficient equipment and eco-friendly supplies, and recycling your electronics. Your electric bill and Planet Earth will thank you. Here are some tips. For selected resources, see the Appendix.

TOP TIPS (AND MYTHS) FOR A GREEN OFFICE

Turn it off. It's old-school, but it works: When you leave a room, turn off the lights. Turn off your printer and other machines not in frequent use.

Invest in multitasking machines. For example, printers that also scan, copy, and fax save power and space.

Use power strips. Flip one switch; turn off multiple appliances. By cutting connection to the power source, you also eradicate "phantom" or standby power load (the power a turned-off appliance uses), which for home office equipment could be 20 to 40 watts per item.

Unplug chargers or adapters when you're not using them or after charging.

Myth: Leaving equipment on twenty-four hours a day isn't a big energy drain. **Truth:** Running machines 24/7 increases your power bill, exposes your equipment to more power surges, and pulls in dust.

Myth: Screen savers save energy. **Truth:** Letting your monitor go to sleep or turning it off saves power.

Score a triple-save. Enable power management features (power-save, sleep mode) on your equipment. You'll save power, cool your equipment, and save on your AC bill.

Use disks and drives without the detriments. Look into recycled disks and earth-friendly flash drives free of lead, mercury, cadmium, or other toxic chemicals.

Pick your paper. Compare recycled paper products' postconsumer content (discarded consumer material). Get the highest level you can find. Look for chlorine-free processing.

Flip it over; cut it up. Flip over paper printed on one side and put it in your printer tray to print on the blank side. Or cut it into quarters and use the blank side for notes (junk mail's good for this, too).

Keep landfills cleaner and leaner: Donate or recycle your electronics. If your equipment works (or can be repaired), donate it. Otherwise recycle it so metals, plastics, glass, and more can be harvested for reuse and harmful materials disposed of. For donation or recycling programs, check your state or local government website. For a list of questions to ask recyclers (including how they destroy personal data), log onto E-cycling Central (ecyclingcentral.com/faqs).

Donate your phone. Cell phones, chargers, and the like can be donated to programs that provide them to charities or sell them at a discount to the needy. Be sure your service contract is terminated and all personal data is erased (manually and by removing the SIM card, and/or get instructions from the manufacturer or service provider, or use a tool that erases data). To find out about cell phone mail-in, drop-off, or collection programs in your community, contact the manufacturer, local retailer, or check out charities and state and local waste programs. Another good resource: the U.S. Environmental Protection Agency's "eCycle Cell Phones" (epa .gov/wastes/partnerships).

STAR POWER

ENERGY STAR (see Appendix) has partnered with more than 17,000 organizations to help citizens and organizations adopt energy-efficient products and practices. Products that earn the ENERGY STAR meet energy efficiency standards set by the U.S. Department of Energy or the U.S. Environmental Protection Agency—for example, ENERGY STAR computers go to "sleep" (i.e., low power) after being inactive for a certain period, "waking" at the touch of key or mouse. Make sure the features are enabled.

ENERGY STAR lamps and compact fluorescent light bulbs (CFLs) last up to ten times longer than standard incandescent bulbs and use 75 percent less energy.

Look for the ENERGY STAR label on the product or on its packaging, literature, and online.

When all's said and done, your office doesn't have to suit anyone but you, for the work you love and do.

"I wish my office weren't also a guest room and that I didn't have to use fifty percent of my real estate on a bed. But I love that, on the wall over the bed, is the sign from the café I owned—it represents my first foray into the business that I now freelance in, and that suits me so perfectly."

"What do I miss about corporate life? A paycheck in my bank account every two weeks."

YOUR FREELANCE PORTFOLIO

Freelancers can't count on paychecks, promotions, or job titles as benchmarks for their value. They have to create their value in the marketplace every day.

I've talked with thousands of freelancers. Nearly all say variable income in a world of regular expenses is their biggest stressor: "I keep a certain amount in the bank. If it drops below that amount, I'll consider returning to corporate America. So far it hasn't, but it's getting very close, and I'm more worried than usual. It's not good for me." But there's a flip side. Not to minimize the challenges, but one freelancer astutely commented, "I think the danger in freelancing is that we can easily condition ourselves to struggle."

You can think of freelancing as volatile and risky, or as flexible and opportunity-rich. Doesn't having multiple sources of income and multiple moneymaking skills sound less risky than putting all your eggs in an employer's basket? It's no accident that during the 2008 recession, Nebraska had one of the nation's lowest unemployment rates (4.8 percent), partly because many Nebraskans held more than one job (a farmer might also do equipment repair).

Freelancing lets you shift gears when the world does.

When you look at freelancing that way, the question becomes not "How can I keep the ups and downs from happening?" but "How can I ride the waves?" Enter the Freelance Portfolio.

THE FREELANCE PORTFOLIO

A Freelance Portfolio is similar to a financial portfolio. A financial portfolio spreads your money across multiple investments with varying levels of risk and return. The goal is to diversify your holdings to provide maximum income while protecting you from the market's volatility: When one investment's down, another's up; some are low-return/low-risk; some are higher-return/higher-risk, and so on.

Your Freelance Portfolio helps you balance the risks and rewards of your freelance life. It helps you weigh how much time and energy to "invest" in projects, and change the mix depending on the work market and your income needs. It lets you decide how work fits into *your* plans, not the other way around.

The Freelance Portfolio has four levels, explained in more detail below:

Level 1 | The Blue Chips

Level 2 | Growth Investments

Level 3 | One-Shots and Long Shots

Level 4 | New Ventures and Growth

You want to balance these levels so your Freelance Portfolio meets these three goals:

Goal 1 | Have enough clients of the right kind: not too few and not more than you can handle, who pay well and/or can advance your career in some way.

Goal 2 | Bring in enough steady income to reduce cash flow highs and lows.

Goal 3 | Meet your total income goals.

LIFE IN THE BALANCED LANE

What does a balanced Freelance Portfolio look like? Here's what it *doesn't* look like (and what you can do about it):

Imbalance: Your pipeline's full, you're working like crazy, but barely making ends meet.

Rebalance: Reassess your portfolio for Goal 1.

Imbalance: You're making a decent income, but the payments are so far apart you struggle to meet your monthly expenses.

Rebalance: Focus on Goals 1 and 2.

Imbalance: You've got some great clients and gigs, but the money's lousy.

Rebalance: Retuning all three goals may be necessary.

Portfolio planning isn't just about how busy you are, but about finding *a client mix that delivers maximum value for your time and effort.* This boils down to a handy equation:

---

optimal clients + steady cash flow + meeting your income goals = balanced freelance portfolio

---

Here are the benefits of a balanced Freelance Portfolio:

No more living project-to-project. Changeable schedules are part of freelance life: "Project schedules inevitably shift and collide, so some weeks are insane with work and others are very quiet. If you averaged it out, it would probably look something like a normal workload, but it never feels that way!"

When these fits and starts happen to a freelancer with a balanced portfolio, other prospects and possibilities are quietly simmering. If a project gets back-burnered or a client pays late or fades away, you're more likely to be able to quickly turn up the heat and land a gig or two to fill the gap.

No more "pipeline perspective." A full pipeline's only as good as the projects in it. Your portfolio lets you weigh your projects and craft a mix that serves your income goals.

No more "Oops, forgot to network." "If you don't divide your time between looking for new work and doing your current work, you'll finish your project and be tearing your hair because you don't have any work lined up." Your portfolio lets you track your workload, anticipate quiet periods, and ramp up your marketing. There may still be dry times, but odds are they'll be fewer and shorter.

No more "fire, ready, aim." Your portfolio lets you see holes and change your goals—whether it's landing or replacing a Blue Chip, growing your network, increasing your cash flow, or building your future with new products or services.

Let's look at each level in more detail. At the end of the chapter is a template for making your own Freelance Portfolio.

LEVEL 1: THE BLUE CHIPS

WHAT THEY ARE

Your Blue Chips are the core of your Freelance Portfolio. Like blue-chip stocks, they're your buy-and-hold investments: major clients (large or small in size) that you maintain and monitor carefully as sources of regular income.

WHAT'S TO LIKE

Income anchors. Blue Chips are your hedges against marketplace rock-and-roll. They keep the lights on. They are your priority.

Rich relationships. A positive Blue Chip relationship can be rewarding on every level. You get to know and respect one another as professionals and people. Your work together deepens and sharpens. It's satisfying, lucrative, and just plain nice. Holiday cards and treats may be exchanged.

Referrals. You'll likely get referrals, or if your contacts move to other companies, they may seed new Blue Chips.

WHAT'S CHALLENGING

Systems and shifts. You might be at the mercy of corporate bureaucracy and politics: glacial payment schedules and protocols, projects scrapped or delayed at the whim of the suits. If they're small companies, you may be buffeted by their fitful cash flow or changing strategies in their struggle for market traction.

Great project, awful people. You may have to suck it up until you can groom another Blue Chip.

Great people, awful project. See above.

COMMUNITY
ALERT

LOVE THEORY AND YOUR FREELANCE PORTFOLIO Just signed a new Blue Chip and overwhelmed with work? Subcontract! Hack that gig into pieces and contract a fellow freelancer (or several) to do portions under your supervision. Get someone good at time-consuming tasks like transcribing or photo research, or someone starting out who needs experience and mentoring. Make sure your agreement specifies that you're the intermediary with the client and they can't go around you to be hired directly. Talk to your accountant to make sure you comply with tax requirements when subcontracting. (For more on subcontracting, see Chapters 11 and 15.)

Of course, you'd never subcontract to someone you don't trust. You build trust through relationship. You build relationship by giving—info, help, and (eventually, with trust) shared work. That's Love Banking. These relationships aren't business transactions so much as the outgrowth of how you choose to live your life, working and playing with lots of people you enjoy and care about.

Speaking of subcontracting, you can have Blue Chips as a subcontractor, too. Maybe there's a sole proprietor who needs to offer services like yours. It's a great strategy for regular cash flow if repeat clients aren't common in your type of work, or if you hate prospecting: Someone else gathers the pollen; you're the worker bee.

Poof! Like anything else in business, Blue Chip gigs can disappear overnight: "Due to the economy, the company where I had a major consulting contract made some big cuts. Mine was one of the accounts that got cut. Even when you have a great relationship, sometimes the situation's out of their hands."

BALANCING BLUE CHIPS

Have more than one. So if you lose one, you've got at least one other.

Keep Level 2 prospects simmering. You can get lulled into a comfortable place with Blue Chips (see "Poof!" above). Cultivating Level 2 prospects keeps you nimble. Can't stand a particular Blue Chip? Don't get mad; get a new one and phase out the old (or raise your rates to make them worth the aggravation).

Remember boundaries. Sometimes you'll go the extra mile for a Blue Chip, letting a project bulge out of scope. Be friendly but clear that this is a sometimes thing, so everyone's expectations stay in line. With tough Blue Chips, boundaries are essential. You shouldn't tolerate what the staff has to put up with to keep their jobs.

LEVEL 2: GROWTH INVESTMENTS

WHAT THEY ARE

Level 2 is the growing edge of your business and your Blue Chip incubator. The gigs turn over faster than Level 1 and generate income by their volume while enriching your client base. The more you nurture Level 2, the more it can stabilize your career.

You'll get Level 2s from client referrals, other freelancers, and your own prospecting, so it's about networking. While not every lead pans out, over time, as you expand and refine your strategy and bring in more and more projects, most of which bring good revenue or referrals for more work, your net return will be positive.

WHAT'S TO LIKE

You're in control. You decide what prospects to pursue and how you want to be viewed. It's you saying, "This is what I do, and how my work can help you." Way more powerful than, "Tell me what you need and I'll do it." The business world not only expects people to communicate their value clearly, but rewards it.

Nice and smart. Level 2 is where profitable opportunities are born. Example: You spot an opportunity that more specialized company workers don't see. You bring it to a client with whom you've worked well. Of course, you suggest how you could help make it happen, with just enough detail to show how big you could deliver. Suddenly, you've got a new gig. But even if not, you've made a huge impression (how many of their employees are this proactive?) and just moved to the front of the line for the next time they need outside help. Nice. And smart.

WHAT'S CHALLENGING

Juggling. When Level 2 gets rolling, you'll have lots going on. This is the beating heart of freelancing. Make sure you have love banked in case you need a hand, a favor, or advice from a fellow freelancer.

Hitting your stride with networking. Reputation and word of mouth will only take you so far: "I had a track record and initially built a clientele from that. But I didn't promote myself.

I'm a private, retiring person and never thought about marketing myself. I was under the misassumption that people knew my name." Everyone can network successfully. It's about finding the approach that works for you and brings you the level of projects you want. We'll talk about finding your own networking style and get into specifics in later chapters.

BALANCING LEVEL 2

Price to compete. In Level 2, you want to price yourself high enough to weed out low-paying, time-suck gigs, but not so high that good prospects assume they can't afford you (such as a promising start-up that could become a Blue Chip, or a high-visibility, lower-budget nonprofit). It might help to itemize pricing on some components of your work. An à la carte approach might make you affordable to a wider market without lowering your price.

Persist, persist (did I say persist?). "I get work because I put it out there and put it out there and put it out there and put it out there some more. I just keep knocking on doors. That, combined with the fact that I'm friendly and likeable—and talented—gets me work."

. . . but be selective. Trust your gut. If you sense a prospect will cost more to keep than lose—haggling over nothing, making constant changes, expecting way more than they're paying for—find other prospects worth working hard for. You'll be happier, more productive, and in the long run probably no worse off in the pocketbook.

LEVEL 3: ONE-SHOTS AND LONG SHOTS

WHAT THEY ARE

These are opportunistic gigs that fill time or income gaps (as in "I need money *now!*") or let you make the gig-getting aspects of freelancing more plug-and-play. I group sources of Level 3 gigs into two categories:

1 **Passive intermediaries, or what I call "listers."** These sources list available jobs and leave the rest of the process up to you and the client. They include print classifieds, online job boards such as Craigslist, Monster, Freelancers Union, and MediaBistro, and professional association job board listings.

2 **Active intermediaries.** These entities more actively manage the freelancer/work provider relationship; for example, by handling payment, instituting systems for communication or workflow, or providing some benefits. Temp and staffing agencies are in this category. So are work exchanges: on-demand workforce websites that have proliferated alongside the expanding freelance workforce as companies trim staff and start-ups can't afford to hire, but both need work done.

Put simply (and ideally), independent contractors post their profiles; work providers post their projects; the twain meet to their mutual benefit, while the host website oversees payment and facilitates interactions for a fee. Some examples as of this writing include Elance, oDesk, and Guru.com.

Both categories are useful in aggregating projects in one place. So—duh!—everyone's cruising them. Check them often enough to stay current, grab a good gig, or mobilize fast for cash, but you shouldn't spend a lot of time trolling these über-competitive spaces. Especially in the case of work exchanges or staffing agency jobs, the pay rarely warrants it.

WHAT'S TO LIKE

Opportunities at a glance. As mentioned, these sources aggregate leads for quick scanning and comparison shopping.

No cold calls or networking. Prospects are looking to hear from you—one reason why it's easy to get sucked into online gig-hunting at the expense of networking.

Easy application. If your résumé or application materials are ready to go or if your profile's posted, you can move fast.

Supplemental income, seasoning, and selection. Work exchanges can be handy for picking up work in a pinch or supplementing your income. They're also useful if you're new to your industry, new to networking, are returning after a break, or want to control your workload—for example, there's a new baby at home, you're job-hunting, or anytime you want or need more short-term, self-contained projects.

With work exchange sites, no chasing payment. These sites advertise project approval, systems to ensure payment if you meet the work provider's benchmarks, and protocols for disputes. While there are no guarantees of a smooth ride, these safeguards can reduce the risk of working with an entity you don't know.

You might find some Blue Chips. This shouldn't be your rationale for trolling these sources, though.

WHAT'S CHALLENGING

Welcome to the cattle call. You may not be networking, but you are auditioning. Applying for these gigs can feel like a Broadway casting call where hundreds wait for hours in the rain to tap dance for thirty seconds, and a handful make the cut.

Checking in, or checking up? While technology can help workers and clients find each other, it also allows more monitoring of workers' performance. Work exchange websites have systems that electronically track freelancers' progress and hours as part of managing projects long-distance and ensuring payment for work completed. Some call it transparency; others call it an intrusion that takes the "independent" out of independent contractor and veers unacceptably close to the kinds of oversight employers are entitled to exercise over employees—but without the benefits employees are entitled to in return. Employers can't have their cake and eat it, too: getting a capable "on-demand" workforce free of the obligation to provide any benefits, yet with the power to limit their work product and freedom as if they were employees.

Beware of bargain-basement pricing. The pricing on job boards is hugely variable. On work exchanges, it's generally low. Since you're competing with a global talent pool, a) you'll spend time applying for positions with less chance of getting them, and b) prices are pushed down when the labor supply exceeds demand. That's why I recommend that you not put all your eggs in the Level 3 basket. Remember the mantra of the balanced Freelance Portfolio: *a client mix that delivers maximum value for your time and effort.*

If you need income, you do what you gotta do. Otherwise, consider whether you'd be better off working Level 2 and holding out for quality over quantity in your portfolio.

Remember, too, that as a freelancer you have the option to work outside your usual frame. For example, one of the sample Key Skills lists in Chapter 1 listed "math tutor" alongside sophisticated accounting skills. Maybe that freelancer would think, "I'm not getting any enjoyment, new skills, or reputation value from these Level 3 gigs. For the same pay, I could pick up some math tutoring, which

I love doing. Plus, I can do that during off-hours and still have time to look for other work." Freelancing gives you that flexibility; staff jobs don't.

Here's another reason to be leery of bargain-basement pricing. When companies can choose from a giant pool of available talent responding to online work listings, it drives prices to artificial lows that don't reflect the true value of the skill required for the work. Freelancers' main strategy has to be increasing economic power so as not to be dependent on getting work online. Freelancers need to think twice before taking bottom-feeder jobs and hold the standard for higher value to be placed on their work. We also need to build freelancers' political power to make sure the practices on work exchange sites are fair.

BALANCING LEVEL 3

See Level 3s for what they are: ways to get short-term gigs, work experience, or quick/incremental/supplemental income—not as your primary income source.

Limit trolling time. The time you invest should be in proportion to the income potential. Level 3 shouldn't be mined at the expense of Level 2.

Ask your Brain Trust and other freelancers if they've gotten work this way. What was it like for them? How did they make it work?

Look for the three Ps: price, projects, and people. Focus on higher-paying, higher-quality projects that will boost your skills or credits, and for clients you feel you'll work well with. Their positive testimonials will boost your earning potential. And they may become Level 2 or Blue Chip clients.

Focus on specific kinds of projects. Once again, a specialty helps.

Be clear on payment procedures, oversight, and dispute policies. Are you paid by the hour or getting a fixed price? How are payments triggered? Exactly how do the oversight and dispute policies work?

Make sure the project description, directions, and deliverables are well defined. If not, ask. A good outcome is in everyone's interest. Showing you want to get it right impresses clients, too.

Bring your best game. Take the tests and ace them. Tailor your pitches to the projects. Get great testimonials. That's how these sites work, so make them work for you.

ASK SARA

Q Dear Sara, What about temping?

A I'd put temp or staffing agencies at Level 3. These agencies match workers with employers needing particular skills, in exchange for a fee from the employer or a percentage of the worker's salary. It used to be that you'd register with one agency and become eligible for benefits by accruing hours. Now, it's usually necessary to register with multiple agencies to make ends meet, reducing the likelihood of accruing enough hours though one agency to be eligible for benefits.

Upside: Someone else finds the gig and handles payment and administration, while you have a chance to make a good impression on the employer, which might lead to future gigs.

Downside: not much choice in the work, and lower pay.

Getting work through an agency can be useful during a long dry spell or if you need experience: "I know I'm very good at what I do, but I couldn't point to multiple-year experience. When I set out as a freelancer, I networked as best I could. And when I couldn't get any new assignments, I got temp jobs doing administrative support until I could get work."

LEVEL 4: NEW VENTURES AND GROWTH

> "I want to shift the balance of my work so I'm doing more writing and less editing. I'd like to be more thoughtful about the big picture, and more bold about setting goals for myself."

Level 4 is in some ways the most speculative part of your Freelance Portfolio, but it's also the most exciting. Here, you're building the services, products, and alliances that will bring income in the long-term future.

These are ventures you're creating on your own or with others: developing a seminar, pursuing speaking gigs, teaching classes, writing a book, collaborating to offer expanded services. You might test-drive them for free or use them as "freemiums" to build your profile, but the ultimate aim is to position you for a profitable future. As one freelancer said, "A huge factor in my staying in business was that I've reinvented myself many times while staying in the same industry. To be on your own you have to generate ideas, and you have to see where the market will be a few years from now."

Level 4 ventures need to be phased and planned so they stay on your radar but don't take over and cut into the time you need to make your living. We'll talk more about them in later chapters, but here are some ways to cultivate Level 4 no matter how busy you are:

Don't set yearly goals. At least, not the "set and forget" way most people do. Instead, set yearly goals and then make a monthly, even weekly, breakdown of small, achievable steps to get there.

For example, if your goal is to lead seminars but you've never spoken in public, steps might include reading books on public speaking; taking a class on speaking; volunteering for public roles in your professional organization, your kids' school, or in your community or spiritual group; attending seminars and asking the speakers afterward how they plan their events; outlining a topic for a short talk about your profession, then pitching and giving the talk; et cetera.

Take steps, not leaps. Shuffle if necessary. One goal achieved is better than many unmet. Very small steps make for steady progress, which motivates you and helps you correct your course as you go. To take the seminar example above, if that seems like too much to do in a year, set a goal to read some books and take a class.

Put each step in your calendar. Just do it, even if it's "Make a list of steps."

Treat yourself like a client. Treat Level 4 projects as you'd treat a project: Break it down, identify trouble spots, set up a schedule, project-manage it.

"DRY TIME" — WHAT TO DO WHEN NOTHING'S COMING IN

A short dry spell after a busy period can be a luxurious chance to sleep in, get back to the gym, and catch up on filing. But when you're spending half a morning swabbing grunge off your keyboard . . . not so fun. Not just because no money's coming in, but because freelancers like to have stuff to do. If they wanted to spend time perfecting how to say "Not my job," they'd be trolling for company positions.

Dry time bites when you lose a Blue Chip and get caught with your network down. Or when one *bleh* thing happens after another: A project's postponed, another's canceled in a budget cut, a client pays late, and prospects you were certain would lead to gigs don't.

Dry time is a tough reality for freelancers. Our 2011 survey showed that:

• 79 percent of independent workers surveyed didn't have enough work in the last year (2010).

• 49 percent experienced periods with no work, with an average of fifteen weeks without any work.

Of those who had trouble finding work:

• 35 percent dipped into savings intended for other purposes (such as retirement).

• 35 percent used credit cards.

• 3 percent had to rely on some form of government assistance.

FOUR BENEFITS OF DRY TIME

Benefit 1: Dry Time Pushes You to Do "The Ask."
There's no shame in asking for work. You're letting people know your skills are available. Try something like . . .

"Hi. I finished that big project and am open for new work, so if you hear of anyone who needs online marketing, I hope you'll recommend me or let me know. And now we can finally meet for coffee and catch up! When's a good time?"

"Dear Ms. Major: Sam Prescott at X Corp. recommended I contact you. Sam and I worked on several online marketing projects together. I develop social media campaigns and have had particular success with [pertinent example]. I'd like to set up a brief call or meeting to learn more about Major Productions and whether there are ways I might be able to help. I've attached some information about my work . . . [et cetera]."

"Hi, Jane. It was great meeting you at the school Halloween party and talking briefly about your company, Major Productions. As I mentioned, I develop social media campaigns and have worked with X Corp. and others. I've had particular success with [pertinent example]. I'd love to have a short call or meeting to learn more about Major Productions and whether there are ways I might be able to help. I've attached some information about my work. When would be a good time for you?"

"Hey—just wanted to let you know I've got some open time, so if you hear of work or if there's something you'd like to subcontract out, I'm in the market. Thanks!"

Benefit 2: Dry Time Reminds You That Work Can Come from Anywhere.

"Last month was my slowest month so far. And it came on the heels of an expensive home repair. After some financial hand-wringing, in desperation, I reached out to two contacts that had cooled a bit. With one, I asked—in my best nondesperate tone—if he had any work. He did! It's good work, pays well, and has a quick turnaround. The second contact was happy to hear from me, and we set up a meeting for this week to catch up. He has national clients and a great reputation. Now I have a wildly busy six weeks ahead of me."

Benefit 3: Dry Time Reminds You to Tend Your Portfolio.

"I've been freelancing for less than a year, and I really haven't created any long-term schedule. I've been lucky to get work just in time to get my bills paid. Hitting a slow time made me think more about planning, strategy, and diversifying my client list. And frankly, I think I need to work harder when I have the chance. I've skated a bit, and it's come back to bite me. I have to keep my motivation up."

Benefit 4: Prolonged Dry Time May Point to Market Changes.

Working all the levels of your portfolio and still long time, no gigs? Maybe market demand is changing. Do you need to add new skills to your bag of tricks? Seek clients in a broader range of businesses? Make alliances to expand your offerings? Temp or do virtual assistant work while you retool? Talk to your Brain Trust: "Is it the market? Is it me?" This is your time of need, so be sure you give back to those who help with insights, advice, or leads.

THIRTEEN TACTICS FOR DRY TIME DAMAGE CONTROL

1 Keep a routine. Treat your work days like any other, but *you're* the project: touching base with former clients and potential Blue Chips (Level 1), prospecting, cold-calling, seeking referrals, following up with new contacts, going to events where you can network (all Level 2), and checking job boards and work exchanges (Level 3). Save time by creating several form pitch letters you can customize (like several of the "ask" letters in Benefit 1).

2 Connect. Not only because you never know where the next gig might come from, but because de-isolation reduces the loneliness of dry time.

3 Tidy up. Tackle the administrative stuff you've been meaning to get to.

4 Ask for testimonials from satisfied clients. Say you're working on your website or updating your professional profile online and would appreciate being able to post a testimonial.

5 Clean up your act online. If you find things a prospect might misunderstand or find objectionable in your social media activity, modify or delete them. Update your bio across platforms. Add recent accomplishments, awards, testimonials, or other achievements. Is it clear what your specialties are? Is it clear what value you deliver? Is it clear what clients are likely to benefit from your work?

6 Evaluate your business model. Dry time's more stressful if you suspect you've been undercharging. Research where your fees fall on the spectrum for your profession. Are there some tasks you've subcontracted that you can do yourself? Have your business and personal spending crept up? Setting up consistent bookkeeping and budgeting systems can help you track and compare—see Chapters 14 and 17.

7 Add skills. Take online tutorials or get coaching from a fellow freelancer. If you can afford it, enroll in a course or certification program that'll add to your marketability (then update your bio!). Visit blogs and websites for insights and advice about your industry, marketing tips, financial planning info, and productivity strategies. Books on all these abound—your library's a free resource.

8 Consider bartering. Sometimes when money's tight, a friend or fellow freelancer will do you a favor by offering their free expertise—maybe making some fixes on your website. And you'll return the favor—maybe helping them set up a better accounting system. If you barter services, know that it carries tax implications (you're receiving value that should be reported) and check your accountant before getting into any serious bartering (for additional info, see Chapters 11 and 15).

9 Do pro bono or volunteer work. It feels great, and you'll find new friends, connections, and community. Maybe it'll lead to some work, that's not the point. Connecting is intrinsically good.

10 Make dry time "you time." If your business has predictable slow periods (post-holidays, post-taxes, post-wedding season, post-school year), prepare a financial cushion during your busy time so you can take that down time for rest and personal development: your vacation, a class, or anything you want. Planned dry time keeps it from being so dry.

11 Work Level 4. Step up your brainstorming and development of new income ideas (more on this in Chapter 10). Deepen your social networking: Start or get back to your blog; add contacts, connections, friends, and followers (for ideas, check Chapter 9). Remember all the times work came from unexpected places. You truly never know where your efforts will lead.

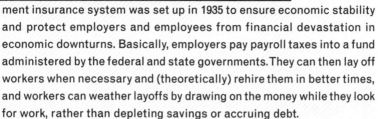

UNEMPLOYMENT INSURANCE FOR INDEPENDENT WORKERS The unemployment insurance system was set up in 1935 to ensure economic stability and protect employers and employees from financial devastation in economic downturns. Basically, employers pay payroll taxes into a fund administered by the federal and state governments. They can then lay off workers when necessary and (theoretically) rehire them in better times, and workers can weather layoffs by drawing on the money while they look for work, rather than depleting savings or accruing debt.

Recent downturns have strained this system, and its power to protect the economy will only weaken as the independent workforce grows. Freelancers Union is advocating for reforms. Self-employed workers should be able to contribute pretax dollars each year to build their own financial cushion to draw on during unemployment. So-called "permalancers" or "permatemps"—people who work long-term for one employer doing work very similar to permanent employees but who are denied employee status and benefits—need easier recourse to prove their eligibility for unemployment, and temp and part-time workers need easier access to this protection. Dry time may never be stress-free, but freelancers shouldn't be forced to live perilously close to the edge financially as a matter of course.

12 Revisit your Key Skills List. Are you using them all? Are there some you can add? Look at the whole you. Serious knitter? Start a knitting instruction group. Serious swimmer? Take lifeguard training and bring in some summertime cash. Great with a specific kind of software? Get gigs teaching it.

13 Be scrappy. If you take absurdly low-paying gigs for a while because you really need the money, so what? If you take temp jobs, work in a café, or do handyman work for a while, so what? You're making a living. That's what counts.

WORKING FOR FREE: SHOULD YOU?

The answer is "it depends"—on whether you can afford it, have the time, are looking to build connections, develop experience, or just plain want to: "I work for free when it's for a good cause, like a friend's start-up publication or contribution work for a nonprofit organization I care about."

Working for free can help you build experience and a body of work: "I often tell my students this is how they can get some of their best portfolio pieces—it's proven to be the case for me."

Doing pro bono work during dry time keeps you sharp and busy—and nothing attracts business like a busy person: "It helps to be busy. Then prospective clients know other people are using your talents." (P.S. You don't have to tell them you're working pro bono.)

Doing a self-contained task gratis can be good business. It showcases your chops, builds goodwill, potential word of mouth, and, maybe, the possibility of pay for more. Pro bono work for nonprofits is rewarding and may bring recognition and referrals in time. And if nothing comes of it, that comes with the territory: "You exchange thoughtful emails for a while with a client, hoping it'll turn into a marvelous project. Nine times out of ten, it doesn't."

If you work for free, I believe you have to do it with no expectation of anything other than the satisfaction of your contribution. That's a personal decision: "I've learned not to work for free. When I was starting my agency, I worked with a writer on a book concept. Every week we'd work on it, and every week he'd start over. After months of banging my head against the wall with nothing to show for it, one of us realized we had two separate ideas. I'm not sure I got much from this except frustration and migraines." Also, sometimes people value what they pay for: "I've done appearances for free, but I didn't find it successful. I was showing up and *no one* knew I was coming. Now I charge a fee, and when I arrive it's a big deal."

Be cautious before accepting goods in lieu of payment. Not only are there tax issues with bartering, as mentioned, but there are times when there's no substitute for cold, hard cash: "One client wanted to pay me with a gorgeous, drop-dead outfit. I wavered and then realized that as lovely as the outfit was, I had no place to wear such a beauty. It was a good thing I said no and wanted cash. As I drove home, my car died. I managed to pull to the curb, and as I was calling the mechanic (who had just repaired it!) a passerby said, 'Hey, lady, your car's on fire!' I ran to a safe distance and called the fire department. The money owed that day went for a down payment on a new car."

When it comes to doing good in the community, freelancers have a special opportunity to put their skills to use. An accountant in a corporation may crunch numbers all week and volunteer in a soup kitchen on weekends. Very admirable, but somewhat segmented. A freelance accountant may be able to put in a few hours a week doing the books for a fledgling nonprofit that desperately needs accounting help. The income's tiny or nonexistent, but there's something hugely gratifying about discovering your skills *really* matter; in fact, they make a survival difference to that organization. As a freelancer, you can ply your trade for whomever you choose—for no other reason than that it matters to you.

Thinking back to the freelancer whose comment opened this chapter, I'm reminded of the two sides of freelancing: the freedom of it, and the responsibility of it. They're really two sides of the same coin, and the Freelance Portfolio unites them. OK, so you don't have a staff job and can't do your work with one hand, check the sports scores with the other, and still pull down a regular paycheck. But you're no office drudge waiting for the weekend, retirement, the axe, or permission to take time off. Instead of checking the scores, you can decide to take the day off and go to the game. Instead of waiting for the weekend, you can start your weekend any day of the week. You can rearrange your life to make time for your passions, for play, for purpose, and for projects and people you care about.

Your Freelance Portfolio gives you the freedom to live the life you love—and to spread that love around—while fulfilling your professional and personal responsibility to make a living and do it well. It keeps you connected with your larger life plan. It enables you to change that plan when your life goals change. And it reminds you that all work is noble when you're working for something you believe in: yourself.

MY FREELANCE PORTFOLIO

LEVEL 1: BLUE CHIPS
The core of your Freelance Portfolio. Like so-called blue-chip stocks, they're your buy-and-hold investments: major clients (large or small in size) that provide regular income and work.

LEVEL 2: GROWTH INVESTMENTS
The growing edge of your business and the incubator of Blue Chips. Level 2s come from referrals, client testimonials, maintaining your network, and cultivating new contacts and prospects.

LEVEL 3: ONE-SHOTS AND LONG SHOTS
Opportunistic gigs that fill time or income gaps.

LEVEL 4: NEW VENTURES AND GROWTH
In Level 4, you're building the services, products, and alliances that will produce income in the long-term future.

PART 2:
GETTING WORK

> "You can't be a pest, but your name has to come to mind when they need someone."

Chapter 4

GETTING CLIENTS

Freelancing is associated with working alone, but no one really works alone. Success depends on connecting with people—and the first lesson of getting clients is that the connection has to be genuine. Otherwise you'll come off looking devious, desperate, or both. "I think I came across as desperate at first," one freelancer remembers. "I was, though."

Networking and prospecting just narrow the field to the small number of people you'll ultimately work with. It's not like you'll get work from 90 percent of the people you meet. So set your expectations accordingly, think long-term, and relax into it. When you do, you'll connect naturally (we'll talk about how in this chapter and go deeper in Chapter 8), alert to possibility, but not coming off like those creepy people who see everyone as a sales target.

This isn't to criticize people who are truly desperate for work. There's no shame in going after whatever work you need to make ends meet. All work has dignity—because dignity is in the worker. My aim is to help you set up your freelance life so you have many more calm and productive stretches and fewer desperate-feeling ones.

GETTING RIGHT-MINDED ABOUT GETTING CLIENTS

The most wildly successful freelancers motivate others to *want* to work with them. Gigs are constantly booked. What's their secret?

First, the not-so-secret secret: They're excellent, so they get repeat business and word of mouth. The X-factor: They have the ability to influence people.

SIX INFLUENTIAL FUNDAMENTALS

The kind of influence I'm talking about doesn't require money or status. Social psychologist Robert Cialdini has pinpointed six key elements of influence or persuasion. We all use them. Once they're on your radar, you'll spot them everywhere. You can apply them to make a connection, strengthen a bond, stand out, or even navigate tricky situations.

Fundamental 1: Reciprocity
We learn early that giving helps us get on in life. Share the blocks and you can build a bigger tower together. Invite Janie to your sleepover, and she'll probably invite you to the water park. That's reciprocity.

Reciprocity is most powerful when the gift is unexpected and costs the giver something in time, energy, or other resources. It's doing a good deed not because you have to, but because you want to. It's Love Theory in action: Build your Love Bank account, and your relationships will compound in value over time.

For example: Talk yourself up too much and people will flee your blowhard vibe. Instead, talk up others—refer them for gigs, make introductions—and they'll likely reciprocate.

Sharing information is a big Love Bank gift: "Hey, Jackie, I met someone who needs a writer for a dog-training book. With your work in animal rescue and fostering, you'd be perfect. I told him about you. He wants to talk. Here's his number. Good luck!"

In sales, reciprocity is the free trial, sample, or consult; the discount, "buy one/get one . . . "; the recession and early-bird specials; and gifts to say "Thanks" or "Happy holidays!"—all actions that keep customers coming back.

In negotiation, it's each of you giving some to seal the deal: "That delivery date's doable if we do the two-color version instead of the four-color." "That price works for two revision rounds. If you'd like more, how about if we set a price per additional round?"

Fundamental 2: Consistency

When someone calls me and says something like, "Because of your work getting health benefits for freelancers, I was hoping I could ask for some advice about a health-care project I'm trying to launch," I listen. Why? Because helping out would be *consistent* with my interest in health care and with my reputation as an advocate for affordable health benefits.

Here's how consistency might look in networking: "Thanks so much for recommending me as a language tutor last year. Your recommendation helped me land a client I'm still working with. The tutoring has gotten so popular that I've created a webinar series to help more students. Attached is a brief announcement about it. If you know families or teachers who might be interested in knowing about it, I hope you'll forward it. Thanks again—and let me know if I can help you out in any way!"

Here's how it might look in a pitch: "I know you're serious about education because of your long membership on our school board. Since you led the campaign to get funding for the computer lab, I thought you might be interested to hear about the language webinar series I've developed for high school students, from my work as a language tutor. My goal is to offer these at our school. Could I meet with you briefly to show you some material about the program?"

You can even use it in negotiations: "I assume the payout will be consistent with what we agreed in our last contract."

Fundamental 3: Social Validation

Looking for a romantic restaurant? Get friends' recommendations. Hunting for a preschool? Ask parents you trust. Got a call from a prospect? Talk to contacts who used to work there. We've all done things like this.

Life throws us tons of decisions, from what toothpaste to buy to what candidate to vote for. Finding out what other people are doing can help us size up our options fast. Marketers, of course, know this. Which is why we're told how many copies were sold, how many patrons were served, how many subscribers the newsletter has, and how many votes the candidate got (or didn't).

You're invoking social validation when you:

- provide references for a prospect to check
- display testimonials about your work
- build your number of social media connections
- let people know you're setting up more seminars because the current one is sold out
- post news about getting a professional award
- tell prospects about other clients you've worked with or projects you've done

All suggest you're a freelancer worth choosing, because others have chosen you.

You can even use social validation in negotiating: "I've never been asked to delete this language from my contract."

Fundamental 4: Liking

I'm curious about people and want to know what they're all about. So when I meet people, I ask questions. Doing this almost always leads us to something we have in common—whether it's our interest in freelancers, a film we just saw, or our passion for flea markets.

We tend to feel more open with people if we share some kind of bond. Maybe we went to the same school, belong to the same professional group, or go to the same place of worship. Paying someone a genuine compliment shows a shared value. So does cooperating to meet a goal: doing a community project, organizing a panel, or helping to coach the team. There are so many ways to build liking.

Liking is one reason why friends and family can be your best sales force and maybe your first customers. It's why industry veterans get glowing referrals from colleagues they've worked with over the years. It's why networking with fellow high school or college alums, members of a professional organization, or your neighborhood, school, or spiritual community makes sense. It's why, when you and a client get along great, often you'll both give up some negotiating points to strike a deal.

When you meet people, look for a common connection, but don't be ridiculous about it. You've got a minute or two to get to know each other, and you either find that connection or you don't. Be genuine and interested and you'll have the best chance of finding the place where liking happens. In the groups you're involved with, step up, volunteer, be helpful, and you'll discover how quickly the good energy spreads and just how many people like you—and yes, maybe even love you.

Fundamental 5: Authority

All the doctors I've ever been to display their diplomas in their offices. It promotes trust in their authority. You can do the same in many places and ways: your résumé, website bio, portfolio, client list, professional titles, memberships, certifications, special training, and awards.

With prospects, mention your experience: "I recently worked for a photo house, and I know this budget will only buy about two-thirds of the images you want."

Fundamental 6: Scarcity

I have a friend who says that at dinnertime, her husband points to the largest piece of food and says, "That's mine." She thinks it's from growing up in a large family, where he had to lay claim to his share.

Scarcity definitely pushes our survival buttons. Scarcity of the coveted holiday toy can drive mall stampedes. Scarcity of goods drives prices up as people pay more for what they need. Scarcity of gigs drives freelance wages down as freelancers take what they can get. Even scarce information skyrockets in value—think of media fights over the exclusive celebrity interview.

In your freelance life, scarcity can look like this: "limited edition prints." "Only three slots left!" "Sale ends tomorrow!" "These contract terms are available until X date." "Class size is limited—enroll early!" "The first fifty people to sign up get a twenty-percent discount." "Exclusive rights to the image will cost X." Or even: "I just got a cancellation for five p.m. tomorrow. You mentioned your back was hurting, so I wondered if you might like to schedule a massage."

NETWORKING NEED-TO-KNOW

Sometimes gigs drop in your lap, but mostly they come from networking. We'll talk about networking in more detail in later chapters, but here are some "best practices" for connecting with pretty much anyone as you start looking for gigs.

FIND YOUR NETWORKING STYLE

Networking gets a bad rap because of people who do it wrong. You know, the ones who are scanning the room while they're talking to you . . . who spew business cards . . . who call only when they want something . . . who don't reciprocate . . . who never *really* want to know how you're doing . . . and other obnoxious behaviors.

So if networking makes you feel vaguely dirty, call it something else—reaching out, connecting, talking, sharing, contacting, or meeting.

I'm serious. Use another word.

The best networking is networking you'll stick with doing. Your style should mesh with your personality and habits, with gentle stretches in new directions.

If working the room at meet-ups isn't for you, join a professional association and go to their events. Make small talk; get to know people. Keep showing up and you'll soon be a regular welcoming the newbies. Then a meet-up might not feel like such a dread fest.

If you feel allergic at the thought of going to conferences and introducing yourself to strangers who look at your name tag first, to see if you're "worth" talking to, don't go there. Or don't *start* there. Try smaller-scale seminars like the ones we have at Freelancers Union on finances, taxes, and marketing. Everyone's there to learn and meet people. Work your way up to larger groups.

If you take lunch or coffee breaks during your workday, turn a couple of those every week into get-togethers with freelancers you'd like to know better.

If you're most relaxed when doing something, your best networking op might be standing on a stepladder working with other parents

ASK SARA

Q Dear Sara, I just graduated and I'm new to freelancing. I don't know how to network. Where should I start?

A You *do* know how to network. Your first day on campus, you didn't know a soul. Now you know your roommates, dorm-mates, classmates, club-mates, teammates, and professors.

Everyone has a network. Imagine concentric circles. In the inner circle are your parents, siblings, immediate relatives, closest friends, and close family friends. The next ring might be good friends, their families, school connections, and people you've worked with or for. Next might be people you meet through your activities, sports, alumnae organization, or spiritual community. Next would be contacts you make through people in all of these circles. And so on.

Start with your inner circle, and don't worry about a polished pitch. Their questions and feedback will help you get a handle on your goals and the possible markets for your work. By the time you're ready for the next circle, you'll have more refined goals and an improved elevator speech. That's when you'll start zeroing in on people and professions for prospecting.

But work leads can come from anywhere. Now's *not* the time to be embarrassed when loved ones brag about you. As one freelancer said, "A significant percentage of my work and income has come from reaching out to friends, letting them know what I'm doing, and asking if they know of anything going on." Maybe you can offer a price break on some services in exchange for an introduction. It's important not to make anyone feel obligated, though, or sound like you're always pitching.

Make sure you show the love to thank that inner circle who listened, gave feedback, or offered help or kindness. They're just as important as people who can more directly get you gigs. Write them a note, bake them a cake, take them to lunch.

If you're on social media, remember it's based on face-to-face networking fundamentals and was built to help people with shared interests find one another. That includes professional interests. If you meet local people you like online, see if you can meet in person.

to fix up the gym for the school carnival, or serving on a committee at your house of worship or your favorite charity.

OPEN YOUR LOVE BANK ACCOUNT

Start networking by thinking of all the ways you can be helpful and start giving. You're building your Love Bank account. After some robust giving, you can start to ask for help, advice, brainstorming, et cetera. Often when people think of networking, they think, *What can I get?* That leads either to the obnoxious networking mentioned earlier or to anxiety-ridden encounters where you feel you failed if you came away with "nothing." Change your mindset to "What can I give?" and it gets much easier because there's nothing to worry about or fail at.

So, meet in their neighborhood. Pay for the coffee or the lunch (especially if you did the inviting—unless you've agreed to go dutch). Invite them to an event as your guest. Offer a work lead, some industry info, or an idea for solving a problem they're dealing with. Introduce them to people you know.

In some professions, sharing is more the norm than in others: "Freelance publicists tend to be very giving. We share media contacts with one another, as well as potential clients." If your business is stingy, what would happen if you set a different standard?

When reciprocity is working as it should, others will give back in their way. If you feel all the love's coming from you, move on and show it to someone who appreciates what you bring to the party.

In addition to the six fundamentals of influence above, here are a couple of other unwritten rules for Love Banking:

1 **People don't appreciate those who expect a "get" for every "give."** "I was recently recommended for a *huge* project by another freelancer who couldn't take it on herself. She's even spending some time giving me direction on how to proceed. This is by contrast to

another freelancer who used to refer work to me and ask for a kick-back for the referral."

2 When someone gives you something, don't ask for more.
"A freelancer friend and I were at a lecture and I introduced him to a guy I'd worked with on a couple of projects. It turned out my friend and this guy had contacts in common and started talking about them. Later my friend suggested I put in a word about this guy hiring him! I was annoyed. I'd introduced them, they'd hit it off, and now it was up to my friend. In the time it took him to ask me, he could have contacted the guy himself and made a date to continue their great conversation. *And* he had built-in references from contacts they had in common!"

DO THE FOLLOW-UP THREE-STEP

Say you meet some interesting people at an event and collect their cards or contact info. Do the Follow-Up Three-Step:

1 When you get home, jot down some key words on their cards about what you talked about, including personal details.

2 Add them to your contacts list and *include the notes.*

3 A couple of days later, call or email one or two of your new contacts and suggest getting together. Get into this habit and see how it accelerates your networking. Send emails to the others (create a form email that you personalize) saying it was nice to meet them and talk about such-and-such.

If you don't get in touch right away, don't write off the contact. It's never too late. It's kind of flattering for someone to be remembered after time has passed. Here's where those notes on what you talked about come in:

"Dear Barb, We met in December at the public library lecture. I'm still laughing about your story of your toddler and the pancake batter!

I'm interested to hear more about your work. I think there might be ways we could help each other. . . ."

"Hi, Ben: I can't believe the write-a-thon happened almost a year ago! You were a great writing buddy. I'd love to get together and catch up. . . ."

"Dear Jon, This article reminded me of our conversation at Gizmofest about educational toys. How've you been? Do you have time to meet and catch up?"

PRACTICE CREATIVE (NOT CREEPY) CONTACT

Don't be one of those "calls-only-when-they-want-something" networkers. Email and voicemail make the soft reach-out easy:

Send something: An article or video clip they might be interested in; a link to a good discussion board; a funny video you know they'll like.

Congratulate them on something:

A deal: "I saw in *Industry Weekly* that you landed the Big Kahuna project. Congrats! I've been busy finishing up [describe] . . ."

A promotion: "I saw the announcement of your promotion. Congratulations and best wishes for continued success. I hope you've been well. I've been busy . . . [et cetera]"

A new job: "I heard about your new job at Goliath Corp. That's great news! [Et cetera]"

A new product: "I saw your product at the trade show. It's amazing! I hope it's a great success, and that you've been well. I've been busy . . ."

Ask them something: "Have you tried that new software? It's constantly crashing on me. If you have any advice, the drinks are on me!" A genuine appeal to someone's authority or skill motivates them to be consistent by sharing their know-how with you.

You can sign off any way you want—including with a suggestion about getting together: "It would be great to get together later this summer and catch up" or an invitation: "I'd love to get together and catch up. How about coffee later this month?"

RESPECT THEIR TIME

Be sensitive to their time: "I really enjoyed our conversation at the Freelancers Union meet-up the other night. Do you have a minute or two now to talk?" If they're busy, ask if there's a better time for you to call.

Start with some small talk to revive your connection. Then get to your point with a clear transition (assume they're multitasking!): "So, Nate, I'm calling to find out . . . to see if we could get together . . . to ask your advice . . ."

Let them talk: "What do you think?" "What's your opinion?" "Have you ever tried that?" A conversation's a two-way street. You don't have to carry it alone.

Keep your asks modest: "Do you know anything about X Corp.? I'm planning to pitch them and haven't found much info on their R & D."

Better yet, just call because you'd like to get to know them better.

TWO WORDS THAT NEVER GET OLD

"Thank you" has boundless power. Especially when someone gives you work leads, thank them and let them know what happened, even if it didn't work out.

PROSPECTING FOR FUN AND PROFIT

Successful prospecting can seem like a secret formula: "I'm good at making contacts, but I don't feel I've acquired the skills or comfort level to get in front of the people who do the hiring." or luck: "I've been lucky enough to connect with two local media outlets I enjoy working with. For both, it was about meeting and pitching an editor on the spot, and having it work."

The reality's somewhere in between. Prospecting combines strategy, Love Banking, and throwing yourself in the path of opportunity.

THE THREE GOALS OF PROSPECTING

Successful prospecting has three goals:

1 **To start a conversation with the right people.** Make sure you're contacting *prequalified prospects:* people with hiring responsibility in healthy professions or businesses that could conceivably, at some point, use your services. More on that below.

2 **To make a connection.** Treat it like an informational interview. You don't ask for a job. You talk and learn how you might be able to help them out. Ask about their business, their needs, and their view of the industry. If you're a newbie, ask their opinions about your goals, good resources to read or consult, and other people you could talk to.

This might segue to a talk about how you might be able to work with them, or introductions they could make. If not, that's OK—you've made a new contact. Know when to get out of their hair. While an interview may not lead to a yes, there are lots of interesting "not-quite-nos": "Send me some information." "Call me in three months." "You should talk to Sam Prescott at X Corp. Tell him I told you to call." If things don't click, it doesn't mean they never will. More often than not, people return to the table eventually. "I request informational interviews from anyone I'm referred to, or from people I read or hear about in industry news. I've found that, while most people can't offer work, they're happy to meet with you, and you can't have too many contacts. These contacts often lead to others down the road. One of my informational interviews led to four short-term and long-term jobs."

3 To be top of mind when they need someone like you. How do you do that? By staying touch without being creepy, doing a lot of what you do when networking: tuning into their interests and sending info you think they might like, congratulating them on successes, and sharing ideas for how you might be able to work together. You'll have a better chance of being top of mind when they finally do need someone like you. As one manager, now a consultant, told me, "I rarely hired outside contractors, but when I did, I always needed someone right away—and I could never think of anyone! If someone with good skills had been in touch with me a month or so earlier, they'd have gotten my call. Whenever I feel weird about prospecting, I remind myself of that." A graphic designer says, "I send samples to people who haven't hired me in a while saying, 'Here are some designs I recently did for so-and-so, and I wanted you to see them.' I've gotten many new jobs that way."

ARE YOU SABOTAGING YOURSELF AT PROSPECTING? A QUIZ

A lot of prospecting is about staying positive. Are you subtly sabotaging yourself? Take the true/false quiz below and find out.

1 **True/False:** I'm bothering people who'd rather be doing something else.

False. If you've determined beforehand that they could be a qualified prospect, then anyone with any business sense should be willing to at least get to know you. In a few years, they might be looking for work and you'll be looking to subcontract. If they really don't want to talk, they'll say so. Remember, you're not spamming people who couldn't care less about your work, you're talking to people you know you can help—now or in the future.

2 True/False: I'm terrible at selling myself.

False. You're not *selling you;* you're *connecting with them.* You're talking shop. You're great at that. A lot of people who talk shop everywhere else somehow assume they'll be tongue-tied on calls like these.

3 True/False: People will ask questions I can't answer.

False. Asking questions means you've started a conversation— that's half the battle! Chances are you can easily answer questions about what you do. See also: Know What You'll Do If They Ask, "What Are Your Rates?"

4 True/False: I don't know if they'll need me.

True, but you've done enough homework to think they *might* need you—maybe just not yet. I don't need a plumber til I'm mopping the floor with one hand and dialing 800-UNCLOGG with the other. Moral: Nobody needs anybody—until they need somebody. You want to be top of mind when that happens.

5 True/False: There's so much rejection.

True, but rejection helps you prospect efficiently. It lets you focus on prospects who say "not right now," "maybe," "not yet," or "let's talk."

6 True/False: There are so many people to contact, it's overwhelming.

Partly true: More people want to know about you than you might think! And *partly false:* If you carefully qualify your candidates, you'll be narrowing the ocean to a river, river to lake, lake to stream. So when you cast your line, you'll be more confident that these fish may want to bite.

7 **True/False:** Most of them won't lead anywhere.

True. In fact, a lot of the time you'll be getting voicemail. If you get a small number who are mildly interested, you're doing pretty well. Remember, the goal isn't to walk out with a gig (though anything can happen!), but to start a conversation, build your network, and start building your Love Bank account.

THE PROSPECTING ROAD MAP

Though there's no formula for successful prospecting, there are ways to boost your effectiveness and stay on track.

CHOOSE YOUR PROSPECTS

Review your Key Skills List from Chapter 1. Which businesses, professions, industries, or companies might need what you do? Start a list.

Then rank them, from ideal candidates on down. What makes them ideal? Their fit with your skills? Their pay scale? Their size (big and stable . . . midsize and busy . . . start-up and growing)? Their reputation? Their Blue Chip potential? Recently had layoffs and might need outside help?

Next, find contact info for the people who commonly hire people like you. The Internet has made this so much easier. You can search by industry keywords, trade associations, company names, or people's names and titles.

Think about where your prospects go, in person and online. What organizations do they join? What websites, blogs, or discussion groups do they visit? Where do they go to hire people like you? "A lot of my writing gigs come through literary agents looking to match their clients with collaborators," Dan says. "So one day I looked up the website for the Association of Authors' Representatives, an organization several agents I knew belong to. I clicked on the 'Agents' tab, and voilà! Up came a member directory of more than four hundred agents, including contact information, websites, and blogs. The site also had links to other publishing associations I could research. It was an amazing resource."

WRITE A SHORT SCRIPT

No, you won't read it. You'll have it in front of you, so well practiced that you're just glancing at it for key points. It could be in large type with important words or phrases in boldface, a list of talking points, or a flowchart on a legal pad. Your script says who you are and what you do. It asks if they ever hire people who do what you do. It states what you'll do if they're interested. Generally, your goal is to take your conversation a step deeper, usually by sending them some information about yourself and/or setting up a brief meeting, or opening up the possibility of contacting them again. Remember, you're not looking to secure a gig, just to start a conversation.

Personalizing your script a bit helps build liking. Maybe you belong to the same professional group, your kids go to the same school, you attended the same conference recently, or you heard the person give a talk. Mention something you learned about this contact from your research, or how you found the contact: "I read about your work and found your contact information in the Landscape Architects Association membership list . . . on your company's website . . . in the Landscape Architects Expo conference program." If someone referred you, say so.

PRACTICE, PRACTICE

Try out your script with some folks in your Brain Trust. It's better to call than send an email (even a voicemail pitch is more personal than an email pitch—which might get deleted unread). Rehearse both leaving a message and getting them on the phone. Ask your rehearsal partner to respond in different ways—welcoming, terse, in a hurry.

WORK YOUR WAY UP YOUR LIST

Contact less-important prospects first to warm up and get relaxed with your script. Start with industries where you already have work, know your spiel, and feel the strongest match with your skills, rather than industries you're looking to break into.

LISTEN TO YOUR GUT

Some people prospect in ways you'll find impossibly pushy. Don't go there if it's not your style. There's no one way to do this. If your gut's screaming, "Don't go up to that guy and shove your card in his face even though your friends say that's what networking is," then don't do it. It won't work if it doesn't feel genuine. That doesn't mean you shouldn't try new things. But you know the difference between being a little nervous about a new situation and gut-screaming aversion.

DON'T OBSESS ABOUT HOW YOU SAY IT

Don't worry if your delivery isn't perfect. Normal speech isn't. Actually, sounding too rehearsed can make people uncomfortable.

A good way to sound less scripted is to practice verbal mirroring: using words your prospects use. If they're more formal, be a little more formal. If they're less formal, mirror that. For example, if they say, "We're all about the customer here," you'll sound weird if you say, "I applaud your mission to prioritize customer service." You'll be more in sync if you say, "Being all about the customer is a great goal!"

KNOW WHAT YOU'LL DO IF THEY ASK, "WHAT ARE YOUR RATES?"

"My prospecting goes OK until they ask about my rates. Then I freeze, afraid I'll screw up." First, congratulations on getting them interested enough to ask! See how fast a prospecting conversation can morph into a negotiation?

Now's your chance to ask *them* some questions. You probably don't know enough yet about their needs to talk pricing. You might say something like, "I'd be glad to talk about pricing, but first I need a little more information about what your needs are." Then ask your questions.

If you do give pricing in these early conversations, a price range (make sure it's one you're comfortable with—i.e., not leading with your lowest price) will give you some wiggle room and potentially segue to more specific conversation: "Well, depending on its components, which we can talk more about, a pledge campaign could cost from X to X." For more strategies on negotiating pricing, see Chapter 5.

HAVE A FOLLOW-UP PLAN

Suppose things go OK on the call or in the meeting, but they don't have work right now. Have a next step in mind. Such as:

> "I don't want to take any more of your time, but I'd like to send you some information about my work for your files."

> "I'd love to talk with you when you have more time or think you might need the kind of work I do. Would you mind if I checked in with you periodically? Thanks, I appreciate it."

"Thank you so much for your time. Are there others you think I should be talking to?"

"I really appreciate your taking time to meet with me. Are there some books or other resources you think would be good for me to look at to learn more about this side of the business?"

"I'm so glad we got to meet. Thanks so much for your time. By the way, I write an email newsletter about industry goings-on. I'd like to send it to you. Just let me know by responding to this email [or] I'll send it to you." (Make sure your newsletter has an "unsubscribe" option. See Chapter 9 for more about email newsletters.)

KNOW WHEN TO PERSIST OR DESIST

As with networking, following up without being creepy is key. Yes, you'll do the chasing, because getting gigs is up to you. But know when to stop.

You might start by leaving a message, then follow up a week or so later. You might email an article you think they'd find interesting a few weeks after that. Then send some news about your work a month after that. Any signs of life?

If you keep trying and never hear back, or if you decide they're not really a prospect, you might choose to stop. Certainly stop if someone asks you to.

TRACK YOUR PITCHES AND FOLLOW-UPS

Track your prospecting so it's easy to pick up where you left off: when you called or emailed and what you sent; what follow-up you promised; even your impressions and information (reluctant, great vibe, distracted; prepping convention speech; son had soccer tournament coming up) to jog your memory and help you craft your next contact.

Your system could be a file folder and follow-up reminders in your calendar; it could be a spreadsheet; it could be a more sophisticated contact management system or CMS (check out listings online). Just find a system that works for you and maintain it as carefully as you would your financial records. After all, this *is* an investment record—of your time and energy.

In the end, networking and prospecting are about connecting with like-minded people. When you work from that win-win place, your confidence is strong and your enthusiasm contagious. You start to see that life is filled with opportunities to connect, ply your trade, and attract people and projects. As this writer's story shows, it's freelancing at its best:

"I was on the road, writing a music segment for my local public radio station. Early one morning, I found a small coffee shop adjacent to a surprisingly pretty public parking lot. I noticed five or six people in the lot working with large-format cameras—the 'old school' ones on wooden tripods with the long accordion-style lens casing and the black sheet you put over your head to use the viewfinder.

"I instantly saw there was a story here. I'd been listening to public radio for fifteen years and knew this would interest listeners. I had my field recorder in my bag, and I simply walked up to one of the folks and asked what he was doing. It turned out I was seeing a class being taught by a guy who's been designing and building large-format cameras for thirty years. The students had traveled from as far away as London to take the class. The rush of finding something like that, interviewing all of them, and having a great story in the can that day was one of the best feelings I've ever had."

Chapter 5

CLOSING THE DEAL

A good contract distills a relationship, explaining everyone's rights and obligations and describing what happens if bad stuff happens. The word's Latin root, *contrahere*—"to draw together"—pretty much says it all.

Negotiating is about finding out what's fair for you and the other guy. I'm not from the adversarial I-got-everything-I-needed school of contracts. If all your deals are "show me the money" transactions, freelance life will be pretty miserable, and most of your clients won't want to work with you again.

A master negotiator knows when to stand firm and when to bend. This chapter is about helping you figure that out. You'll learn to gauge your negotiating leverage and why a signed contract is your best protection. Then we'll review the main points you'll find in many contracts, with ideas for handling them. Finally, we'll talk negotiating strategy.

THE THREE KEYS TO NEGOTIATING LEVERAGE

Negotiating isn't about putting on a show of bravado. It's about knowing your power relationship with the client.

1 Know your industry's deal norms.

2 Know the market's needs.

3 Know your market value.

KEY 1: KNOW YOUR INDUSTRY'S DEAL NORMS

Demanding terms way outside industry norms makes you look clueless. Get deal help from your freelance community and give it. Join professional discussion groups online. Some organizations have suggested pay rates. Some have model contracts. If yours doesn't, propose it. We're doing it at Freelancers Union.

KEY 2: KNOW THE MARKET'S NEEDS

If you've done your homework, you know your prospects' needs. The greater their need, the greater your leverage.

KEY 3: KNOW YOUR MARKET VALUE

Your negotiating mojo rises with skill and experience. A twenty-one-year-old newbie has less leverage than a forty-one-year-old with twenty years' experience. Also, different types of skills are compensated differently. Not happy with where you stand? Get training, find markets with bigger budgets or need, or work for less money until you gain experience that will be rewarded with higher pay.

WHERE DOES THIS CLIENT FIT?

Next, judge the importance of this client and project.

1 Does it fit my Freelance Portfolio?
2 Does it fit my life?
3 Does it fit *me*?

DOES IT FIT MY FREELANCE PORTFOLIO?

For a potential Blue Chip or a Level 2 growth gig, you might be more flexible. Drive too hard a deal and even if you get it, they may not want to work with you again. Level 3 gigs are often (though not always) mostly about the money on both sides, so use your network to learn the market rate.

If the giving is too one-sided—for example, they won't budge on pricing or their contract would make Attila the Hun call his mother in tears—know why you're taking this on (quick cash? career boost?), because you don't intend an encore.

DOES IT FIT MY LIFE?

Freelancing can fit your life in ways staff work can't. If you're handling a personal issue and need easier, lower-paying work because it's steady and undemanding, do it.

DOES IT FIT *ME?*

Recently a coworker talked about "coming to work with your full self." If a gig feels perfect, you might negotiate differently. If not, you can still take the deal, work well, and gain experience. Save your full self for a more reciprocal relationship.

HANDSHAKES ARE NICE. CONTRACTS ARE BETTER.

That was the headline of a Freelancers Union postcard campaign urging freelancers to try out the Contract Creator tool on our website to better protect themselves when making deals and getting paid.

A signed contract is your strongest evidence that a) a deal existed, and b) the terms were mutually agreed on. That's critical if a dispute is taken to a higher authority.

If you and another person decide over lunch to work together, you've reached an agreement—which is the basis for a legal contract. But there's no *proof* of your agreement. What's your leverage if the client remembers the conversation differently?

An email thread beats a verbal agreement. Even better: a deal memo. But a contract signed by all is your best protection. That's why we at Freelancers Union say you should have one—and why we worked closely with our members to come up with Contract Creator, an amazing, easy tool Freelancers Union members can use to help formulate a fairer contract.

If clients insist on using their contract, you can review it and suggest revisions. You can create your own contract, in friendly or formal language. As mentioned, some professional groups have sample agreements. Someone in your network might recommend a lawyer (see Hiring a Lawyer) or have a template you could adapt: "When I landed my first big deal, I told a colleague who's also a lawyer that I'd hire her to draft a contract for me. Her reply? 'Oh, please!' and she sent me the one she uses, plus a contract checklist from an industry association. I nearly cried with gratitude."

At minimum, send a deal letter or memo recapping the terms and saying, basically: "This is my understanding of what we've agreed." You can end it with: "If I don't hear back from you, I will assume these terms are acceptable to you." This is called an adoptive admission. Or: "I look forward to getting started once I receive confirmation of these terms." Or tell them when you'll send your contract or ask when you can expect theirs.

If you send your contract or deal letter via certified mail, return receipt requested, you'll have proof that the client got it.

HIRING A LAWYER

If a contract is pretty standard, you may not need a lawyer, though having a lawyer vet a few contracts can teach you a lot about negotiating. But a complex or big-money contract or project is a reason to hire one. A negotiating issue quickly zapped by a lawyer can cost twenty to forty times more to untangle in a legal battle—very possibly beyond the claim's worth.

A lawyer can draft your contract, an independent contractor agreement (for subcontracting), and a nondisclosure agreement when a project requires confidentiality; pursue deadbeat clients; and coach you through representing yourself in small claims court or when a legal perspective can help.

Get recommendations from your Brain Trust and freelancers in your industry. Ask accountants and financial advisers. Your local bar association may have a referral service. For a guide to legal resources by state, log onto the American Bar Association website's "Consumers' Guide to Legal Help" (americanbar.org).

Some questions to ask:

- Would a big, "name" firm benefit me, and would I get enough attention—or should I go with a smaller firm?
- Does this attorney understand my needs and my industry and communicate clearly?
- Do they work on a contingency basis, a billable hours basis, on retainer, or some other fee structure?
- Are there ways to reduce fees, for example, by working with junior members sometimes?
- Can I get an idea of what this may cost, and could we establish a cost ceiling?

THE ONE-HOUR CONTRACT

Your contract should address anything that could cost you *money, time,* or *skill*—the three key commodities of business.

Below is an overview of common contractual issues for freelancers. It's not exhaustive, as every profession (and practically every contract) is unique, but you can use these points as a general road map. You should be guided by your industry's norms and by an attorney who knows your situation.

WHO, WHAT, WHEN, WHERE, HOW—AND HOW MUCH: TERMS

"I've learned it's extremely important to make sure clients understand not only my responsibilities, but also theirs."

Your contract should spell out what you'll do, what you'll be paid, *and what's expected of the client.*

The more detailed the terms, the better: "I undercharged for a project that had a million revisions. Next time, I'd set a limit on the amount of revisions and then start to charge for them."

Below are brief descriptions of terms that are commonly found in contracts.

Statement of the Work

A summary sentence or two describing what you'll deliver. State the services you'll provide in broad yet clear strokes, which will then be detailed in the sections on project scope, deliverables, and deadlines.

Project Scope and Deliverables

Here's where you prevent scope creep. Define the deliverables: What are you designing, writing, building, cooking, teaching, photographing, filming, performing?

Quantify the deliverables: How many items, hours, words, recipes, guests, students, photos, performances?

Nail down detailed specifications: What formats, programs, procedures, dimensions, colors, locations, subjects?

How and where will this be produced, delivered, shipped, prepared, taught, set up and dismantled, performed?

What have you agreed about the process, such as: review/revision cycles, meetings, fittings, tastings, rehearsals?

Should you address additional work? For example, pricing for additional changes, that the rates may go up, or that additional work will be covered in another agreement on terms to be agreed.

Deadline(s)

When are deliverables due? If in stages, when? What if you need more time? Is there a grace period?

Approvals

What's the criterion for satisfactory completion? Will the client have approval over the final product and interim stages? Are there approval time frames? What if the client misses them? If the client doesn't approve the final, must the client provide specifics about changes?

What's a reasonable revision period? What if the client still doesn't approve (see It's Over: Termination, which follows)?

After approval, how will additional questions, consults, or changes be handled (some for free, with a charge for more? with a service contract?)?

What if errors or problems are found post-approval?

Payment Structure

Payment in stages evens out your cash flow, covers project-related expenses, builds in timely feedback, and can alert you to slow-paying or deadbeat clients. Make sure the milestones are doable. If they need it ASAP, will you charge a rush rate?

Payment structure depends on your industry. Ask other freelancers what they do: "I send invoices with the lowest total I can. For instance, if someone's paying me two hundred fifty dollars per script read-through, I'll bill five hundred dollars for every two scripts instead of twenty-five hundred dollars for ten scripts. I think paying smaller increments makes a psychological difference for my client, who has to approve each bill for payment. To help me track what's paid and what's outstanding, I break the payments into different amounts—one invoice for five hundred dollars; one for seven hundred fifty dollars; then one for two hundred fifty dollars—so all the checks aren't for the same amount."

Try for an up-front payment. A large portion is a good idea with out-of-state clients, since it's hard to collect a judgment from them. That goes double for international clients. (P.S.: Payment in U.S. dollars eliminates conversion issues.)

If up-front payment is acceptable in your field but the client is reluctant, maybe they're just uninformed, or maybe it signals potential payment problems. Be careful about working too far past an outstanding payment.

Your contract should specify when payment is due and what happens if it's late. You can include a grace period or a late fee—such as a percentage of the total. (For more on nonpayment, see Chapter 7.)

ADVOCACY ALERT

BAD CONTRACT Some companies will pay you faster if you agree to a discount on your fee. Please excuse us if we don't tug our forelocks, bob a curtsy, and say, "Much obliged."

Instead we say bad contract! Freelancers shouldn't have to pay to get paid. Share this kind of intel with other freelancers and use our Client Scorecard to out these offenders. Start a movement in your professional group to take a stand against them.

WHO PAYS: EXPENSES

In some professions, outlay is significant: supplies, permits, equipment, rentals, travel. Will you be reimbursed, or will expenses be built into your price?

NONCOMPETE LANGUAGE

The client may want to prohibit you from working with competitors. It's understandable, but it can limit your making a living. If this is a problem, talk early about less restrictive language.

OWNERSHIP

The contract should state who owns the final product. If that's you and you'll be licensing it to the client, some issues to work out include format, territory, duration, exclusivity, and what, if any, ongoing compensation you receive (a royalty or some percentage of the income?). See the discussion of intellectual property, page 136.

WARRANTIES, REPRESENTATIONS, AND COVENANTS

Think of these as guarantees you each make. If they're untrue or broken, you could be sued for damages and the deal could end. Keeping the warranties reasonable is key.

Some common examples include warranting that you're free to make this agreement (you might not be if, say, you have a noncompete agreement with a competitor). Or that your service or product doesn't damage or injure others or infringe on their rights. Don't guarantee things you can't control.

Think about these and other covenants your client should make. What do you need from your client to meet your obligations? Could be production specs, financial data, artwork, research, interview time, guest list, or other resources.

Both of you might want confidentiality about material you share with each other—both yours and the client's. Specify what you can say publicly about your involvement with the project as part of building your business.

At some point in your freelance travels, you'll likely encounter a nondisclosure agreement (NDA) or confidentiality agreement. An NDA prevents trade secrets from being shared. It can cover confidential information from both parties, or one. You may be asked to sign one, or you can ask prospects, clients, and subcontractors to sign one.

Among other things, an NDA should define what can't be divulged, whether there's a time limit for maintaining secrecy, and how disputes and breaches will be handled.

Read an NDA carefully, especially since some documents with the NDA heading are actually waivers of confidentiality that *remove* your trade secret from protection by stating, in essence, that sharing the information does not mean there is confidentiality between the parties.

Most freelancer contracts have a clause stating that you're an independent contractor, not an employee, so the client doesn't have an employer's obligation to you (such as paying wages and benefits). Just make sure it's also clear that you don't have an employee's obligations toward your client (such as letting them control when, where, and how you work).

Liability or indemnification language covers who's legally responsible if a negative event happens, and the limits of each party's liability. If you do the kind of work where liability could be an issue, you're not sure what the language means, or think it should be changed, consult a lawyer.

If you're a licensed professional, you're responsible personally for malpractice and you should have liability insurance. Even if you're not a licensed professional, consider liability insurance depending on the kind of work you do.

TERM AND RENEWAL

There might be language stating how long the agreement will last and whether it's renewable. Repeat business is sweet—but not necessarily on the same terms. How about a percentage increase, or renewal on terms to be agreed? Nix language that automatically renews the contract unless you terminate it in a certain time frame. You don't want to be opted in if you forget to opt out!

IT'S THE LAW: GOVERNING LAW

This clause specifies which state's laws apply in a dispute—important if the laws for your profession vary state to state.

YOUR STATE OR MINE? JURISDICTION

This clause spells out where disputes would be heard. Try to keep it in your state and county. Traveling is expensive, plus there's the cost of hiring local counsel. Generally it's wiser to handle disputes through arbitration or other alternatives—see Disputes, below.

FORCE MAJEURE

This language says the parties won't be liable if an event beyond their control, such as a natural disaster or other calamity, makes it impossible to meet their obligations. Look into what would be considered force majeure in your field; find out if your professional association has info on this. If you're still not sure or have specific questions, consult an attorney.

THIS IS IT: ENTIRE AGREEMENT

This basically says that this agreement supersedes any other communications between you, and that any changes have to be made in writing. So make sure the contract fully reflects your understanding.

IT'S OVER: TERMINATION

Sadly, gigs sometimes die an untimely death. Every contract should address how and why that could happen. Possible examples: for warranty breach, nondelivery, nonpayment, unacceptability of deliverables. It's best to spell these out so everyone is clear: "I had an agreement for a multipart writing assignment. I turned in the first part and received my fee. Then the client felt the publisher was going to do the next part, so she didn't need me to do it—or pay me for it. I should have had a clearer arrangement so I'd get paid no matter what happened."

You've got four negotiating goals:

1 **Define the grounds for termination.**

2 **Make them as balanced as possible** (i.e., you're not carrying all the risk). Beware of termination language favoring the client far more than you, or allowing termination for less-than-major reasons.

3 **Define the payment scheme.** Can you keep amounts paid?

Would the client ever be required to pay additional amounts, such as reimbursing expenses incurred? Some professions have cancellation policies. Others stipulate a kill fee. If the initial payment becomes the kill fee, is the amount acceptable? "In sixteen years, I've been 'fired' once, and it was a mutual decision. Thank God, I had a termination fee—I earned it. The people I was working with were known to be difficult, so I built combat pay into my fee."

4 Specify how notice will be given. The parties might have to give each other advance written notice of a breach and a reasonable period to try to fix things before termination kicks in. But there might be times when you could terminate immediately; for example, if the client is breaking the law, injuring or violating the rights of others (you included), putting you in such a position, or acting in ways that could hurt your reputation.

DISPUTES

The cost of resolving disputes can be so high that even winning can feel like losing. Which is why Freelancers Union is so clear on ADR— alternative dispute resolution. It saves money and time, so companies typically appreciate it, too. I believe no freelancer contract should be without an ADR provision unless there's a really good reason. Here are three ADR approaches:

1 Mediation. The parties hire a trained mediator to help them get to a settlement. The mediator is not making the final decision, so the parties have to want to reach a solution.

2 Arbitration. You each present your case to an arbitrator (sometimes more than one), who renders a decision called an award. Unlike judges, arbitrators don't have to follow case precedents or law; they can assess the case based on their sense of fairness. Although arbitration isn't as formal as a trial, there are costs, which may include hiring a lawyer.

3 **Negotiation.** The parties or their attorneys negotiate and arrive at a settlement.

Often an arbitration clause names the organization that would handle arbitration, frequently the American Arbitration Association, JAMS (Judicial Arbitration and Mediation Services), or the National Arbitration Forum (see Appendix). (For information about small claims court, see Chapter 7.)

INTELLECTUAL PROPERTY: PROTECTING WHAT'S YOURS (AND WHAT *IS* YOURS?)

If you'll turn to Article 1, Section 8 of your pocket copy of the U.S. Constitution, you'll find that Congress has the power "To promote the Progress of Science and useful Arts, by securing for limited Times to Authors and Inventors the exclusive Right to their respective Writings and Discoveries."

That's forefather-speak for intellectual property rights residing with their owners for a period of time. So highly did our nation's founders value creative workers' contributions that the power to declare war got lower billing!

Your intellectual property (IP) is the product of your skills and experience. It can bring direct income (such as a book), lead to income (such as your fabulously annotated mailing list), or be integral to your professional identity (such as a business name, product name, or logo).

Intellectual property can span software technology to toys; databases to music scores; websites to blueprints—there are even special copyright forms for hulls and masks!

If you've ever tried to negotiate IP ownership in a contract and gotten major push-back, it's because IP has value. How much, and how

FREELANCERS SPEAK **The Little Book That Could** This freelancer's story reveals just how important your intellectual property can be to Level 4 of your Freelance Portfolio, leading to new ventures and income streams:

"About twenty years ago, a publisher paid me a $25,000 advance to write a book. After several years, they reverted the rights to me as copyright holder. My agent resold the rights to another publisher for $7,000 to republish the book. Eventually, we got the rights back again. Then we licensed custom edition rights to a retailer. It sold like crazy for several years (my first experience of royalties!). Then we licensed the remaining rights to another publisher for a $7,500 advance and published a new version. Recently, I successfully got those rights reverted to me. Now I'm considering retooling some of the content into short digital pieces.

"So far, this content has had four lives and earned thousands of dollars. It wasn't until its third edition that it actually sold really well—not only bringing income, but enabling me to market myself as an author whose book had sold more than 100,000 copies. If I'd written it as a work for hire and hadn't held the copyright, I wouldn't have that credential, and I wouldn't have profited from anything but the first edition."

far you're willing to go to protect it, generally has to be decided case by case.

Freelancers should grant the minimum rights possible. Leveraging this depends on your industry's norms and your negotiating power. But on principle, retaining your rights is a good policy, because technology and business are spinning so fast you never know how your IP could profit you down the road.

I'd like to see freelancers avoid signing contracts that give up "all rights" for an unlimited time, and contracts that grab "future" rights not yet invented—since how can a fair value be assigned to rights that don't yet exist?

Freelancers Union aims to drag these kinds of practices into the light, since changes in negotiating policy usually happen only when workers unite against them. We need to push for rights models that are legitimate and fair and not let industries extract all rights as the norm and pay less and less for them. Until we prevail, there will be contracts like this out there, but we're on a mission to see them gone.

Protecting your intellectual property involves two steps:

1 Formally registering your IP with the appropriate agency (for trademarks and patents, it's the U.S. Patent and Trademark Office (USPTO); for copyright, it's the U.S. Copyright Office—see Appendix).

2 Being vigilant about protecting your rights. You can lose your trademark, for example, if you're not vigilant, so keep up with your industry and be alert to new products and launches.

Trade secrets lose that status if they become known or knowable in your profession, so secure your premises, protect your files, put notices on confidential material, and make sure anyone who has contact with proprietary material signs a nondisclosure agreement. Be alert to unauthorized sales or use of your copyrighted material. If you spot possible infringements, consult your attorney.

If intellectual property is important to you or you aren't sure whether it should be, consider consulting an attorney specializing in IP. Do this early, especially with anything relating to patents, since there are time limits for getting patent protection.

A DOZEN NEGOTIATING DOS AND DON'TS

What and how you negotiate depends on your leverage, best practices in your profession, and the advice of your attorney if you hire one, but here are some dos and don'ts to keep in mind.

1: DON'T GO IN BLIND.

Learn about your prospect (they probably learned about you). Read financials, press, reviews, complaints. Visit their website, blog, and social media feeds. Ask your Brain Trust what they know.

2: DO PICK YOUR SHOTS.

Pick several points you consider must-haves; several you can give up, and several you could go either way on. You'll feel calmer knowing your deal breakers and what you can trade depending on how the negotiation's going.

3: DO NAIL DOWN SPECS AND EXPECTATIONS.

I can't overstress this. Failure here can cause freelancer pain off the Richter scale. So find out things like:

What's considered within the project's scope, what isn't, and what happens if the scope changes? How many revision rounds, reception guests, or platters of hors d'oeuvres will there be? Approximately how many hours might this project take? When your client says "animation," does that mean rough animation, cleanup, or both? Will illustrations be delivered as hard copy or electronic files? What software version will be used? What are "reasonable" changes? What's considered "acceptable"? How long does the client have for approvals? What happens if the client wants more work done? What expenses will you incur? Do you cover expenses or does the client? You can even specify that if the project scope changes, the price may go up.

Make a checklist of scope issues for your kind of work and check off items as you finalize the deal.

4: DO SHOW VALUE, VALUE, VALUE.

One freelancer got this negotiating advice: "Explain everything you'll be doing so you can justify your price. Explain how you're adding value to their project."

When you focus on your value, you're not haggling over money, but explaining why your skills are a great match for their project. Every skill has a price.

"Too expensive," client says? Offer a different level of service at a different price. Fewer dollars buys fewer services.

If your value arguments don't work, let them look for their price. You look for a client willing to pay for your value.

5: DON'T LET THINGS DRAG ON.

If you need time to run costs or aren't available, say when you'll respond. But promptness should be a two-way street: Waiting months for contracts and payments can wreck your cash flow and workflow. Maybe add a little scarcity and put a reasonable clock on your terms:

"If we have a signed agreement and initial payment by September 1, we can deliver by your deadline."

"The cost of supplies goes up on the first of the year, so work done after that point will be billed at the higher rate."

6: BUT DO TAKE A STEP BACK IF YOU NEED TO.

It's OK to say, "I need a little time to think this over." "I'll need to rerun the numbers for those quantities." You want your answer to be right, not rushed.

7: DO THINK TWICE BEFORE LOWERING YOUR PRICE.

There are reasons for coming down slightly on price—like a one-time discount to fill an income gap, break a dry spell, or bag a Blue Chip. But too much price flexibility suggests your work has no clear value. Don't expect your client to respect your worth if you don't. Also, if word gets around about your rates, it can be tough to raise them.

Instead, adjust services offered, or break the work into separately priced segments: "A lot of people don't want to get locked into a long-term arrangement until they get to know you better, so break the job into pieces." Or throw in something as a one-time extra. Finding ways to work things out can help fill your pipeline while helping clients stretch their budgets.

8: DON'T ASSUME ALL CLIENTS AND PROJECTS ARE CREATED EQUAL.

Decide how you prefer to be paid and know what's standard in your industry (project fee? hourly rate? retainer?). But reserve the right to change things up depending on your needs. Hourly pay can work if you have no clue about the project's scope. A defined project fee is reassuring for the client and might help you finalize a deal with one you really want—but make sure you know what the project involves. A retainer can even out your cash flow if the client's willing to commit to it.

You may charge more to squeeze a client onto your full plate or to take on a high-maintenance client who'll leave you less time for other work. You might accept less money in a dry time. For a Blue Chip, a high-paying client, or for a project or business you believe in, you might give a one-time pass on scope creep: "I took care of it, but it cost X/added X hours/was outside the scope of our contract. I'd be glad to continue to do it; we just need to amend our financial agreement to cover it." That's smart Love Banking.

9: DO USE SILENCE, SOMETIMES.

Silence takes control of the dialogue, which can't continue without you. Often people rush to fill it:

Prospect: "We can only offer you [abysmally low amount]."

You: [*silence*]

Prospect: "We might be able to come up a little . . ."

You: "What did you have in mind?"

Prospect: "Maybe [the bottom of your range]?"

You: "Hm. Well, in that range, we could do A and B."

Prospect: "Not C, D, and E?"

You: "How about if we do A and B at the rate you suggested, and include pricing for C, D, and E so you can add them later if you want."

10: DO BE COOL ABOUT TALKING MONEY.

People *expect* you to. Some will respect you for bringing it up, or be relieved they didn't have to.

You can learn to talk money even if you never get totally comfortable with it. Here are some strategies:

Arrive early. By the time you get to contract stage, you should have had several money conversations with your prospect. Talking money early also lets you weed out tire kickers who pump you for advice. Just offer glimpses of your value: "One thing I'd address is . . . ," If they push for details, say something like, "I'd need to know more about the project and your needs, and that means getting more specifics and talking about pricing."

Suss out their expectations. Some ways to ask: "Do you have a project budget?" "Do you have a range in mind?" "What did you pay last time?" "What's affordable?" Then talk about what services that would buy.

Listen for concerns. Say they balk at the up-front payment. Find out what's driving that. Cash flow problem? You might be able to take a bit less up front and add an interim payment a few months in. Price too high? You could adjust the services or the project scope: "Sometimes I suggest we just edit one chapter, if they're reluctant to commit to a whole manuscript. They see what I can do and come to trust me. Often we just keep going. Small steps put them in control—*and* help me price the project." That's bending to make a fair contract. It's better than insisting on your top price and maybe getting it, but meanwhile the other party, feeling you stuck it to them, has already decided to replace you for the next gig.

Think "costs," not "fees." If they ask, "What's your fee?" turn it around to talk tasks and value: "Let's talk about what you want to do. Then we can talk about what that would cost."

Even if you charge by the hour, you can say, "Writing costs X per hour" vs. "I charge X per hour." That leaves the option to charge differently for a different service. Instead of lowering your writing rate if the client thinks it's too high, you say, "Well, I could edit your draft, which costs X per hour."

Think ranges or options. Instead of a single price, quote a range. It gives you latitude for scope creep: "I find complex jobs tend to get bigger and more complex, and the terms you negotiated don't cover the new tasks at hand. Then you're faced with earning five dollars an hour under the original terms or trying to renegotiate new terms, which makes it look like you're being tricky (bait and switch). It's important to build in some 'wiggle room.'"

Or give an array of prices: "That could cost X, or Y, or Z." This helps loop them in if they have no clue about costs. Then you can tell them what services those amounts will buy. It's a win-win: You're tailoring your services to their needs, not quoting too high (for them) or too low (for you).

Beware of low-ball offers. Comments like "Our budget is tiny" or "There's no budget" could mean they're very price-driven.

This is where knowing market rates helps. Learn the project scope, pick a price range high enough so you won't be annoyed if they turn out to be tough customers, and quote it.

Doesn't fly? Modify your services so you can charge less. No go? Cut them loose: "I'm sorry we won't have a chance to work together, but I hope the project is a great success!" If you hear backpedaling: "Maybe we can work something out," that's your cue to say, "When should we talk again?"

If they won't give enough info about the project scope so you can price it, you might say, "It's hard to cost out a project accurately without more information. I'd be glad to talk some other time, once you know more." Sometimes prospects need to shop around. They may come back to you. If they find someone at their price, good for them (though more than one freelancer has had a prospect hire them later to fix the work of the "better deal"—great leverage for you when this happens.)

If things are going nowhere and you've had enough, you could just say, "I've given this some thought, and I don't think I'm the right fit for the project, but thank you for thinking of me."

11: DO VALUE YOUR TIME.

Suppose your price is on the table, and . . . no word. Maybe inject some scarcity: "I'd really like to work with you, but my schedule's getting full. If the contract isn't signed and initial payment received by [date], the project will need to be done at a rush rate, which would be [specify]." Or "I'd really like to work with you, but my schedule's quickly filling up. If the contract isn't signed and initial payment received by [date], I won't be able to do it."

12: DO TRUST YOUR AUTHORITY.

Businesspeople can make decisions that are seriously dumb and shockingly subjective. "It's challenging to be in a 'horserace' where a client is considering different freelancers," one freelancer notes. "I lost a race once because Freelancer A promised he could accomplish the work in something like one month. My time estimate was more like six months. Freelancer A either had no idea what he was talking about, or was lying to get the job. Which he did."

The best way to stay confident is to do the homework we've been talking about: know the market norms, pricing, your value, and the project's fit in your Freelance Portfolio. Then you can go in knowing you've optimized your chances of landing the gig.

Finally, go in knowing your walkaways:

"Know the lowest price you will do the project for and balance that with what may come out of it for you. Contacts? Something you can mention on your website? The possibility of more work down the road?"

"I won't do free work just to prove I know what I'm doing. I think this is exploitative. If people want to see a sample of your work, offer to do a brief sample for free or do a longer sample for a fee."

"I work hard to get to an agreement with prospects. So when I say no, they know I'm not bluffing. By then they usually feel my walking away would be a loss for their project, and they're more willing to work things out."

"At the end of the day, it's about who needs whom more. That's why I think economic security is a freelancer's most important bargaining tool. If I know I can walk away from a negotiation or fire a client if I have to because I can survive financially without them, that's my negotiating ace in the hole. I've never had to do it, but knowing I can gives me confidence."

If things don't work out, learn from all the info you've gathered from the experience—even the rejection. Remember these people are not God; don't let them make you feel inadequate.

If you're constantly striking out, assess: Are you outpricing your market or trying to sell a service no one wants? Learn, correct course, and move ahead.

Negotiating can feel nerve-wracking. But if you've done your industry homework, have a community you trust to consult with and coach you, and know your own skills, you've got the basis of your negotiating platform. The rest you learn on the job.

"You can read all the books and talk to all the people in the world about freelancing, but until you start your own freelance career, you won't truly get it. You have to actually go through the process and learn as you go. You have to create your own path. Only you can envision where the path is heading. You are the captain of your own ship."

"When I started, I was afraid my phone wouldn't ring. Now I worry how I'll get it all done!"

Chapter 6

CLIENTS 360°

How do you give great service to each client when you get really busy (and you *will* get busy)? In this chapter we'll look at how to give clients what they want without losing sight of what *you* want—from your day-to-day interactions and best practices to some important legal issues freelancers need to know about.

THE THREE MOST IMPORTANT WAYS TO KEEP CLIENTS HAPPY

Do these three things most of the time, and most clients will show amazing tolerance if (OK, *when*) you mess up sometimes:

1 Be there. **2** Prepare. **3** Care.

1: BE THERE

Being there means looking out for your clients' interests—often just requiring garden-variety best practices:

Turn in your best work, on time. It's the ultimate be-there.

Say what you *can* do, not what you can't.

Be on time for meetings and calls. People might not comment on it, but lateness is noticed. Even a few minutes rankles some closet control freaks.

"I CAN'T" STATEMENT	"I CAN" STATEMENT
"I can't do a call until three p.m."	"I'm here from three p.m. until five p.m. When would be a good time?"
"That deadline's too tight."	"I can deliver it by _____."
"I can't start for three months."	"I'd love to work with you, if we can start in June."
"I can't start until I receive the initial payment."	"I look forward to starting work after receipt of the initial payment."

Don't multitask on calls. Think clients won't hear your computer's cheery "Hello, I'm turning on!" song? Keys clicking? Email-distracted pauses? Don't you?

Unless you're butt-deep in a crisis, don't take calls during calls or meetings with clients. It's like dating: Clients know you see other people, but they don't want to think about it.

Be helpful, even when it's not your job. Your clients should be in your Love Bank. Drop off a package to save them sending a courier. Bring an extra copy to the meeting. Don't charge for the first time they cancel a session (with a friendly warning: "Normally, I charge for a cancelled session, but you get a free pass the first time.").

Stay in touch. Not just when you're paid to be.

> "Hi, Dave. I saw a Gizmofest ad today and thought of you. You're probably getting ready to go. Have a great show."

> "Hi, Daria, Happy New Year! I wondered how things were going with your script submissions."

> "Hey, Devon. Great blog post yesterday! I shared the link."

It's not that you always have to be there. But when you're there, you're *there*. "A client once told me, 'You had a hundred deadlines, but I never felt you didn't have time for me. If I called when you were busy, you'd say, "I'd love to talk about that; let's set up a time. How about tomorrow morning?" You always made me feel important, you knew how to manage your time, and you found time for me somehow.'"

2: PREPARE

Preparation tells clients they're important. Keeping your office and yourself organized will help. For strategies on that, see Chapters 2, 13, and 14. Meanwhile, some tips:

Let them know you prepared: "I looked at your website . . ." "I did some preliminary research . . ." "I was reviewing my notes . . ." "I read your latest book . . ."

Get up to speed: "Let me call you when I have the document on-screen." "I'll touch base after I've read your memo."

Respect their time: "You said you had another call at eleven. I've got a couple more questions and then we'll wrap up."

3: CARE

Caring takes surprisingly little effort and builds shining palaces of goodwill. Transparency shows caring and builds trust—especially important with new clients, since people are generally most vigilant at the start of a relationship: "When I start editing a client's manuscript, I give a reason for every suggestion," Luke says. "Once they trust me, we can communicate in shorthand. Ultimately, things move faster, they get a better book, and I get really happy clients."

Personal caring counts hugely: "Years ago, I was scheduled to meet a prospect who was coming into town for a lot of meetings. The day before, he left a voicemail cancelling his trip because his wife had a health emergency. I left him a message saying I hoped his wife was OK. That was years ago. He's never forgotten that I was the only one who called to express concern for his wife."

ON THE FRONT LINES WITH CLIENTS

Company workers handling a tough client can hide behind company policy, bring in reinforcements (the boss), or even heavy artillery (the legal department).

You, freelancer, are infantry, general, and artillery rolled into one. You have to establish your policies, communicate them, and enforce them. Thus the funky whiplash feeling you get playing good cop/bad cop—seeing as how you're the only cop in the room: "We're on track for the deadline. But we need to discuss the payment that was due last month."

The best way to have great client relationships is to map out the strategy, tell your client what to expect, and then keep the campaign on track. After all, who knows more about getting your job done than you?

"I WILL DO THIS, NOT THAT."

It starts with your first conversation, where you explain what you provide for your price, how you'll meet your obligations, and what you'll need from your client in order to do so. In psychobabble, you're setting boundaries. In business, you're managing expectations.

Boundaries are best set *before* they're violated. Just be collaborative yet confident: "I've found this works [describe]. I think it'll work here. What do you think?" You're building trust and setting the project up for success and so it works for you.

SETTING BOUNDARIES: A CHECKLIST

Use or adapt this checklist to set your boundaries with clients. Be willing to give a little, and they should, too. One person getting everything their way usually signals a dangerous imbalance in the relationship (more on that in Chapter 7).

1 **Anything else we need to discuss?** Presumably you nailed down project specs and scope in your agreement, but if there are any loose ends, handle them now: "I'm all set to start, as soon as we work out a few final details." If necessary, do a contract amendment or send a confirming email or letter: "Here's what we agreed on today. I look forward to working with you."

2 **My communication practices:** Some freelancers check email

and phone messages at specific times. If you do, say so. Try not to make exceptions at the start.

3 My weekend availability: Some freelancers work on weekends just like weekdays. Some work but don't answer emails or calls. Some take weekends completely off. Some (like party planners or musicians) may be busiest on weekends and take time off during the week. Explain your policy. Any later exceptions are nice Love Bank things to do.

4 My availability during the workday: If all hell breaks loose when your kids get home from school, you might say, "I don't take phone calls after four p.m. because of family obligations. I've worked this way with all my clients [social validation] and it's never caused problems." You don't have to explain. Maybe Wednesday afternoons are for sports, yoga, personal writing, museum visits, recipe testing, bookkeeping, visiting a relative, volunteering, writing your blog or newsletter, or working on Level 4 projects. Just make an "I can" statement: "On Wednesdays, I'm available until two p.m."

5 How we'll do check-ins: Will you email weekly progress reports? Say so. Hate to be interrupted? Flag it: "When I'm writing, calls go to voicemail. But you can always leave me a message. I'll get back to you in twenty-four hours."

6 How we'll structure feedback and approvals: Try to suss out the decision tree: Who makes the decisions? Are there layers of approval? Ideally, put specifics in the deal (see Chapter 5). Be clear that you're a team, with shared accountability: "Let's set up a feedback system so delays don't jeopardize the schedule." Then make sure it happens.

7 What's the best way for me to work with you? "A client mentioned he's a morning person, so I try to schedule our calls then."

"I noticed a client was emailing me on Sundays—obviously when she was carving out time for our project. I try to set up my work-flow so I can send her material on Fridays."

8 Do you have any policies or procedures I should know about? Do they need layouts by three p.m. Monday for their ten a.m. Tuesday marketing meetings? Do they cut checks on Thursdays and need three weeks to process invoices?

TELL 'EM WHAT YOU'RE GONNA SAY. SAY IT. THEN TELL 'EM WHAT YOU SAID.

The clients you want to work with—the grown-ups of the business world—notice good communication: "I'm a great communicator and rarely let things fall through the cracks. On the rare times that it seems I'm going to miss a deadline, I'm in communication, and my clients appreciate that."

Employees work in a living laboratory for communication, but freelancers have to learn on their own. Read up on communication and study people who do it well. Here are some ground rules:

Be the expert on you.

Even if your client has worked with freelancers before, everyone's different. Put a page on your website about how you work. Tell your client how you operate. Use the Setting Boundaries checklist. Explain your next steps on their project.

Lead by following.

That means helping clients figure out what they want; then tactfully escorting them toward decisions:

"How do you envision the event?"

"Why do you think the competition is outselling you?"

"What do you think isn't working in the ad campaign?"

Stay in touch.

Unlike bosses, clients can't see how hard you're working. So tell 'em:

"I'm starting the next section today."

"The mock-up will be ready next week."

"I fixed the coding glitches."

If problems arise, they'll know you were on top of things. You're also giving them an opening to give you information:

"I have new data for that section."

"I'm on jury duty next week, so take more time if you want."

And it keeps everyone on point about his or her responsibilities:

You: "The photo research is almost done and ready for you to start clearing the permissions."

Client: "I thought you were doing that."

You: "Actually, our contract says I'm doing the photo research and you're clearing the permissions."

Offer choices—but only ones you can deliver on.

Ask which versions . . . colors . . . desserts . . . formats . . . they'd like. Narrow the options to a few you recommend, and say why. Asking for too much input makes you look indecisive, and your clients will expect unlimited input on everything.

Document, document.

When you reach agreement on a key issue, send a quick email recap or do a contract amendment if it's major. It's good protection for everyone. Suppose your contact or the person who green-lighted the project leaves or is laid off, or the boss hates the campaign. You need paperwork to confirm that yes, the budget was authorized, the deadline was extended, and the colors were approved.

Respond, respond.

Even if it's just: "I got your email and will proceed as instructed. Thanks." When you don't respond—especially about a problem—you're putting your reputation into someone else's hands. Get in there and manage perceptions. Even just saying, "I need to look into your questions. I'll get back to you by [date or time frame]" lets them know you're on the case.

Decide which communication method to use.

Whether it's face-to-face, phone, texting, email, fax, or snail-mail depends on your purpose and planned impact.

Email is fine much of the time. Just choose it; don't default to it. A client who emails you may be assuming you'll respond in kind (same goes for the phone). But if you think the conversation can be more productive in another mode, you can, for example, decide to call to discuss their email. Consider the client's comfort level and what will move things forward.

Don't assume people will read long emails, especially since so many read messages on their smartphone. Get to the point, list your questions or options, and when appropriate suggest a date to finalize a plan.

When you're angry, step away from the keyboard! Angry written words last forever. A phone call or meeting could be a smarter choice.

The phone is great for getting a quick decision, brainstorming, and persuading, and it gives you valuable clues from the person's tone. It's powerful for subtle or sensitive communication, from negotiations to troubleshooting.

Snail mail is high-impact because it's increasingly rare: usually reserved for "official" communications such as formal proposals, contracts, and legal correspondence. You can email the doc as an attachment for quick receipt and follow it with a snail-mailed hard copy.

Then there's the handwritten note: warm, rare, high-impact. A typewritten thank-you note is impressive; a handwritten one is exceptional.

Choose your words. Proofread, proofread.

If you've got something tough to write, draft it in chunks. Start with the sections where ideas and words are flowing, or sections you can adapt from other material. That way you make progress and get inspiration for the harder parts. Or try drawing a flowchart or diagram to map out your ideas.

Proofread more than once; don't trust your computer spelling and grammar check to catch everything. If it's really important, ask your mate or a Brain Trust buddy to proofread and give feedback. Double-check to make sure people you want cc'd on an email (or not) are included (or aren't).

With international clients, avoid slang, metaphors, or abbreviations that could be misunderstood.

Be sensitive to intergenerational issues. If a client is older or younger than you, there might be differences in communication style and understanding of technology.

BREAKING BAD NEWS

A freelancer told me this story: "I took riding lessons as a kid, and one horse was really nasty and liked to kick people. The safest way to walk behind him was to approach where he could see you, get up close, and then slide around his rump, keeping in contact. If he tried to kick, you were too close for him to do real damage."

Bad news can put distance between you and your client, so stay close. Instead of writing an email, maybe pick up the phone, or meet.

Stay close while you're fixing it, too. Let them know you're working on it. Ask how they'd like to receive your progress report: "Would you like me to call or send you an email?" Staying close helps you manage perceptions. Allow too much time and distance, and they might wind up for a kick.

CRITICISM: TAKING IT, GIVING IT

Feedback means everything to a freelancer. And it's one of the hardest things to control. When you send off a project and hear nothing for days or even weeks, as one freelancer said, "You assume 'they hated it,' when in fact often they're so busy they haven't even looked at it."

Then you either get too much feedback (groupthink) or not enough: "I busted my rear for nine months on a project and the feedback basically consisted of two sentences! Good thing the first two words were 'great job.'"

Or it's totally contradictory: "Sometimes—OK, often—clients don't quite know what they want, and a project can go merrily in one direction and then suddenly shift. I'm currently working on a project using a particular piece of music. When the company heard the demo they thought it sounded stuffy and boring even though they'd approved it. Back to Square One."

SIX STRATEGIES FOR GETTING IT

Here are six ways to make getting feedback easier:

1 Prep your client. Tell them changes, revisions, and corrections are part of the process. A sketch, mockup, or sample is just that. You'll work with them to shape it.

2 Prep yourself. It's hard to be detached, but listening to your client is part of your work, too: "I need time to think over feedback. So I say, 'I'm just going to listen and take notes right now.' That way they don't expect me to respond immediately."

3 If the feedback's negative, could communication be better? Are there key questions you should have asked? Were wrong assumptions made? Suggest ways to avoid future problems: more check-ins? showing material in earlier stages?

> "Working in an office, you have days when you earn your keep and days when you don't. When you freelance, payment is tied to what you deliver."

4 Stay cool (even if they aren't). "I knew an executive who used to call composers he'd hired and leave a message, 'Got the song. We have a lot of problems. Call me,' and slam down the receiver. Years later, I met one of the composers, who told me when she got those calls it took her all day to get up the courage to call back. But when she did, she would ask, 'Do you like the melody?' 'The melody's fine.' 'The tempo?' 'That's fine.' 'Um . . . , the guitar?' 'I like the guitar.' This would go on until she went through the entire arrangement and would finally say, 'Is it the tuba?' and the exec would say, 'Ugh, I *hate* the tuba!'" She'd take out the tuba—and all would be well. So if you hear some version of 'We hate it,' don't panic. Peel the layers of the onion to figure out *what* they hate. It isn't easy—but it's part of freelance life."

For serious problems, have the conversation face-to-face if you can, in person or by video call.

5 Agree on how you'll proceed together from here. How far are things from where they need to be? What's a reasonable time frame for fixing the problems?

6 Send a confirming email. And give yourself props for coming up with a masterful plan.

What if what the client wants falls outside the project's scope? Be quick, be calm: Flag what's out of scope and talk terms and logistics (for more on handling this and other problems, see Chapter 7).

SIX STRATEGIES FOR GIVING IT

It may seem surprising, but part of your job is actually to give your client criticism—in the form of constructive suggestions about what you need in order to do your job well. Here are six strategies to try:

1 Stay project-focused. "I frame it in terms of what will help the project," Tom says. "It keeps things objective. Even if they disagree, they can't argue with my wanting to do right by the work."

2 **Collect your thoughts.** Jot down your points if necessary: "I've been doing some thinking, and . . ."

3 **Be honest yet respectful, and expect the same.** "Next time, just tell me if you don't like the design concepts. I'd rather spend time finding new ideas than developing ones you don't like."

4 **Suggest solutions.** "I have some ideas for next steps. . . ."

5 **Cite positives.** "I think your idea is great. The thing is, it would make a big dent in the budget, and you'd have to let go of some other features you want." "We covered a lot of ground today." "I'm glad we've got a plan." "I'm glad we had this conversation."

6 **Follow up in writing and get buy-in.** "Thanks for our conversation today. I just wanted to recap the main points and the plan we worked out. . . . Is this your understanding?"

REPUTATION = POWER

Reputation is the respect you're accorded in your profession. Although it's fundamentally about you, you build it by being fundamentally about others: client by client, project by project, extra mile by extra mile. It's about putting excellence above personal agendas. A good reputation gives you the power to pursue the highest-level work and relationships.

The respect you get is only as great as the respect you give, in these fundamental ways:

THE FOUR CORNERSTONES OF REPUTATION

1 **Apply your skills honestly.** We all know talented people who leave messes for others to clean up. When you work with integrity, you do a good job regardless of the project's prestige or pay scale. You market yourself truthfully.

2 Respect your clients' time. Meeting deadlines is the obvious example. "The worst mistake I ever made was overestimating how much I could do as a working mother/freelancer. I accepted a job that paid a *lot* of money, but I couldn't finish all of it. I was distressed, humiliated, embarrassed. I had to do less work and accept less money, and I damaged my reputation."

It's also about not wasting people's time with substandard or disappointing work—far better to underpromise and overdeliver. And it's about returning the favor when people take time to help you professionally, and being concise and punctual.

3 Be responsible about money. Stick to the budget, report spending and earnings honestly, communicate clearly about money, and keep your financial commitments.

4 Be honorable. Word gets out about the bad apples who sour relationships and don't help their businesses or the industry. Eventually, they become isolated.

Reputation comes from putting Love Theory into action: "The morning after my father died, I had to have some dental work done. The dentist greeted me, asked how I was—and I started crying! We then had an amazing conversation about parents before he

HELP
YOURSELF
ALERT

THE BEST CLIENT IS A HAPPY CLIENT You delivered the job, and it's awesome. Take pride. Your client's praise is well deserved.

Now is the moment when they're most willing to reciprocate.

No, you won't suck up for favors. But you'll send your invoice promptly, while the memory of your awesomeness is fresh. You'll tie up loose ends, such as expense reimbursements. And not too long from now, you'll ask if they're willing to provide a testimonial, or whether you could use a short clip, or some images, or their name as a reference, or whether they could make an introduction to someone they know, to help you grow your business.

got down to work. The next day, a fruit basket arrived with a note. He was a healer that day in every sense. I'll be his client forever."

THE OFFICE EPISODE: WORKING ON-SITE

If you're working on a project at a client's office, your main concerns are making a good impression, advocating tactfully for yourself, and fitting in as someone who's on the team, though not part of the gang.

SIX STRATEGIES FOR FREELANCERS WORKING ON-SITE

Strategy 1: Ask the Project Supervisor for Guidelines.
Your contract should spell out your responsibilities and project and payment schedule, but ask about the day-to-day:

- How often should you report on progress?
- Is there anyone else you should loop in?
- If there are project meetings, should you attend?
- Who should you talk to if you have questions?

Strategy 2: Be Friendly and Respect Their Sandbox.
Introduce yourself and offer to do something: "Hi, I'm John Smith. I'm here for a few weeks working on the website update. I'm going to get some coffee. Can I get you anything?"

Mirror office norms. If no one wears headphones, you'll look anti-social if you do. If others don't eat at their desks, don't. But some things the staff gets away with will be noticed if you do them, so make like a good houseguest: Wash your coffee mug and tidy up after yourself.

Some staffers might not bother to make friends since there's nothing in it for them. Or they might see you as competition. Take a project-focused, how-can-we-get-this-done approach. If an employee is rude or undermining you, talk to the project supervisor about what you need in order to do your work, and what you've done to try to improve things.

Strategy 3: Roll with Things, but Ask for What You Need.
Maybe you'll suddenly have to share a workspace or move. Talk with the project supervisor about what you require to work well: "There are a couple of things I need for my workspace." "I have some questions about the project. When would be a good time to talk?"

Strategy 4: Contribute, Diplomatically.
Fresh ideas are why they hired you for this project, so put yours in the mix, tactfully. It's all in the delivery: "I noticed ... Have you ever tried ...?" "I've found this sometimes works: ..."

Strategy 5: Ask Before You Eat the Pizza.
Offices are deeply social places. There are holiday parties, birthday parties, baby showers, and TGIF pizza. You don't want to be a crasher, but hunkering in your cube while revels unfold around you might make you look like a drudge or an apple-polisher. When in doubt, ask the project supervisor: "I'd love to come, if that's appropriate."

Strategy 6: Be Alert to Misclassification.
For that, read on.

LOOK OUT FOR MISCLASSIFICATION!

When I was about thirty, I was a labor lawyer looking for a job in a tough market. Eventually, I heard the magic words: "We'd love to hire you." I was hired as an independent contractor, receiving tax Form 1099 instead of the Form W-2 received by employees. I upped my hourly pay by five dollars to cover buying my own benefits and was grateful to have a job.

Eventually, though, I discovered I was an employee in every practical sense—other than the small matters of salary and benefits. I worked on the premises, had the same client work and schedule as the W-2'd lawyers, was listed in the company directory, had business cards sporting the firm's name, and was referred to as a lawyer for the firm. And yet no salary, raises, bonus, health benefits, paid vacation, or unemployment insurance. Several of us were in this boat.

I understand the economic reasons why businesses misclassify workers (a savings of 30 percent or more on payroll costs, just for starters). But while you're performing the same work as your coworkers, they're getting the full package of New Deal safeguards—unemployment protection, race/gender/age bias protection, and benefits, all overseen by the Department of Labor—and you're not.

There's an emotional cost to misclassification, too. I worked really hard, but that didn't seem to merit the same treatment as my peers. It wore on me.

Being misclassified got me interested in the needs of the growing independent workforce. Eventually, I left to continue that inquiry in grad school, and then to found Freelancers Union. It seems prophetic that at my going-away party, the junior lawyers unveiled stationery for a mock organization we'd formed called The Transient Workers Union. Its motto? "The Union Makes Us . . . Not So Weak." Its president? Me.

MISCLASSIFICATION 101

Misclassification is generally defined as hiring a person as a self-employed independent contractor or paying them off the books, when they're doing the work of a full-time employee and should be entitled to:

The legal protections of employment: including wage and hour protections and overtime, and protection against discrimination due to race, age, gender, and in some municipalities sexual orientation.

WHAT YOU GET	WHAT THEY GET
A fixed pay rate.	Raises and bonuses that boost career earning and saving power.
No pay for days you don't work.	Paid vacation, sick days, and parental leave.
100 percent responsibility for buying your health insurance.	Employer-sponsored plans (leaving more money to save, invest, and spend), and employer payments into Medicare.
100 percent responsibility for retirement saving.	Employer-sponsored retirement instruments (which can include matching contributions), and payments into Social Security.
No unemployment benefits if you're laid off.	Financial cushion of collecting unemployment while looking for a new job.

Public benefits: such as workers' compensation, unemployment insurance, Social Security, and Medicare.

Employer-sponsored benefits: such as health insurance, retirement programs, family leave, and medical leave.

Intentional or not, misclassification:

1 Violates labor and tax laws.

2 Exploits workers.

3 Robs the country of unemployment funds and workers' comp premiums.

4 Puts the burden on workers to calculate, report, and pay taxes which, if incorrectly calculated, diminish state and federal revenue and Social Security.

5 Gives misclassifying businesses an unfair advantage over those that properly hire and compensate their employees (one study estimates that misclassifying employees can cut a company's labor costs by 20 to 40 percent).

The exact scope and cost of misclassification aren't clear. But in a 2000 study, 10 to 30 percent of employers audited had misclassified some employees. A 2009 report attributed an estimated $54 billion in underreported employment tax.

Misclassified workers may not realize they've been misclassified until they seek a protection reserved for employees—like filing a wage complaint for failure to pay overtime—and find they're not entitled to it.

Fortunately, we have two 800-pound gorillas battling alongside us:

Quick Fact 1: The more employees a company has, the higher its employment taxes. Which is why the IRS is *very* interested in rooting out and punishing misclassification as the independent workforce has grown—and especially since the Great Recession's assault on state and federal budgets. Employers who misclassify workers may have to pay their unpaid unemployment insurance premiums, and state court rulings are on the books requiring employers to pay millions in back unemployment taxes.

Quick Fact 2: Unions are on the alert to misclassification within their professions.

AN INDEPENDENT CONTRACTOR IS *INDEPENDENT*

Classification boils down to control versus independence. An employee grants an employer the right to control specific aspects of the relationship in return for specific guarantees of economic security. Although there's no set formula and factors and practices differ across industries, the IRS evaluates three areas:

1 **Behavioral control:** Does the business have the right to control or direct what you do, where you do it, and how?

2 **Financial control:** Does the business have the right to control the business facets of your work, such as whether you can market and offer your services to other clients?

3 **The type of relationship:** The actual working relationship between you and the business also counts in the equation, regardless of what may be stated in a contract. For example, is this an ongoing relationship, not tied to specific project or time frame?

There are multiple factors in these categories to evaluate, and in the end it's a matter of looking at the whole relationship for its balance of control and independence.

MISCLASSIFICATION HELP AND PREVENTION

Assessing for misclassification is more complex than we can cover here, but if you think you may be owed health insurance and retirement because your wage isn't covering these costs, one option is to file a complaint through your state department of labor or contact the U.S. Department of Labor's Wage and Hour Division (dol.gov) or call toll-free 866-4USWAGE (866-487-9243).

As for prevention, a good first step is knowing misclassification exists and being on the lookout for it. Having a contract also can carry weight because it spells out both parties' intentions.

Q Dear Sara, Over the past year, I worked a total of thirty-eight weeks for a media company. Am I being misclassified?

A Freelancers ask me this all the time. Actually, the number of weeks they work differs, but the question doesn't. Which is exactly the problem. Many workers *think* a rule exists about how much time constitutes full-time employment—and thus entitlement to benefits. But there's no clear actual rule. It depends on all the factors we've outlined in this chapter.

I have a theory that all the corporate lawyers convene annually at a top-secret luxury location where they eat, drink, enjoy sporting games, and devise that year's new mythical "rule" about the work schedule, designed to keep full-time employment just out of reach. They might like us to believe this decree came from Mount Olympus. I suspect it was jotted down on a scorecard somewhere on the back nine. No one really knows. Least of all freelancers.

Check out the U.S. Government Accountability Office (GAO) Report to Congressional Requesters: *Employee Misclassification: Improved Coordination, Outreach, and Targeting Could Better Ensure Detection and Prevention* (August 2009) [GAO-09-717] (gao.gov).

BUT WAIT—THERE'S MORE.

There's a more insidious type of misclassification, less on the radar but equally toxic for freelancers. Ironically, it's a reaction to the government's crackdown on the type of misclassification just described. Here's how it typically works.

Hypothetical Mega-Company wants to avoid tangling with the aforementioned 800-pound gorillas over misclassification. It puts its best minds on the case, and . . . voilà! Introducing XYZ Temp Agency (which may be located—surprise, surprise—on Mega-Company premises).

Now when you, freelancer, get hired, it's not by Mega-Company, but by XYZ Temp Agency, who hires you out to Mega-Company. You may be called a permatemp. You get a W-2 from XYZ Temp Agency. IRS gets its due. Unions can't cry foul. Nice and tidy.

Here's how it (still) rips you off:

For the period covered by the W-2, you can't take tax deductions as an independent contractor. So, for example, if that period covered 50 percent of your total work time, you'd lose 50 percent of your deductions. There's also a big murky gray area as to who's your real employer if any kind of legal issues come up. And you still might end up having to buy your own benefits.

The companies that do this tend to be fairly large, with the kind of long-term, regular work many freelancers want, and with money to pay. So a gig that normally would be a cause for celebration ("a Blue Chip—great!") becomes a weird changeup: "For every day of steady work, I lose my freelance tax breaks. "

Yes, it's a very special no-win just for freelancers:

Either you're really an employee but you're misclassified as a freelancer.

Or you're really a freelancer but are misclassified as a permatemp.

In the first case, the IRS cares because they want the taxes that proper classification would bring. In the second case, no one seems to care, except those whose boat is tied to yours (like your family) . . . and Freelancers Union.

GETTING BUSY? WORKING SOLO DOESN'T MEAN WORKING ALONE

What do you do when, like the freelancer at the beginning of this chapter, you start wondering how you'll get it all done?

In the short term, you may have to turn down some work. If so, leave a positive vibe by recommending another freelancer who might be a good match (and while that good vibe's happening, build your Level 4 by asking if they'd like to be included on your mailing list for your email newsletter or periodic updates from you).

Then let that freelancer know you recommended them. Referrals add to your Love Bank and forge relationships you might later build into teams for tackling big projects together.

In the longer term, realize that landing big projects is the reward you've been working so hard for. If you're turning down good gigs, consider whether it's time to weed out smaller, lower-paying gigs (raising your rates can help) and open up time for bigger projects. Also, you may need to work out a strategy for subcontracting work and project-managing the job, as liaison with the client.

Subcontracting works the other way around, too: If you're in a dry spell, you can say to your freelance friends, "I see you're really busy. I'm in a dry spell right now, so if you need an extra pair of hands, I would be more than happy to work out a subcontracting arrangement." We'll talk more about subcontracting in Chapter 11.

If it's a gig you don't want, you might decline as part of managing your Freelance Portfolio. Employees are often assigned work or clients they don't like. You, freelancer, are not assigned anything and can always say no. But don't toss sludge to your network.

Exactly what you say depends on why you're bowing out and whether you want to leave the door open for future business. Here are some options (you can tack a referral onto the first three):

Another time, perhaps? "I'm working on some projects that will keep me busy for a while. But I'd really like to work with you, and I'd like to stay in touch. I'll be available in [time frame]. I'll touch base with you then."

Sorry, but no. "Unfortunately, I'm booked solid/my plate is full/ I'm not taking new clients at this time."

POWER IN NUMBERS By focusing on the first type of misclassification, the IRS can get the taxes they're after and say they're declaring war on misclassification. But they're not addressing the second type, which allows companies to tap the ever-growing pool of independent talent in a way that remains unfair to workers. By some measures, it's expected that by 2020, contingent workers will comprise more than 40 percent of U.S. workers. Misclassification won't go away and will likely only become more entrenched. The government needs a comprehensive plan to address misclassification as it's really happening in the workforce today. We need to change the laws so freelancing pays "a fair day's wages for a fair day's work."

Freelancers Union is working to unite workers across professions to make things fair for freelancers.

We need to know exactly how many freelancers are being misclassified so we can calculate the financial losses to freelancers and the government and make the money case for policy change. It's a huge reason why the government has to do a better, more consistent job categorizing and counting freelancers, as I mentioned in the Introduction.

Some changes Freelancers Union is working for:

• Streamline the misclassification claims filing process

• Increase misclassified workers' knowledge about their rights

• Encourage better state-level tests for classification

• Change tax laws so independent contractors and employees have the same level economic playing field.

If you need to take jobs that misclassify you, try to find other work you can transition to that won't penalize you for being a freelancer. Get a movement started in your professional group to raise awareness of misclassification. And join groups like Freelancers Union to share your experiences, add your voice to our phone campaigns, your feet to our marches, your ideas to our meetings with political candidates, and your contribution to our Political Action Committee (PAC) (freelancersunion .org). Your involvement can make change happen.

It's not you, it's me. "I don't think I'm a strong fit with the project, but thank you for thinking of me."

I wouldn't wish you on my worst enemy [if asked for referrals]. "Hm, I can't think of anyone offhand, but if I do, I'll let you know."

BECAUSE CLONING YOURSELF ISN'T (YET) AN OPTION

If you're drowning in email, appointments, correspondence, billing, and filing, consider whether a virtual assistant (VA) could free you to do what only *you*, freelancer, can do: Get the projects in and get 'em done.

A virtual assistant interacts with you electronically and can live anywhere and help you with pretty much anything, only when you need it, working as an independent contractor. Some tasks include: typing correspondence, scheduling appointments, proofreading, filling orders, managing email, and setting up and maintaining online files. Or they can do bigger tasks such as research, writing, helping manage social networking, or handling your billing and collecting (you compose the letter; they send).

You can sign up for a virtual assistant service offering different levels of assistance. Read the terms of service to find out about their processes, including billing, quality control, complaints, and especially security (working with confidential material, having passwords or account numbers, and the like). Make sure you're comfortable with the service, its policies, and the people you're working with.

A private arrangement might involve working with a student who needs a side gig or an industry newbie you can mentor. Obviously, the same issues of procedure and duties, billing, quality control, and security have to be worked out.

As I finished this chapter, I could see that being a good freelancer is really about bringing your higher self to your work. You show it in the transparency, thoroughness, and fairness of your policies and practices. You show it in the empathy you bring to your client relationships. It's present in all your dealings. When it's there, clients know it. There's no better way to serve them. Best of all, it serves you, too.

Chapter 7

TROUBLESHOOTING

As your career grows, you'll start getting challenging projects and clients. Stuff will happen. Problems are opportunities to show your chops and become indispensable. A single crisis, awesomely resolved, can win undying client love.

This chapter will help you prevent the avoidable and suggest game plans for the unavoidable, the unforeseen, and some of the toughest freelancing problems, including a huge drain on freelancers' resources: late-paying or deadbeat clients.

THE POWER OF PUTTING IT IN WRITING

As you read this chapter, you'll see that you have much more leverage in troubleshooting if you have a contract, letter of agreement, deal memo, adoptive admission, or even just a confirming email about what was agreed upon (see Chapter 5). A lot of the troubleshooting we'll talk about can be handled by having a good agreement in place. I'm saying it here so I won't have to sound like a broken record repeating it throughout this chapter.

For the same reason, put decisions, approvals, changes of direction, and other important benchmarks in writing as you proceed on a project: "Glad you liked the chapter overall. I agree it needs more examples." "Thanks for approving the mock-up. We'll proceed to final and I'll send an invoice for the payment due on design approval." "Thanks for our meeting today with the photographer and the stylist. As discussed, we'll set up the shoot for next week, with a steampunk theme."

Keep notes on your conversations: "I have a spiral notebook for each client that's a running phone log and project notes. So if questions come up, I can tactfully say, 'My notes say that last month we talked about . . .'"

TRIPLE-A TROUBLESHOOTING

This troubleshooting strategy has an easy acronym so you can remember it in a pinch:

1 Acknowledge it.   2 Analyze it.   3 Act on it.

1: ACKNOWLEDGE IT

Stare down the problem, in all its ugly splendor. Tips to keep from blinking:

Acknowledging ≠ Admitting

If your client has a problem, so do you. It doesn't mean they're right about everything.

Trust Your Gut

You're the expert, so if you smell a problem, check it out. You might head off a crisis. Then you can relax and have a drink. Better yet, tell your client: "This happened. I took care of it." *Then* have a drink.

Sometimes, of course, the client's the problem. "Often you aren't the first freelancer to work on a project. You may figure it out by finding another person's notes, or from vague references to someone named 'Jane' whose role is never made clear, or you'll be told Jane was terribly inept."

This is where your network can save you: "If at all possible, contact Jane before accepting the job. She can tell you what *really* happened." Getting the back story might help you negotiate a tighter contract or avoid a nightmare client altogether.

2: ANALYZE IT

Don't let the client beat you to the problem. Get there first with your own solutions, which you'll probably like better than theirs, plus get points for laying out the issues so they don't have to. Here's how.

Determine What's at Stake

Is it a missed interim deadline or the final one? Is the photo shoot delayed a week or a month? The stakes determine what you do, how fast, and what it'll cost. You may have to negotiate additional payment, an extension, eat some time and costs, or all of the above.

Play out the immediate, middle-range, and long-range consequences. Brainstorm ways to prevent or minimize negative outcomes.

If the problem's potentially serious—financial losses or other damage, or possible legal repercussions—consult your attorney.

On overload? Call someone in your network with dry time to assist or handle your day-to-day stuff.

Toss What Hasn't Worked

Research shows we tend to persist with decisions or plans that aren't working—especially when we're responsible for them. Look at anything you or the client did that contributed to the problem.

Have Good Reasons

Have a "why" for every recommendation. The best one's inarguable: "for the good of the project." Propose what's feasible in the time frame and budget. Tell your client you want to address the problem but can't make unrealistic promises.

Remember Not All Clients Are Created Equal

When deciding how far to go to fix a problem, ask yourself where this client fits in your Freelance Portfolio.

For a Blue Chip, a project you believe in, a career builder, or someone you hope to work with again, you might decide to pour in hours or take losses.

If you've been treated badly, you might decide to finish as well as you can, make sure you get paid, and move on.

Don't be unprofessional. But do be strategic about using your resources, because crisis drains them.

3: ACT ON IT

We're wired from infancy to notice the responsiveness of the adults around us. It's the beginning of communication. That's why responding to a client problem is so important. It shows you care about what this client needs—and clients notice. In fact, it turns out that even if you can't totally solve the problem, your level of responsiveness counts. Think about some of your own experiences as a customer. You're disappointed that the store doesn't have the shirt in your size, but you appreciate that the salesperson checked the stockroom and called the neighboring store to see if they carried it; you're annoyed because your order got lost in the system but gratified that customer service is putting a rush on delivery. So when trouble strikes, responding with prompt and clear communication is critical.

Twelve Acts of Über-Communication

Since problems are often rooted in communication lapses at the contract level, the day-to-day level, or both, good communication is crucial for putting fixes in place.

1 **Protect yourself, protect the project.** If something happens that could derail a project, go on record. "This is outside the project's scope, but I'd be glad to do it. We just need to set up compensation and a schedule." "If I don't get the designer's mock-ups by Monday, I'll hire another designer. I'll keep you posted." "I have bad news. There's a family emergency and I need to revise the deadline."

Reasonable clients appreciate honesty that comes from wanting to do right by the project and can be surprisingly flexible in working out solutions. "I've learned not to get caught up in emotion or the particulars. I focus on the job at hand. My approach is, 'How can I help you to finish this project?' I try to remind clients that we're on the same team and that my efforts are in service to the project. This attitude almost always gets us back on track."

2 **Stay close.** Remember my friend in Chapter 6 who avoided getting kicked by staying close to the orncry horse? The more upset or ornery your client, the closer you should stay. Tell them you'll get back to them ASAP with a plan. Send updates: "Here's what I'm doing to look into the problem," or "I haven't heard anything from the designer yet. I'll let you know when I do." Give them no space to wonder about lining up another freelancer. You want to be the architect of a workable solution and indispensable to its execution.

3 Pre-Communicate. Are you waiting for the right moment to bring up a problem? Or maybe you can't reach the phone from your fetal position under the desk? Pre-communication helps prepare everyone for an important conversation: "There's something I need to talk with you about. When could I call you?"

4 Choose the medium. For really sensitive conversations, face-to-face gives you access to the full range of human communication: words, facial expressions, and body language. Video calling makes this doable from anywhere.

Email puts things on record, but choose your words and tone carefully.

While you may not choose it for time-sensitive communication, snail mail can be official (a notice about payment) or personal (a note of apology), and can impress on a client that you're serious.

5 If they need to vent, let them. Emotions trump logic. If a client's really upset, you may need to let them get it out: "I want to know what's on your mind."

Don't interrupt or make encouraging listening noises; even the touchy-feely "I hear what you're saying" can be irritating.

Eventually, you'll sense them winding down. Now you can have an actual conversation: "I wanted to know what you were thinking. And I have some thoughts, too. And a few questions. And some ideas for where we go from here."

6 Stay in conversation. This dials down the heat and helps you drive toward a solution. To raise the bar above finger-pointing, ask questions to get actionable data: "What do you think happened to make the project go off-track?" "You chose a mock-up, but you're saying you never liked it. What didn't you like?"

Use the info to get to next steps: "Good point about faster response time. One idea I have is . . ." "So, you thought the graphics were fine, but the colors didn't pop?"

7 Look for good news. This keeps the client from trashing everything: "The good news is the files of the previous version were backed up. So while the lost work needs to be reconstructed, we're far from being at square one." "The new schedule is very tight, but we've set up a super-efficient review system with your team over the months."

8 Hand them solutions, not problems. Remember, problems are opportunities to become indispensable. "Here's what I've done to fix this." "Here's how we can prevent this from happening again." "Here are portfolios from three new designers. Each can start immediately."

The more plug-and-play you make the solution for the client, the easier it is for the client to say yes. "The cost of a new design is ... Once you confirm the price, we're good to go." "The printer can start as soon as we send revised files. I'm willing to do the revisions free of charge, if you'll absorb the remaining costs."

This is how you have to work to be successful. It's especially how you have to work through a crisis.

9 Don't take blame for what isn't your fault, but take responsibility when it is. If something's your fault, get out in front of it. "I shouldn't have waited that extra week to hear from the designer." Communicate, don't confess. Then move quickly to solution.

10 Don't overpromise. You want to stop the bleeding and succeed, not make it worse and fail.

11 Put the resolution in writing. Don't let misunderstandings undo your all your repair work.

12 Communicate the Triple-A way. See chart, page 180.

SITUATION	TRIPLE-A COMMUNICATION:
Lapse in communication	"I'm sorry I've been out of touch [ACKNOWLEDGE]. Here's an update on where things stand ... Going forward, I think it would help to add checkpoints for updates and feedback [ANALYZE]. How about a short weekly call where I can update you and we can discuss any questions or concerns [ACT]?"

SITUATION	TRIPLE-A COMMUNICATION:
Schedule in jeopardy or lost	"We're X weeks behind schedule. [ACKNOWLEDGE]. Delays on my end were caused by ... Delays were also caused by ... [THEIR ACCOUNTABILITY] [ANALYZE]. Here's a revised schedule and a plan for going forward: ... [ACT]."

SITUATION	TRIPLE-A COMMUNICATION:
Errors on your end	"I apologize for the errors. Although I have safeguards against this sort of thing happening, obviously these got past them. We don't want that to happen again [ACKNOWLEDGE]. Part of what caused this were the additional revision rounds, which shortened our time for checking the work [ANALYZE].

| Errors on your end (cont'd) | Some solutions might be for you to budget for a proofreader, and/or to compress your team's feedback. Here are some proofreaders who could be hired, and a schedule going forward: ... [ACT]." |

Six Plays for Resetting Boundaries

Problems can happen if you weren't totally clear about the job scope, your services, price, or your day-to-day policies and practices. Or maybe your client is just brazenly expecting more attention, calls, meetings, fittings, sessions, revisions, touch-ups, or retakes.

Here are six plays for when clients go out-of-bounds:

1 **The Smooth Move.** Hide the boundary in a plug-and-play solution:

"Sure, I can do that. It would cost . . . Let me know how you'd like to proceed."

2 **The Flying Change.** Fix it in real time:

"I should mention that I no longer do weekend calls. Of course, we can talk today, since you didn't know about the change—I just wanted you to know the policy going forward."

3 **The Straight Arm.** Ward off the tackle:

"I'm happy to answer your questions, but I suggest we bundle them into a phone consultation, to make sure everything has been answered. The cost of a phone consult is: . . . " (Even if you don't charge, you could suggest the call to reduce interruptions.)

4 **The Ounce of Prevention.** Set up a system to handle it:

"That's a great question. It's actually one of the FAQs on my website/in my brochure. I've pasted the answer below, with a link to the others, in case they're helpful."

5 The Charge for Refills. If an issue crops up a lot, maybe it's a clue to a new service. Example: different price levels of support packages (X number of follow-up questions, revisions, or consults). If old clients return, make sure they know:

"I have a new service plan—here's the link with the info."

6 The Lemon Squeeze. Turn a problem into a product. For an accountant, it might be:

Your e-book: *The 100 Most Asked Small-Business Tax Questions.* Free to clients with Premium-level service.

Your workshop: Audit-Proof Your Business! Clients get a discount.

Your webinar: The Top Ten Tax FAQs for Small Business Owners. Clients get a discount.

AND NOW, JUST FOR YOU

After a client crisis, do a postmortem. Go with a freelancer friend for a walk, a run, or a stagger to the nearest watering hole. Laugh, cry, beat a pillow, whatever. Get it all out about what went wrong, losses incurred (dollars, time, reputation) and lessons learned. What were the red flags? What could you put in your agreement that would prevent problems? Was the project description vague? Did you take on more than you could do for the time or money? Did you communicate often and clearly enough?

Good communication in a tense situation can take a load off your mind and might even save you from getting fired, as these freelancers learned:

"I edit publications for a company where the schedules are always tight. On one very tough project, the client asked me to return a hundred pages within one workday—coincidentally, a day my toddler was home from school.

"They'd asked the impossible. I let them know I couldn't do it same day but would return it the following morning. I got no response. I spoke with the company's local rep, who said the rep had been talking to them about their tight schedules. I'm adding a thirty percent surcharge for any future work from this client requiring less than a week's turnaround. Even if it costs me some work, I hope it will encourage them to respect my time—or at least their own budgets—a bit more."

"I was under the gun to finish my first freelance design assignment and ended up turning in a version that was a little rough around the edges. I assumed I'd have a chance to rework it after the client responded. Instead, he sent it out to others for feedback. When it didn't pass with flying colors, he fired me. Lessons learned: I need to explain the back-and-forth of the design process. Also, if I'm running out of time, I'll ask for more time. I'll *never* again hand in less than my best work. Of course, your best work should be done *on time*. But if it's not, ask for more time. (Side note: The client ended up going through several designers. So I didn't beat myself up too badly. Still, it was a good learning experience.)"

SITUATIONS AND SOLUTIONS

Below are symptoms, treatments, and prevention tips for common client ailments. They may not fit your problem exactly and won't replace legal advice, but I hope you can adapt some to your situation.

SITUATION: "WE'RE OFF-SCHEDULE."

Symptom 1: Client is slow to respond.

Treatment: Bring it up as soon as you see the pattern: "We need to discuss the feedback process. It's taking longer than it should." Be on record: "I know you don't mean to jeopardize the schedule, but this does." Suggest a fix: A weekly call, a revised schedule. Monitor in writing: "I know you're busy, but please continue to give this project your priority." "The delivery date cannot be met unless I hear from you by..."

Prevention: Protect against client delays in your contract. Examples:

- Client will be available for consultations, interviews, approvals, et cetera.

- Client will provide necessary materials, data, and information.

- You can terminate the contract and be paid a kill fee if the client fails to meet these obligations after a reasonable number of requests.

- Set deadlines for feedback and/or approvals.

- If no response is received in X time period, materials are considered approved.

- You won't be held to your delivery dates if the client doesn't respond in the time period specified.

- If there are client delays, rush rates may be charged to deliver on time.

Symptom 2: Client is making too many changes.

Treatment: Make sure you both agree about the project's direction. Remind the client in writing of what's been approved, so you have a paper trail preventing them from reworking approved material or rejecting the final. Set deadlines for changes and stick to them. Say you won't be able to meet the project's deadlines if there are changes after these points.

Prevention: Build into your contract:

- Specify the number of revision rounds—you get paid extra for any additional rounds.

- Stipulate payment at an hourly rate for changes beyond a "reasonable level."

Symptom 3: Client is indecisive/keeps changing her mind.

Treatment: Part of your job may be to help the client narrow things down. Offer fewer options. Offer opinions. Suggest group conferences where everyone gives feedback at once.

Prevention: Specify in your contract:

- The number of mock-ups, drafts, or samples you'll provide.

- A time frame for the client's response (see "Symptom 1: Client is slow to respond").

Symptom 4: Doing the work is taking longer than you thought.

Treatment: Alert the client and team up to solve it. "We need to work out a new schedule. Here's why." How you handle compensation depends on who's responsible for the schedule problem. If it's your fault, you may have to do extra work without pay, compress stages, subcontract work, pull long hours, or all of the above.

If both of you had responsibility, discuss how you can both take on some of the burden. If the schedule's blown because the client wants more than was agreed, instead of saying no, think about what you'd charge so you can say you'd be happy to accommodate them, for X price.

Prevention: Build an automatic extension into your contract for some cushion on the deadline. Log your time on projects for a more accurate idea of how long tasks take.

Symptom 5: You have too much other work.

Treatment: Negotiate extensions on less-critical projects. Subcontract portions, and/or get temporary help (another freelancer, a student, your mate, a virtual assistant) to handle routine work. Engage or barter help for child care or home chores. If missing the deadline is unavoidable, check your contract for consequences for late delivery, nondelivery, and termination. Then alert the client and use the communication skills in this chapter to work out a solution.

Prevention: See "Doing the work is taking longer than you thought." To help keep projects from colliding, set start-date schedules with your clients (maybe with a deposit to hold that date). Let them know they may lose their "spot" in the lineup and/or the delivery date if the project doesn't start on time.

Symptom 6: You have a serious personal or family issue/crisis.

Treatment: Figure out how much you can realistically do. Consider subcontracting portions, or other projects. Depending on the situation (for example, it'll be very distracting or prolonged) and the client (you have a friendly, personal relationship), you might clue in the client: "I'm dealing with a family problem. This is how it affects the project: ... " Or: "This won't affect the project, but there'll be times when I'm less available [or whatever]." If you decide you must resign from the project, check your contract for termination and repayment terms. Consult your attorney if there could be legal repercussions. If you do pull out, suggest candidates you think could pick up from here.

Prevention: Keep your network active so you can find subcontractors or, if necessary, people you trust to replace you.

SITUATION: "WE'RE OVER BUDGET/WE'RE PUTTING THE PROJECT ON HOLD."

Symptom 1: Client cuts the budget.

Treatment: Submit revised project specs/services. Be polite but firm about what's possible.

Prevention: Write the budget (or a minimum) into your contract, and/or stipulate that if the budget changes, the project specifications will be revised accordingly.

Symptom 2: Client puts the project on hold due to financial or organizational changes.

Treatment: Let the client know you're suspending work until the issues are worked out. Discuss how you'll be paid for work completed/expenses incurred to date.

Prevention: Put the budget in your contract. Include how you'll be paid if the project is delayed or suspended for reasons beyond your control. Build in a kill fee or nonrefundable up-front payment or deposit.

Symptom 3: Your expenses/costs are coming in way over projection.

Treatment: Tell the client the costs are higher than anticipated. Consider changing vendors or subcontractors. Discuss modifying the project. You may have to take a hit financially if the client refuses.

Prevention: Create a cushion by giving a cost range. Make sure you're getting accurate estimates. Specify in the contract that you're not responsible if costs go up as a result of delays or late start by the client. Be transparent in costing out the project so if there are problems, you can partner with your client to brainstorm solutions together.

SITUATION: "THIS ISN'T WHAT WE AGREED."

Symptom: Client wants something more than what was originally agreed.

Treatment: If the contract doesn't specify or you have no contract, use emails or notes from your conversations to remind the client of what was decided. Negotiate the additional cost or time required for anything different.

Note: If you charge by the hour, don't just rack up the time and start pricing tickets for your beach vacation. If the bill is way over what the client expects, you might be sitting in small claims court instead. Give the client a chance to bring the project back in scope.

Prevention: Put detailed specifications about the job scope in a contract, deal memo, or confirming email. Keep a phone log and email records. Confirm procedures and approvals in writing. Use your experience to anticipate scope creep and suggest ways to expand your role, adjust the terms, or hold firm to the deal.

SITUATION: "THAT'S NOT TRUE."

Symptom: Client rejects the final, says they never liked it, or claims you didn't deliver what was promised.

Treatment: Keep/show documentation of approvals, decisions, or pattern of unresponsiveness despite your attempts (see "We're Off-Schedule").

Prevention: Sometimes clients forget what they approved or change their minds. Either way, it's not your responsibility. Ask questions at the start about the client's ideas. If the client's expectations aren't realistic, educate them. See previous prevention tips re keeping good records and written confirmations. Tie payments to approval stages—this documents approvals and ensures you won't lose a lot of money if they dispute the final payment. Make sure the contract specifies how disputes will be handled (for more on dispute terms, see Chapter 5). Assess their place in your Freelance Portfolio. For a Blue Chip, try to work things out. For a one-off, finish as well as you can and move on.

SITUATION: "UH-OH."

Symptom 1: A mistake or oversight.

Treatment: If it's your error, you have to fix it, make your deadlines, and eat the costs—unless the client is a mensch and will cover some costs or extend the deadline. If it's the client's error, the same applies in reverse. If you're the mensch, you've banked a lot of love with this client, which might be priceless for future business. But don't say yes with that expectation.

Prevention: Live and learn. Look into professional liability insurance or other kinds of coverage (see Chapter 10).

Symptom 2: Something unexpected happens that's no one's fault (client gets laid off, event is called off, equipment fails or is stolen,

Never Assume Sometimes you might think asking questions might make you look bad; other times misunderstandings just happen. Better to ask than have to fix it later at your own cost.

Just saying "This might seem like an obvious question, but . . ." gets it done. If you do mess up, being a class act can pay off: "I had to write a piece for two investment advisers. I'd worked with the personal banking division of their parent company, but not the investments side. The banking side had a very specific brand voice that I was familiar with. I wrote the piece using that voice. I learned very quickly that banking and investments are very different markets—at least at this company. I apologized, talked with my contact, who explained the difference—he was very understanding about it—and rewrote the document in the style they wanted. I spent a lot of time reading their website, thinking about the brand, and made sure I had it right in the new document. They loved it and I've worked on several projects with them since then."

shipments are delayed or damaged, personal emergency, natural disasters, et cetera).

Treatment: Damage control is paramount. In the case of a major glitch or disaster, inform each other right away and keep the updates coming. Make a disaster plan together to stop, rethink, or revise the plans. If your contact's been laid off, there's not much you can do other than find out who your new contact is, take steps to connect and quickly bring the new person up to speed, and show your value in being clear about what you've done so far and what you will do to finish the work per the terms of your contract.

Prevention: To the extent that insurance, preparedness, padded deadlines, and contract terms such as force majeure language, non-refundable deposits, kill fees, and expense reimbursement help, do them.

DAMAGE CONTROL: WHEN YOU MESS UP, BIG-TIME

Even if it isn't your fault, the financial, reputational, and stress price of a major error can be high. That's why you may want to check out liability insurance (see Chapter 10). It's easy to get in some fields; tough in others. Check professional associations, search online for liability insurance in your profession, and talk to other freelancers in your field. Licensed professionals should always have malpractice insurance.

FREELANCERS SPEAK **The Importance of Facing the Mess** "I'm a freelance food writer and recipe developer and had written an article, including several recipes, for a major magazine. Between the time I did the work and the time the story ran, I realized one of the recipes was dangerously close, copyright-wise, to something I'd done for another client. I laid awake for a couple of nights worrying about it, vacillating between telling myself that no one would ever realize the similarities and telling myself that I had to come clean and tell my editor, even though I was convinced that if I did, I'd probably never work for that magazine, and maybe any other, again.

"I realized I had to clean up my mess—that any work I did after that would be on *top* of a mess and could therefore never feel good or satisfying. So I took a deep breath, called my editor, and explained what I'd realized. I also completely apologized for being so irresponsible and said I'd do whatever it took to make it right. The editor's response was, 'Your food is delicious. Now, give me a few more details and we'll figure out what to do.'

"In the end, the most major repercussion was that I had to reformulate the recipe a bit. No big deal. And in the process, I learned how much my editor appreciated my work and ended up acknowledging me for my integrity. Bottom line—in all kinds of relationships, work or otherwise, it's always better to speak up. There may be some work involved in cleaning up a mess, but in my case I found that the relationship was better, stronger, for having done it."

If you make a mistake that has (or could have) damaging repercussions for the client, for you, or both, everything we've been talking about moves to warp-speed level.

If you have a contract, check the language to make sure you know your obligations and the client's, and how termination and disputes would be handled. You might consult a lawyer and your accountant about legal or financial fallout (one reason why it's smart to have a lawyer and accountant who are already familiar with your business). (For tips on choosing a lawyer, see Chapter 5; for tips on choosing an accountant, see Chapter 15.)

SEEING 3-D: DISSATISFIED, DISGRUNTLED, OR DISRESPECTFUL CLIENTS

Employees can recruit their posse to keep ornery clients in line: "My boss says . . . the sales director wants . . . it's not company policy . . ." Freelancers don't have that built-in protection. What to do?

First, accept human nature. The longer you freelance, the more likely you'll hook a client like this now and then.

Second, mentor yourself. Read up on psychology and communication; learn how to deal with tough customers.

Third, freelancers have to mentor one another. Tap into your Brain Trust at times like these.

Fourth, freelancing gives you more freedom to walk away than the company worker who's handcuffed to the benefits, retirement plan, and paycheck and has to grin and bear it. Some tips for keeping your freelance freedom:

Protect yourself on paper. Negotiate deal terms protecting you from the most common client toxicities (scope creep, delays, unreasonable demands, late payment/nonpayment, unclear direction). For negotiation tactics, see Chapter 5.

Have an exit strategy. You can't walk away if you can't afford to. When you sense a 3-D client, keep killer records of every transaction and conversation. And start working to line up a replacement gig. It might take time, so don't wait until you're desperate. If your 3-D is a big name, that's leverage to help you get an even bigger (let's hope nicer) one.

Don't let one client dominate. Work every level of your Freelance Portfolio. Have two or more Blue Chips. All it takes is one bad hire at the company you count on for your freelance life to become suddenly, significantly miserable.

Add combat pay. If you get a bad vibe from a prospect but need the income or the career boost, build high maintenance into your price. The time you spend babysitting a 3-D is time lost from other ventures.

And here are some strategies to help you deal until you're out of there:

Kill 'em with kindness. Don't sink to their level. Be proud of how you handled things in the end.

Find something to like. It could be a common interest in sports, or even their dedication to their work (which, uh, compels them to call you on Sunday evenings). It can help create a connection, however fragile, between you.

Use positive pressure. Most 3-D types are hiding insecurities or have an inflated ego. So, appeal to their past performance, which they'll want to uphold: "You tend to have clear ideas about things, so I'm surprised you haven't sent your thoughts on the mock-ups."

Be gently assertive. You know how things are typically done in your industry, so feel free to lead, saying, tactfully, "This is how it works; this is what we're doing."

MELTDOWN MANAGEMENT

Handling a true client meltdown? Here are two fixes.

Short-Term Fix: Draw the Line

If their venting gets personal, tell them this is getting too personal and you'll have to call them back, and say when. Use the break to cool down and gather your thoughts for the callback. Maybe they will, too.

Or you can say something like, "You know, I can't be spoken to that way. I hear you're very upset and I'll work with you to get to the bottom of the problem. But we're both professionals, and we need to treat each other professionally."

Longer-Term Fix: 3-D Freedom

Your ultimate ticket to 3-D freedom is having the reputation and the financial stability not to work with clients who don't respect you. Network and prospect, build your chops to work with the best and charge top dollar, and systematically save money and reduce debt. It may seem like a lot to do, but effort accrues over time.

THE FOURTH D: DEADBEAT CLIENTS

What do 44 percent, more than $10,000, and thirty-six hours have in common? They're just a few of the sad stats about late-paying clients and freelancers:

- 44 percent = the percentage of independent workers who had trouble getting paid in 2010, according to Freelancers Union's survey of more than 2,500 respondents.

- $10,071 = the average amount paid late.

- 36 hours = the average amount of time spent chasing payment.

Of those who had trouble getting paid in 2010, 81 percent were paid late, and 37 percent were never paid. The average amount they couldn't collect: $4,643.

In the best of times, freelancers struggled against the drag of slow-paying or nonpaying clients. And it hasn't been the best of times for a long time. The Great Recession pushed record numbers of businesses into cash-flow crises or out of business.

Freelancers felt that pain. According to one study, in New York State alone, 42 percent of the state's 900,000 independent workers experienced problems getting paid in 2009. Average amount owed: $12,000—for a whopping estimated $4.7 billion total.

These factors don't help:

- Freelancers without contracts have less leverage for collection.

- Freelancers' economic instability makes them fear pursuing collection because they can't afford to lose the client or referrals. Even collecting is a losing proposition:

- There are caps on what you can collect in small claims court.

- Every minute you spend chasing collection (calls, letters, small claims court, obsessing) is time lost for paid work.

- You may not be able to afford to hire a lawyer to pursue deadbeat clients. (Compare this with company employees, who get free help from the Department of Labor to investigate and recover unpaid wages.)

- If you win in court, trying to collect on the judgment costs more time and money.

Freelancers also pay a longer-term price for deadbeats' delinquency:

- To pay business expenses, freelancers divert income they might have put toward retirement savings.

ADVOCACY ALERT

- They're sometimes forced to draw on retirement income to meet daily living expenses.

- They may have problems paying their taxes.

While companies that default on their payroll are severely liable (including the threat of criminal proceedings), at this writing, no labor laws exist to deter deadbeat clients.

How can one-third of the U.S. workforce be left twisting in the wind when trying to secure payment for an honest day's work? This undermines the spending power of a large segment of the population.

WHO THEY ARE

There are basically four types of nonpaying clients:

1 **Well-intentioned nonpayers.** These clients can't pay for legit reasons. Suggest smaller increments. Confirm a timetable in writing. Contact them the day before to confirm they'll be making the payment.

If they say it's a cash flow thing and they're expecting money by X date, suggest paying you some now, with the balance due when that payment comes in.

2 Unhappy nonpayers. These nonpayers are unhappy with you. Maybe you made errors or underestimated the job. If you made errors, apologize and work out an adjusted pay scheme. Taking a hit now might preserve future business.

As for underestimating a gig, lobbing a giant invoice into an unsuspecting client's inbox is asking for trouble—and your post-delivery leverage is zip. Try to work something out with the client as soon as you realize the problem.

If they're unhappy for unreasonable reasons, see "This Isn't What We Agreed," "That's Not True," and "Seeing 3-D," above, for some options.

3 Serial nonpayers. These folks may pay some, then no more. Chances are, there's a trail of stiffed freelancers in their wake. Ask your network and check Freelancers Union's Client Scorecard archive before signing on. If you suspect a nonpayer, get paid up front or get a deposit before starting, don't work too far ahead of the payment installments, and if possible in your profession, try not to deliver the final until you're paid. For additional tactics, see "Seeing 3-D." Your gut can alert you, too: "Only once was I stiffed by a client. She walked out with my work and never paid me the nine hundred dollars she owed me. She came in all flustered and jittery, saying someone had tried to rob her. She promised to come back and pay me. Something didn't quite ring true. I should have listened to my instincts and not taken her on."

4 Mega-corp nonpayers. These businesses delay or stiff you because they can. They're big, you're little, and they set policies that sweeten their cash flow. If you manage to shoehorn an arbitration clause into their contract, gold star for you. Another trend in a down economy: Accountants advise small businesses and others to put freelancers on a ninety-day payment cycle, effectively treating them like any account receivable. That policy is conveniently blind to the human toll on freelancers, who don't have larger vendors' cash flow cushion.

Diversify your Freelance Portfolio so your boat isn't moored to these monoliths. And fill out a Client Scorecard for posterity.

SEVEN REMEDIES FOR A DEADBEAT CLIENT

Remedy 1: Have a Payment Policy

State your policy at deal time. If you get push-back, it's your choice to negotiate or stand your ground. Some options to build into your policy:

- Negotiate a time limit. If their policy is 90 days and yours is 30, maybe you can agree on 60.

- Specify a late fee, often a percentage of the amount, in your contract and on your invoices. You could even specify more hard-line stuff, such as no delivery if interim payments aren't made.

Remedy 2: Get a Portion Paid Up-Front

Get paid something to reserve the time slot... on signing the contract... before starting work... or some other early benchmark. Not standard in your industry? Maybe you can set the precedent if you're in demand, thanks to your excellence.

Remedy 3: Write "Dispute Resolution" Terms into Your Contract

Put arbitration or mediation language in your contract (see Chapter 5). Especially with out-of-state clients, specify where jurisdiction will be—ideally in your state/county. Getting a judgment is hard enough, but the really hard part is collecting on it. You don't want to have to hire a lawyer in another state and try to collect there.

Remedy 4: Practice Prompt, Preventive Invoicing

Your invoices should:

- Be sent promptly post-delivery, while everyone's in love with your work. No love? All the more reason to bill them and close the books.

• Be sent in triplicate: snail mail, email, and a phone message saying the invoice was sent. If this is what you do on Round One, let them imagine what Round Three will be like.

• Be dated, for tracking lateness.

• Include your full contact information.

• Include all the data for payment processing, such as the project's name, project codes or identifying numbers, itemization of services, your payee name and tax ID number, and instructions for payment method (including sending).

• Reflect lateness ("Second notice—30 days past due").

• Reflect any late-payment charges.

Remedy 5: Make Friends with Someone in Accounting
You'll glean info on their procedures, get to know someone in a position to help, and keep your primary contact unsullied by the money thing: "I know you're busy. Is there someone in accounting I could reach out to?"

Remedy 6: Delegate It to the Cloud
Documentation is nine-tenths of the collection game. You can hire an online service to track your time on projects, invoice for them (including late payment follow-up), and handle the payment transaction. It's one time when making things less personal can work. Make sure you're comfortable with the site's security and backup practices. Search under "online invoicing" or "online billing."

Remedy 7: Have a Follow-Up System
Your system is up to you. It could start with an email, friendly but firm, along these lines: "Our records show you haven't paid [details: invoice date, amount due, job name]. You might have forgotten, so this is a quick reminder. Let me know if you have any questions. Thank you for giving this your prompt attention."

If there's no response or you aren't paid in a week or so, a more formal notice could be next, recapping the billing info and saying in part: "This payment is now [how many days/weeks] late. Please contact me to discuss this serious matter." I know a freelancer who created an alter ego in the form of someone who works for her inquiring into the matter of nonpayment.

If you and the client work out a payment plan, summarize it in an email for the record. Keep copies of every letter and email and a phone log. You're building documentation for possible use in court or for a collections agency.

Don't procrastinate on follow-up. The older the debt, the harder to collect.

Keep your tone professional, factual, and solution-oriented, focused in a positive way on what can be done to resolve this.

It's essential not to say or do anything that could be viewed as harassment. Don't get personal or list their failures. If they ask you to stop calling, stop; if they tell you to call back later, ask when would be a good time and call back then; don't contact them multiple times a day, and don't make threats or criticisms. There are strict regulations around the debt collection process. You want to comply fully to avoid any appearance of harassment. To find out more about federal and state regulations, type "consumer debt collection and regulation" into your browser. If you have any questions about how to proceed, consult an attorney.

KICKING IT TO THE NEXT LEVEL

You might ask an attorney to send a letter after your initial attempts, or pay a collection agency to send letters or make calls.

If your client's using work you've done, you could talk to your lawyer about whether they can be ordered to stop. You could propose mediation (see Chapter 5). If the debt's large, has been pending awhile, and collection looks dim, you could offer a discounted payment to clear the slate. Put it in writing, put a deadline on it, and be clear that this offer is only happening once. If it works, formalize the deal with a legal agreement called a mutual release and settlement.

If you hand the whole sorry mess over to a collection agency, they'll generally pay you 50 percent of what they recover. For information on collection services, check out the Commercial Collection Agency Association (ccaacollect.com).

As a final stop before lawsuit lane, you could send a demand letter that a) briefly, clearly, politely recaps the history of your grievance, b) proposes a resolution, such as X amount, paid by X date, and c) states that if they choose not to do this, you'll file a lawsuit. If that doesn't work, you might be able to present the letter in court as part of summarizing your dispute.

If all else fails, you'll have to decide whether to sue or let it go. It costs time and money to pursue legal action. Sometimes people decide to take the loss, move on, and let the universe dole out its brand of what-goes-around-comes-around justice. Others choose to take it to court.

Before you hire a lawyer, do your math and get a realistic assessment of the expenses, because the fees may exceed the debt.

Small Claims Court at a Glance

What it is: Small claims court is a venue for resolving relatively small disputes over money and sometimes other issues (depending on the state). While it's not costly, it does take time. You can represent yourself or (again, depending on your state) you could have a lawyer represent you, but make sure the cost of paying the lawyer makes sense for what you're looking to recover.

Where it is: Ask the small claims clerk in your city about any regulations regarding where you can sue. It might be in the defendant's state of residence or business, which can add to costs and time.

How it works: It's a relatively informal process similar to arbitration. You (the plaintiff) present your evidence to the judge; the other guy (the defendant) does the same; and the judge rules on it. The judge might encourage you to have the case mediated (see Chapter 5). If you do, you probably won't be able to go back to the judge.

Why you shouldn't wait too long to file: States have statutes of limitations on how long you have to bring a lawsuit. Check the rules for yours.

How much you can recover: Each state limits how much you can recover in small claims court. It's usually somewhere from $3,000 to $10,000 (which makes a case to break payments into amounts that fall below your state's limit—but keep in mind that you can sue only for one cause of action; you can't break a large payment into multiple parts and seek to collect on more than one. That's why small claims court doesn't work for recovering larger amounts. It's designed for very small matters, hence the term *small claims court*. Check your state to find out limits.

Tips and tactics: While you can represent yourself, it could help to pay a lawyer for a coaching consult or two. Also, carefully compile the evidence you'll bring to persuade the judge. It could be your written and spoken communications with the client; copies of your contract, letter of agreement, or deal memo; and invoices. It could be photos. Or witnesses.

Winning ≠ collecting: If you win, the fun has just begun. If the client doesn't pay up, you have to pursue payment, a process in itself requiring more time and (yes) more money.

Resource: To get information on small claims court in your area and learn more about the procedure, type "small claims court" and your state's name into your browser, and look for official government websites, which end in .gov or .us.

Woody Allen famously said, "Eighty percent of success is showing up." I believe the other 20 percent is keeping going, especially when problems come up. It's about resilience. In Chapter 6 I told my misclassification story. It was rough while it was happening. But in hindsight, there's a weird symmetry. Without that experience, I wouldn't have had the idea for Freelancers Union and found the work I love and am uniquely suited to do.

No, I won't segue to mystical ravings about silver linings and lessons learned from adversity. There are bad work situations that defy positive spin. We all have them. They push us to learn from our mistakes, protect ourselves better, and in the end be better at what we do. They make us smarter about finding good projects and good clients—the ones who are appreciative, intelligent, accommodating, honest, and happy to pay us what we're worth, on time. And they make the hard-won rewards of freelancing—chief among them the opportunity to work with great people—even sweeter.

PART 3: GROWING YOUR BUSINESS

Chapter 8

MARKETING YOU

Recently I went to a regularly held conference for social entrepreneurs I hadn't attended in several years. It had started as a clutch of upstarts. Now the world knows about this field. The convention's a big deal and much more business-focused.

Seeing how happening this little convention had become was a lesson in staying connected even when crazy-busy. As one freelancer said, "I forgot that a few years pass and new people enter a business and build new connections."

Here's how Holly has kept her freelance pipeline full so far: "I'm good at quick turnarounds, and I fill a niche working with small businesses on tight budgets." But she admits, "I depend on word of mouth. I'd like to know how to market my skills better."

Word of mouth alone usually won't turbocharge a freelance career. You can't control who calls. And if your market or contacts dry up, you'd better have a plan unless you want to do the same.

Employees, surrounded by coworkers, can practically bathe in their network. Freelancers have to create theirs.

"I suck at this part," one freelancer laments. "I'm good at what I do, but I can't say I've got a strategy for getting work. About as bold as I get is gentle email reminders that I'm available."

You need a marketing method you're comfortable with that can grow with you. In this chapter we'll look at extending your outreach and developing your marketing style alongside your freelance career.

A FISH TALE

Once upon a time, there were two hungry fishermen. One drags his tackle to the end of a pier, drops in his hook baited with leftovers, anchors his rod in a bucket of sand, and goes home to do chores.

The other fisherman rows to a place he's learned trout gather, when he knows they tend to be there. He drops his line, juicy worm thereon, and waits awhile. Then he rows to a different spot and casts again. He observes the ways of the river and the fish. He enjoys the beauty of the day.

Which fisherman is more likely to:

a) Catch a fish (or two or three)?

b) Have a better chance of catching fish next time?

c) Feel happier?

We don't question the common sense of knowing what kind of fish you want, going where they go, and learning the best ways to catch them. Fishing for clients isn't that different. There's a simple trifecta for happy marketing:

1 Have a strategy.

2 Let go of strategy.

3 Think give, not get.

HAVE A STRATEGY

Without a marketing strategy, the choices of where to drop your line (pond? lake? river?) and for whom (trout? salmon? grouper?) get overwhelming. A lot of freelancers troll for gigs online and talk to other freelancers in discussion groups. By themselves, these tactics are like Fisherman 1's line-in-a-bucket approach: relatively easy; not very effective. You want to find prospects not by accident but by design, and network with people you're pretty sure can help you as much as you can help them. That strategy's driven by a very different philosophy. It's not about finding people who want you, but about finding the people you want.

For that, legwork and face-to-face networking remain the gold standards—with straight shots of Internet added.

First, Know Who You Are

You can't catch a fish without the right bait. So review your Key Skills List from Chapter 1, and your fabulous human traits—the intangibles that make you unique. Get the specialties your market wants. Specialists can charge more and be choosier about gigs. (Fisherman 2 developed a way with trout; Fisherman 1 had to take whatever he could get.)

Maybe you'll develop a special service: massage therapist magical at shiatsu. Or an industry specialty: financial writer for banking institutions. Business size can be a specialty: website developer for start-ups. Specialists know their market's likes, dislikes, aches, and pains and can quickly build a bond.

How much you market depends on client turnover. Freelancers with mostly one-time clients have to cast wider and more often than freelancers with lots of ongoing business. (For the one-time types, Level 4 products can add income streams; social media can broaden your reach.)

If you don't deep-down know who you are and what you're looking for, no one else will, either.

Know Where They Are

Where's the growing edge of your market—the innovation, the energy, the spending? That's where your chances are best for gigs now and later.

What's the growing edge worried, wondering, or excited about? Look for what's trending. Position your skills and services to the needs of that growing edge.

Then go where those fish go. Find out what they read, what organizations they belong to, what discussion groups they visit, what blogs they follow. Where do they network, get training, or look to hire people? Who are the players? "I read industry publications and make lists of people to contact," Dave says.

Use the Internet to follow prospects. Check out their social media posts, blog, or newsletter. Study their website. Read articles mentioning or quoting them.

All this gives you something to talk with them about. Imagine the lame, generic lines tossed out to industry big fish. You'll be able to connect much better because you're attuned to their world.

While it's fun to network with your own kind, you also need to fish in different waters to grow your freelance business. The shiatsu specialist might network with acupuncturists, yoga teachers, physical therapists, sports medicine professionals, and athletic coaches. Discussion groups can eat time, so lurk to learn whether they fit your networking needs before joining the conversation.

Be choosy about professional groups, too. Check them out online. If an event's open to nonmembers, go. Look for groups with good reputations, a membership you want to meet, and events where you can learn and network. Join because you want to get involved.

Conferences and conventions can cost time and money. Again, focus on the opportunities to learn and connect: "When I was trying without much luck to break into food writing, I went to a panel called 'What Magazine Editors Want Today,'" Alison recalls. "The panelists, editors from the big food magazines, talked about how they preferred story ideas to be pitched. One mentioned the importance of talking about food in pitches. She said something like, 'My mouth should be watering over your delicious food.' I realized I'd spent most of my queries talking about why my ideas were good for their magazines, forgetting to talk about the delicious, amazing food I'd be writing about! From then on, I spent more time describing the recipes that'd be in my stories. Almost immediately I started getting more assignments."

Have a question for the Q & A session. This gives you an opening to introduce yourself afterward (do that anyway): "Thanks for answering my question about runners' knee problems. I'm a shiatsu practitioner and I'm interested in helping athletes recover from injuries. I'd love to know more about your work. Do you have a card?" Or email them to thank them for their talk, and ask your question.

You can even contact people you didn't meet: "I was at Gizmofest last week and was impressed by your booth. I'm sorry we didn't meet, because I'm interested in your work [et cetera]."

Here's how one freelancer's natural enthusiasm and smart conference prospecting paid off: "I attended a panel where one of the speakers was someone I hadn't met who was newly assigning stories for a magazine I'd worked for a lot, but not since he started assigning. I got there early, got a seat directly in front of him, and adjusted my name tag so he couldn't help but see my name (I knew he'd recognize it). I paid rapt attention to everything he said. The moment the session ended, I popped out of my chair, extended my hand, and introduced myself. He immediately said, 'We have to get you back in the magazine!' That one sentence made my attendance at the conference worthwhile. Even better, later that day I pitched him a few story ideas, and about a week later, he assigned one to me! It covered the price of the conference and then some."

Do What Works

You could have the best idea since fish bait, but if your target market isn't interested, it's the wrong bait. Rethink your market, your bait, or both. Some guidelines:

Try stuff out. A journalist says: "I used to send editors longer, more detailed story ideas, and only one per query. But I think including several ideas makes an editor more likely to choose one he or she likes best, and making them briefer and less specific makes it easier for the editor to read what might interest him or her into the ideas. So 'more, briefer ideas' is one of my strategies for selling stories."

Success? Share it with other freelancers and ask what works for them.

Have one request or question, not ten. "I wondered if you ever hire outside contractors to do . . ." "I wondered which newsletters or professional groups you think would be good to check out." "I'm interested in how you established your freelance business. You're doing things I'd like to do someday." If all goes well, you'll have other chances to talk.

No reports, please. Julie says, "I met this guy at a meet-up who started reciting a list of his achievements. It wasn't a conversation. It was a monologue." Linguistics expert Deborah Tannen calls this "report-talk." It's more like a presentation, whereas "rapport-talk" invites connection.

Fish with focus. Don't just stick your rod in a bucket and leave.

Fish a little every day: Spend half an hour a day on some kind of self-marketing: research a new contact; visit a discussion group or blog; find a new list of names; write or call a couple of people; or reconnect with someone. That nagging thought, *I should be doing more marketing*, will vanish.

Track your catch. Make it easy to pick up where you left off. Track who you contacted (or want to), when, what you discussed, and your follow-ups. It could be on a spreadsheet or a legal pad: "I keep a running list of people with whom I like to keep in touch and a list of new people to contact. I call them my 'master plans,' because they remind me that living in the day-to-day doesn't preclude dreams." Or try a technology-based method such as a contact management system (CMS) or customer relationship management (CRM).

Make mini-casts. At events, talk to a minimum of, say, three people for five-plus minutes. Or invite one person you met to get together with you.

Have some give-and-tell. Examples: "I'll send you a video clip of my latest animation project." "I've attached an audio file of our new release. Enjoy!" "Here's a postcard about my book/my class/my next show. It was fun talking with you about it. Thanks for your encouragement!" (See Think Give, Not Get.)

Come away saying, "I learned something." Such as: how to contact them; people, ideas, books, a website, or an organization to check out; a shared interest; the answer to a question about their business, their market, or the kind of contractors they hire; or that they'd like to receive some info about you, receive your newsletter, or get together again.

Follow up all leads you're given. Yes, all. Not following up on someone's suggestion basically trashes their time and info—and the time you spent getting it. So follow up. Let them know you did. Thank them again.

Know what you'll do with "No." I like hearing no because it's useful information. It sends me right into: "Thanks for your time. Is there anyone you'd recommend I talk to? Books or places with good information?"

You could handle nonresponses that way, too. Getting no response doesn't necessarily mean no. It could mean: "Not now." "I don't know." "Maybe, but I can't talk about it." "I'll look at this later." "Any email older than yesterday is dead to me."

Find out what's working. When prospects contact you, ask how they heard about you. Was it from a member of a networking or professional group you're in? Which discussion groups are driving hits on your website? Where are your mailing list sign-ups coming from? Knowing where it's working helps you know where to row your boat.

LET GO OF STRATEGY

Here's where we talk about enjoying the beauty of the day while learning the ways of the fish. About pursuing activities not just to make contacts, but because you want to. About enjoying the process, apart from the results.

No chanting or candles necessary. This actually makes rational sense.

When you hyperfocus, you miss stuff. Like the little stream of bubbles a few yards upriver, where the fish are really biting.

Part of your marketing strategy should be letting go of strategy. Once your line's in the water, relax and tune in to the moment. You'll be more likely to pick up useful information. And you'll enjoy yourself more. Here are some tips that may help.

Make Friends, Not Contacts

When I reach out to new organizations, I want to find out who's the smartest, most helpful, or most knowledgeable person there. That's not necessarily the person at the top.

Be democratic about your networking. Hierarchy and status aren't the only barometers for meaningful contacts. Not every decision rests with senior management. The most important person in the room may *not* be the one you should meet.

Also, be low-key. Always selling is like having bad breath: No one will tell you, but everyone notices ("He must really need work," "Oh, God, here she comes again."). Josh says, "Not long ago I thought about recommending a guy I know for a project. I didn't because he's such a relentless networker that I was afraid he'd never stop calling me."

Allow for Coincidence

When I was at the Kennedy School, I met a woman I'll call Jane who'd recently left her position at a foundation. When I told her I was thinking about starting a freelancers organization, she suggested I call a friend of hers who was an executive at another foundation. Because of Jane, this woman was willing to talk with me, though initially she didn't see a funding fit with her organization. But after an hour-plus of conversation, she said, "You know what? Let's move it to the next phase."

Ultimately, she became my first funder. Jane was the bridge connecting us. It never would have happened if I'd decided Jane wasn't worth talking to because she wasn't in a position to help me directly. But I wasn't thinking strategically. I was just out there sharing my dream. There are people like Jane who'll want to help you. Allow for coincidence and you'll find them.

Be open to the serendipitous meeting—the idle conversation, the doing of a thing that seems to lead nowhere. The calculated life isn't much fun. And it may not be as productive.

Sociologist Mark Granovetter studied and wrote about "the strength of weak ties": the idea that each of us has strong ties with some people and weak ties with others we'd call acquaintances—and that it's our acquaintances, with strong ties of their own, who are bridges to people, information, and opportunities we wouldn't otherwise find.

Amazing coincidences can happen when you're openly doing what you love. When Freelancers Union was new, we were desperately seeking an insurance company to partner with us to offer health insurance to members. We were striking out. One of my coworkers went to a lecture on a topic she was interested in. Coincidentally, she sat next to an insurance executive—who ended up helping set up our first health insurance plan for freelancers. We didn't send her there saying, "Go find people who can help us." She was pursuing an interest. Once there, when she met someone in a position to help, her passion was galvanizing.

Years ago, I had a fear of flying. The only thing that helped was talking (OK, babbling) to the passenger next to me. So, on a flight to California, I babbled on about Freelancers Union to the nice man beside me. I must have given him my card, because after I returned to New York, out of the blue I got a $250 check from him for Freelancers Union, with a note wishing me luck.

I'm not suggesting you depend on coincidence to get work. Just don't be too stuck in your usual habits of going about your business to tap into it. Do your best marketing; then get out and live. Go wide, go long. Pursue your interests. Share what you do. What you stand for. In places like these:

- Alumnae groups: high school, college, postgrad

- Hobbies/activities: teammates, book group buddies, hiking club members, et cetera

- Community groups, from civic groups to food co-ops to block associations

- Your Chamber of Commerce
- Your local Rotary Club, Y, or Junior League
- Your spiritual community
- Your kids' school, camp, and sports groups; parent groups
- Volunteer/charitable work
- Political involvement

Joining groups like these beautifully integrates work and life. It accelerates your networking because you have something in common with the members, which fosters liking, trust, and connection. Ply your trade for the cause: Design the postcard or brochure, raffle off a free consult, make the refreshments, be the event photographer or videographer, write the press release or the pitch letter, do the books, donate the fund-raiser favors (the goody bag at our first Freelancers Union gala contained handmade soap, lip balm, discount offers, and other items from members, which put their work in front of more than 200 people).

Be Up to Something

Who knows if it comes from a primordial urge to hook up with the most energetic (presumably the healthiest) specimen in the bunch, but there's nothing more alluring than someone who's got a lot of interesting stuff going on. Being into something—paid or pro bono, ventures you're trying to launch, or any work you love doing—is attractive. When you give off that vibe, others will want to play in your sandbox. You're busy being the capable person they could hire or recommend.

"Before I had any contracts for gigs, I prospected by talking about projects under serious discussion," Travis says. "It was impressive to say, 'I'm talking with the director of X firm about helping them with a new project, and I'm meeting with Y type of professional about a project on Z general topic . . .' I made sure not to give away any confidential details. I'd see prospects' eyes widen. They went from passive listening to active thinking. And they realized that if they wanted to hire me, they'd better get on it."

There's nothing like a little social validation ("What's that feeding frenzy going on over there?") and scarcity ("Wow, better take this bait before someone else does!") to tempt the fish to bite, as Jody learned: "Last year, I had an opportunity to travel to Paris for a project. As exciting as this was, I was ambivalent about going, as I'd just begun courting producers and directors in Los Angeles toward developing a feature film for which a tiny window had opened. In Hollywood, it's a game of striking when the iron is hot. I feared my iron would be stone cold by the time I returned.

"One reason feature film projects take so long to gain momentum is the time it takes to get everyone on board. This is heightened by studios and agents who might take days or weeks to return your calls . . . *if* they do.

"This phenomenon changed when I accepted the Paris job. I stayed up long enough for LA to awaken and to place my calls. It worked like a charm! First, because my calls were unusually noteworthy: I was calling from *Paris*. Second, the assistants in LA were quick to note my limited window of availability, creating an almost incidental call to action. I've never had such success in generating returned calls, new appointments, teleconferences.

"I'm experimenting with ways to re-create this phenomenon at home. I've discovered that not articulating when I'm available suggests that my schedule creates me and not the other way around, affording others a looseness in their actions that isn't very rewarding."

Being up to something interesting can change how you network, as Carrie found: "I meet a lot of people who are potential clients, and I often ask them, 'Do you ever hire my kind of work?' It's always been a little embarrassing—not necessarily because I'm asking, but because it's never felt like a very powerful way to ask. Recently, at a conference dinner, the marketing director of a very big company and his PR agency contact happened to be at my table. It was late enough in the conference that I'd sort of given up doing a lot of 'work,' so we all just had a great time over dinner. At the end of the evening, instead of my usual, tentative, 'Do you ever need what I do?' I said, "It's my goal for this year to do more X-type of work, so if there's ever anything I can do for you, here's my card!' And they both said, 'We were thinking we'd like to work with you!' Since then, I *have* worked with them. To me the lesson is that instead of asking potential clients and contacts yes-or-no questions, which asks them to immediately accept or reject my proposition, it's much more effective to let them know what I am interested in and invite them to play. I told those potential clients what I was committed to, and they wanted to participate. So that's my new strategy: share what inspires me and invite potential clients to play."

THINK GIVE, NOT GET

I'll never forget the excitement and honor of being invited to the World Economic Forum Annual Meeting in Davos Klosters, Switzerland. As a start-up nonprofit among heads of major corporations and foundations, I felt like a goldfish in a pod of whales.

In one workshop, I spotted the CEO of a major company who I knew slightly. I wanted to talk with him but knew he had no incentive to spend time with me. I started thinking about what I had to offer that would be interesting or helpful to him.

One thing I knew was philanthropy. So I wrote out ten ideas for what his philanthropy strategy could be. As we were walking out I kind of cornered him, reintroduced myself as one of the nonprofit attendees, and said something like, "By the way, I've been thinking about ways you might develop a philanthropy strategy and came up with these ten ideas."

We ended up talking for close to an hour. It drove home the point that if you want to connect with a major player, while all the others are scheming how to get their pound of flesh, you might get that person's attention by thinking about what you can give, not what you can get.

When you do, you're building a kind of wealth called social capital. As political scientist Robert Putnam notes, it's the trust that grows from the give-and-take between individuals and groups.

I think we're turned off by people who are always selling because we sense they just want to take something from us. It's also why, once you find the people, places, and groups that might be receptive to your work, you need to spend time just hanging with them, not starting in with requests. Participate. Give. Become trusted as a regular. You'll build genuine relationships that genuinely help your work. And you'll be a happier fisherman.

TEN TERRIFIC GIVES

1 **Attend the events.** "For years, I paid dues to a professional women's group and never attended the events! Finally, I decided I'd either save the money or go and get to know people. I've enjoyed it much more than I expected."

2 **Help organize something.** Join or form a committee. Suggest an event and lead the effort. Volunteer to tweak the website or assist with social media outreach. Help set up seating for the lecture. Step up.

3 **Post comments on the group discussion board.** Or spearhead starting one.

4 **Start your own professional group.** (See Chapter 12.)

5 **Make introductions; give referrals.** If you know people others would like to meet, set them up. Give referrals and let the person know you referred them.

6 Share things. Share stuff you know your contacts and prospects will appreciate: an article about an industry trend, the link to a cool blog, a review of a movie they wanted to see.

7 Comarket with other businesses. Link to one another's websites; put postcards or flyers in one another's offices; serve your catered hors d'oeuvres at their gallery show; colead a workshop.

8 Offer to speak or teach for free. It's great give-and-tell for your skills or specialty. Could be a lecture, workshop, or webinar; business-to-business or for the public. It could be sponsored by a professional group or through a local business, school, or nonprofit (maybe with a pay-what-you-wish donation for the venue). All of you can promote the event to your respective contacts (including the media).

9 Help out at a trade conference. Conferences are prime fishing spots. Ask how you could help: "I saw a blurb in a trade magazine about a new conference. I figured the organizers might be open to event ideas, so I talked with my professional group and we pitched a panel discussion. The organizers loved it. The next year, we did two sessions. They just contacted us about year three. We pass out brochures and cards and get free admission to the exhibit hall and all the workshops."

10 Give to your clients, too. Give your Blue Chips a discount or throw in an extra service for being such loyal clients. Check in with clients you haven't talked to in a while—not to ask about available work, but just "how's it going?" Send a suggestion and don't frame it as a pitch. Give a short talk on something that's happening in your industry and invite clients and friends. Have a reception, holiday party, or "business birthday" party for clients, contacts, and prospects. Celebrate a year of getting to know all these cool and interesting people. Have examples of your work on display and a spot where guests can pick up your card, brochure, goody bag, or other take-aways.

Working for Free: Giving Too Much?

Some freelancers are fine with working for free: "As someone who has written for a living for more than twenty years, I respect anyone who has actually taken the time to write. I'll read work from friends, acquaintances, and business associates and offer constructive comments for free."

Working for free isn't the same as doing work on spec, because no one asked you to. True giving is freely given and feels great. Only you can judge when it's that way for you.

Keep the task short in scope and schedule so it pops like the one-time, special thing it is. Or do free work only for people and projects you feel a strong connection to: "I work for free when it's for a good cause, like a friend's start-up or a nonprofit organization I care about."

If you're new to freelancing or looking to break into a new type of work, working for free can add to your credentials and spread word about you. It can be a win/win: "I've done a lot of work for free, mostly freelancing while working a day job. Almost all of it led to paying work, mostly from building experience and being able to show future clients my work or my knowledge of a subject."

But in case that doesn't happen, you should be totally OK with doing the work for its own sake.

It's smart to set up pro bono work in writing so everyone's clear. Some items to include:

• A description of what you'll do, any drafts or revision rounds, and delivery date(s).

• Any assistance, materials, or resources the organization will provide (Copying? Envelope stuffing? Tables/chairs set-up? Screen, podium, and mic?)

• The type and manner of any credit you receive (in the show program or the gala journal; on the website; on the video?) or reward (free gala ticket? free admission to the exhibit hall?)

- Whether you can include the organization in your client list and mention or show the work on your website or in your portfolio.

- Whether you can use metrics for self-marketing: funds raised, tickets sold, website traffic increased.

- A testimonial for self-marketing if they like your work.

IT'S NOT THE PITCH, IT'S THE PERSON

The Internet is an amazing marketing space—we'll talk about it in Chapter 9. But a website is basically a digital wallflower that sits there with millions of others, hoping to be noticed (thus the competition for top placement in search results).

Online searches and pitches—emails, job boards, bidding sites—all have their place. But you're always one of many vying for attention. And an email pitch, no matter how customized, is still just words on a screen.

You are a walking, talking, thinking, movable feast of potential: flexible and responsive to any time, place, or person you encounter. When you network and prospect in a way that's the right fit for you, lavishing your wonderfulness on the right people and places, you're working your Freelance Portfolio Level 2 like a master. You'll spend a lot less time wondering where the next gig's coming from. And you'll be one of the fortunate freelancers who gets gigs by competing *less,* connecting *more.*

SEVEN KEYS TO NATURAL NETWORKING

At the law firm where I worked, I struck up a mentoring relationship of sorts with a woman several years younger than I. Eventually, it became clear that she couldn't give back in the reciprocal way natural to networking. She just didn't get that I was a person, not an endless source of professional advice.

It made me realize that networking is really about being genuinely interested in the other person, and ultimately about how you live your relationships over time. And that's about knowing how you interact with people.

In Chapter 4, we talked about how the best marketing happens when your marketing style feels natural to you. Here are seven keys for refining the fit:

1 Go your own way. Make it clear you're on a path: "I've been tutoring kids and coaching sports for years. I want to add a teaching component to my paid work." People will respond to your passion and have a better idea of how to help you.

2 Practice varying your pitch. Have a technical one for professionals; a super-short, laid-back one for the backyard barbecue; and a medium-size, understandable-to-the-masses one. When the "What do you do?" question comes, relax and answer naturally.

3 Cultivate your connections. The Internet makes this easy. Joe's company just launched a new product. Bob has an amazing, opinionated industry blog. Heather has been posting about the trade show. You can congratulate Joe on the new product launch (which could lead to a conversation about how Joe's company markets its products, and eventually maybe how you can help). When you tell Bob, "Your blog posts are fierce! How do you come up with your topics?" Bob will love talking with you about that. Now when you comment on his posts, he'll recognize you. To Heather, you can say, "Your posts are so good that I've been sharing them in my social network. I'm thinking about exhibiting at the show next year. Do you think it's worth the expense?" Now you've built the basis for connecting around mutual interests and reciprocity.

4 Let them get to know you. Have ways people can learn about you. It starts with the info on your card. It might continue with your "Thanks for our talk" email: "I've attached the video clip I mentioned. If you'd like to receive my newsletter, just click on the link below." And then there's your website, portfolio, video or audio clips, press packet, bio, or anything else that helps people know what you do.

5 Don't buy into status marketing. You'd be surprised what you can do with just a handful of business cards and a professional profile posted online, or a basic website. Maybe others have achieved self-marketing world domination (website-blog-newsletter; social media moguldom, ubiquity at lectures, workshops, and conventions; professional memberships out the wazoo). All that can come later, if you want. Don't let anything stop you from getting out there now: "I started with homemade business cards, a one-page bio, and a one-page résumé that I emailed to people. Later I posted my bio on some professional websites so people could find me there. Then I started posting comments on social media. But with just the cards and the two docs, I had enough to get started. My pipeline filled pretty fast."

6 Keep it up. Like friendships, contacts fade with disuse, leading to scrambles for work. So don't wait until you need something. Do a little something daily to stay in touch. Eventually, you'll have a lot of active connections to mine for info and work.

7 Take steps toward financial stability. Being more financially secure will help you network with confidence and not give off that frantic vibe that puts people off and alerts prospects that they can have their way with you at the negotiating table. For some quick financial relief, look for ways to pare your expenses in the short term. Chip away at longer-range stuff: pay down debt, save small amounts regularly, and even look at where and how you live. You can't change everything at once, but making your life fit better with freelancing is a huge pressure-reliever.

"I network intuitively—and I pride myself on being good at it."

THE CARD THING

To give or not to give your business card? Actually, the question is how to do it well and not come off like the March Hare ("Here's my card, here's my card..."), Attila the Hun (*"Take. My. Card."*), or Homer Simpson ("Forgot 'em...*D'oh!*").

You also want others' cards so you can build a list of people who might want to know about your products and services, or receive your amazing info (stuff we'll talk about in later chapters).

Some ways to do the handoff:

Give something. Promise to send information about something you've discussed. Of course, you'll need their contact info...which you'll get when you exchange cards.

Just ask. "I've really enjoyed talking with you. Do you have a card?" If they don't, ask them to write their contact info on the back of one of yours for you to keep, and then give them one of your cards.

Segue to it. "If you'd like more info about that, it's on my website, listed here on my card." Or, "I can email you some info about that. Do you have a card?"

Keep your cards in a convenient pocket or in your bag (no undignified digging!).

If they're barely holding up their end of the conversation, consider them card-UNworthy and make your exit: "It's been nice talking with you."

TOP TIPS FOR PEOPLE WHO HATE TO NETWORK

If you're introverted or think you're no good at networking, read on.

THINK OF IT AS LISTENING AND HELPING

The best networkers are master listeners, able to draw people out. Think of your elevator pitch as explaining how you help people. Or envision your quintessential client—and describe that person.

FIND THE RIGHT-SIZED GROUP FOR YOU

Make smaller events your specialty, like the meet-ups at Freelancers Union, with twenty-five to thirty people or fewer. Lisa says, "My professional group recently started having small dinners at members' houses with about eight people, where we really get to know each other. It makes the larger luncheon events easier, because I know people from the dinners."

DO THINGS THAT WILL PUT YOU MORE AT EASE

"I've learned to work with my shyness so it works for me. I tell myself, 'You're gonna go to the premeal mingling because once you sit down, it's harder to network.' So I do that. Before I sit, I wait for my tablemates to show up and introduce myself. Hardly anyone else does this, and they like it. There's no awkwardness about avoiding eye contact with people across the table because you don't know their names. Then when I say good-bye, I ask for business cards. The next meeting's that much easier."

"Probably the biggest reason I don't make pitches as often as I could or should is because there are a million other things I'd rather do."

Other tactics:

Keep expectations low at first. You don't even have to talk to people. Just stroll the space and scope things out.

Get there ahead of the crowd. It can be tough to walk into a roomful of people. Arrive before it gets crowded. Then you can start conversations as others arrive.

Get involved. Get on a planning committee and you'll get to know all the committee members. Bad at names? Ask to give out the nametags. Professional organizations need volunteers for everything. It's a natural way to meet people, give, and get your mind off yourself so you can relax.

Ask about the other guy. Remember they're looking to talk to you about what they're doing. Ask questions; show your natural interest; let the conversation develop. When it's your turn to talk, you'll be relaxed and ready.

Have a give-and-tell. Maybe after your handshake, you give out a fun little freebie, or a postcard for a first session/first purchase discount. You'll stand out and it's a great conversation starter.

LET SOMEONE ELSE DO IT

If you're willing to pay for the service or share the profits, partnering with a great networker can work: "The best years I've had were when other people marketed my skills. I had agents represent me. It was worth the percentage. My income soared." Or hire someone to help you hone your own—a career or marketing coach specializing in solopreneurs.

TOP TIPS FOR PEOPLE WHO LOVE TO NETWORK

Super-social folks can get so excited by all the great people to meet and things to do that their marketing can lose focus.

BE SELECTIVE TO BE EFFECTIVE

There are only so many people with whom you can develop the kind of relationship that builds real trust, referrals, and work. Consider what will really propel your career, learning, or enjoyment, and focus on those relationships.

DEPTH BEATS BREADTH

Choose some subjects you want to get really knowledgeable about and go to those events. You'll get more out of groups personally and professionally if you get involved—so how many can you realistically join? People will notice if you're doing more flitting than fitting in.

TALK LESS, LISTEN MORE

Listen to yourself network. Are you sucking up all the oxygen in the room? Ask at least two questions of every person you meet.

"I can walk into any room and network. I enjoy talking with people, learning about their business, and figuring out a way we might partner to grow our businesses together."

"WHAT DID I LEARN?"

As you sort through the business cards you picked up at an event, ask yourself what you learned from each person. It's a good test of "Did you talk less, listen more?"

Self-marketing should not be about selling to anyone who'll listen, but about finding people who want to listen. And it's about relaxing and knowing that wherever you go, something might happen that could help you in ways you can't begin to imagine. It might happen at the event you attend with your meet-the-players plan. Or it might happen in the conversation you strike up with the stranger sitting beside you on the plane.

What it takes to be a successful freelancer is really what it takes to have a successful life. You care enough to have a plan. You care enough to put yourself out there. You care enough to help others who are doing the same. The most powerful marketing is letting people see and feel that you care—in the integrity, commitment, and quality you deliver in real time, over time. The best marketing plan is the one that elevates your game and shows your best self. That's how you'll find clients worth keeping.

Chapter 9

MARKETING YOURSELF ONLINE

The Internet gives you a seat at the global table. It extends your reach to people you might never meet, lets you be everywhere at once, and works while you're not: You might be asleep or going all in on your best poker hand in months while someone nine time zones away is sipping coffee, browsing your website, and deciding you're the best person for the job he needs done.

Turning Up the Volume Online marketing should amplify, not replace, in-person marketing. These freelancers tell how they use it to stay on contacts' radar:

"When I updated my website last year, I sent an email blast to all my contacts. And every six months or so if things are slow, I send an email, basically saying, 'Hi, I'm here for you if you need anything.' I get responses."

"In my professional group's monthly meetings, I might talk with a member 6 times a year, about 10 minutes each time. Would I expect him to trust me with a major project based on an hour of small talk? No. But if we do that *and* connect online, it really pushes my marketing momentum. He reads my social media posts; I read and comment on his. I send him interesting articles. If I do 5 posts a day, 3 days a week, that's 15 posts per week, or 750 posts a year (allowing 2 weeks' vacation!). I've made up to 750 additional impressions on him, compared to 6."

You're busy and the Internet's vast, so be strategic and find the online marketing methods that work for you. This chapter aims to help you figure that out.

VIRTUAL VOCAB

The Internet hums with millions of conversations. Your challenge: finding the people who want to tune in to you. Thus a ridiculous amount of attention is paid to some terms and practices you should know about.

SEARCH ENGINES

I've done it. You've done it.

I refer to the shameless-yet-smart practice of looking yourself up online.

When you do, you're using a search engine, which trawls the Internet finding and listing all the places where your name appears.

Search engines are information hoarders that chug around cyber-space 24/7, tracking changes constantly. You want to harness their info-hoarding talents.

KEYWORDS

In Chapter 4, you learned about mirroring prospects' language to build trust. The Internet version: online content using words and phrases people use to search for products and services like yours.

Search engines know those keywords in excruciating statistical detail. So can you, using analytic tools (some free, some paid) such as Google Adwords: Keyword Tool (adwords.google.com). Ask your peers how they'd look up someone like you. Try searches using different keywords and study the top-listed websites.

SEARCH ENGINE OPTIMIZATION (SEO)

The more you use your prospects' language, the more relevant search engines may deem you on those topics, and the higher you may show in search listings. It's like being at eye-level on a store shelf, in an *optimized* position to be noticed.

Of course, it's not really that simple. Search engines also notice your content's relevance to the keywords searchers use, links to your content found elsewhere on the Internet, and other factors. All are weighed, or indexed, using secret algorithms to calculate your potential relevance to searchers, and thus your ranking. It's not a perfect imitation of how humans size people up, but it's all the Internet's got.

Because search engines are constantly chugging, you have lots of chances to optimize your ranking by updating your content, refining your keywords and creating relevant content, making friends online by linking to others and having them link to you, and most important being an active, informative presence. This is the "have a strategy" aspect of the marketing trifecta we talked about in Chapter 8.

Of course, just finding a product at eye level on the store shelf doesn't mean you'll buy it. Which is why slick SEO strategy is no substitute for having a product or service people really want. True relevance to your customers, coupled with knowing how to express that relevance in ways search engines understand, is smart SEO.

Because SEO is so complicated, once you're involved in a real marketing campaign, you might want to hire another freelancer who can do all the stuff that needs doing to help you show up higher in a search. It's kind of like hiring an accountant: Sometimes it pays to hire an expert. Hey—maybe this is a good barter opportunity (see Chapters 11 and 15).

SOCIAL MEDIA OPTIMIZATION (SMO)

Think about products and services you like and recommend. We might say you have a relationship with them. Social media optimization involves building online relationships with people who might become or connect you with customers. You do this using Chapter 8's "think give, not get" approach: offering useful, appealing, interesting information that encourages people to visit you online, share your coolness with others, and maybe, in time, become clients. That buzz around your content gets noticed by search engines.

CONTENT AND LINKS: SEO'S DYNAMIC DUO

Dressing thin content in catchy keywords won't get you into the SEO party. You need content that's rich in utility *and* optimal keywords in website page titles, headlines, and opening material (what pops up in searches), so people click on your stuff. Then your high-quality, keyword-rich content might link to pages deeper in your site, so people stay there, browsing and enjoying. You should also link to others' website pages that you find useful, delightful, or important. Become a hub for awesome information online.

The more people appreciate your content, the more apt they are to share your links. The greater the sharer's influence, the more likely they'll drive traffic to your site.

All of this boosts SEO. Do a handspring! If any of these folks eventually becomes a customer, do a handspring *and* a cartwheel.

Keep an Idea File

An idea file can help keep your digital content quality high. Save every idea and relevant link you could share. Here are some to get you started (for more, see Blog or Slog?):

Opinion pieces. Weigh in on an industry issue.

Problems/solutions/explanations/FAQs. Show your chops: Explain how you solve a common problem, answer a client question, or tell or show how a process or product works. It might become a webinar or tutorial.

Inside views. Reveal what pros know that customers often don't.

Product reviews. Help readers be smart consumers and show your knowledge of industry best practices.

YOUR BASE IN CYBERSPACE

What will be your base in cyberspace? Will you have your own website? A bio on a professional site? A business page on a social media site? All of the above? Choose a focal point to concentrate your efforts.

THE WELL-APPOINTED WEBSITE

"My website has been worth every nickel, though it's a hassle to keep it updated," Jing, a children's songwriter, says. "Often the first thing people do is look you up online. If you don't have a website that catches their attention, odds are that's where it'll end. When I perform at schools, every teacher thinks they've already met me because they've seen my video on my website."

Below we'll look at three levels of website complexity. First, some general guidelines.

The well-appointed website:

Knows what works and what doesn't. Become a website voyeur. Study other websites' design, content, and navigability. What draws you in, tosses you out? But remember, your website needs to show who you are. Don't go for a corporate look if that's not you. Ask your network how they built their sites and why. Read and take some classes or webinars on website development and online marketing.

Stays current. Since search engines notice change, even minor updates to your website—a photo and a little text—are good things. Your website shouldn't require more than you're willing to do to maintain and keep it fresh.

Knows what interests visitors. A successful website engages visitors from the instant it opens and is structured by what they want to know.

Reflects your style. Corporate websites have to be all things to all people, but you can give your website your own spin. Being yourself also helps you qualify prospects: You're more likely to attract good matches.

Makes you easy to find. Make it easy to contact you from any page on the site. Make it easy for visitors to provide their contact info so you can build a mailing list. Remember "think give, not get" and offer something in exchange: A free article, a resource list, a recipe, an exercise, a song.

Answers frequently asked questions. It saves everyone's time and communicates how you work.

Listing your rates is a personal decision. Some freelancers with fixed or minimum rates find it eliminates tire-kickers. Clients may like the transparency. Or try an optional section where prospects can tell you what they need and select their budget range from a menu.

Shows you off. Share your background and training, a client list, work samples (get clients' permission first—build it into your contracts if possible), video or audio clips, and client testimonials: "I got a superlative endorsement and put it on my website. It wasn't exactly unexpected, since I'd asked for it. But I didn't expect it to be so stupendous. It made me feel great about the work I'd done."

Protects your rights and your visitors'. Explain your policy on not sharing visitors' contact or personal information. Protect your copyright in your site. Do you need to include other terms and conditions, disclosures, policies, or disclaimers? Discuss this with a lawyer.

Apprentice Level

First step: buying a domain name. Search online under "domain name registration" to find registrars, see if the name you want is available, and buy it for a modest fee.

It could be your business name (which could be or include your name), ideally ending with .com, or your own name (or a version), depending on availability.

Your choice of hosting service (prices and capabilities vary) depends on your needs and the complexity and capability (current and anticipated) of your website. Read reviews and ask other freelancers.

Could a prepackaged, hosted website be for you? The design and technology are licensed to you; you just supply the content. You sacrifice some uniqueness and customization for lower cost and easy setup—but it's a no-fail, reasonably priced, website recipe you can season with a few of your own flavors and quickly serve up a site that won't embarrass you, without hiring a developer or designer.

A prepackaged option may not be for you if you plan to fast-track your site's growth or have a really specific vision. Before you commit, read the terms of service and know exactly what the package will let you do. Want to upload audio or video? Get the file size limits. Want to sell products (or plan to)? Find out how orders are processed, including security and fulfillment.

If someone's visiting your site, they're motivated to learn about you. So make sure your home page looks great, directs visitors clearly, and links to other social media spaces where they can find you.

SEO start-up: Include links to your website anywhere you're visible online and in your email signature file.

ASK SARA

Q Dear Sara, I'm a professional bookkeeper, and I also make and sell jewelry. Can I have both on my website?

A Freelancing lets you pursue multiple passions for profit. But if you combine them in one website, some prospects might question how you can be equally good at and dedicated to such different things. ("Is she doing my monthly billing or prepping for the craft show?") If one activity pays less or is perceived as lower-status, it might devalue your services.

If you have any concerns about perception, set up a dedicated website for your craftwork or join a professional online group such as Etsy (etsy.com).

A DEVELOPING STORY If you're hiring a website developer, ask how they prime a website to be adaptable as technology changes. What's their experience with features you might want to add? Do they test performance on multiple browsers (which?), and processes such as secure payment? How will their work facilitate SEO? Also important: building in security against malware. And what's their support policy?

HELP
YOURSELF
ALERT

Journeyman Level

Want to step up? There are choices to make. And possibly more expense, if you're hiring help (see A Developing Story).

Think how visitors to your site would want to use it. How would someone make an online appointment or purchase? Is it likely that they'll be using a smartphone to access your site? Will your website look great and be fully usable on different-size screens and types of devices? Discuss the possibilities with your designer and developer.

On the SEO side: Lurk less; comment and share more. Work on building relationships with and linking to other sites. Keep updating your site with new blog posts, articles, or other content.

Master Level

If you want a website that looks fierce, markets you like a rock star, and functions like a geek's fever dream, these abilities don't usually come rolled into one person. You may need to hire a website designer, website developer, and a marketing consultant.

A designer focuses on the site's look and visitors' experience. The developer should be expert at programming and function. An online marketing consultant should help you figure out your customers' needs and what features your website should have.

Get deeper into tutorials, newsletters, and blogs on online marketing and websites. Talk to freelancers with great websites; ask who they hired. The clearer you can be about what you want, the better your team should be able to cost out the job and deliver what you need.

Make your website scalable: built to accommodate added features, growing traffic, and technological change. If e-commerce is your goal, work with your developer to set up your store so products and services can be added. And keep your security up-to-date.

THE DRILL ON DIGITAL MARKETING

You already know the key to good digital marketing: Be helpful on subjects where you're knowledgeable, and you build visibility, trust, and a following. With or without a website, you can pursue any of the items below.

BUILD YOUR EMAIL CONTACTS LIST

It's your digital goldmine: an instant, low-cost, direct line to people who've trusted you enough to provide their contact info. (Important note: This doesn't mean they've opted in for mailings.) A good mailing list is:

Democratic: Everyone has or can develop one.

Versatile: You can email one person, handpick a group, or reach hundreds with a click.

Trackable: You can tell who opens your emails, clicks on the links, opts in or out, enrolls, registers, votes, or buys.

Any Level 4 ventures (see page 89) stand a better chance if your mailing list is current.

EMAIL LIST ETIQUETTE AND LEGALITIES

Our email inboxes have become like digital dens. We don't like it when people drop in uninvited. Drop in on your email contacts this way and you might end up in the trash or deleted as spam.

There are legal penalties for violating anti-spam laws, so play it very safe. Some tips:

- Always get consent before adding anyone to your mailing list.

- Include a clear opt-out or unsubscribe.

- Include a valid return email address, your company name, and your physical mailing address.

- Don't ever supply email addresses to others.

Check out "CAN-SPAM Act: A Compliance Guide for Business" from the Federal Trade Commission's Bureau of Consumer Protection Business Center (http://business.ftc.gov/documents/bus61-can-spam-act-compliance-guide-business). Unsure how the law applies to your situation? Consult a lawyer.

And remember:

Think give, not get. Give people a little something in exchange for signing up to your mailing list.

Always be relevant. If people hear from you too often about stuff they're not interested in, you'll lose them.

EMAIL NEWSLETTER: A CLASSIC, UPDATED

An email newsletter is a digital upgrade of a time-tested marketing tool. While websites and blogs wait to be visited, an email newsletter goes visiting (to fully consenting recipients, as just discussed), bearing enticing links to your website or blog.

No website or blog? An email newsletter is a super-fast, super-cheap way to remind people about your products and services and launch new ones.

Hate public speaking? An email newsletter lets you build an audience without putting on a tie, wearing heels, or suffering an attack of dry mouth.

What would your readers find interesting, helpful, or diverting? Ask your network how they create, design, send, and manage their newsletters.

Not into doing your own? If your professional group has one, ask if members can contribute content. Pitch some ideas. Your byline can include your website and contact info.

SEVEN EMAIL NEWSLETTER DOS

1: DO HAVE A CONSISTENT SENDER LINE.

Trust in the sender is critical in getting people to open an email. Consistently use your name or business name as the sender.

2: DO GIVE IT A TITLE.

Putting your e-newsletter title in the subject line builds trust and branding.

3: DO HAVE A FAMILY RESEMBLANCE.

If possible, pick up some design elements of your website or business materials.

4: DO KEEP IT SHORT.

A lot of people read email in a viewing panel, so make your lead compelling and your entries short. Or give digests, with links to a deeper dive: blog posts, articles, video, photos.

5: DO HAVE A SCHEDULE.

Write it into your calendar. Work on it a little each day. You risk losing momentum and credibility if you send out a couple issues, followed by silence.

6: DO PLUG IT.

Put opt-in language in your email signature file, on your website, and on your blog. Ask prospects if they'd like to receive your email newsletter. If you give talks, pass a signup sheet or ask people to give you their business card if they'd like to be added to your mailing list.

7: DO REMEMBER CONTENT AND LINKS.

SEO's Dynamic Duo!

BLOG OR SLOG?

A blog (short for web log—a term no one uses) is an online log of your thoughts, ideas, insights, opinions, discoveries, and perceptions. Blogs can be text-, video-, or image-based, or a microblog: a mix of super-short posts with visuals and links.

You can quickly set up a blog on a free blog site, integrate your blog into your website, use a blog instead of a website, or start a blog as precursor to a website.

Blogs are SEO boosters and marketing tools because:

1 You can update them anytime with fresh, relevant, keyword-rich content.

2 They're a platform for linking to others' content, and vice versa.

3 They let you cultivate relationships online: Readers can comment on your posts and you can respond.

4 They can funnel subscribers to your email newsletter.

5 You can incubate ideas by seeing what generates comments and interest.

6 You can build the trust that can pave the way to business.

A good blog is a significant time investment. Committed bloggers post every day. Be prepared to do weekly posts or several per month minimum. Consistency is key. We talked in Chapter 6 about being there for your clients. This is being there online.

It helps to have a goal. Do you want to get paying customers? It's not easy to make money directly from a blog unless it's from ad display (assuming your blog subject is attractive to advertisers). Instead, you might try an email newsletter, which goes to people who've already confirmed their interest in you. Do you want to connect with prospects? Make sure your content addresses their interests—this sounds obvious, but it's surprisingly easy to lose focus.

What to Blog About?

It's totally up to you. But keep it real, not too formal, and informative, like a good conversation. Some topics:

• What you've always wanted people to know about your industry: why it's cool, frustrating, freaky, weird, wonderful, or wildly unpredictable. It's your very own virtual soapbox. Climb up and wave your arms.

• New developments in your field and what they mean for your customers

• A list of really good resources

• Inside tips, tactics, strategies, warnings, or updates

• Examples of how you work and why

• What you learned from attending a workshop, seminar, show, or speech

- Interviews with pros in your field (a great excuse to call prospects and cross-link to other websites or blogs)
- What to ask or look for when hiring professionals like you
- Product reviews
- Regular features: a weekly summary, recipe, or project; a monthly digest; a "best of" list; an annual roundup
- A demonstration of how something is done or of how something works (or what to do when it doesn't)
- Themed posts tied to holidays or seasons
- Ways to save time, energy, money, or all three

End some posts with "What do you think?" You want your blog to be "rapport-talk," not "report talk," as mentioned in Chapter 8.

Beginning to Blog

You can start by following some blogs that get good traffic, are read by people in your target markets, and that you like.

Then start commenting on a few. Don't crash the party; introduce yourself with a few words about what you do. Show appreciation of the posts and of others' comments, and contribute your own. Link to helpful resources. Ask questions. Become familiar as a regular. (Once you start blogging, your comments might sometimes include links to relevant blog posts you've written, but they shouldn't be excuses for self-promotion. Link to others' content, too.)

A next step might be guest-blogging. Choose blogs your prospects read. Study the content, length, tone, and format of the posts, and check their policies on guest posts before pitching ideas. Blogs with a more modest readership might be more responsive than super-popular ones.

You might leave it at that. Guest-blogging can be a great way to build your visibility online.

You can share a blog: "My professional group started a blog. We share the responsibility to post, comment, and spread the word through our contacts."

Before launching your blog, you might stockpile several weeks' worth of posts. Build in links between them. Doing so invites readers to stay engaged with your blog and makes it seem robust from the start.

Schedule blog work just like your other work, so you can prep seasonal or holiday posts, do interviews, keyword research, arrange guest posts (while you're on vacation!), or plan a series.

Blogs and the Law

It's smart to check with your lawyer about any legal issues (state, federal, and international) if you intend to blog, including libel, invasion of privacy or right of publicity, protection of intellectual property and trade secrets (yours and others'), and not violating noncompete and nondisclosure agreements, to name some.

SEVEN BLOG DOS

1: DO BE YOURSELF.

Be informative, but be yourself. Some bloggers are known for analysis and stats. Others go short-form, packed with tips, lists, and links.

2: DO KEEP IT SHORT.

Around 500 words or so.

3: DO VARY THE FORMAT.

Pairing a photo per post really livens things up. Make sure you're cleared to use it, and include a credit line. Or feature fellow freelancers' pix, with credit line and link to their site. Or take your own if you're good at it (ask someone for their brutally honest opinion). Try bullet points, lists, subheads, videos, or flowcharts. All promote sharability.

> "Social media is my main source of professional news. I recently got three project inquiries that way, so it's starting to become a resource for paying work, too."

4: DO USE KEYWORDS STRATEGICALLY.

Especially in headlines and first paragraph.

5: DO REPLY.

If someone's commenting on your posts, congrats! It's like getting a prospect callback. Make sure you answer, getting a thread of good discussion going, or saying simply: "Glad the post was helpful!" "Thanks for your comment!" "Great idea!" "Thanks for pointing that out." "I hadn't thought of that . . ." et cetera. You can block or remove comments from "trolls" (cranks who are nasty or profane). People who respectfully disagree aren't trolls. They could be opportunities to show how you handle differences of opinion.

6: DO BUTTON UP.

Have buttons so readers can click 'n' share on the social media platform of their choice.

7: DO GIVE.

Offer a free article or a short video or podcast. It's a taste of what people could have if they hired you.

OTHER OPTIONS

Not into writing? Too busy to blog? Try microblogging, a short-form, highly fluid platform. A current example is Tumblr (tumblr.com), where you can post short written bytes, videos, images, links, or a combination of all, or Twitter (twitter.com). (See Microblogging at a Glance.)

Posting reviews positions you as an authority. Are you an IT pro? Review new electronics and software. Caterer? Review local restaurants. Writer or editor? Review books.

Post short videos demoing a process (exactly how does one debone a chicken, replace spark plugs, or give the cat a pill?) or showing you performing (a song, dance, or a short presentation). If you give a talk that's videotaped or recorded, ask if you can use a brief clip for promotional purposes).

Audio podcasts let your work travel with people on the go. Offer them on your website as free content, or post them on a hosting service and announce them on social media. This plus blogging makes you findable in multiple media, all over the Internet.

SOCIAL MEDIA: MAGNET OR MADNESS?

Freelancers' feelings about social media are all over the map. Take the quick quiz below and then read what your answers say about your relationship with social media:

"I'm active in social media, but I've never gotten a job through it. I don't know how helpful it really is."

SOCIAL MEDIA AND YOU: A QUIZ

Which of these statements best describes your relationship with social media?

1 I love it.

2 I thought this was supposed to help my business—nothing's happening.

3 It's been great for reconnecting with people I know.

4 I'm not sure it's for me.

5 I'm just starting to learn about it.

Analysis

1 Into It. You're off and running with social media. But do you have a plan for using it as a professional? How do you want to influence others?

2 Results Seeker. You understand how social media can help your business, but building trust takes time and focused effort. Maybe concentrate on one social media space for now, setting a deadline to assess results.

3 Connector. You've mastered the relationship side of social media. Now add a professional focus: Where can you do the most good *and* be the most successful?

4 Undecided. You haven't decided whether social media is for you. Is there any social media space where you'd feel comfortable at some level of engagement? If you have *no* presence, you might be significantly limiting your market outreach unless your personal network and word-of-mouth are thriving.

5 Learner. Maybe you've been reading about it and talking to other freelancers about their social media practices. Maybe you've been lurking online, watching how it's done. All very smart moves. But eventually, you have to learn by doing.

Where you fit on this spectrum might depend on where you are in your freelance career, your comfort level with technology—maybe even what day you're asked. Some have abandoned blogging for the speed and agility of social media. Many use it as an amplifier for their other online marketing.

This section will help you figure out an approach that works for you. First, let's profile the major players.

PROFESSIONAL NETWORKING SITES AT A GLANCE

What they are: LinkedIn (linkedin.com) is an example of a professional networking site. Check out these networking spaces if your primary aim is to connect with other professionals in specific fields. The conversations and the site's overall thrust are more business-focused than on social networking sites, where professional identity and marketing may or may not enter in.

Basic uses: You can post your profile, contact info, links to your website, blog, and other social media, and testimonials about your work, and you can join discussion groups. If you don't have a website, it's a way to be findable online.

Prospecting positives: It's a great way to find contacts old and new: "I've found people I forgot I ever worked with. And I've located contacts in minutes that it would have taken me days to track down, if ever." You can then reach out to new contacts through those you've already made. For example, you might discover that your cube-mate from your first job now knows the CFO at a company where you'd like to get a gig and can make an introduction. You can also get known by participating in discussion groups not just of freelancers, but also of professionals you'd like to work with in various fields.

Tips for connecting: Give testimonials without being asked. If others return the favor, great, but this is about the Love Bank. Ask clients if they'd be willing to provide testimonials you can post (or ask if one they gave you for other marketing can be posted).

If there's a discussion group topic you're knowledgeable about, respond with helpful information and links to web pages, articles you've read, or relevant content on your website or blog. As you get to know the regulars, send them invitations to connect. This is how group members become contacts, and eventually maybe freelance friends or clients.

SOCIAL NETWORKING SITES AT A GLANCE

What they are: Facebook (facebook.com) is an example of a social networking site with both a social component and a business side for those who want to use it professionally.

Possible uses: Everything from reconnecting with old friends to connecting with people with common interests (professional or personal) to launching business events and products.

Finding the mix: How much of your personal self you share might depend on your industry, the image you want to project, and whether showing a personal side is good for your business. Talk to your network; find out what they're doing and how well they feel it's working. Make sure the site's privacy settings are set exactly the way you want them and you know exactly what others see when viewing your content. Be vigilant about what others post on your page; remove what doesn't fit your mix.

If you have a personal page and a business page, put a more professional photo on your business page, link to your website and/or blog, and publicize this page in all your business networking.

Whatever you do, apply the classic email advice: Never post anything you wouldn't want seen by the world.

Website replacement? Possibly, but not necessarily. Pluses include fast, do-it-yourself setup with social networking functions quickly in place, and a hotline to your devoted peeps and all of their peeps.

Some drawbacks: You have to work within the site's design and function parameters and follow its rules, which can change at any time; low traffic can create a "dead page" perception; traffic is limited to site members; eventually your content or number of products may outgrow your page; and there's the possibility, however remote, that the site might cease to exist.

You could start with a business page and then transition to a free-standing website, or have a page that ultimately drives traffic to your site.

MICROBLOGGING AT A GLANCE

What it is: Twitter (twitter.com) is one example of a microblog: very short-form blogging (Twitter limits posts to 140 characters) where people share everything from what they're up to at that moment to ideas, thoughts, information, opinions, jokes, breaking news, rallying cries, questions, and links to engaging content (their own and others'). Twitter has shown its amplifying power in everything from political transformation in the Middle East to marches on Wall Street—and this area is changing quickly, with new technologies emerging by the season.

Best business uses: If your target market's in this space, it can be a way to build profile as a source of useful, interesting, quirky, creative (or whatever other adjective you want to be known for professionally) content, and drive traffic to your website or other spaces where people can learn more about you.

Since space is limited, it's critical to remember the basic rule of social media: Share, don't sell. Any blog topic you can think of can be pared to microblog size to help others gain impressions of you—short blurts about what you're working on, events you attended expressing opinions, asking questions, or alerting people to goodies coming from you (a new blog post, a webinar or talk, a discount, a freebie). The Love Bank cyberetiquette about sharing others' links and giving credit where it's due applies big-time.

How it helps: As you build visibility and credibility through your posts, others will share your posts with their connections, who may in turn share with theirs, and so on. That's how your name and what you do can become known to total strangers, potentially all over the world. It's digital word of mouth. As mentioned, all this can drive traffic to your social media pages, website, blog, or email newsletter. And some might inquire about doing business with you.

Tips for traffic: Make your handle your name or your business name if possible, or what you do. In your profile, include keywords and a link to your website or other online bio info. Be relevant. Share others' links as well as your own.

MAKE IT YOUR OWN

Since social media marketing costs so little (unless you're hiring a consultant) and can reach so many, it has huge potential for freelancers compared to the expense of traditional marketing campaigns. Yes, it takes time and there are no guarantees of success, but that's true of the traditional methods, too.

Social media also fits freelancing because it's based on personal connection—something freelancers have in spades that big companies struggle to emulate. The keys are being authentic and being in control of the process, from choosing the tools to using them.

SEVEN SOCIAL MEDIA DOS

1: DO HAVE A POLICY AND SET GOALS.

Some people "friend" everyone who asks and "follow" everyone who follows them. Others apply traditional friendship or networking standards. Just like your other business policies (do you take phone calls in the evenings? work on weekends?) know your policy and follow or change it by choice, depending on your goals: "When I first joined LinkedIn, I only connected with people I knew personally. Now that I'm starting to connect with people in discussion groups, I may have to change my policy."

Set goals, ideally measurable ones. (See "Do Regularly Review Results.") Do you want to:

- Get more clients?

- Grow your network?

- Drive traffic to your website or blog?

- Increase subscriptions to your email newsletter?

- Increase product purchases?

- What else?

All of these might be goals for you. If so, rank them so you can a) concentrate your efforts for best results, and b) build one goal atop another. You might need to grow your network before you can get more clients. You might need to start a newsletter or microblog intensively before you can increase traffic to your website. You might need more traffic to your website before you'll see a spike in product purchases.

Your goals will also influence your social media decisions.

If you want more clients, find the social media spaces where they hang out.

If you want more email newsletter subscribers, blog readers, or webinar students, your posts have to be interesting conversation-starters and direct people to other great info from you on your website, where they can sign up for your newsletter (the opt-in will be prominently displayed, right?).

If you want to grow your network, connect with other freelancers: "LinkedIn lets me learn about people I've met or want to meet, and it has connected me to old friends in new ways. For instance, it turns out the husband of an old family friend does much the same kind of work as I do—which I only know because LinkedIn told me so. It could have taken years of holiday parties to find this out! We're now collaborating on a project."

2: DO FIND YOUR MARKETS, AND BUILD SLOWLY.

If they're not microblogging, don't put your effort there. If they're commenting on blogs, join in.

Start in one social media space and build from there. If you spread yourself too thin, you won't be able to judge how well it's working. If you're in multiple social media spaces, integrate them so your posts in one show up in the others. You'll save time and look like a social media party animal! That way, too, people can respond and share in whatever space they're most comfortable.

3: DO SHARE THE BEST, AND LEARN FROM EARLY ADOPTERS.

Not only will you become trusted for the excellence of what you share, but it's efficient: You'll do less scouting for good content. And you might establish an authentic connection with these influencers over time. Also study the Internet practices of people who adopt new social media practices early. It could be they're pointing toward the future.

4: DO ASK QUESTIONS.

Asking for help and opinions draws a crowd. "Prepping a blog post on tax FAQs. What are yours? Ask me anything!" Post a link to the finished piece, saying, "Thanks for your great questions!" Or "What's your fave homemade cookie?" Create a recipe for the most-nominated one and offer it as a free download. "Making a book video trailer. Any advice?" Post the finished trailer and thank those who offered help.

You've also got a readymade research pool for Level 4 ventures. Create surveys or quizzes and invite people to take and share them. Your new products and services can be launched in the same space: "You spoke, we listened!"

5: DO GIVE, BUT HELP PEOPLE COMMIT OR BUY.

For example, when they click on a link that takes them to your website, offer them something of value for free for joining your mailing list. It's bad form to hard-sell in social media, but once they decide to opt in, sign up, register, or buy, make that process fast and effortless.

6: DO MAKE A SCHEDULE.

Says one freelancer: "I try to assign a deadline for updating my website. But sometimes that doesn't work." Says another: "I find social media addictive." They pretty much sum up the two extremes of digital marketing. It takes time, and there are only so many hours in your day.

First, set a kick-off date for your new online marketing venture—be it your first blog post or first Tweet. Work backward to schedule pre-launch to-dos: market research, tutorials, lurking, reading and commenting on other blogs, setting up your account, drafting your first post(s), et cetera.

Remember activity's essential for SEO, so to keep momentum once you're rolling, break down tasks in your calendar: writing your blog posts, composing your email newsletter, updating online profiles, visiting discussion groups, commenting on industry blogs.

Choose a pace you know can maintain and gradually increase it. Shoot for several times a week on social media. Or do some every day, or break it into two or three short sessions daily. Investigate tools (some are free, some paid) to integrate and manage your social media. Ask freelancers who are active online how they get it done.

7: DO REGULARLY REVIEW RESULTS.

Networking relationships aren't built overnight, and online relationships are no exception. Give it six months or so of consistent effort. Then ask:

- How close have I come to meeting my goals?
- Do I need to revise my goals?
- Do I need to break my goals into smaller increments?
- If I step up my commitment, what can I reasonably do?
- Should I change my strategy (including my content) in specific ways?
- Should I change my platform or mix of platforms?
- When will I check progress again?
Use metrics (see Measuring Success) to help you evaluate.

MEASURING SUCCESS

- Which social media space is driving the most traffic to your website?
- Once visitors get there, how many bounce (leave), how many browse, and how many buy a product or sign up for your webinar or other offering?
- Who's linking to your site?
- Who's subscribing to your blog, versus dropping in?
- Was there a spike in views of your video?
- Which keywords are more heavily searched than others, and are they in your online content?
- What search terms bring up your website, and which ones result in actual visits?

- How many people opened your email newsletter—and then clicked on the link to the promo you were running?

You can answer questions like these by using analytic tools (free or paid). There are numerous options. A familiar, free resource for starters is Google, specifically Google Analytics (google.com/analytics/index .html), Google AdWords: Keyword Tool, and Webmasters Google (google.com/webmasters). If your blog hosting service offers analytics, study them; the same goes for where you post your videos. For other free ways to get started, type "free web analytics" into your browser.

The Internet gives you an opportunity to become part of a community far beyond your physical reach. And like other aspects of freelancing, the rewards can be far more than monetary. "Somebody once compared social media to a giant party line," Maryann says. "Sometimes I think it's more like being at a giant party. People ask for advice, opinions, and directions. They share information, ideas, and consolation. There's a lot of laughter. And there's an amazing collective bullshit detector at work on the Internet. If you're doing something good and genuine, and you go public with it in a good and genuine way, that shines through. And connection can come from the most surprising places."

When you market yourself online, you never really know where the results will come from. But that's business—actually, life—writ large. You plan, strategize, analyze. That's preparation for opportunity. But in the end, like any interaction between people, you have to let go of strategy and go in there and be real, in order to get something real in return. Fortunately, being real is something that freelancers, bold individualists, know how to do.

Chapter 10

MOVING YOUR FREELANCING TO THE NEXT LEVEL

Sometimes your freelance career grows under the radar. Sometimes others see our growth before we do. Sometimes the push to grow comes as a nagging dissatisfaction.

Striking a balance between organic and intentional growth is important; otherwise you might end up with an unfocused career that never reaches potential or an overmanaged one that blinds you to unexpected opportunity. In the end, you want to be a self-reinventing freelancer—able to direct your growth and roll with things, too. In this chapter, we'll look at ways to grow, from raising your rates to rethinking your business setup and more.

QUIZ: HOW DO YOU KNOW IT'S TIME TO GROW?

And if so, how? Here are some questions and answers to get you started.
Do you answer "Yes" to any of the statements below?:

1 I have more work than I can handle most of the time.
Ways to grow:

• Raise your prices.

• Market yourself to higher-tier clients.

• Be selective about what you take on.

• Subcontract work (see Chapter 11).

• Develop passive income streams.

2 Increasingly, I don't have enough work to do.
Ways to grow:

• Develop new client services.

• Get additional training.

• Study the major players in your current market and aim new products and services at the growing edge.

• Research new markets.

• Develop multiple income streams.

3 I know I could market myself better.
Ways to grow:

• Get systematic about online and in-person marketing.

• Get back in touch with past clients.

• Package your services in new combinations.

• Network with/learn from freelancers who market themselves well.

4 I'm working long hours and cutting costs—and still barely meeting my expenses.
Ways to grow:

• Track your time on tasks to make sure your time/price ratio is accurate.

• Raise your rates (especially if you haven't in years) to ratchet up your client level and your perceived value.

• Study how higher-tier freelancers package and market themselves.

• Upgrade/revise your marketing materials.

5 I don't have time to focus on the kinds of projects or marketing I really want to do.
Ways to grow:

• Phase out or subcontract lower-priced services (see Chapter 11) and lower-level clients.

• Raise your rates.

• Phase in marketing to higher-tier clients.

6 I need to update/expand/upgrade my technology/space/tools. *Ways to grow:*

• Budget a percentage of each client payment for a tech/tools fund.

• Investigate coworking or renting space (see Chapter 2).

• Check into cloud computing for mobile productivity or to facilitate working with teams.

REBALANCE YOUR FREELANCE PORTFOLIO

Go back to your Freelance Portfolio and see if some rebalancing would help you grow.

1 Are your Blue Chips too dominant?

2 Are you prospecting mostly on the bidding sites (maybe because that's where your early gigs came from)?

3 Are you networking to meet *new* people, not just the same people?

4 When was the last time you worked on Level 4?

Here are some ideas for rebalancing:

FIVE FREELANCE PORTFOLIO REBALANCERS

1 Rethink your assumptions. Subcontract work you're doing on automatic pilot, freeing yourself for new ventures (see Chapter 11). Is it time to phase out a client? A service? Raise your rates to encourage natural attrition?

2 Make contacts at levels you aspire to, not levels you're at now.

3 Get more visible in every group you're in. Help at events. Step up and lead.

4 Up the ante on social networking. Been lurking? Start commenting. Been commenting? Comment more, in more visible spaces. Been blogging? Increase your posts, include more links, take on more topical professional subjects.

5 Treat Level 4 ideas like clients' projects. They're that important: "I have a 'Ventures' file where I dump every idea I have. Seeing it reminds me to grab an idea to work on."

SUBWAY THINKING AND THE ONE-PAGER

A BUSINESS MICROPLAN FOR THE NIMBLE FREELANCER

When I'm growing new ideas, I play a game called Subway Thinking. There's one rule: I have to be able to describe my idea in a single subway stop. (No subway? Try variants: between traffic lights, fifty steps on the treadmill, landmarks on your morning run).

To get my idea that small, I have to make it big. Which clues me into its potential. Which is how I'll get others on board.

Then I develop what at Freelancers Union we call a one-pager: a single page describing the what, why, and how of the idea.

It might take a day, a week, or three to write. But we don't turn it into a slog or use a template. We make that page fierce.

Will we raise money using this document? No. But we share it and get feedback for crafting a killer proposal. Like an elevator speech, the one-pager gives people a basic idea of what we're doing. It's a great way to incubate growth.

Try it! Here are some hints:

Get the big picture down in the first paragraph, but make sure you have the tactical things you'll do in the first year or two. Business is changing fast. You can revisit and tweak the plan as you go.

The one-page limit is slightly arbitrary. But only slightly. You want a super-short form you can quickly share and ask, "Whaddya think?" Think of what would help you pitch. After a quick summary, you should be able to say, "I've got a one-pager I can send you." Then you follow up after they've had a chance to think it over.

Share it first with your inner circle, thoughtful people who can give you smart feedback. These could be people in your Brain Trust, in your industry, or other wise ones. If you'll be seeking funding, maybe it's someone expert at giving or getting financing. You could bounce it off your lawyer and accountant, too.

Use your uncommon sense. If someone asks a question you can't answer, tell yourself, "Good to know this might come up." Assess its relevance, but use your uncommon sense to avoid doing things just because someone else would do them that way. If it fits and improves your concept, great.

You can add teeth to your one-pager by incorporating elements of a financial plan, which might include your customer base, costs, profit margins, monthly budget, growth goals, and strategies for achieving them.

IS IT TIME TO REVISIT YOUR BUSINESS STRUCTURE?

Your choices about business structure will affect your record keeping, tax procedures, and personal liability, among other things—so consult your accountant and attorney. Below are profiles of common structures to get you started. Make sure you investigate federal, state, and local regulations and tax laws for any business entity you might form. (For example, partnerships, LLCs/LLPs, and S corporations don't pay federal tax but might have to pay state and city tax.) For selected resources on small business, see the Appendix.

SOLE PROPRIETORSHIP AT A GLANCE

What it is: As a sole proprietor, you alone own your unincorporated business. In many states, sole proprietors must operate under their own names unless they file a trade name ("Doing Business As," or DBA). Check with your state business entity registration office.

Tax issues: You report your business income on your personal return, filing Form 1040 with Schedule C, distinguishing between your personal and business finances. Self-employment tax is paid using Schedule SE. You may have to pay estimated taxes quarterly.

Potential pros: Setup (and dissolution) is easy. Other than any required licenses or permits, there are no fees or forms. Maintenance is minimal compared to corporations. And you're the boss, answerable only to yourself.

Caveats: You're personally liable for any debts or legal problems in the business. Proper insurance is important as part of managing your risk. Getting financing and transferring ownership can be tough.

PARTNERSHIP AT A GLANCE

What it is: In a partnership, two or more people put in money, labor, or other contributions, and share profits and losses. A general partnership equally divides labor, liability, and profits—or if not, the specifics are spelled out in the partnership agreement. A limited partnership has limited partners whose liability and input are based on their level of investment. In addition to any necessary licenses and permits, partnerships must be registered with the state and have a business name.

Tax issues: The partnership reports income to the IRS but pays no income tax. Instead, profits or losses pass through to the partners, who each report their share and pay self-employment tax and estimated taxes.

Potential pros: You're joining forces to be stronger together than alone—not only for the work itself, but potentially helpful when seeking financing or credit; also, the partnership pays no income tax.

Caveats: Make sure you have a partnership agreement specifying your individual duties and powers, the division of profits, how decisions will be made and disputes handled, how partners can be added or bought out, and how the partnership would be dissolved. Unless the partnership is an LLP or a corporation (see below), partners are liable for their own *and* their partners' business debts and actions. So choose your partner(s) carefully, make a sound and fair partnership agreement, and communicate well.

INCORPORATION AT A GLANCE

What it is: A corporation is a separate entity that pays taxes and distributes profits to its shareholder owners, whether as dividends, salaries, or bonuses. There are C corporations and S corporations (both named for subchapters of the Internal Revenue Code). Also, an LLC or Limited Liability Company can elect corporate classification. (See LLC at a Glance.)

A corporation and its business name are registered in a state, generally via articles of incorporation filed with the state's secretary of state office. Check with your state for specific requirements.

Potential pros: You may be more protected from personal liability, though it's no substitute for having liability insurance and other precautions. A corporation can be a good choice if you're looking for investors. Corporations can raise funds though stock sale, they can survive beyond the shareholders, and ownership transfer is straightforward.

Caveats: The setup costs money, and you'll probably need an attorney's help. Then there are mandated ongoing procedures and costs—for example, shareholders' meetings, paperwork, and filing separate tax returns for the corporation.

You may have to sign personally as well as for the corporation to get a loan or credit, so your personal liability protection isn't ironclad—or you can compromise your protection if you put the corporation's legitimacy at risk by not following the rules for maintaining it.

Tax issues: The tax benefits of incorporating start to manifest when you're earning more than $100,000 per year. Corporations and owners file taxes separately. The corporation is taxed at a corporate tax rate generally lower than the personal rate. But there can be a double whammy: The corporation pays state and federal taxes on its profits; then the shareholders pay tax on their dividends. This can be offset somewhat by having the corporation pay you and other shareholders working in the company salaries, which the corporation can deduct as business expenses. Note: The IRS has rules defining reasonable payment.

C corporation potential pros: A C corporation can be a choice if you plan to pour your profits into the company and take a modest salary. This eliminates double taxation because only the corporation will have to pay tax on its profits, and not you as well (other than tax you pay on your salary). Double taxation would become an issue if you decided to take out some profits, whether as dividends or as a higher salary, at which point you and your accountant would need to work out the best way to handle it.

C corporation caveats: The C corporation has to pay taxes separately from the shareholders, and there's the associated additional paperwork and cost, plus the work and cost of following required corporate procedures. You can avoid the C corporation's double taxation by setting up an S corporation or an LLC.

S corporation: An S corporation must be domestic, and its shareholders can't be partnerships, corporations, or nonresident aliens. An S corporation is filed in your state of incorporation; you also file S corporation status with the IRS (Form 2553).

S corporation tax issues: Setting up an S corporation eliminates double taxation: The S corporation files a tax return, but its profits and losses are apportioned to shareholders as profits or losses to file on their personal federal returns (though there are some items the S corporation is taxed on). Tax regulations for S corporations differ among states, so find out your state's rules.

S corporation potential pros: A major positive: elimination of double taxation. An S corporation can be a happy medium if your sole proprietorship no longer serves you tax-wise but you don't need or want a C corporation.

S corporation caveats: As a corporation, an S corporation must follow specific procedures, meaning more accounting and legal costs. Consult your attorney and accountant. Also, the IRS assumes you work for the S corporation, so must receive a salary. Those wages are taxable even if the business reports a loss. Remember the IRS has rules for reasonable wages. If they deem you underpaid, they can determine other distributions you get from the corporation should be classified and taxed as wages.

Additional note: An LLC can request S corporation status. (See LLC (and LLP) at a Glance.)

LLC (AND LLP) AT A GLANCE

What it is: An LLC (Limited Liability Company) has the liability protections of the corporation and the tax advantages of a partnership. If you have one or more partners, you can form an LLP, or Limited Liability Partnership. A single member LLC, or SMLLC, is recognized in certain states. Talk to your attorney and accountant for other state and federal conditions.

You file in your state, and your status will be designated by "LLC" after your business name. LLCs don't need to register their names in addition. Different states have different regulations about procedures, including setup and dissolution, so check. You may be required to locally publicize the fact that you formed your LLC. You may or may not need an operating agreement, but you should have one if you have multiple members. If you do out-of-state business, find out what the status of your LLC will be there.

Tax issues: Because it's not viewed (and thus taxed) as a separate entity by the federal government, an LLC avoids the additional filing fees and double taxation issues of corporations by passing profits and losses to the members, who report them on their taxes. However, LLCs are taxed like corporations in certain states, so consult your accountant and attorney and your state income tax agency.

If you want your LLC to be taxed as a corporation (for example, as an S corporation—see "LLC/S corporation combo" below), you must file Form 8832 with the IRS. Otherwise, the IRS will tax it as a sole proprietorship or a partnership, whichever applies.

Potential pros: As mentioned, LLCs aren't subject to the double taxation of corporations and cost less to start, but like corporation shareholders, LLC owners (known as members) have personal liability protection from the LLC's debts or acts. An LLC is easier and less costly to operate than an S corporation, and the division of profit, investment, and labor between members is less regulated. An LLP is more complex and costly to start than a partnership, but in an LLP your personal liability is limited to your actions, not your partners'.

Caveats: LLC members are personally protected from the LLC's debts or legal issues, but note the term *limited liability*—members may not be protected from their own (or employees') tort actions.

It costs less to run an LLC than a corporation, but as mentioned, LLCs are taxed like corporations in certain states, so check with your state, your accountant, and your attorney, and make sure your accountant is experienced in handling LLC accounting and taxes. Also check with your state to see if the business has to be dissolved if a member leaves and a new LLC formed. If so, your operating agreement can stipulate what happens if members depart.

LLC/S corporation combo: As mentioned, you can be an LLC legally but can ask the IRS to apply S corporation tax treatment to your LLC if you submit Form 2553 in accordance with specific deadlines. Doing this can reduce your employment taxes, since these will be calculated on your wages as an S corporation shareholder/employee rather than on the business's net income. Consult your attorney and accountant. See if the savings offset the accounting costs involved with S corporations. Also find out if your state accepts this type of election, and how the process works.

INSURANCE, ANYONE?

Years of work can be wiped out faster than you can say "fire." Insurance buys peace of mind. There's a lot to consider and everyone's situation is unique, but here are some initial questions:

- What property do you own for your business?

- Could a product or service you sell cause harm?

- If you store products or expensive supplies, is there a risk of loss?

- Do you (or might you) hire others?

- Are there safety steps you can take to get discounts on premiums?

- Are you making sure you aren't buying insurance that overlaps with coverage you already have?

- Can you add coverage to a policy you have?

- Have you read the *entire* policy and do you know what is (*and isn't!*) covered, in detail?

Do an annual insurance checkup. Did you buy new equipment? Add higher-liability services? Expand your business online? These are just a few examples that could require a change in coverage.

Below are short profiles of common types of insurance. (For tips on insurance related to subcontracting and staffing, see Chapter 11. For information on health insurance, see Chapter 17.)

INSURANCE PACKAGES

Package policies are mash-ups of multiple coverages. If you work from home, chances are your homeowners' policy coverage for home business is minimal to nonexistent. If so, an in-home package policy might be cost-effective if you meet the requirements.

There are also small-business insurance policies. A Business Owner's Policy, or BOP, may cover property, on-site injury to others, and more.

PROPERTY

There is all-risks coverage against property loss and named-peril coverage, which lists the dangers it covers. With named-peril, if it's not on the list, it's excluded. Even with the all-risks coverage, give it a close read, note what's excluded, and consider whether you need extra coverage based on your location and your work.

A replacement cost policy lets you replace property at current market price. These policies have a total cost cap. If you don't get one that revises the cap for inflation, revisit it each year to see if it's still sufficient.

LIABILITY

A client falls in your office and sprains a wrist. Or is harmed by mistakes in your work. That's the kind of stuff liability insurance is for. Read the fine print so you understand what is and isn't covered.

Pretty much anyone whose work entails a fair degree of skill might be at risk of a lawsuit resulting from errors on the job. Talk to your insurance professional about your needs for professional liability insurance. It might cost less if bought through professional groups or trade associations. Shop around, review carefully. Ask members what they think of the coverage.

Professional liability insurance is available in some fields, but not in others. Often if it's available, it's expensive, not comprehensive, or both. These are not good things. You might contact insurance agencies in your area to see if they provide liability insurance in your field.

Freelancers Union is working on creating umbrella liability insurance for freelancers.

...AND MORE

Other kinds of insurance include:

Dependent properties. If your business depends on the existence of another (such as products or materials you store at another location), consider whether "dependent properties" insurance could be for you.

Auto. Does your insurance cover business use of your car?

Business interruption. Trees are beautiful . . . except when they fall on your office roof. Business interruption insurance can cover your lost profits (based on earnings history—one more reason to keep good records) and pay your expenses while you're closed for repairs, and possibly ramp-up time after reopening.

Web insurance. Would you suffer business damage if your business website service were compromised?

Disability. If sickness or accident really knocks you out of commission, the consequences for your business can be devastating. Disability insurance (short-term or long-term) pays a percentage of your average earned income during the time you can't work. There's a waiting period before coverage kicks in.

Life insurance. This may be required for a business loan. If you're a sole proprietor with no employees, generally the family's protection is to get a personal life insurance policy.

Umbrella policy. You can also get what's known as umbrella coverage that covers payments and liabilities that fall outside your other coverage.

WHAT ABOUT A LOAN?

When it comes to loans, freelancers are penalized for being who they are. Even when their income averages out OK by year's end, it's episodic by definition. Lenders like to see a steady-Eddie income stream rolling in every month: proof that you're a good risk for repaying a loan.

No steady-Eddie? Then they either deny the loan application or pass the risk to you by making you pay more on the loan. Even small business loan programs aren't scaled to fit most freelancers. Result: It can be hard to capitalize your business when you want to grow.

Before you get into the loan application and business plan–writing thing, do the math to figure out if you'd be able to live—i.e., pay your regular, everyday living expenses—if your plan doesn't go well and you're stuck with a loan to repay and not much else. If not, rethink the time and effort you're putting into looking for financing.

LOANS: THE CRASH COURSE

A loan entails borrowing money, known as the principal, and repaying it to the lender with interest at regular intervals over a set period of time, a process called amortization. Borrowers also pledge collateral: assets the lender could sell if the loan isn't repaid. This is called debt financing, in contrast to equity financing, in which an investor invests in your venture in exchange for some stake in the business.

FINANCING FIT FOR FREELANCERS Freelancers' businesses aren't like big businesses—or even like many small businesses. But when financers size up freelancers, those are the benchmarks they often apply.

Those benchmarks are stuck in the manufacturing era, when income was more predictable for more of us. Instead of rethinking their risk models so they can invest in the growth of today's workforce, lenders deny the loan or dump the risk on the freelancer: higher repayment terms.

Successful microcredit programs exist. Grameen Bank in Bangladesh provides collateral-free loans with interest limits and incremental repayment. The bank's mostly borrower-owned, a cooperative, self-monitoring model helping ensure loan repayment.

Freelancers Union aims to do for loans what we've done for health insurance:

1 Start by looking to ourselves for answers in professional or voluntary associations, co-ops, unions, et cetera. This is not where government has all the answers.

2 Create alliances to develop freelance-friendly local models. Start with your network or social media sites or civic groups to see if others have the same problems or opportunities and find a local place to meet and see if you can join together to achieve your collective goal.

3 Incubate successes using those models.

4 Build the business and policy case by showing how these models benefit freelancers and the economy and can be scaled up for broad use.

For more on ways to change the conversation about freelancers in business and in government, see Chapter 12. Meantime, your best defense against loan prejudice is to shore up your finances on every front: Save steadily. Reduce and resist debt. (For both, see Chapter 17.) And work on balancing your Freelance Portfolio to even out your income.

Want to play with some loan scenarios? Search under "amortization calculator" to find a template and plug in numbers.

Upside: Unlike equity financing, you're not sharing ownership when you get a loan. And the interest is tax-deductible.

Downside: It's all on you. You can't be late on payments. You're personally liable if you were required to guarantee the loan personally. You could lose property if you used it as collateral to secure the loan.

Which bank? There's no single answer. If you already have a bank you like, check their offerings. A big bank might have more choice of services, but a community bank may offer a more personal relationship, which may help move along the process. Better yet, see if you can join a credit union. (See Appendix.) Search online for a credit union in your city, state, or professional field. You want to feel comfortable with the bank, its practices, and the people you'd be dealing with. Do they understand your goals? Has the bank worked with businesses in your profession? Does it loan to other freelancers?

If you're approved for a loan, read everything carefully before you sign. Find out the penalty for repaying ahead of schedule, or prepayment. You'd think they'd be cheering—but *noooooo*. Questions? Talk to your attorney or accountant. Going forward, loop in your banker on how things are going. You want this person to be an informed advocate with the higher-ups.

Not approved? Stay positive. Find out why so you can work to improve your business, your business plan, or both.

Another interesting model is peer-to-peer lending of the kind you see on Prosper (prosper.com), where people evaluate risk and are willing to give you a loan where a bank may not.

How to Think Like a Bank

You'd rather not? Relax, it's temporary. Here are some of the questions lenders will want answered.

How successful are you? Lenders want evidence of your ability to repay a loan. They'll assess your financial statements for profitability and cash flow. If your business is new or if profits have been low or spotty, you'll need to make a strong case for your business's growth prospects and your ability to pay off the loan.

What's your collateral? The value of your collateral is important, since theoretically the bank would sell it (at a discount from full value) if you defaulted on the loan.

Do you really know what your goals are, and why you want this loan? This is where a one-pager can help you. How will this venture, purchase, or investment help you achieve your goals?

What's happening in your profession? Is it growing? Contracting? Do your goals fit where the industry is going? Who's your competition? If you've been keeping up with your prospecting, you should be a master market observer.

How good is your credit? If you haven't checked your credit report in the past year or plan to seek a loan in the coming months, get your credit report. You can do this for free from each of the three credit reporting companies once in any twelve-month period. Correcting any errors or repairing your credit takes time, so start early. *Note:* Not every bank views every credit report alike. For more on your credit report and credit score, see Chapter 17.

How much equity does your business have? Lenders look for investment in the business (whether your own or an investor's) and to see that the business's debts aren't way out of proportion to its equity, which makes it potentially less hardy.

What's the dollars-to-debt flow? Lenders want to know whether your income will arrive in time to pay your bills. You may have to provide a cash flow projection.

Loan Applications, Business Plans, et Cetera

Your one-pagers may be all you need to grow your freelance career. But if you pursue debt or equity financing, they can become the foundation of your loan application and business plan.

These documents are blueprints that lay out a comprehensive case for financing, with detailed financial paperwork. Doing them right helps expedite the decision-making process. It's the finance equivalent of a job interview. So you want to go full-out.

You're too busy to spin your wheels, so read up on financing, loan applications, and business plans before tackling them. One great resource is the U.S. Small Business Administration (sba.gov). Also check out SCORE (Service Corps of Retired Executives), a national volunteer small business mentoring program that offers mentoring, workshops, and other info (score.org).

PASSIVE INCOME: THE FREELANCER'S BEST FRIEND

> "The only way I'd like to change or grow is to keep doing the same thing, but make more money at it."

Sounds good! But how do you make more money when you can juggle only so many projects and raise prices only so far?

Enter passive income.

The term *passive income* gets thrown around a lot. While the IRS has a very specific definition of "passive activity" (which you should apply when doing your taxes), in common parlance and for our purposes, passive income is often used to describe anything that brings in income without further labor on your part once the initial work is done. A few examples: a book, video, or audio product. The idea is that they make money while you do other things. Passive income is really part of a larger concept: multiple revenue streams.

The quest for ways to augment and diversify income is as old as the first ancestor who discovered that not only could you sell what you grew, but you could also preserve, age, ferment, churn, spin, weave, or otherwise transform it into other commodities you could sell to grow your wealth in good times and sustain you in lean.

Multiple income streams free you from living project to project. They help you meet expenses, invest or save for the future, or have some extra money to throw around: "I keep a dozen or so copies of my books in my car trunk to sell. I make a few bucks per book—no big shakes, but it puts a little spending money in my wallet. And it's really fun and rewarding to sign a book for someone." They're your best offense *and* defense: They'll grow your business *and* help protect you from freelancing's biggest stressor—episodic income.

SWIMMING IN REVENUE STREAMS

Coming up with ideas for revenue streams takes Level 4 thinking. Find some time and a place where you can focus. Write down every idea you can think of. Nothing's off-limits.

Below are just a few examples. I hope they'll spark your ideas. Any of these products or services may give rise to any of the others and can be scaled down or expanded. They could be free or paid, depending on your goals (gaining experience? building a mailing list? creating a range of different-priced products?). All can be promoted anywhere you go, including online. All can help you collect contact info and marketing data for future ventures.

"A friend recently told me she'd set up a basement studio for video blogging. I suggested she rent it out to other entrepreneurs making marketing videos."

Look for ways to slice, dice, expand, and retool your ideas. A talk can become a webinar, maybe recorded and sold online. That webinar could become a series; maybe bundled and sold as a course. For listeners or readers, your material could be developed into an audiobook or an e-book.

Lectures, Talks, Workshops, Seminars

Imagine you could network not just with one person at a time, but to a whole room, and talk about anything you wanted. Enter lectures and workshops. Pitch a talk tailored to an organization whose membership or customers would be a good match with your topic. They provide the venue and promote to their mailing list and media contacts; you reach out to your peeps, including online. You bring your amazing self and your knowledge, plus some goodies to give away and/or sell.

There's no perfect formula for figuring admission, but factor in how in-demand you are as a speaker, a realistic guess at audience size and how much they're willing or able to pay, your costs for the event, and the price of your products if that's built in.

Teleclasses

You can conduct these by phone to an audience dialing into a common number. They're a great low-tech, low-cost way to extend a popular talk or seminar or test-drive ideas you might develop into classes, webinars, podcasts, or books.

Webinars/Webcasts

Both of these are conducted via the Internet. A webcast may have more of a "talking to" feeling. A webinar has a "talking with" aspect, allowing communication between speaker and audience. Try typing "webinar services" or "webcast services" into your browser to research pricing and features of online services. Some offer free trials. You could charge for the live webinar, for a recording of it, or for products you promote within it. You might create several paid or free webinars to later sell as a series. Or spin e-books out of the content.

Articles, White Papers, and Reports

Craft your expert info into articles. Build your mailing list by giving them away online in exchange for contact info. Print them and use them as handouts at speaking events. Give them to prospects when you meet.

Books

Publishing a book used to be something most people could only aspire to. No more. There are still many publishers out there doing the

Q Dear Sara, How do I decide what should be free versus what I should sell?

A Free stuff—articles, talks, samples, initial consults, and the like—gives prospects a taste of your awesomeness and should be part of your "think give, not get" philosophy. To a point.

Too much free stuff conditions customers to devalue your work, dragging down the earning potential of everyone in your industry. It can erode quality: "Hey," some unprofessional professionals might say, "it's not like they can demand their money back if they're not satisfied." And it builds customer loyalty to the freebie, not the freelancer. All of this ultimately reduces value for everyone.

So:

1 Ask other freelancers who are growing their businesses how they deal with "free."

2 Analyze your free-to-paid conversion rate: How much paying business comes from free events?

3 Look at your needs and goals. Not all are monetary. Giving can help you build a community or do surveys before you launch new products. For example: You write a blog post that gets lots of comments. You expand it into a free podcast. Which leads to a speaking invitation from someone who downloads it. Which leads to a standing-room-only speaking event, a boost to your mailing list, and some local media hits. Which leads you to develop a paid webinar. Then a multipart telecourse. Then maybe an e-book. All of which you make available to your growing community, which drives more traffic, community building, and, ultimately sales.

You never know where "free" can go. But you have to take it there.

standard publishing arrangement, but if that route's not for you, you can pursue self-publishing: making your own arrangements directly with a publishing service, publishing digital books (e-books) or physical books (print-on-demand technology makes storing inventory a thing of the past).

Audio/Video Products

Posting short videos online is a great way to show off your expertise, boost your profile online, and drive interest in paid products. A builder could show how to use specific tools or do home repairs. A decorator could share low-cost home deco makeovers. A trainer could demo exercises. A computer pro could review new apps.

Audio podcasts let you editorialize, advise, or interview people in your field. You can record using a headset mic, edit yourself using audio editing software, and offer it via your website or blog.

Online Ads

Got a popular blog or a website? You might get revenue from hosting keyword advertising. These ads are keyword-driven, so what appears will depend on the keywords in your content. Blogs let you play with lots of keywords. Generally, you get paid if people visiting your site click on the ads. Rates vary and may be very low, but it's a revenue stream that can grow for some. You can choose to allow ads on your online videos or video blog, too.

Some professions lend themselves to these ads better than others. Are there products or services that are highly relevant to your online content? If you're a caterer, it could be cooking equipment, utensils, foods, and party stuff. If you're a tech expert, you could review products, post about tech troubleshooting, and host ads for tech equipment. A landscape architect? Ads for gardening tools, supplies, plants, and seeds. Be careful of papering your site with ads, though. It can annoy visitors and the revenue may not be worth that.

Blog Income

If you're an ace blogger, people might hire you to blog. If your blog is a super-informative and popular destination, related businesses might sponsor it. Or visitors might pay to subscribe. These developments can be great when they happen, but they're really about making blogging a business in itself, and the potential varies widely depending on your industry and on your willingness to pursue it based on your time, interest level, writing ability, and how a blog-based business fits with your goals.

Affiliate Marketing

Affiliate marketing is a form of advertising where you put links (often to products or services) in your website or blog content, and you're paid a commission if a sale is made through your referral, or if the person you referred does something else the advertiser wants, such as taking a survey or providing their contact info (the arrangement varies).

This could be an option if your website or blog lends itself to discussion of products and services (writer blogging about books; software developer reviewing products; musician profiling new releases). You might research affiliate programs related to your topic if you're considering blogging.

It's important to maintain visitors' trust, so don't oversell or promote bad products or products you don't know about or don't believe in. If you write product reviews, make them objective.

How you disclose that these are affiliate links is something to discuss with your lawyer and with people who do affiliate marketing.

Co-Ventures

Many of these ideas could be developed with other freelancers. Share the work; share the profits. An accountant and a bookkeeper might lead a tax prep talk. If you really click, you could formalize a business agreement to offer services to clients as a team and cross-promote on each others' websites. You've instantly added outreach and services without having to develop them yourself.

GROWING YOUR SKILLS

Companies invest in employee training and education. Freelancers have to invest in themselves. Some professionals are required to pursue ongoing education. Seminars, workshops, certification programs, or degrees can help you build new revenue streams and raise your rates. Add learning to your Level 4 planning.

"I'm taking a design class so I can handle the more straightforward aspects of preparing files for print. I hate having to pay someone for work I could do myself."

It doesn't have to cost a lot. You can take free online tutorials to learn computer skills, trade how-to with a fellow freelancer, or get a group together and hire someone to teach you all. Look for lectures and workshops through professional associations (Freelancers Union offers low-cost lectures and webinars on taxes, marketing, finances, and more).

If you can get a teaching gig, you may be able to take classes for free or at a discount. "My wife is a freelance graphic artist and teaches at the local college. She's getting a master's degree there. It'll make her marketable for more teaching gigs, which is steady work. She gets a huge break on tuition."

Some professional education is tax deductible, so check with your accountant.

Now it's your turn to brainstorm your growth plan. Here are some questions to get you rolling.

What's Your Growth Plan?

- Do you have a specific income goal for the coming year?

- Do you have ideas for a product, a service, a plan for modifying your current services, or other ideas for achieving that goal?

- Are there books you could read or other research you could do to learn more?

- Are there knowledgeable people you could talk to?

• Are your plans or ideas connected to other things you already do? If so, marketing along with your other services will be easier.

• How do you plan to make contact with the market? And then launch and sell?

• Do your plans or ideas require you to put in effort and time on a continuing basis?

• How unique are your ideas compared to what's out there?

• What should the price point be, based on your market research?

• Are there manufacturing, storage, and fulfillment costs? Any safety or legal issues to look into?

• How could you grow this, if it's successful?

• Is there something you can do for free to test interest?

• Try a one-pager. Do you like what you see? Who could give you good feedback?

• How might you develop your plans in the coming weeks, months, or year?

Chapter 11

THE NIMBLE FREELANCER: SUBCONTRACTING AND BUILDING TEAMS

No one's nimbler than freelancers. Fearless wranglers of unruly projects, lean but not mean, ever mindful of where the buck stops, they're ingenious at finding the quickest way to get it the job done. They have to be.

But as your projects get bigger and your pipeline fuller, you might need help. Maybe you bag a super-size Blue Chip. Or a family emergency strikes and you need to be sixteen places at once—your desk not being one of them. Or subcontracting and hiring are written into your growth plan. (You've got a plan? Impressive.)

Thanks to the freelance population explosion, there's a ton of talent to tap into. You can turn on a dime and assemble a team to win a big project, enlist a buddy to help you push to the finish on a gargantuan gig, or engage a fellow freelancer to cover your work so you can untangle a problem at home. When the crunch is over, the team might disband until the next opportunity (or calamity) comes along.

As informal as a "Yikes!" phone call or as structured as a partnership agreement, these relationships spread the marketplace goodies around so when one freelancer wins, so do others. As John F. Kennedy famously said: "A rising tide lifts all boats."

Staying nimble in this context means knowing how to get the right help and set things up to run smoothly. In this chapter, we'll talk about bartering as one way to tap into skills or services you need. Then we'll lay the groundwork for subcontracting and team building. Finally, we'll look at some issues to consider when hiring staff.

BARTERING

Bartering efficiently puts two humans together who each have something the other needs or wants.

When I was young, my parents and several other families formed a babysitting co-op. A family would babysit someone else's child, logging hours to "buy" babysitting time for their kids from other parents in the co-op. This system is formally known as Time Dollars.

Time Dollars systems can be scaled to different communities and extended across professions. A wedding videographer might earn, say,

Q Dear Sara, What's the difference between a free-lancer and a small business owner?

A Good question, and interesting that there's no definitive answer. Some people use the term *microentrepreneur* to describe very small business enterprises. Even if it's just you slogging away in your sweats, don't you still consider yourself to be running a business?

But there are differences in how freelancers and small businesses are viewed and treated—by society and by organizations that assist, represent, and finance small business. And yup, once again freelancers tend to drop out of the net.

My own quick and dirty definition? If you sometimes engage help or even have up to a couple of employees, you're more freelancer than small business owner. But once you have four or more people working with or for you on any kind of regular basis, then you start moving into the small business realm.

---

five Time Dollars filming another community member's wedding and can use those units to buy services from anyone in the group, from dental cleaning to window cleaning.

Pretty much anything can be bartered. You can barter services to help each other grow ("I write your brochure; you design my website."). Or exchange client services ("I, contractor, put up your shelves; you, massage therapist, give me a massage."). Or personal tasks ("I babysit your kids, you mow my lawn."). Or mentoring: ("I, social media wunderkind, teach you the basics of online marketing; you, former corporate account exec, coach me through a client relations crisis."). It's another way for freelancers to de-isolate and build strength.

"I'd happily write a press release or edit web content in exchange for professional pictures of my kids, housecleaning, graphic design, car maintenance, eyebrow shaping ...!"

Bartering is definitely up in a down economy, when cash is tight. People can barter directly, post ads online (Craigslist is one example), or join a barter exchange.

Make sure you trust anyone you barter with. Do your homework (look them up online; get references; ask questions). Be business-like—that means a signed agreement and keeping detailed accounting records, because you need documentation for tax reporting. For selected resources on bartering, see the Appendix.

JOIN THE CLUB: BARTER EXCHANGES

In barter exchanges or clubs, you pay to become a member and pay the club a percentage of each transaction. Members' accounts are credited or debited for exchanges (typically as units called barter or trade dollars) based on a service's fair market value. Members can spend their units anytime, for anything they need. What you receive needs to be reported as taxable income, as if you'd been paid cash.

Using trade dollars helps prevent inequities where one party gets a far more valuable good or service than the other. Barter exchanges also aid in IRS reporting, since in most cases they have to file Form 1099-B, so the IRS receives a record of all transactions, as do exchange members for tax reporting purposes.

BARTERING AND TAXES

The IRS defines bartering as the exchange or trade of goods or services, generally without the exchange of money. Taxes are due on bartered goods and services. You must report on your taxes the fair market value of any goods or services exchanged. There may be state taxes, too. For more information, see Chapter 15.

SUBCONTRACTING: WHEN TO DO IT, HOW TO DO IT

The day when federal and state governments all have plans in place for economic security for freelancers, the day when we win all the freelancers' safety net rights we're lobbying for—on that day, you can turn down work.

Until that day, don't turn down work. That's just a rule of being a freelancer.

OK, let me amend that. Turn down crappy work and work that doesn't fit your Freelance Portfolio, assuming you've got plenty to do and dough to live on. But you shouldn't have to turn down good work just because the job's too big to do alone, you don't have some of the needed skills, you'll be on vacation, your life is nuts, or you promised your mate you'd stop working until midnight every night.

Good managers set things up so work can continue whether they're there or not. Whether it's an ad-hoc thing or a formal contract where you partner on projects or tasks, share the work with someone else— or several someone elses—and all of you can bank the rewards.

WHO'S ON YOUR SPEED-DIAL?

Think of your work like a doctor's practice: You need at least one other excellent, trusted person who can be on call, and for whom you'd do the same. Developing those relationships means getting to know people over time.

It starts with networking. Go to meet-ups, strike up conversations with people sitting next to you at professional meetings, trade business cards, participate in professional discussion groups online, and keep your contact list in shining order. Ask people in your network who they call in a pinch or who they think is excellent. Choose some people you get a good vibe from who you'd like to know better. Email back and forth, have a few coffees or beers, swap war stories and advice, and generally keep up with one another. By the time you need that person on speed-dial, you should have a sense of what he can do, how good he is, how fast he is, how nice he is, and how he might be able to help you in your hour of need—and he should have the same sense about you.

Q Dear Sara, If I'm paying someone else to work, how could I be making more money than if I do the work myself?

A Paying someone else to do work allows you to make money by extracting surplus value. It's why Karl Marx didn't like capitalists. Example: Capitalist Freelancer (that would be you) engages a worker to produce a product and pays that person, say, $10. Capitalist Freelancer then sells that product to a customer for $20. Capitalist Freelancer has extracted $10 of surplus value.

Couldn't Capitalist Freelancer just make the product herself, sell it for $10, and get her value that way? Yes, but if she subcontracts that work, she frees herself up to do other profitable work: Maybe perform a service she wouldn't have had time to do . . . develop a new product to sell at a higher price . . . prospect for new business . . . or sleep so she can be bright-eyed for the Blue Chip pitch the next morning. That's how you can make more money paying someone else to work rather than doing it yourself.

Was the worker who got paid $10 a loser? Not if she's fairly paid. Actually, she might have paid another worker $5 to help her assemble the product, so she got $5 of surplus value. Or if not, she's got $10 she wouldn't otherwise have had. The process breaks down only if the system gets exploitative on the production side (abysmal rates for sweatshop work), the selling side (gouge-level prices), or both—which Comrade Marx thought was pretty much all the time.

You might already have done favors for each other and have good Love Bank accounts between you. You might have even done a few small gigs for each other to test-drive the relationship. You're smart to do that before trusting someone with a big subcontracting job.

You can do this even as a new freelancer working on a shoestring. Get to know others who are starting out, too. Share knowledge and skills. For example, if someone else has figured out the new software, pay her for a tutorial or barter a skill in return. That's the start of a speed-dial relationship.

A veteran freelancer can subcontract to new freelancers. It's a win for the veteran (new freelancers won't be as expensive as peers), and a win for new freelancers (who get connected with a pro who can mentor and recommend them). Subcontracting to new freelancers can invigorate your work with novel ideas and perceptions.

Three Key Questions to Ask Yourself

1 **What do I really need to subcontract?** What parts of projects could you spin off to someone else who could do them better, faster, or more patiently than you, freeing you to do the work you are best at doing (and prospect for it, too)?

2 **How much record keeping do I want to do?** If you're paying anyone with any degree of frequency, you may have to do tax-related paperwork. (Read on and see Chapter 15.)

3 **How much formality do I want?** Is this an ad-hoc, as-needed deal, or something more formal where there's a contract setting out your obligations? Do you want to try one small venture as an experiment and go from there? A referral network of people you call on when needed is the least structured. A subcontracting relationship would be medium-structured. You might want a contract or confirming emails.

MAKE A SUBCONTRACTING TASK LIST

What to subcontract? Think delegate. And for some—OK, maybe a lot—of us, that's not easy: "I'm a hands-on worker, but sometimes I do busywork to avoid doing the career-advancing stuff that comes harder for me, like marketing and prospecting. I realized there was a surprisingly short list of things I really *had* to do myself: networking, prospecting, negotiating, tax and legal stuff, and the high-skill aspects of my project work. Anything else could be delegated if I chose to." One way to figure this out: Break tasks down into their component parts. You'll see a sequence or routine emerge. Letting others perform parts of the routine lets you produce more (earn more, too), just the way a nurse practitioner in a doctor's office allows the practice to assist more patients because the doctor can be performing more specialized tasks while the nurse practitioner is performing multiple others.

If you've never looked at your work this way before, you might be surprised at just how much you're doing—and how much you might be able to let someone else do so you can concentrate on things that *only you* can do.

What could you subcontract? Make your list.

FIVE KEYS FOR WORKING WITH SUBCONTRACTORS

1 **Figure out the skill level you really need.** A big part of subcontracting success is breaking the job down correctly to match tasks to skills. An overqualified subcontractor might be a bored and overpaid subcontractor. An underqualified one might spell disaster.

2 **Be clear about the task.** What exactly are their duties or deliverables? The deadline? "Engaging other freelancers raises money issues. This is a negotiation. I always took the other person's point of view too much into account. As a result, part-time assistants, designers, and others took advantage of me."

3 **Check in, but don't hover.** You want to make sure your instructions are understood, work's progressing, and that your subcontractor feels you are available to answer questions. But a subcontractor is a freelancer, just like you, and you're a client, not their employer. Remember from reading about misclassification in Chapter 6: Employers can exercise specific controls over

employees, including behavioral control, in exchange for meeting certain financial obligations. You don't want to appear to be dictating or controlling how your subcontractors do the work. So set the objectives and let them get on with it. If there are problems, it's their job to fix them for you, the client.

4 Don't assume everyone works the way you do. Different freelancers may have different levels of training and skills. While it's not your job to train, you do need to figure out what people can do and where they might need some guidance.

5 Look for good work ethic and attitude. The best subcontractors want to be your go-to person and will work with that kind of integrity. Once you have a solid foundation, the relationship can grow.

DOES THE CLIENT NEED TO KNOW? NO!

A company executive doesn't tell the client his assistant drafted and typed the letter he signed. The exec's still responsible for the letter's contents, as you are for the subcontracted work. What matters is that your client be satisfied with the work, which you've guaranteed will be delivered at a certain quality and price. That's why the people you subcontract to must be excellent: They're stand-ins for you.

If the work's shoddy? Presumably you've built in checkpoints to head off disaster before it happens: you reviewed a portion before they proceeded with the rest; you've seen rough drafts; a rough cut; early sketches; preliminary spreadsheets—plus revisions or other key stages that would alert you to any problems, and you allowed time in the schedule for your subcontractor to fix it if it needs more work before you can send it to the client. Otherwise you'll have to line up a rescue subcontractor ASAP (rush rates—ugh) or fix it yourself—in which case it's going to be a very long night.

SUBCONTRACTING LEGALITIES

Check out Chapter 5 for details on the what, why, and how of deal making—including the importance of having a written agreement and what should be in it. The same principles and practicalities apply to hiring subcontractors. It's a good idea to talk with an attorney about drawing up a boilerplate subcontracting agreement, especially if you expect to subcontract on a regular basis—or if you're a subcontractor yourself. Here's a cheat sheet to begin:

- Business terms (e.g.: the services being provided, the deliverables, the deadlines, the price, the payout). Research industry rates and ask your network for advice on payment terms for various services.

- Your legal protections and responsibilities

- Grounds and terms for termination

- Dispute resolution (see Chapter 5 for a discussion of the virtues of arbitration)

- Confidentiality/nondisclosure

- Noncompete (If included, make it restrictive enough to protect you and your client from harm that could come from the contractor working for a competitor while working for you, but lenient enough to permit the subcontractor to make a living—and if you need a noncompete, that might be an indicator that you need a lawyer to properly draft the agreement to protect you.)

- Language stipulating that the subcontractor can't do an end run around you to be engaged by your client (again a place where a lawyer can be helpful)

- Intellectual property (make sure the intellectual property rights in the work product will belong to you, so you can adhere to whatever your intellectual property arrangement is with your client—yet another reason to consult a lawyer)

• Independent contractor status (clarifies that this is not an employer/employee relationship).

SUBCONTRACTING FINANCIALS

Start budgeting for subcontracting before you need it. When your marketing starts to pay off and you start to see that major gigs are gettable, start a subcontractor savings project, so when you need reinforcements, the money is there.

How much you set aside depends on what tasks you want to subcontract, and for how long. Look at the task list you made and pull out a couple that could help you the most. Ask around in your network about pay rate if you aren't sure: "I once needed help transcribing audio recordings of interviews and didn't know what to charge. I posted the question in a discussion group I belong to on an online networking site. I got many responses, including leads for transcribers."

For information on setting up subcontractors for taxes, see Chapter 15.

THE POWER OF PARTNERING

Sometimes you have such a great relationship with another freelancer that you decide to team up in a more formal, ongoing way, maybe because you each bring skills the other can use to offer more services to clients: a tax accountant teams up with a financial planner; a small business coach teams up with a web developer; a personal trainer teams up with a physical therapist.

You can cross-promote or feature each other on your websites and mailings. You might guest-blog for each other. Or teach, give talks, or coauthor articles or books together. You work out the finances to reflect what each of you brings to the other's party and formalize it in a written agreement.

You could do this with one other person or with several. Who knows, you might end your solopreneur existence and launch a partnership!

TEAMS: THE NEWER, NIMBLER WAY TO WORK

I like watching the beehive of preflight activity around airplanes at the gate. Fuel trucks, baggage trucks, mechanics, cleaning staff, and more all walk, climb, drive around, fill up, load, unload, stock, check, repair, replace, and otherwise make sure this giant thing will get off the ground. Then the passengers board; the plane departs, and all that activity quietly disperses—until the next plane arrives.

That's how I picture teams of freelancers that nimbly assemble and disband on a project-by-project basis: the right people with the right skills, applying their excellence precisely when and where needed. Swift, scalable, and sustainable. The essence of work in the twenty-first century.

Today's fluid workforce lets you expand and contract in tune with opportunity. These are high-trust, collaborative relationships: Brain Trust buddies, longtime subcontractors, or fellow corporate refugees you worked with in-house. You can form *diverse-skill teams* (e.g., an editor, cover designer, text designer, marketer, and publicist team up to help an author write and self-publish a book). This is a good reason to network across skill sets, not just hang out with your own. Or you can form *same-skill teams* (e.g., a band of animators cranks out a cartoon).

You might head the team as project manager. Or you might be a team of equals. One of you might be the rainmaker who brings in the business and serves as client liaison. Or the whole team might pitch or prospect, individually or together as a dog and pony show. For a Super Blue Chip gig, you might even form a mini-corporation, and then let the corporation go dormant or dissolve it when it's no longer needed.

Into it? Here are some things to consider:

Location. Will you all work from your own workspaces, assemble in a common space (whose? or would it be a coworking space?), or some of both? (See Make the Connection, below.)

Liability. Do you have the insurance you need to cover yourselves? If you work out of your place, do you need additional insurance to cover someone getting injured there?

Job descriptions. Exactly how'll this work? Make a flowchart, outline, or some other record of each person's responsibilities.

M.O. The financial, contractual, and tax issues for subcontractors grows in proportion to the size of your team, its level of permanence, and the complexity of the projects you tackle. If you're at this point in your freelance career, talk with your attorney and accountant about the best moves to set up legal protections and financials for you and the group.

Even if you've got your team, keep networking. Behind every great team is a great network. If you've got that, you've got the infrastructure to never have to refuse work because the project's too big to do alone.

MAKE THE CONNECTION You and your team can get big-company results without big-company IT costs. Using the Internet for secure file-sharing lets you do the equivalent of passing a project from desk to desk or collaborating in real time from hundreds of miles away, and serves as backup to your hard drives, too. With Internet-based video and phone conferencing, you can get all the heads in a room. Time-tracking tools can help you stay on budget by keeping tabs on time spent per task. To start checking out the possibilities, search under "online collaboration."

HELP
YOURSELF
ALERT

STAFF AND STUFF

We understand. If you'd wanted to run a business with staff, you probably wouldn't have bought this book. But sometimes freelancers grow a new vision for themselves as their career develops. Hiring employees becomes a way to take on more complex projects and goals.

You don't have to hire full-time help. And it might be another freelancer who could use a regular gig.

How can you tell if it's time to hire more than subcontractors? There's no way to know for sure, but here are some gauges.

Don't go by outside events such as, "Just landed the mother of all gigs!" That gig could be gone tomorrow: your contact gets fired and the new guy kills the old guy's projects; the company gets sold and the new owner puts all projects on hold; bad management or creative accounting come back to roost; and so it goes. You have to believe that by taking on staff, you can build greater profit over time, even in leaner times, thanks to greater built-in capacity. Other signs: if you know you're on the growing edge of your profession and often have more work than you can do.

> "I don't want all the work and costs that go with hiring and managing people who also own their own business."

On the interpersonal side, you have to be willing to let go of some control over the tasks you've been doing yourself all this time. Sure, you need to ensure quality (that's the purpose of job descriptions and performance reviews), but you also need to be willing to get out of the way and let your (presumably highly qualified) employees do what they do so well.

One way to explore the fit between you and staffing is to hire temporary help through a temp agency during busy periods. The temporary help company matches worker to job description, so you're saved the search. You also don't have to pay unemployment, health benefits, or the other protections employers commonly have to provide. Make sure you find out what kind of worker's compensation and liability insurance the temp company carries; you don't want to be swamped by a claim. Ask how they find their workers and monitor performance, and what happens if the temp isn't a good match for the job. Request references from other clients and ask what trade associations the company belongs to (for example, the American Staffing Association), which can be a barometer of the company's ethics, currency, and commitment.

Find out if colleges in your area offer internships. Interns might be paid a stipend, or might work gratis. It's a great way to mentor young people into your profession, and who knows—they might stay and become a dream employee!

For part-time workers, consider students: Their schedule allows it and their pay scale may be lower, although their schoolwork or other activities might make them less dependable. Also consider retirees. Generally, their schedules are flexible, they're glad for extra income, and often they're veterans of the business world. Another possible resource: parents who want and need some paid work, but can't work full-time because of their parenting responsibilities.

Here are some differences between hiring staff and hiring subcontractors.

Controls. If you become an employer, you'll have the right to exercise the behavioral, financial, and relationship controls that employers have. You'll be able to set up exactly what the job is, and how and where you want it done. In exchange, you'll have responsibilities toward your staff. (See below.)

Forms and tax issues. As an employer, you'll be paying employment taxes, unemployment tax, and withholding income tax. You'll also need to receive and send various forms. For details, see Chapter 15.

Intellectual property and ownership. You own any work product that your staff creates as employees. But it's still best to have a signed agreement spelling this out.

Fair employment laws. You may be subject to state and federal employment antidiscrimination laws.

On the spectrum between freelancer and small business that we talked about at the beginning of this chapter, you're moving more toward the small-business side. Start reading up on small-business issues, and specifically employment. Books, magazines, and articles abound. Talk with your accountant and attorney about your plans and possible next steps.

We started this chapter with the idea of nimbleness. You're plenty nimble alone. Teaming up should make you feel nimble, too—as though you can leap even higher hurdles with the strength of the team propelling you forward. There's a sense of possibility and joy as together you take on and master new challenges. Everyone's lifted, everyone benefits. It's an amazing feeling to know you've built something more powerful than you can be alone. I hope you'll have the opportunity to experience that.

Chapter 12

COMMUNITY—
WHERE PERSONAL AND PROFESSIONAL MEET

In Chapter 6, I mentioned how, at the company where we were misclassified as independent workers, my coworkers created a mock union called The Transient Workers Union, with the slogan "The Union Makes Us . . . Not So Weak."

It was truer than they knew for freelancers. While unions grew up around certain trades, until Freelancers Union came along, no organization spoke for all freelancers as a group. Getting the government to adopt freelance-friendly policies is a numbers game that can be won only if freelancers come together across professions as a diverse yet unified community and become a voting force to be reckoned with.

There's a bonus when they do: They find one another!

Freelancers Union is part of a growing wave of grass-roots solidarity among freelancers to share workspace, ideas, skills, strategy, and energy. In this chapter, we'll look at how community helps freelancers succeed as individuals and as a group—and how freelancers can start creating this community right where they are. Indie workers are amazing people. Get them together and there's no limit to what they can do.

NEW MUTUALISM: WORKING TOGETHER FOR PROBLEM-SOLVING AND PROFIT

The image of freelancer-in-café-with-laptop is a cliché for a reason. Most of us do better when we hang with others at least some of the time. After all, our ancient ancestors shared brains and brawn to outwit predators, thrive in tough environments, and live to procreate another day. Community and productivity go hand in hand in humans.

But despite many examples of profitable cooperative communities (trade guilds, work and farm cooperatives, credit associations, and communities in developing countries and in Italy's Emilia-Romagna), until recently experts have mainly focused on how hierarchies and markets drive profits.

Lately, though, the link between profit and community has gotten a closer look—I think because the 2008 Great Recession was an excruciating lesson in how markets and hierarchies gone wild can land us in a steaming pile of trouble.

The recession was a tipping point for other reasons, too: The freelance population explosion due to layoffs, the strain on social safety nets such as unemployment and Social Security due to long-term joblessness, and Americans' crisis of confidence in the ability of large institutions to serve their economic and political interests all collided with the rising viral power of the Internet.

Result: People are creating their own communities, from local to global, to help one another in the times we live in now. We're returning to a pre-industrial model of human-scaled, self-caring communities that were the norm in the United States for generations—but with a new awareness that our solutions must be cost-effective in the short term and sustainable in the long term, and with technology accelerating the pace, breadth, and depth of our contact. At Freelancers Union, we call it New Mutualism.

New Mutualism is everywhere.

Local love. There's been a resurgence of food co-ops, farmers' markets, and the demand for local products where our dollars fuel the economy where we live.

Artisanal production. We want to know the people behind the products we buy.

Trading, lending, and giving communities. Our hunger for the handmade and the personal has been scaled up into giant Internet communities of people exchanging goods and services on Craigslist, eBay, and Etsy. Credit associations have surged in popularity as a more local, personal way to do banking and get loans. There's even a trend toward peer-to-peer lending through sources such as Lending Club, bypassing the bank as economic gatekeeper. And with grants for local projects hard to come by, locals are stepping up. I recently learned about "soup groups" springing up in major cities to fund local projects. People donate a small amount to gather and enjoy a tasty soup meal, listen to short pitches for community project funding, and vote at the end to decide who will receive the collected donations. At this writing, microgrants from the Brooklyn-based group exceed $17,000.

Online review sites and customer forums. These spaces afford public oversight of companies and products.

Democratizing of resources. Technology makes open-source software available to the smallest start-up, as well as crowd-sourced ideas and funds for business innovation.

Mutualist organizations. Freelancers Insurance Company (FIC), is one example. wholly owned by a membership association and obligated to respond to members' needs.

A new, super-connected, local-global age has arrived. And freelancers are poised to lead and gain from the change.

WHY THE MOST SUCCESSFUL FREELANCERS ARE GIVERS

Freelancers are the perfect group to both demonstrate and benefit from this rediscovered connection between community and profit. We've been talking in previous chapters about the Love Bank—freelancers helping, informing, teaching, networking, strategizing, and advocating for and with one another. The Love Bank is New Mutualism in action; it's the antidote to freelance isolation and the path to sustainable freelance success.

While traditional employees can bond just by walking down the hall or prairie-dogging over the cube partitions, freelancers have to consciously connect. And it starts with you. It's nice when others contact you and start the ball rolling, and that certainly happens. But the reality is that everyone's busy—and sometimes people (freelancers included) are a little leery of trusting one another. A community can become giving only when the individuals in it give.

When you do, everyone benefits. How else can freelancers hold the line against downward mobility through lower and lower pay? How else will you all know, for example, if a company misclassifies freelancers or strong-arms freelancers into accepting substandard contract terms? How else will companies stop exploiting freelancers unless freelancers out them and insist as a group on being treated with respect? I believe freelancers *must* connect. If they don't, they'll be less successful and their collective voice won't be heard in the workforce debates going on today.

Because the Love Bank emphasizes giving over getting, it turns the market model on its head. In a market-driven world, community is the end result of the members getting their material needs met (i.e., no need to compete for resources). The motto might be: "Prosperity breeds community."

In New Mutualism, community around shared interests fosters collaboration, which advances success. New Mutualism's motto might be: "Community breeds prosperity."

New Mutualism isn't about group hugs or grand gestures. It's boots-on-the-ground stuff, and unless you have the social conscience of a sea slug, you're probably already doing it—if, for example, you've helped a fellow indie in any of these ways:

- Referred someone for a gig
- Warned about a deadbeat client
- Helped negotiate a contract
- Talked through a professional problem
- Brainstormed ideas
- Called a new freelancer to ask how it's going
- Posted a testimonial or linked to others' websites or other online content

- Offered tech support
- Explained how you did something

I'm sure you've done all these and more. I'll bet you know exactly who's done them for you, too: "When I lost my job, a number of people called offering to console me over coffee or lunch. But one person, Rob, whom I'd met just two weeks earlier, called with a very different offer: He said he might have a project for me and wanted to know if the payment he was offering was acceptable (it was more than I would have charged!). I started approaching others and got other projects. That call was the best thing that could have happened to me. I wouldn't have considered freelancing if it hadn't been for Rob's offer and his confidence in me."

A single act of giving—in this case, someone trusting a new freelancer with a good gig—can change someone's life. We all know this is true; I'm just suggesting we all be a bit more conscious about it.

Giving makes the giver succeed, too. Reciprocity's part of it—people we give to often return the favor. But in today's local-global world, eventually your giving reverberates and is sensed on a larger scale. You get that to-die-for marketing result: positive branding. When your giving touches hearts and minds, you become truly golden, the kind of person everyone wants to work with, recommend, and befriend forever.

Mutualist relationships can have different levels of formality and structure. The least structured might be just building a great network. Medium structured might be cultivating subcontracting relationships or teams. The most structured could be a co-op or partnership with a legal structure.

WHAT FREELANCERS NEED FROM ONE ANOTHER

What's your experience of Love Banking and New Mutualism?
    Has it been all too rare:

"Honestly, I find the community of freelance writers a bit difficult. Understandably, everyone's trying to survive out there. But in the twenty-five years I've been engaging freelance writers, only one ever returned the favor."

Too networky:

"I'd love a casual, social way to meet other freelancers, not necessarily focused on talking about work or 'networking.' "

Too one-sided:

"I find I'm giving more help than I'm getting. I don't want to take advantage of people or deny advice to those I can help, but I do need to take a closer look at how and where my networking is helping or hindering my income."

Or a good place to be:

"I'm always afraid about sharing too much information with other freelancers about what I'm doing for who, and for how much, and I'm always a little nervous about others sharing too much about all that with me. Usually, though, it turns out to have been a good idea."

"I like that other freelancers—particularly those with young children—really get the crazy, irregular pace of working in this way."

When freelancers help one another navigate market changes big and small, every freelancer finds more stability, and the group becomes more resilient and self-sustaining, too.

BUILDING YOUR FREELANCE COMMUNITY

Imagine your ideal freelance community. What would it be like? What kinds of people would be in it? What would help you most (work leads? industry news? business advice? contacts for subcontracting or team-building? help at home? good listeners? all of the above?)

What can you do to build the kind of community you're looking for? I find that when I have a need, the best thing I can do is to give. Big needs? Give big. It's what people least expect—and most value and remember.

Start by creating your community wish list.

MY COMMUNITY WISH LIST

- I'd like to connect with people who . . .
- I'd like to be in a community that . . .
- Some things I can do to find or build the kind of community I'm looking for . . .

Here are two very different sample lists—one from a new freelancer; one from someone who's been freelancing for a while.

SAMPLE 1: MY COMMUNITY WISH LIST— NEW FREELANCER

I'd like to connect with people who:

1 Are starting out or have been freelancing for a few years.

2 Have some skills I don't have.

3 Aren't super-competitive.

4 Like to work but also like to play.

5 Have the types of clients I'd like to have.

I'd like to be in a community that:

1 Shares work leads.

2 Talks about how to deal with clients.

3 Shares negotiating strategies.

4 Brings in new people to network with.

5 Stays in touch/gets together regularly.

Some things I can do to find or build the kind of community I'm looking for:

1 Get active in my alumnae group to meet new or recent grads in my field.

2 Join a professional association and get to know the local members.

3 Join Freelancers Union and go to the member meet-ups.

4 Start a Friday Night Freelance group to meet at my place and talk about about the week.

5 Join some professional discussion groups online.

SAMPLE 2: MY COMMUNITY WISH LIST— EXPERIENCED FREELANCER

I'd like to connect with people who:

1 Have been doing this as long as I have, in my field and related fields.

2 Want to kick their business to a new level.

3 Work hard but make time for family.

4 Are interested in teaming up for new ventures.

5 Can be trusted with confidential info about my business.

I'd like to be in a community that:

1 Shares work leads.

2 Discusses industry trends.

3 Collaborates well.

4 Likes to talk about new business ideas, especially for marketing.

5 Is hand picked and not too big.

Some things I can do to find or build the kind of community I'm looking for:

1 Be the person I want to attract to this group: Step up in my professional organization(s) to head committees, organize events, and be visible.

2 Go to seminars and conventions to meet people in related fields.

3 Sign up for Freelancers Union workshops on marketing, legal issues, and finance to network and learn about growing my business.

4 Start a small monthly coaching group of freelancers looking to start new ventures.

5 Mentor some younger freelancers I could eventually subcontract work to, freeing up time for Level 4 projects.

Ready to build your ideal community? You already have communities to draw from. There's your Brain Trust, with whom you can be totally frank about what's happening in your freelance life. But don't stop there. Pull from other groups: family, friends, alums, former coworkers, parents at your kids' school, volunteer groups, your spiritual group, even your workout mates: "Last night I started talking with a guy before our cardio class. We went from workouts to work. Turns out he does exactly what I do! It just proves the right person could be right next to you—but you have to connect."

Think of online discussion groups, too, where you can connect with freelancers worldwide to get and give info and support: "Someone posted a question asking if anyone had ever had to fire a client. There were tons of interesting, informative responses. I've had members send me private messages saying they liked my comments and asking about my work."

No one freelances alone. You have lots more connections than you realize.

GROWING YOUR LOVE BANK ACCOUNT

In Chapter 8 we talked about a Love Bank ground rule: Think give, not get. Go there if you'd like a refresher; then read on for more ways to give to fellow freelancers:

Teach. Teaching's a great way to prospect in your community, but freelancers can learn from you, too. Yoga instructor? Give some yoga love to your computer-contorted, smartphone-spasmed cohorts. Accountant? Offer a workshop on tax deductions for freelancers, tax-record keeping, or using tax-prep software. Lawyer? Talk to creatives about intellectual property protection. Running a formal freelance group or hosting a more ad-hoc Jelly group (described below)? Invite freelancers to give talks, or pool your resources and pay someone to give a training workshop.

Do good, do well. Get behind causes and events in your neighborhood, school district, religious community, or town. It's a great way to meet like-minded people, including freelancers.

Get smarter with barter. Bartering lets you trade skills with other freelancers even when money's tight. While you have to track the value of the exchange for tax reasons (see Chapters 11 and 15), there's something refreshingly pure about bartering: You feel like you're working against the tyranny of the dollar.

Start your own freelancers group. Could be your smartest give ever. Complete the My Community Wish List above to figure out your goals. Make it a virtual group if you want.

Consider joining Freelancers Union. For one thing, it's free! And through our member platform, you can find Freelancers Union members anywhere in the United States. Maybe you're looking to increase your freelance network in your neighborhood, town, or city. Or maybe you're traveling or moving and want to connect with freelancers in another city. You have a ready-made way to reach out.

Get involved in the groups you're in—though be careful about spreading yourself too thin. Joining online professional discussion groups lets you bond with freelancers far and wide. Answer questions and ask them. If there's someone you feel a good vibe with, send a direct message to ask more about their work or just to say you really appreciate their posts. "I joined too many groups at first and got overwhelmed by the number of discussions!" Pam says. "I'm realizing that the ones I enjoy most are the ones I participate in the most. I'm planning to winnow down my groups and go for quality over quantity."

Join or start a coworking group. Freelancers need to create the water-cooler conversations employees have all the time to get advice, trade gossip, or share a laugh. We've talked about coworking in other chapters as a great way to build community with other indies, plus have workspace outside your home without the expense of renting turf. There are coworking spaces to fit all kinds of professions, practical needs, budgets, and personalities.

Want an arrangement that's free and more fluid? Join a Jelly group—indie workers hanging at someone's house, sharing couch, tables, and Wi-Fi, or meeting in a coffee shop or other Internet-accessible space where they can talk and help one another while getting on with their work.

Interested in starting a coworking group? Try starting a Jelly group—just an informal but focused group—to see if you like running the show and to test the mix that makes it work. Starting a coworking space is more complex (getting space and figuring fees and such). You might read up on it (see the Appendix for selected coworking and Jelly group resources) and join one to see how it works from the inside.

Mentor. You've probably got a metric ton or two of wisdom to offer a start-up freelancer or someone new to your field. Employees have

GET A GROUP Can't find a group that's just right? Start your own!

Choose the mix of social to professional, who and how many you'll invite, where and how often you'll meet, and how structured it'll be:

• **Purely pro:** Want to ramp up your career? Form a group that helps members meet business goals. Keep it small and build it by group invitation as you meet freelancers with solid reputations who can be trusted to respect confidentiality, who are ready to grow, and who can support others in doing the same. Write up some group guidelines, so everyone's on the same page.

• **Mostly pro:** "I belong to a group of local freelancers in my industry. We meet for a monthly brown-bag lunch and keep membership to the max that'll fit around our dining-room tables. We swap news, deals, who's working where, and negotiating strategies. Every few months, we order in sandwiches and invite industry guests to speak—people who could send clients our way, but sometimes experts in a field we need to learn about to serve our clients better. We invited a social media consultant to speak at one meeting. We have a brochure, a website, and started a blog. Anyone can suggest a new member. We meet them, look at their creds, and vote. The main requirement is that everyone's been in the business at least 15 years. There's a modest new-member fee. Otherwise we hit up members when we need money to print more brochures or fund the guest lunches. I've gotten a number of work inquiries through the website. Although we refer prospects to one another, everyone's completely independent. It's a great blend of community and autonomy."

• **Semisocial/semipro:** "A bunch of us who worked together on staff at one company meet for dinner every few months. We've met at restaurants and at people's apartments, where we order pizza and everyone brings wine. Some of us are sole proprietors; some work in big companies, some run small businesses, so it's a great industry cross-section. We talk about work news, world news, gossip, vacations, and personal stuff, amid much laughter and wine. It's never about getting work, but I landed a major project thanks to a referral from someone in this group."

wall-to-wall help. Freelancers have to find, teach, and learn from one another.

Get involved in your alumnae association or school career planning office to help new grads get started in your industry. Start a mentoring program in the professional group you belong to: "My professional group mentors young women studying or interning in the business. We meet for coffee, answer their business or job-hunting questions; whatever's on their minds. A lot of what they need is tips on being professional and how to deal with businesspeople."

Involve interns and new grads while they learn the ropes.

Have there been layoffs? Find out who's been let go and ask if they'd be interested in some subcontracting work. You never know where this kind of team-up can lead.

Advocate. Shine a light on what freelancers need as a group. We are, at Freelancers Union, and it's working. We're also having a lot of fun—pizza-fueled brainstorming sessions, gangs of freelancers ditching their gigs to work the phones and take field trips to the state capital, launching click-'n'-shoot email campaigns to state representatives, crowd-sourcing our Contract Creator tool for freelancers.

WHAT FREELANCERS NEED—AND HOW COMMUNITY HELPS THEM GET IT

Freelancers have always had to make their own safety nets—most notably in finding health insurance and saving for retirement—while employees have long enjoyed these benefits by law. And a few late-paying or deadbeat clients with a "so, sue me" attitude can decimate a freelancer's livelihood, whereas companies that don't make their payroll get major legal smackdown. Those are just a few examples of how freelancers are vulnerable in ways other workers aren't.

The lack of affordable health care for freelancers was my main reason for starting Freelancers Union, because freelancers repeatedly told me this was a huge mental and financial stressor. I wanted to see whether addressing this issue could help stabilize freelancers' lives, and whether we could do it in a way that was accountable to freelancers themselves. So we set up an insurance company wholly owned by a membership association. We've been able to offer group-rate health plans to freelancers at prices unavailable on the individual market without relying on government institutions, and group benefits for dental, life insurance, and disability. The state of New York now recognizes our model. We're scaling it up for other states. And we're building the same thing for retirement and other benefits.

Freelancers Union encourages community by making membership free. Members can connect via our job board, through our blog, at member meetings, and through affordable workshops and webinars on taxes, finances, and other freelance need-to-knows. We've made alliances with retailers for member discounts on everything from office supplies, billing services, and coworking spaces to gym memberships, car rentals, and ordering flowers.

Ten years in, Freelancers Union is financially self-sufficient and membership at this writing is nearing 200,000.

So I can say with some conviction that community and New Mutualism are alive, well, and proven effective at Freelancers Union. Which is a really good thing, since we've entered an era where the new normal is, "If it's broken, fix it yourself."

In the new economy, our best chance of securing what freelancers need is to provide as much of it as we can ourselves through the groups freelancers are connected to—organizations like Freelancers Union, professional associations, faith-based communities and other nonprofits, and micro communities formed by freelancers themselves—and then approach lawmakers as a collective unit and let them know that it's really getting to be ridiculous that freelancers continue to grow in number, continue to pay all these taxes (see Update the Tax Code, below), continue to proactively develop sustainable, cooperative ways to achieve security—yet continue to get no consideration in the safety net discussions where change has to happen at the policy level.

I believe in many cases we can form cooperative solutions to solve freelancers' problems better than government can. I'm sure freelancers could teach everyone a thing or two about belt-tightening. But there are some things that lawmakers need to do.

FIX THE HEAD COUNT

For starters, the government must do a better job of counting freelancers. The General Accounting Office (GAO) has eight different categories of independent workers, the Current Population Survey only tracks part-timers and the self-employed, and the Bureau of Labor Statistics (BLS) usually doesn't include freelancers in its reports at all! Could the left hand please talk to the right hand? It's actually kind of weird, considering its fiscal interests, that Uncle Sam doesn't have a better handle on exactly how much freelancers' work contributes to the economy. And since BLS numbers are used for budget- and policy-making, how else will freelancers get a fair slice of the pie?

UPDATE THE TAX CODE

The tax code is way, way too complicated—for everyone, but it's even more complex and costly for freelancers. Employers pay payroll taxes for their employees, but because they're both boss and worker, freelancers have to pay taxes as both. And while employers regularly withhold tax from employees' paychecks, freelancers have to make quarterly estimated tax payments, adding to their paperwork and accounting costs. Employees get a nice neat W-2 from their employer at tax time; freelancers get (and may have to prepare and send) fist-fuls of 1099s. Keeping the required records for all this, plus tracking tax deductions, pulls them away from paying work and often requires the purchase of tax software and hiring accounting and bookkeeping help. Yes, freelancers expect and want to pay their taxes. But do you have to make it so hard? Freelancers Union successfully reformed the Unincorporated Business Tax (UBT) in New York City, so people earning under $100,000 per year no longer have to pay, and those earning up to $150,000 pay a reduced tax. However, similar taxes still exist in Philadelphia (as the Business Privilege Tax) and other cities. Do taxes really have to be so onerous and so complicated?

INCLUDE FREELANCERS IN LENDING PROGRAMS

The Small Business Administration (SBA) does a huge amount of good work and provides amazing information. But freelancers really need a lending program scaled to their finances. Grameen Bank in Bangladesh is just one model of successful microcredit. Talk about looking bad on paper! Grameen violates pretty much every standard practice of a loan program: It offers collateral-free loans to the very poor, repaid in very small installments with limits on the interest that can be charged, and the bank is 95 percent owned by the borrowers themselves. Borrowers' loan repayment is overseen in part by their peers and exceeds 96 percent, with more than 8 million borrowers (all statistics as of October 2011). The bank and its founder, Muhammad Yunus, received a Nobel Peace Prize in 2006.

As a large and growing sector of the economy, freelancers could contribute even more if there were loan models that didn't penalize them for the episodic income that is the norm for most freelancing. I believe freelancers have to start looking for—and we need to start building—new institutions that give freelancers funding options beyond simply going to a bank for a loan. These new institutions need to be based on the idea of self-help and mutuality. We need to pool our economic strength because if we don't, there will be no other institution in place to help us. As the rural poor in India learned, without Grameen, no one would give them a loan. Freelancers Union wants to enable these new institutions—whether we build them, partner with others who do, or help tee up the idea so some budding social entrepreneur can make it happen.

WAGE WAR ON UNPAID WAGES

The 2011 Freelancers Union survey found that 44 percent of independent workers had problems getting paid in 2010, which comes to billions all told. Our grass-roots Get Paid, Not Played campaign and Client Scorecard both raise awareness, outing businesses that rob freelancers of rightful pay (and the government of taxes).

But this problem also needs pressure from the top. Lawmakers need to recognize the economic contributions and rights of freelancers by supporting payment protection for them, just as they do for employees.

WIDEN THE NET ON MISCLASSIFICATION

It's great that the Department of Labor and the IRS are playing hardball with employers who misclassify workers. But they're missing that tricky other type of misclassification where companies set up ersatz temp agencies and hire workers from the agency (hey, no need to pay benefits—the agency takes care of it, wink, wink). Well, the agency doesn't always. And freelancers can't take any tax deductions for this work because they're employees, not independent contractors. Penalized for having steady work? What kind of labor policy is that?

THE THREE LEVELS OF ADVOCACY

The biggest lesson I've learned from founding Freelancers Union is that the best help to freelancers comes from freelancers themselves. They are the experts on what they need.

Advocating for better quality of life for freelancers doesn't have to take a lot of time. In fact, you're already advocating by taking good care of yourself as a person and a professional. That's the self-advocacy part. It starts at home. Advocacy for others happens when freelancers help other freelancers. Community advocacy happens when freelancers advocate as a group.

LEVEL 1: SELF-ADVOCACY

Every day that you handle your freelance life like the pro you are, you're strengthening the freelance community, such as when you:

- Have written agreements for your gigs.
- Negotiate fair terms for yourself.
- Work on balancing your Freelance Portfolio and avoiding misclassification.
- Set reasonable limits with clients.
- Get the professional and personal insurance you need.
- Stay on top of your billing and bookkeeping.
- Pay down/limit your debt and set up savings and retirement programs.
- Learn about health insurance options and get the best you can afford.

LEVEL 2: ADVOCACY FOR OTHERS

This is one or more freelancers helping one another, such as when you:

- Help another freelancer in any way.

- Share work leads.

- Share info on freelance-friendly banks, insurance programs, and other services.

- Join professional associations, Freelancers Union, discussion groups, and other communities where independent workers can connect and share resources.

- Start your own professional group.

- Swap negotiating strategies with fellow freelancers.

- Work to establish industry standards for independent contractor agreements.

- Talk about fees in your industry and what constitutes fair payment.

- Share information about clients (nonpayers, 3-Ders), including using Freelancers Union's Client Scorecard.

- Set up codes of ethics and best practices if your profession doesn't already have them.

LEVEL 3: COMMUNITY ADVOCACY

When freelancers act together to represent their interests to others, that's community advocacy. It's speaking with one voice and knowing and using your political and economic power, such as when you:

- Complete the Freelancers Union annual survey to help us plan initiatives to make laws, systems, and the work world more freelance-friendly.

- Get involved in working for positive change in freelancers' lives through Freelancers Union and/or a professional group.

- Fill out the Freelancers Union Client Scorecard and share it with others.

- Talk with other freelancers about what freelancers need.

- Talk with nonfreelancers about freelance life.

- Support political candidates who advocate for freelancers' issues.

- Buy products and services that offer special discounts or incentives to freelancers.

- Contribute to the Freelancers Union Political Action Committee (PAC) and volunteer to contact elected officials.

New Mutualism isn't just a feel-good thing. It's a survival thing. Everyone—not just freelancers—has to do for themselves and one another what government and social support systems can't do, weren't designed to do, or don't yet exist to do.

So while we advocate for change, we have to make changes where we are. With New Mutualism, we can set up small experiments and models, see what works, and then grow and show them as models to scale up. As we try them out, they become:

- Plausible—rooted in lived experience.
- Durable—able to withstand challenges and integrate change.
- Elegant—containing the greatest possible complexity in the simplest possible way.

That's how informal groups grow into coworking spaces, which the Internet magnifies into vast virtual hives like Etsy. That's how neighborhood babysitting co-ops become Time Dollars communities and barter exchanges. That's how the Get Paid, Not Played campaign becomes the Client Scorecard. Micro meets macro.

And that's where you and community meet. What you do as one freelancer affects all freelancers. What all freelancers do affects you. Take it as assurance, if you needed it, that while you're independent, you're never alone.

TOP TEN USES FOR A COMMUNITY

1 To answer the question, "What should I do?"

2 To share where there's work.

3 To recommend you.

4 To listen.

5 To laugh with.

6 To brainstorm with.

7 To celebrate with.

8 To warn you about clients who aren't freelance-friendly.

9 To march with you in support of freelancers' rights.

10 To give you the opportunity to help someone else.

PART 4: MANAGING YOUR BUSINESS

> "I love having uninterrupted hours to work and feel accomplished at the end of the day."

Chapter 13

MANAGING YOU

The freedom to sculpt your time and work to fit your life is an awesome feeling. Then there are the days when emails torpedo your work plans, you can't settle down, and a project you postponed (OK, procrastinated on) collides with a juicy little rush job that'll bring in good money but is a drop-everything gig. Oh, and did we mention having to run to two meetings on opposite sides of town, pick up antibiotics for the dog, and help paint your best friend's living room? On those days, freelancing can feel crazy.

This slow or rapid descent into chaos can happen to anyone, for different reasons. A new grad might be new to reining in a sprawling project. An exec-turned-indie, suddenly assistantless, can flounder in phone calls and paperwork.

In this chapter, we'll talk about ways to manage your time, energy, and work habits so you can spend more time in "awesome" and less time in chaos. (For a discussion of balancing work, personal, and family needs, see Chapter 16.)

PRODUCTIVITY AND TIME MANAGEMENT

We've talked about how companies have behavioral control over their staff. What if your best time for focused work is smack in the middle of the morning staff meeting? Tough. What if constant interruptions ("we don't screen our calls here") keep you from getting stuff done? Suck it up; work late. What if your night-owl nature often has you creeping in half an hour late, toting your double-grande java? Expect to discuss it in your performance review.

As a freelancer, *you* decide how you'll work:

"The corporate world was my benchmark. After factoring in the lunch hour, conversations with coworkers, wanderings down the hall, and personal calls, the time spent doing actual work was, well, not exactly as advertised. So as a freelancer, I decided that six hours without interruption was a good day's work. With the phone on mute and the answering machine on, it was fairly easy to shut out the world."

"I've learned that whatever work I do at night—no matter how good I think it is—is subpar in the light of day. So unless I've got a critical deadline, I leave well enough alone and veg out in the evening."

. . . and how hard:

"I work harder now than I worked in my corporate life (and I worked hard!). But because I'm working on projects I choose, in the way I choose, I have lots more energy and contentment while working."

> "My best work days are when my car doesn't leave the garage—and the best weeks are when I can string together several days like that."

"I really like that I'm the boss of me and that, to be honest, I don't have to work that hard."

And you can change things based on what's happening in your life:

"There's no such thing as a 'typical day' for me."

"Instead of watching the clock, I get to follow the rhythms of my family through the day."

Being productive as a freelancer shouldn't be about forcing yourself to follow systems, methods, or others' rules about productivity. Actually, I think most of us know deep down what makes us productive and when we're going off-track.

Here's a working definition of productivity:

---

productivity: doing the right work, at the right time, for the right amount of time

---

Let's figure out what that means for you.

QUIZ: WHAT'S YOUR IDEAL DAY?

What does your ideal workday look like? Complete the quiz on the following page—write your answers down and see how well your ideal and your reality match up. We want detail! Keep your answers in mind as you read.

	MY IDEAL	WHAT REALLY HAPPENS
What time do you get up?		
What's your morning prework routine?		
What time do you sit down to work?		
How long do you generally work in one sitting?		
Describe your morning work time.		
When do you usually make calls and answer emails?		
When do you take breaks, and what do you do?		
What's your lunch routine?		
What percentage of time in a typical workday do you devote to: project work, marketing, and administrative work?		
When do you run errands (work or personal)?		
Describe how and when you socialize (with other freelancers, family, friends) —in person or via phone/email.		
When do you have meetings?		
Describe your afternoon work time.		
When do you exercise, and what do you do?		
What happens at dinnertime?		
Do you work after dinner?		
Describe your evening routine.		
When do you go to bed?		

WORKING WITH INTENT

Let's assume you mostly like your work and want to get stuff done *not* because you can't wait for it to be over, but because achievement (and getting paid!) feels good. So if you're having problems getting work done despite your best intentions, something in your approach may need adjusting. It turns out there's a big difference between *intending* to work and working with *intent*.

Where Do You Like to Work?

Some people love working at home: "I do house cleaning or meal prep on my work breaks. I feel more caught up with everything at day's end." Others are maddened by the home/work combo: "Just once I wish I could lock myself in my tower and have someone else cook dinner while I had my inspired moment." And some don't like the twain to meet: "I have a separate office. I can work at home if I want to—but it's better to keep them separate."

What's the geographic ideal for you?

Experiment! Try one morning a week in a café or at the library. Check out the coworking and Jelly group info in previous chapters. Are you more productive at home, out of it, or does mixing it up do the trick? "I get things done at home, but it's so much easier to get work done quickly at a coffee shop or the library, where there's no laundry to do, no bills to pay, and I have more incentive to get the job done so I can close my laptop and get back to my life."

Your needs might change, too—so allow for that fluidity.

Where Does the Time Go?

You can see exactly where it goes by keeping a time log for a few days, the way people keep food logs. Log every minute spent on work and nonwork stuff. The results can be both eye- and time-opening: "I sometimes spend more time than I should on a project, for instance, doing relatively extensive research for a two-hundred-word article.

I get seduced by the enjoyable projects and forget to be discriminating about my time/income balance."

Tracking your time helps you edit your time commitments and rank your tasks by importance. Otherwise you may take on too much and end up overwhelmed, underpaid, and missing real opportunities to grow your business, maybe by outsourcing smaller fry so you can focus on big game.

When Do You Do Your Best Work? A Pop Quiz
Do you know when your brain's at its best?

- Do you know exactly which hours you're at your best?

- Are you putting your most important work in that space?

- Do you know when your energy starts to taper, and do you downshift to less-demanding work (maybe checking email)?

- Do you know when you're out of gas and should stop pushing?

- Are you forcing a productivity strategy that isn't working (get up early! take frequent breaks! write every day!)?

- Do you often feel stalled out, distracted, or feel you could be doing "more"? "I wish I got up earlier and started my work day earlier. I always feel like I'm behind and/or not productive enough and/or allowing myself to be distracted. I finish each day feeling like there are two or three more things I really should've done that day that a better, more productive, smarter person—one more committed to money and success—would've done."

Depending on your answers, maybe you're working on the wrong things at the wrong times. Alongside your time log, set up a focus log, jotting down your mental sharpness throughout the day.

Energy level is an individual thing for every freelancer. Here's what one figured out: "I try to focus on one project all morning, checking email as infrequently as possible. I eat lunch and watch TV around

TIME AND FOCUS LOG

TIME	TASK	FOCUS LEVEL*

(on a scale of 1–5; 1 = totally tapped out; 5 = laser-sharp)

twelve thirty, possibly also squeezing in a little housework, then get back to work in the afternoon, which is usually my most creative and productive time."

What Type of Work Do You Need to Do?

Writing a manuscript . . . developing a business plan . . . making a film. Big-project work demands fierce mental bandwidth. Now that you've figured out your best work times, is your work synced up to them?

It's not just about having time, but about having the right *quality* of time. Maybe summer when the kids are home from school isn't the time to expect major progress on your Level 4 projects. Prospecting for less-demanding, shorter gigs might be the way to go. As one freelancer says, "My technical work requires calm because it's all about process and order. It's frustrating to be in the middle of a project and be constantly pulled off. It fragments my thinking and I get furious. But I also do craftwork and am researching a writing project. Both of those are easier to pick up and put down."

Knowing your external distractions can help you plan your day as well as your work week and even monthly and yearly calendars to match up your work life to your personal life and preferences.

What Are Your Goals?

You know those days when you bounce from task to task and feel like you got nothing done? When you don't set priorities, other peoples' goals start running your show, or you get mired in busywork.

Time really is money for freelancers. Every minute you spend unprofitably is, well, unprofitable. (P.S.: Wasting or losing time isn't the same as deciding to knock off early and go for a run. That's productive control of time.)

Weight your goals and slot the most important ones into your peak focus times: "I keep a Word document of project status notes, divided into three sections: To Do, On Hold, and Completed (Awaiting Payment). I review it at the beginning of each workday to check that

I've got my priorities in order." Says another freelancer, "I pick three things I must move forward on, write them on a stickie, and slap it right next to my keyboard. I insist on being able to look back on my day and say I made progress on these things."

Does Your Work Routine Work?

You probably do the same thing most nights before bed: Get undressed, wash up, brush teeth, read a little, and then you sleep. Sleep experts recommend poor sleepers develop better "sleep hygiene" routines to prepare body and mind for what's expected.

Freelancers have to create routines for their work because the nine-to-five world isn't there to do it for them: "It's been challenging to set up some structure for myself—specifically, to mark the beginning and end of the workday. I've found the more I do it, the more disciplined I become. I have a much more set schedule now than when I started a year ago."

Analyze what you did on a really productive day. What started it? What kept your energy strong? What tasks did you do, in what order? How did you wrap up? Replicate those elements. Here are some strategies to consider:

Beat bog-down. "In the morning I review yesterday's work and make changes. Then I move forward, organizing and working quickly, without self-editing. I just keep moving."

Gang up appointments and errands. "If I need to run errands (buy groceries, pick up the laundry, go to the bank, visit the doctor) I'll save them for late afternoon if possible so I don't disrupt my workflow."

Hold the phone. "I need quiet. I work inside my head. I don't answer the phone when I'm working."

Hold your fire. "I respond very quickly, but sometimes to the detriment of everything else."

Know how time flies. "I became very good at knowing how long a script, a rewrite, or an article would take to complete and calculated my work hours accordingly. If I was working on a specific project, I knew how many hours I would have to write each day in order to meet my deadlines."

Make a roadmap. "I have a weekly list of things to accomplish from Monday through Friday. Sometimes they don't all get finished, but by now I know which client is going to send things late, which project I needn't rush, and where there's a window for me to work on spec projects or take a break."

Routine ≠ Rut. "In winter, I work at home, cozy with the cat. In the summer, since I don't have air-conditioning, my days follow the forecast. In a heat wave, I get up early and work a couple of hours before breakfast. Then I work out or read until the library opens, where I work for the day (air-conditioning! free wireless!). If I work after dinner, I'll hang out in a café with an iced coffee. I feel like an urban farmer, working according to the weather. It makes me pace myself and reminds me that we humans and our work aren't the center of everything."

Look at your answers to the What's Your Ideal Day? quiz. How could you change your routine to help you settle down to work?

PRESENT/PAST/FUTURE: A NEW WAY TO WORK

Can you relate to any of these?

"When I started freelancing, I had my act together for clients, but administrative stuff was another story. I hadn't looked at or filed my bank statements in eight months. What a mess."

"It's hard to be disciplined when making calls to find work or working on personal projects that aren't necessarily income-generators. But that's when it's most important to keep going."

GIVING YOURSELF A BREAK Do you know when you need a break? It's tempting to keep pushing (and deliver, and get paid). But there's usually a point of diminishing returns. Where is that for you? "When my work's going well, I'm totally energized and stay up until all hours. When it's going badly, I stay up too late trying to get it to a better place. I'm learning to accept that hammering at something when I'm tired won't improve it enough to be worth losing sleep over. I say, 'This will be here tomorrow.' "

Not everyone needs breaks: "I like to work straight through, without interruptions. Call it my 'finish line' mentality." But most of us need at least a few minutes of putting our minds on something else: "On my lunch break, I usually read the paper and distract myself completely from my work."

The body needs a break, too. We talked in Chapter 2 about resting your eyes from computer-screen work. Also, refuel brain and body: "I definitely take a thirty- to forty-five-minute break for lunch."

Experiment and learn what gives you a mini mental vacation: Reading for pleasure in the middle of the day works for some people. For someone else it might be watching TV for half an hour, listening to music and opening the mail, calling a friend, or doing some yard work.

Trust the power of downtime to help you work better—more creatively, more resourcefully, and more happily.

"One thing I hate about freelancing is the freedom to make your own schedule. There's no one telling me what to do and when. If I decide to spend all day walking on the beach, there's no one to tell me I can't do it—but then the work doesn't get done."

Freelancers have so many different tasks to do that it's easy to get sucked into your work and then look up and wonder where the day went. If you feel like your freelance life is running you and not the other way around, try dividing your work into present, past, and future categories—and address each of those categories every day.

PRESENT

"Present" tasks are your current gigs and projects, and time-sensitive tasks. Examples:

- Projects you're working on now, and related calls and emails
- Any deadline-driven tasks (bills that are due, paying estimated taxes or meeting with your accountant for tax prep, sending out your email newsletter, publishing your blog post)
- Important or pressing personal business (making a doctor's appointment for a sick child, going to a parent-teacher conference, calling the store that failed to deliver your new couch)

PAST

"Past" tasks are the administrative stuff you do to clean up after your projects, keep your office and your life going, or maintenance tasks that aren't (yet) time-sensitive. Examples:

- Invoicing and bill-paying
- Bookkeeping/accounting
- Filing (paper and digital)
- Personal admin tasks (processing health insurance claims, kids' school paperwork)
- Related calls and emails

FUTURE

"Future" tasks support your business growth. Examples:

- Networking and prospecting (meetings, calls, emails, going to professional events and meet-ups, market research)
- Online marketing (social media activity, drafting a blog post, working on your website)

- Developing Level 4 projects
- Related calls and emails

Addressing each area daily keeps you from getting lost in, or overwhelmed by them. Even just filing for fifteen minutes will help you feel more on top of things. Doing some marketing and Level 4 work daily will keep you in touch with your freelance dreams and ways to grow your business: "I try to stay aware of what kind of design work is out there by browsing in my local magazine shop or keeping in contact with community websites and blogs. I allow myself some downtime but also reserve a certain number of hours for research."

You might cycle through present/past/future throughout the day, depending on when your mental focus is strongest and what's the most time-sensitive. A super-rush gig might divert 75 percent of your workday. But split the rest over past/future tasks and you'll be keeping up with your billing and not facing an empty pipeline when you stagger out from under Project Kill Me Now.

TECH CONTROL

Technology can answer your phone, remind you of dates, track your deadlines, and tons more. Delegating tasks to technology leaves you free to do the things that only you can do—design a building, write code, counsel a client. Ask other freelancers for their tech tricks of the trade, read product reviews, and take product tutorials to familiarize yourself with what's out there.

DIGITAL DECLUTTERING

News flash: You can't *actually* drown in email. Saving yourself is just a matter of organizing your digital space a little differently as your business grows, as with your physical space.

If your email service lets you set up multiple email addresses, you can segregate your emails—for example, one for newsletters, catalogues, and other subscriptions; another for financial statements; another for emails from website visitors. Living a freelance double life (accountant by day, singer by night and weekend)? Have different email addresses for those very different professional identities.

You probably know you can set up files to archive your emails, just like paper documents. Also experiment with filters, which allow whole categories of emails to automatically bypass your inbox and drop into specially designated files: "I had a project that required a lot of online research. I set up a filter called Murphy Project Research. When I found articles I needed, I'd send the article link in an email to myself, putting the filter name (and a short descriptor) in the subject line. It went right into that file. When I was ready to cull the research, everything was right there."

NEW WAYS TO DO TO-DOS

Computer monitors were never intended as posts for stickies bearing faded inscriptions like: "Find article" and "Call J. re Thurs." and "$300.00!!!" Set up a file on your computer desktop just for to-dos and go there to retrieve your tasks. Need to follow up, make a date, return a call, make your weekly bank deposit? Put that stuff into your calendar and archive related emails.

There are digital to-do trackers. To start looking, search under "to-do list." Portable notes apps can help you stash brainstorms or tasks you need to do that pop into your mind during your morning run or in the checkout line.

PROJECT AND TIME MANAGEMENT

There are free and paid online tools for subduing the wildest mustang of projects, from tracking costs and logging time to who's doing what, when, if you're subcontracting. You want a system robust enough to contain all the project's moving parts, but not so tedious that you won't use it.

Project management systems can also help you track how long specific tasks take, helping you cost out and schedule future projects. To start researching project management tools, type "project management software" and "task management software" into your browser.

> "I spend far too much time drinking coffee, reading the newspaper, and checking my RSS feed. If I really want to procrastinate, I check my social media."

While you're at it, check out apps that will sync your files if you work on different computers or via mobile phone and need to access the latest files from any device.

Think of all this as your digital 24/7/360 (see Chapter 2).

COUNT THE MINUTES AND THE DAYS

I keep an old-fashioned paper calendar, but that's never stopped me from recommending digital calendars to freelancers, especially if you use your datebook on the fly—easy when your smartphone and computer calendars sync up. Count the minutes, too: Set your computer timer for business or personal tasks.

ME, PROCRASTINATE?

Procrastination has been around a long time—it's rooted in the Latin word for "to put off for tomorrow." Experts have studied our baffling tendency to engage in this behavior that we know is self-defeating and sends us toward enticements that provide diversion but ultimately little satisfaction.

There are various ideas about why we procrastinate, one of which has to do with how our decision-making changes over time: We tend to want to do the "right" thing when that thing—say, a deadline—is off in the future, but as the deadline approaches, we're lured by more attainable, immediate rewards.

Most of us know when we're procrastinating; we just can't figure out exactly why or how to stop. Let's leave the "why" to the professionals. And let's accept that everyone procrastinates from time to time, so it's not about stopping so much as about correcting course when it happens.

TEN PROCRASTINATION BUSTERS

Try these ten ways to prevail over procrastination:

1 Are you expecting too much of yourself? It's hard to execute if you expect yourself to get everything right. Give yourself a little reality check that you're no more or less human than anyone else. Which means a) you're capable of great things, and b) you might make mistakes. Welcome to planet Earth. We're glad you're here.

2 Are you doing the wrong things at the wrong times? If you're trying to do high-focus work at low-focus times, procrastination can signal the mismatch.

3 Are you doing enough of one thing at one time? If you're procrastinating because you don't feel you can make real progress in the time you have, try to shift your schedule to free up the chunk of time you need to make the work worth starting: "Whenever I can, I make breakfast or coffee dates instead of lunch dates because I need large blocks of time to do my design work. If I have a lunch date, I feel like I just get settled and get in the zone—and then I have to leave. When I use breakfast and coffee as bookends and put work in the middle, I get a lot more done."

4 Break tasks into increments. "I break projects into ridiculously small steps because I get ridiculously happy when I get each step done—and I can't wait to do more." A task breakdown also helps you match tasks to time and focus level. Not enough time or focus right now for writing? OK, make a few phone calls or do a little research. Chip away at something. Keep moving. Progress begets progress.

5 Withdraw stimulus, impose consequences or rewards, make pacts. These tactics engage the deep-down you that hates procrastinating and yearns to get stuff done. Go offline or log off email for periods of time. Pay your mate five dollars each day the task isn't done. Promise yourself something nice when you finish. Start a group where you report in and help each other meet your goals. Brainstorm strategies that release your inner achiever.

6 Tune in to your body. If your attention's wandering, maybe your brain or body is running on empty and you really *do* need to do something else for a little while. Are you getting hunger pangs or feeling mentally fogged? Maybe you need a snack or a drink. Were you up all night with the baby and are falling asleep at your desk? Maybe you could use a twenty-minute nap. Are you procrastinating because you're wrestling too hard and long with a problem? Maybe you need a change of scene to refresh your mind or it would help to call a freelancer in your network for some advice and a short chat. Rather than fritter time away, take a truly productive break and then come back refreshed.

7 Engage willpower for short kicks. You can push ahead by force of will, and some of the tips above will help you do that, but experts think willpower is akin to a sprint—effective for short periods, not good for marathons.

8 Remember your purpose. When something seems like a slog, remembering the larger goal can inspire, prompt, encourage, or egg you on. "Sometimes I actually procrastinate on depositing my checks! I'd rather work on projects than do bookkeeping. But I *love* to see my account balance go up. So I imagine seeing that little ATM receipt and how proud I'll feel. It helps."

9 Buddy up. Been meaning to learn a new software program? Invite another freelancer over and take the tutorials together. Want to learn more about money but can't find the time? Set a "Friday Finance" call with a friend where you tell each other about an article you've read that week. You get a break, have a little social time, and apply some gentle peer pressure to produce results.

10 Use for good, not evil. If procrastination appears inevitable, put it to some positive use. Surfing the Internet or checking social media? Connect with some freelancers or post some useful info for your professional network. Reading articles? Keep a file of stuff you want to read but don't have time to—industry news, tech topics, finance info, anything that fascinates you that you want to learn more about. Pick one and read it. When you're done, delete or shred it and pick up your work.

DISTRACTIONS AND INTERRUPTIONS

Which of these statements do you identify with—or do you fall somewhere in between:

"I'm easily distracted by other projects and things that need to get done."

"I'm extremely disciplined. I can focus on the project in front of me and not get caught up in the zillions of things that could distract me—chores, snacks, phoning a friend, the Internet, et cetera. For whatever reason, I can put the other stuff aside."

Distractions and interruptions can be necessary and good, and there's the rub. The outside world brings business, information, and contact, but at a dizzying pace.

"When you're looking for work, you have to know what's happening in your industry. So you subscribe to industry websites to keep track of who's buying what and who has what job. Within seconds of a posting from the organization, incoming email starts clicking in at the speed of light. Networking has always been a critical part of any job. But the social media network is networking on steroids."

It's also an incredibly effective way to procrastinate.

"Social media is part of my work, but also a distraction from paying work and from work that's more confronting or challenging."

. . . and in the end, what have you got to show for it?

"By the time you're up-to-date on what's happening around you, nothing's happening to you. At some point it hits you: Being in the know can be a full-time position. Alas, an unpaid one."

Because we're social and curious, social media, emails, texting, and phone calls can be irresistible. In fact, it appears all this mental flea-hopping is habit-forming. It seems our brain gets a chemical feel-good when something interesting suddenly happens—such as an email with good news. It creates a rewarding chemical rush that begs to be repeated—as in *Let's keep checking to see if it happens again!* Thus we constantly check for phone messages or texts, check email, see who's available for chat or who's hanging out on Facebook. When we go without these little stimulus shots, we might feel restless or dulled out: "I actually feel my finger twitching because it 'wants' to click on my email after almost every paragraph I write!" one freelancer says.

You may feel you're getting a lot done by jumping from task to task, but it's been suggested that every time we change gears, there's an adjustment period where we have to exert energy to zero in again, costing time and mental juice (think of taking your foot off the accelerator—you have to hit the gas to get back to cruising speed). One study found it took an average of twenty-five minutes to refocus!

So what's a freelancer to do?

DON'T CALL IT DISTRACTION

First, let's find a kinder, gentler way to deal with the whole subject of distraction.

Humans have agile minds. Being able to detect new stimuli—sometimes in the blink of an eye—and quickly act on our awareness may have helped our forebears respond to danger or opportunity. So let's remove the stigma from our extraordinary ability to sense our world and shift our attention. Instead of calling it distraction, let's call it migration. We are not flawed or bad for being able to do this.

But just because we *can* think fast and respond to interruptions doesn't mean we always *should*.

The IMP Within

It's all too easy to fall into what I call the IMP (Interruption/Migration/Procrastination) Loop—a nasty little number that causes a lot of "bad freelancer" feelings. Watch how it works:

You start the morning with great intentions to focus on your big goal for the day and get it done. You settle down with your coffee and . . . the phone rings (interruption). You pick up (migration). The call's short but exciting—a possible gig. You jump online to do a little research on your new prospect (migration).

Twenty minutes stretches to an hour. You know you should get back to your project (procrastination). But you didn't check email this morning in order to focus on your project. Maybe you'd better take a quick look now (migration).

There are quite a few emails, including several you were waiting for and one that's urgent (interruption). You take care of the urgent one. While your inbox is open, you figure you might as well answer the others (migration).

It's lunchtime and you haven't touched your project. You grab a protein bar and eat at your desk while you play a computer game and chat with some friends (hey, you're basically skipping lunch, so you deserve a little break, right?).

One and a half hours later (procrastination) you finally start your project. You're feeling pretty crappy about how you're doing your day. OK, now. To work. And for an hour, you do. It's going great. Then you remember that the guest blog post you promised to write is due in two days (interruption). Yikes. Your mind scrambles for ideas (migration). Ah, here's one. You start typing notes. Whew, feels good to get these down—but when will you ever learn to put these deadlines in your calendar and start earlier? You're so disorganized.

Oops—time to pick up the kids from school (interruption). Between snacks, homework, and dinner, there's no point trying to work until the kids are in bed. You're cranky with them and you feel guilty—it's not their fault you can't get your act together.

At nine p.m., you sit down and work for an hour but it's slow going; you're a morning person. You keep getting sucked into email and the movie your mate's watching (distraction). Finally, at midnight, you give up and go to bed. Tomorrow you'll have more emails to answer, plus the project you didn't finish, plus the blog post that's due. What happened to the day? You feel like the worst freelancer on the planet.

When I showed this story to a freelancer, she told me it made her feel nauseated. Getting caught in the IMP Loop can be stomach turning. Don't do this to yourself.

THIRTEEN WAYS TO MANAGE MIGRATION

1 Accept migration and work with it. Accept migration as a natural tendency of the mind. When your attention wanders, gently return it to the task. No "bad freelancer" talk. Just, "Oh, there you go. Let's bring you back." (You might recognize this as a meditation technique for quieting the mind.)

2 Find your migration magnets. There are activities, like foods, we can't resist. Keep a time log for all your activities—including your fruitless attempts to beat the fastest time on the daily online jigsaw puzzle. Work on the ones that suck you in the most. Remember the freelancer with the twitchy email finger? "I worked on extending the time I spent writing before checking email. It was uncomfortable at first, but I just kept at it. Pretty soon I noticed a smoother thought pattern."

3 Is this situational migration, or habitual migration? Constantly checking email because you're waiting for an important message is situational migration. Habitual migration is continuing to constantly check email after the important one arrives. From there, it's a short hop to procrastination where time disappears into tasks you never intended to do. Once you know the difference, you can start to catch yourself in the act.

4 Don't hold that thought. Thoughts—ideas, to-dos—steal mental bandwidth. Throw them in a holding tank—a desktop file; a text to yourself; a notepad: "I keep a sheet of paper beside me as I work. If I start thinking about other things I need to do, I write them down as reminders for later." Yes, this interrupts the flow, but it's a quick toss; then you're back on task.

5 Front-load the effort. If you put in more uninterrupted time at the start of a task, you're more likely to rebound faster from later distractions.

6 Try a timer. Set a timer and work like a maniac on your designated task for that time. As soon as the timer goes off, take a break. This can also work to break tasks you hate into short bites, or to contain your migration magnets: "I try to stick to only allowing myself on social media until a certain time."

7 Find your prime time. Freelancers can; office workers can't. If you're an early bird or a night owl, go with it and put your prime projects in your prime time. Stuff the other stuff around the edges. So what if you knock off at three p.m. and then work after dinner until two a.m.? Who needs to know you're calling from the gym locker room or the museum garden? "I don't have to explain my whereabouts to my clients. If I was having lunch with a friend when they called, I just say I was out, or that I had a meeting."

8 Do "just one thing." Choose the single most essential task you need to do today. Put it ahead of everything—your emails, your messages, everything. Too big to finish? Break it down or front-load the effort (see above).

9 Try a procrastination buster.

10 Dangle a carrot. Put something you like at the end of the task: "I make an afternoon date to meet a freelancer who lives near me. The prospect of getting to kick back and relax later makes other distractions less tempting."

11 Remind yourself who's boss. You run this show, in charge of what you do and when you do it. Most callers, texters, chatters, and emailers can wait.

12 Turn off, log off, sign out, shut down. Yes, you hear this advice all the time, but have you done it? Do it, boss. Turn off your cell phone, the ringer, the pinger, the bouncing icons, the gazillion tabs. Log out of email, exit the Internet, ration chat. There are even online tools that'll block access to your favorite migration magnets online. Decide when and how often you'll check in, sign in, log on, turn on. Callers are used to voicemail; just don't leave them hanging too long.

13 See it on the big screen. Cramped computer screens cramp your focus and waste your time as you strain to sort and see priorities in a small space. If a larger screen isn't an option, keep your screen contents as streamlined as possible.

Not feeling it or doing it? Ask other freelancers how they manage time, bust procrastination, and manage migration. Check out books and online resources—to get started, search under "productivity tools."

Go back to the What's Your Ideal Day? quiz earlier in this chapter. Pick one of the smaller places where your ideal and reality are out of sync. Start putting in some fixes there. Don't try to change too much at once. You might just start with some reading, research, or talking with some freelance friends. I guarantee you everyone's got stories and strategies. Try things out and work gently with yourself. This isn't about beating yourself up with "bad freelancer" talk. It's about taking command of your work, doing what helps you do your best, and enjoying your freelance life in all its variety. When you do, it's sweet:

"If you like the feeling of never knowing what will happen from day to day and who is going to contact you, you can probably navigate the ups and downs of being a freelancer. There's no paycheck every two weeks, but there's that great way you feel when you know something possibly amazing will happen. If you think positively, that feeling of anticipation is an awesome one. You don't get that feeling too much working the nine-to-five grind."

Chapter 14

MANAGING YOUR OFFICE

Easy to say, sometimes hard to do. Not because you don't want to be organized, but because of the many different tasks freelancers do. And it's not like filing and bookkeeping rank high on life's big thrill list.

Maybe we can't make organizing exciting, but we can make it clearer and easier—and there *is* great satisfaction in being able to instantly find something you need, or not have to cross the room for that file or paw through drawers with a caller on hold, or have the pleasure of walking into your office on a fine morning and seeing a pristine work surface waiting for you.

Every business is different—and so is every freelancer—so what follows aren't mandates, but options and ideas for getting control of files, piles, email, and more, plus putting some fundamental structures and habits in place for bookkeeping and accounting. You should customize your systems to your industry and situation, including talking with your accountant or if necessary a lawyer about your record-keeping needs. (For information about paperwork relating to subcontracting and hiring, see Chapter 15.)

FIVE REASONS TO KEEP GREAT RECORDS

1: TAX REPORTING

Organized record keeping will save you time and angst at tax time. You'll save money not paying your accountant to tunnel through your records. And you might save your hide with Uncle Sam, because you must have backup to prove tax claims of business income, losses, expenses, and deductions. That includes receipts, credit card statements, bank statements, canceled checks, deposit slips, itemized phone bills, and pretty much any other record relating to the info in your return. You want to easily flip through the 1099-MISC forms sent by clients and check them off against your deposit records. And of course you need to depend on your own records to report any income that doesn't require a 1099.

If, God forbid, you get audited, you want to produce a veritable blizzard of backup—in the form of copious, clear, precise records. Particularly if you're claiming losses, organized bookkeeping lends credibility to your claims. (For a discussion of taxes, see Chapter 15.)

So do yourself a favor and save every receipt or record. You and your accountant can always decide later whether you really need it. Think you'll remember all the details? Do you remember whom you had lunch with on Thursday a year-and-a-half ago, where, what business you discussed, and what it cost? Exactly how many miles you drove to meet Client Twisted Knickers way too many times last summer? Precisely what it cost to fix your computer when it crashed while you were on deadline and witnesses reported seeing a wild-eyed individual in coffee-stained clothing bursting into the computer store, shouting, "Make it start! Make it start!"?

2: LIABILITY CONTROL

For disputes or legal issues, you may need backup to prove actions and interactions: what you or others did (or didn't) say, do, promise, deliver, pay, et cetera. Scary, yes. But it happens. When it does, emails, memos, schedules, financial records, even phone logs can become hugely important.

3: PROJECT DEVELOPMENT, MANAGEMENT, AND HISTORY

You're negotiating a new contract and want to use language from a deal you made two years ago. Where *is* that contract?

You're wrestling with a nightmare project when you suddenly realize you could retrofit the schedule from another project to get this monster under control. Where *is* that schedule?

Your client says, "You sent an email saying you'd do this, remember?" No, you don't. Where *is* that email?

On the way home one night you have a killer business idea. Every detail's clear. A year later, you read someone else has done it and is raking in the dough. You feel sick because you forgot about it after you got home.

4: MARKETING

Your website's in the works! You're going to want to populate it with reviews of the projects you worked on . . . articles about the software you developed . . . tearsheets of the ads you designed. The better records you keep of your achievements, the more effectively you can market yourself.

5: SEEING HOW YOU'RE DOING!

Good records help you keep tabs on how your freelance career is growing. Tracking client payments instantly reveals who's late and when to follow up or warn that work can't continue until they pay. Track your expenses to see whether they're creeping up. Want to know the minimum income you need to meet your annual expenses? A break-even analysis will tell you. Looking for a business partner or funding? Good bookkeeping lets you pull together financial reports for a business plan.

KEEPING IT TOGETHER: THE ORGANIZED OFFICE

When you first start freelancing, you don't always know exactly how you need to organize things. So don't get down on yourself if things haven't been well organized up to now. It's never too late to start.

"I love the way my office looks. I'm not as in love with the way it works."

MANAGING THE STUFF (PILES AND FILES)

Everyone's business is different, but this section will get you thinking in new ways about those piles and files.

DO WHAT WORKS

Your office systems should be realistic for your habits *and* let you work at your best.

It starts with becoming aware about stuff you've been doing that isn't working: "When I get busy, crap piles up. Notes, bills, reminders, subscription forms. This distracts me and makes me feel disorganized."

Next, take tiny steps to challenge your habits: "I'm a nonlinear thinker, and my space reflects that. I try valiantly to throw things out. Slowly I'm getting better at it."

Then ask yourself if you can make some changes that reflect how you naturally work—but let you work at your best. For example, this freelancer knows he's a paper person, so he set up his office to support his paper habit: "I never look back on a conversation or project and wish I'd taken fewer notes. My workspace is filled with folders containing time lines, sketches, flowcharts, and contracts. It can be a struggle keeping things organized, but it's worth it to have all the information about every project at my fingertips and not have to ask clients to repeat themselves. I need ample shelf space to handle the material associated with each project. I like that I can keep everything organized and still work from stacks of books and paper—my preferred organizational method."

And here's a paper minimalist: "I don't keep many files, as I don't like the clutter. If I file it, I tend to never touch it again, so why file? I try to only touch a piece of paper once and then discard it forever."

The key is finding a balance between challenging yourself to change a little and letting your habits run amok: "If what you're doing keeps you organized and you can find a phone number, a piece of research, or a pitch idea almost instantly, you're in good shape."

CHECK YOUR 24/7/360

In Chapter 2 we talked about organizing your workspace around your 24/7/360—what you need constantly (24/7) in arm's reach (360) versus what can be stowed in a drawer, across the room, or out of sight, out of mind. Now we'll take it a step further.

Look at your piles, files, records, notes, papers, and "stuff" and ask yourself what you need to access hourly, daily, weekly, monthly, only for special reasons, or maybe not at all. You might assign levels of high, medium, and low. Right away you'll start looking at your setup differently.

Your 360 is for short-term stuff. The more often or more urgently it needs to be handled, the closer it should be.

Suppose you update your business expense sheet daily at the close of business. You might designate a spot on your desk where you keep the day's receipts. Once they're entered on your expense sheet, you shift them to a file outside your 24/7/360.

But if you update your expense sheet weekly or monthly (say, when you reconcile it to your credit card and bank statements), it's more medium-level than high-level. You need it in your 360, but not under your nose. You might keep medium-level things in labeled hanging files, stacked or standing files, cubbies, boxes, or other containers on your desk turnaround, behind you, or on shelves in your 360—on your radar, but not vying for attention when it's not their turn.

Other possibilities for the 360:

• Files for clients you're dealing with today or this week: "I noticed my doctor has a standing file on his desk for the files of patients he's seeing that day (mine was in there). Good idea."

• Dedicated files for receipts, deposit slips, or other transactions to hold until you get your monthly statements, when you reconcile and file them away

- Files you need in easy reach for personal or family issues in the works (vacation plans, a medical billing problem, a party): "We're landlords of an apartment in our building. If there's an emergency or we're filling a vacancy, it can take up a lot of time."

- "Waiting-to-hear-back" stuff that you'll handle as soon as you do

- Anything you deal with multiple times a week

- Small-scale research projects in process—remember, not everything's on the Internet

- A designated folder to hold instructions, notes, or messages for an assistant, babysitter, your mate, or your kids if they're old enough to be home alone— they can grab it even when you're not there

- Anything pending *in the short term.*

> "I abolished my in-box. I open and sort the mail standing up, filing and pitching as I go. I put checks aside to deposit weekly. I file bank statements but plan to go paperless soon."

Now: See stuff in your 360 that doesn't *have* to be there? Move it out of your orbit and start sorting, pitching, and figuring out what you really must keep, how, and where.

REDUCING THE STACK(S)

If you're a stacker, try standing files where you keep things that will turn over in a week or less. If something's pending longer than that, move it to a box or standing file out of your 24/7/360 until you need it. With standing files, eventually you have to file or pitch.

"I'm a hard-copy reader," Gail says, "My workspace is a mess—I'm drowning in paper." If you're this kind of freelancer, or if your projects require keeping stacks of stuff on tap, have a holding tank for them off your desk until you need them: "I have a grid-style bookcase with sixteen 'cubbies.' I assign one to each project (and one to tech supplies, one to receipts, et cetera). My desk stays clear, and I just haul out the stack for whatever project I'm tackling."

SHRED IT

Recruit a fast-eating shredder with a big mouth and a big belly as your ally against paper clutter and in protecting your personal information. Identity theft is a reality, and you also should take every precaution to protect your own and your clients' proprietary or confidential information. The more your shredder can eat in one gulp and the more it can hold, the easier it is to beat paper piles into trembling submission. Make sure it can eat disks, too. Get recommendations from other freelancers; read product reviews online.

POCKET OR BOX IT

If you have to organize papers of different sizes, bills of various kinds, or swatches or samples, try pocket folders where you can group like with like, or labeled boxes where you can stow papers, CDs, DVDs, notebooks, and the like.

DEALING WITH SNAIL MAIL

Do you open your mail right away or leave it for later? Have a system that matches your habit. I like the freelancer's tip above about opening the mail standing up. I'd add: Stand near your shredder and drop stuff right in. Put checks and bills in designated places to be deposited and paid. For unactionable stuff you plan to read "sometime," stow it in a box or standing file outside your 24/7/360. Go through that box when the pile is flush with the top or the standing file is full. Anything more than a month old, toss it. If you still really want to read it, keep it for your next assessment. This way you have a holding tank for such things, but they don't overwhelm you. "I always grab something on my way out the door to read anytime I'm waiting somewhere. The game is: It never comes back in the house. I have to read and pitch it before I go home."

WHAT GOES IN YOUR DESK DRAWERS

The 24/7/360 rule applies to desk drawers, too. Things you use often enough that you'd be annoyed to have to get up to get them every time (stickies? seam cutters? screwdrivers?) are desk drawer–worthy.

Designate a grab-'n'-go drawer to hold things you grab before heading out the door: business cards, sunglasses, reading glasses, breath mints, pen/small notebook, flash drives, gym lock, or whatever else you need when you're mobile. Consider it a loading dock for your bag, briefcase, or backpack.

OVER THERE

Outside your 24/7/360 is medium-low and low-access stuff. The lower the access, the further away (or higher up) it might be. Current accounting and financial files that you're adding to should be more accessible than files you might need only once a year, if ever. Office supplies you regularly replenish and extra digital equipment might be nearby, too.

You'll want a secure place for tax records, tax returns, permits, licenses, leases, or other official paperwork.

You might have one accessible file for very important papers (the deed to your house, passport, Social Security card, birth certificate, marriage certificate, et cetera) that you can grab if you need to evacuate in an emergency. (And if you're one of those incredibly smart people who actually does this, then you are truly a hero.)

Otherwise, let frequency of use be your guide. If stuff isn't getting filed or you're procrastinating because it's too hard to access certain files, rethink their location. "Over there" materials could include:

- Office supplies
- Finance and accounting logbooks and files
- Tax records and tax returns
- Client files

- Equipment manuals, warranties, and service contracts
- Level 4 idea files
- Media clips about your work
- Reference materials.

Of course, you could create digital files instead of physical ones. You might keep digital and hard copies of important files.

GOING PAPERLESS

Skip this section if you're paperless and proud. Or keep reading and know there'll be no public flogging if you choose not to make this change. It's an individual decision, and one you can take in stages.

A good place to start: shifting things like catalogs and financial prospectuses to email. Then newsletters, professional publications, and other subscriptions. Ready? Get financial statements and bills online. Then maybe pay some bills online, if you feel comfortable. Your bank might offer online bill-paying, which centralizes the process: "My brother pays all his bills online through his bank. That way he doesn't have to provide his bank account info to other entities."

Some bills you might be more hands-on about. For example, if you're not sure you'll have cash to cover bills (especially bills with variable amounts) or need to transfer money between accounts before bills are paid, go slow or be selective about automatic payment.

If your bank statements are coming to a dedicated email address, you need to remember to go there each month, download the statements and save them in your computer system, reconcile them with your physical records, and delete the emails. Put reminders in your calendar. Make sure any urgent or actionable emails, such as bills, get on your radar big-time and don't get mixed in with nonurgent stuff or sit in a file unnoticed!

Then on your computer, you can set up files for, say, your downloaded statements, organized by tax year. When you file away your tax paperwork for the year, burn that year's file to a disk and file it with your hard-copy tax return and tax records. Want a diploma in advanced digital organizing? Scan your receipts and tax records and burn the whole shebang on a disk, with hard copies as backup.

You might decide to go digital in the New Year. Or go incrementally as catalogs arrive, subscriptions are renewed, and bills or statements come in. Also, you can receive bills digitally but pay them manually. Do what works for your situation and comfort level.

CALLING FOR BACKUP

You can't have too much backup because no matter what or how much you have, you're at the mercy of, well, everything. Hard drives, external drives, flash drives, and disks are subject to the assaults of Mother Nature (fire, flood), sticky fingers (theft), old houses (burst pipes), mouthy pets, close encounters with a beverage—or sometimes they just up and die. Internet backup services put you at the mercy of technician error, business busts, or the fine print you didn't read or policy you didn't quite understand. Yeah, it's scary out there. But since when did being scared hold back any freelancer?

> "What's most important in a freelancer's workspace? Being comfortable with your computer setup and backing up your files."

Let's assume you save your work at regular intervals and that your computer's well inoculated against cyber invaders. But you should also save your data externally in case your computer data's compromised or your computer crashes or is stolen or destroyed. And you should back up your backup. Burning disks used to be the only option, but now there are affordable external hard drives that hold lots of data.

To back up your external hard drive (which can meet the same sorry fates as your computer), you could use another external drive and/or disks stowed safely off-premises, use an Internet backup service, or all of the above.

Some people do a "lite" version of Internet storage by emailing important documents to themselves. Official Internet storage entails signing up for a dedicated service. It should be a well-run, stable business with features that meet your needs. Yes, it has happened that these outfits have shut down or suffered technical breakdowns that lose files forever.

There are free and paid versions (your Internet service provider might provide limited storage at no additional charge). Shop around, read product reviews, and talk to freelancers with backup needs similar to yours.

If you have special backup needs (large amounts of data, confidential data, needing to keep data for long periods or indefinitely), consult a knowledgeable specialist.

ACCOUNTING AND BOOKKEEPING BASICS

Maybe that worked before you went solo. But as your freelance business takes off, you should graduate from the shoebox/drawer school of bookkeeping.

Record keeping has two basic components:

1 Accounting books or digital records where you summarize your income and expenses, and

"I don't have a shoebox full of receipts. I have a drawer."

2 What the IRS calls "supporting documents" (examples: receipts, deposit slips, invoices, canceled checks, bills you've paid, et cetera) that provide the data for your books and support your tax claims.

Maintaining both has two components:

1 A system for updating your books during the current tax year, and

2 A system for filing and storing everything safely year by year, usually organizing the supporting documents by type.

Many freelancers have more than one business—graphic artist Monday through Friday, jewelry maker and street fair exhibitor on weekends. If you do, you need to keep entirely separate accounting for each business.

CHOOSE YOUR METHOD

The first year you file a tax return for your freelance business, you have to choose an accounting method (changing it may require IRS approval). There are essentially two types:

1 **Cash method.** Lots of people use this method. You report income and (generally) expenses the year they're received or paid. So if you bill a client $1,000 on December 15 and you're paid on January 12 (i.e., the following tax year), you report receiving that income in the following tax year. Ditto for receiving and paying business bills.

2 **Accrual method.** Usually in this method, income and expenses are reported in the year they're earned or incurred, even though you might not actually have received or paid them yet. Taking the example above of the client you billed on December 15 who pays you on January 12: You report that $1,000 for the tax year ending on December 31, because that's the tax year you earned it. Similarly, you report expenses in the year you incur them, not when you pay them. In this system, you set up books for accounts receivable and accounts payable.

Some use a hybrid. Your choice should depend on the clearest way to document your income and expenses, and what's necessary for your business. You may need to change methods if, for example, you start selling physical products. Not sure? Talk to an accountant or a professional bookkeeper.

Smart freelancers set up a separate checking account just for business use. It makes your bookkeeping and tax prep much easier (no sorting through business and personal transactions). It's also a more transparent documentation of your business income and expenses if any questions arise about your tax return.

Which bank to choose? Up to you. It may depend on the services you need: whether you write a lot of checks (and by hand or electronically), what the bank charges for the transactions you do most, their minimum balance policies, and so on. Shop around; ask other freelancers for recs.

HOW, WHEN, WHAT

There are few hard-and-fast rules about how to keep your records, but here are three guidelines-of-thumb:

1 It has to be a system that works for the profession you're in and the kind of business entity you have (for example, corporations need to keep the minutes from their board of directors' meetings).

2 It has to enable you to maintain the kinds of records you need for the Five Reasons to Keep Great Records mentioned earlier.

3 It has to be one you're able and willing to use.

Some people find spreadsheets are perfect (and the software can add things up so there's less chance of human error): "My spreadsheet-whiz husband made me an invoicing/income grid when I started freelancing. I've used it ever since to keep track of whom I've invoiced, whether I've been paid, and whether I'm on track to meet my earnings goals for the year. He seems to think it's quite simple, but I think it's a marvel."

Or you could sort receipts, bills, and other records into folders or large envelopes with handwritten entries on ruled paper clipped to the outside.

Some go even lower-tech: "I use those monthly planners you buy at office supply stores. That's the best I can manage. I keep copies of all the invoices that go out and photocopy any checks that come in."

"I tape expense receipts into a spiral-bound notebook, scribble notes on the pages, and add it all up at the end of the year."

Ask other freelancers what they do, including any accounting software they use, especially if you think you might want or need to create financial statements as your business grows. There are a lot of exciting digital tools available for organizing your business and finances. What's popular now might be replaced by something even more amazing six months from now. Check out the options and see if any could work for you. Just make sure you understand how to use the system, or serious accounting snarls can happen. Take a class or get good help. Also, make sure your digital records are clear enough to match easily with supporting documents.

Just not into it? Know your limits; pay someone to do it right: "I don't enjoy doing bookkeeping and accounting, so I hired a virtual assistant to manage my books and a CPA to help me manage my tax work. It frees me up to do creative work to build my business." Get bookkeeper recommendations from your accountant, other freelancers, and small business owners you know: "I'm meeting with an accountant next week who does the books for a friend who's been freelancing successfully for several years. It's a simple system that works very well for my friend. I'm confident it will do the trick for me."

When you do your bookkeeping depends on the kind of record it is. You might do your expenses day by day, while the details are fresh, quickly filing any receipts. If you'd rather do them weekly, write it into your calendar and have a place in your 24/7/360 where those receipts are in view, saying "Record me!"

You might have a similar weekly deposit system: a safe spot in your 24/7/360 where you stow checks and a deposit slip you add to as they come in. Bill paying and ATM reconciling can happen weekly, too. Keep all your paper bills in one place in your 24/7/360 or in a digital file if you're paperless. Check what's coming due; write a check or pay it online. Write the check number, date paid, and amount on the bill and in your bookkeeping records and file your hard copies.

Every month, grab your checkbook, reconcile it with your monthly bank statement (including any bank charges), and file the statement.

Also pull your income and expenses into monthly reports, detailing date, client/project, amount, check numbers, and any other pertinent info, with separate reports for direct and indirect business expenses. Seeing what went out and came in every month is a great way to see how your business is doing and can help you make Freelance Portfolio decisions.

If you stay on top of your accounting this way, there's no avalanche of receipts and papers to sift through for taxes. You just pull your monthly expense and income totals into annual summations that you or your accountant use to complete your tax return. Tax prep gets a lot faster and easier, as this freelancer wistfully notes: "At the end of December and through January, I go through everything and make a master list of money received and money expended and ship it off to my accountant—but I wish I entered the info monthly."

Once your tax return is filed, scan your stuff if that's your chosen storage mode, make a backup of any digital records, and store it and your paper records in a safe place.

FUNNEL 'N' FILE

I like to envision this process as a funnel: You're funneling all the transactions from your days into a week's worth; a month's worth, and a year's worth, which then feeds into your tax return. You file papers as you go and then put the whole thing to bed after taxes are filed. If questions arise, you just reverse the process to trace back and find the receipt, bill, or other original supporting documentation.

TRACKING DIRECT AND INDIRECT BUSINESS EXPENSES

You'll be tracking two types of business expenses separately. We'll talk more about these in Chapter 15, but here are the basic definitions.

Direct Expenses

These are expenses solely connected with your business. There are quite a few, but some examples are equipment and furniture used only for business (see Appreciating Depreciation, below), postage, supplies, marketing costs, professional dues and memberships, transportation, and business meals and entertainment.

Indirect Expenses

If you can legitimately claim a home office (see Chapters 2 and 15), you can deduct indirect expenses, which are expenses that span your business *and* home life. Unlike direct expenses, you deduct just the percentage that correlates to the size of your home office compared to the rest of your home. You need to keep these separate from direct expenses.

Here again the list can be long, but some examples include: your electric and other utility bills, your rent or mortgage interest, and property tax.

Make sure your business reason for claiming an expense as a deduction is totally clear, and how you arrived at the amount. That's why supporting documents (paid bills, receipts, et cetera) need to be kept as backup to your claims. Thus the funnel 'n' file process above—and why you write descriptions on your reports rather than relying on your memory.

For meals and entertainment expenses, for example, note the date, the location and/or a description, the business relationship (names, occupations, titles, or the business connection between you), the business purpose for the expense, and the amount.

Break out expenses separately even if they happened together. Suppose you take a client out to dinner and then to a ball game. They need to show up as separate expenses in your records.

A word here about record keeping for travel expenses: Not every travel expense is deductible, so document all your activities and costs and keep all your receipts so you can go over them later and determine what's deductible, or what portions are.

Assuming you can legitimately deduct the travel, you'll need the supporting documents (receipts, bills, et cetera) for your dates of travel, destination, your business reason for the trip, the cost of your transportation, your lodging, and any other costs related to doing business on the road. It's a good idea to note and keep receipts for all your meals, too, until you can decide whether you're using actual costs or will use the IRS's Standard Meal Allowance. For more on travel expenses, see Chapter 15.

APPRECIATING DEPRECIATION

It's common knowledge that you can't necessarily sell something for the same price you paid when you bought it. That's because many items lose value over time. This aging process is called depreciation.

What does this have to do with record keeping? If you're deducting the cost of certain items that have a longer useful life than, say, a year (for example: your computer, your office furniture, your car), you may not be able to deduct the entire cost in the first year. You may have to take depreciation into account. For that you need a record of when and how you came to own it, what you paid for it, when you started using it for business, how much you use it for business (as a percentage, if you also use it for personal purposes), what you paid if you made improvements on it, when and how you sold it (if you did), the sale price (or its fair market value), and any expenses relating to the sale.

Set up a record of assets that you keep with your tax prep materials and can easily update, to use as the basis for depreciation on your taxes. The supporting documents have to be kept, too, things like sales receipts, invoices, and canceled checks.

See Chapter 15 for additional information. And visit the IRS website or talk with your accountant for specifics on what you can depreciate, and exactly how.

TRACKING YOUR CAR MILEAGE

If you use your car for business purposes and want to deduct those expenses, keep a record with your tax prep materials of your car's vital stats: model, make, and year, and the year you started using it for business.

You have two choices for how you track and record your costs.

If you choose the IRS standard mileage rate (a set rate per mile established annually by the IRS) to calculate your mileage, you record each trip: the date, the odometer reading at the start and the end of your trip, your location at the start and where you're headed, the business reason, and the number of miles you drove for this trip.

An easy way to do this is to set up a template for a month's worth of entries, copy it, put the sheets in a binder and throw it in your car. Just fill in the info whenever you go out on a business call. The sheets will eventually be filed away with your tax records for that year. Or record the mileage info in your calendar where you've noted the appointment.

The other method involves tracking the actual expenses for using and maintaining your car, such as fuel, oil, repairs, insurance, licenses,

SELECTED IRS TAX RECORD-KEEPING RESOURCES

Here's a selection of Internal Revenue Service publications you might find helpful as you learn more about tax record keeping. Type the titles into your browser.

IRS Publication 463, *Travel, Entertainment, Gift, and Car Expenses*	IRS Publication 946, *How to Depreciate Property*
IRS Publication 583, *Starting a Business and Keeping Records*	IRS Tax Topics, Topic 704, *Depreciation*

fees (including tolls, parking, and garage), et cetera. For this, you keep receipts for car expenses, and record your odometer reading at the start and the end of the tax year.

If you use your car for business and personal purposes, you can only deduct the percentage correlating to business use, so you'll need to keep a record like the one described above for the standard mileage rate method, adding a designation for personal or business trips. At year's end you figure out what percentage of your trips were for business and use that to calculate the correct percentage of actual expenses you can deduct.

CHECKING YOUR PROGRESS

Read the newspaper every day and you get current on current events. Get updates about new music and you know what's happening with your favorite artists. Watch your favorite shows every week and you can dissect every character and episode.

It works the same way with record keeping. Doing a little every day will make you the resident expert on your business. You'll know exactly how much is coming in and going out. Do your monthly income and expense reports show more going out than coming in? Maybe you need to tighten your belt, charge higher rates, prospect for better-paying clients, look for some Blue Chips, or nudge the slow payers. Are you bringing in more money than last year? You might need to pay more estimated taxes. Good record keeping helps you correct course.

Want to go a step further? With some research and maybe the help of a financial professional, you can slice and dice your data to create various financial statements: profit and loss statements, break-even analyses, and balance sheets. These are the kinds of reports you might do if you're writing a business plan.

It's great to work toward an ideal—your ideal office, filing setup, and organizational habits. But if the setup isn't perfect, don't despair. Just do your usual good work and take baby steps to get to a better place. It'll happen.

"When I started freelancing, my inbox was one square foot of the coffee table. My out-box was the couch, where I put things to be filed or mailed. My desk was a half-moon-shaped table that held—barely—my laptop and my to-do list. The phone sat on a stool by the desk. My files were plastic storage bins. But my little space was flooded with sunlight and it was all mine. In that funky little space, I wrote reams of copy, matched wits with learned people, hatched ideas, and had brainstorms. I learned that good work can happen anywhere. Because good work is up to me."

Chapter 15

TAKING CARE OF TAXES

First, a disclaimer. Everything freelancers need to know about taxes can't be covered in a chapter. Tax regulations also change over time and differ from state to state. We'll focus on federal taxes for the sole proprietor in this chapter, covering some important general tax points for sole proprietors, profiling some of the top tax deductions for freelancers, and outlining the basics of estimated taxes and tax issues when subcontracting or hiring. At the end of the chapter is a Selected IRS Tax Resources section listing IRS publications worth checking out. But don't stop there! The IRS website is packed with useful info that's surprisingly comprehensible, considering the crazy complexity of the tax code. For state and local tax regulations, check your state tax department. Build your knowledge through reading and talking with qualified pros (your accountant; your attorney) about your situation. Also review Chapter 14 for info on record keeping.

Take this short true-or-false quiz:

1 True or False: Freelancers get hit with a bigger tax bill than staff workers.

Answer: *True.* Employers share the burden of paying Medicare and Social Security tax. Freelancers, as boss and worker bee, get to pay both, as self-employment tax.

2 True or False: Self-employed workers' tax returns may get more IRS scrutiny than traditional employees'.

Answer: *The ways of the IRS are known only to the IRS.* What we do know is that the IRS gets a copy of the W-2 form staff workers receive from employers detailing their income. The IRS can just match this against the staffer's tax return and say, "Yep, that checks out."

You, freelancer, aren't an open-and-shut case. You have income from multiple sources. You're deducting business expenses. Both fluctuate. This makes you potentially interesting and possibly complicated to someone whose job description is: "Make sure Uncle Sam gets his due."

3 True or False: Freelancers have to keep more detailed tax records than traditional employees.

Answer: *True*. For the reasons in Statement 2, whether they do their own bookkeeping or hire someone, it costs freelancers time and sometimes money to document their income and maintain detailed records and files to prove their deductions.

4 True or False: Freelancers have to be more consistent about saving money for taxes than staff workers.

Answer: *True*. While everyone has to save for taxes, employers help by withholding and paying taxes from employees' paychecks. Freelancers, lacking that built-in step, often have to save and pay income tax four times a year (estimated tax), keep books on the payments, and often pay an accountant to calculate them.

I'm front-loading the bad news because it helps explain why it pays to get smart about what you can deduct, and why good record keeping and reporting are essential, so you can back up your deductions with confidence. On the upside, there are opportunities not to be missed.

A FEW FUNDAMENTALS

Who You Are

Unless you've selected a different business structure, you're a sole proprietor for tax purposes. There can be valid tax reasons for choosing a different business structure, so discuss this with your accountant.

Your Tax Year

Your tax return covers a tax year, generally twelve consecutive months. Depending on the business, it could be a calendar tax year (January 1 through December 31), a fiscal year (twelve consecutive months that end on the last day of a month other than December), or a fifty-two- or fifty-three-week tax year, which doesn't have the last-day-of-the-month rule. You may have to get IRS approval to change your tax year. With very rare exceptions, a sole proprietor uses the calendar year.

TACKLING SALES TAX

Selling tangible items and even some services can require collecting sales tax from your customers and remitting it to your state by filing sales tax returns. Check with your state or with your accountant beforehand about licensing and procedures, as regulations vary and states take sales tax remittance super-seriously. If you're selling items to an entity that will sell them to the general public (for example, as a wholesaler), you should register with your state and make sure you get a resale certificate from those clients stating, in essence, that they, not you, are responsible for remitting sales tax.

When, What, and Which Forms

For the "when," check out IRS Publication 509, *Tax Calendars*.

The "what" and "which forms" depend on your business structure or organization. Some taxes a sole proprietor may pay include:

• Federal income tax using Form 1040 U.S. Individual Income Tax Return and Schedule C (Form 1040) Profit or Loss From Business (Sole Proprietorship), with separate schedules if there's more than one business.

• Self-employment tax, filing Schedule SE (Form 1040). This is your contribution to Social Security, which offers retirement and disability benefits among others, and hospital insurance via Medicare.

• Estimated tax using Form 1040-ES, Estimated Tax for Individuals (see Estimated Taxes).

• State and local taxes (including estimated taxes).

When to File

Income tax is supposed to be paid as the money is made (hey, even the government doesn't like waiting for payment!). Thus employees have taxes withheld from their paychecks. If you don't have withholding (or if you do, but still need to pay more tax), you might have to pay estimated taxes (see Estimated Taxes).

How You Figure 'Em
Here's a highly simplified snapshot:

You keep careful records of all your earnings (gross income) as a sole proprietor. You and the IRS should receive Form 1099-MISC Miscellaneous Income from clients who paid you $600 or more during the tax year, but you must report all income *whether or not* you received a 1099-MISC. Make sure the amounts on your 1099-MISCs jive with your records. If you spot a discrepancy, alert the sender. If the 1099-MISC is in error, they can file and send you a corrected form.

You also keep careful records of all your business expenses. Some will be "direct expenses"—directly related to the running of your freelance business. Some may be "indirect expenses"—the business-related portion of expenses connected partly with your business and partly with your personal life (more on this is coming up).

You calculate the appropriate tax deductions for your business expenses, based on tax law. Your net income is the difference between your gross income and your deductions. A positive number = a net profit. Negative number? A net loss.

You report all of this truthfully, on time, and pay any tax you owe, because penalties, interest charges, audits, or worse are no way to spend your time and hard-earned money.

"Thank God my accountant saw to it that I paid into Social Security. I didn't even know it was the law."

HIRING AN ACCOUNTANT

Some people really get into the nitty-gritty of taxes and swear by tax software, but if that's not you (or even if it is, but you want another pair of eyes on things), hire a professional to prepare your taxes. A knowledgeable accountant can also help you understand the financial ramifications of business decisions. Vet that person well because you're responsible for your tax return's accuracy, no matter who prepares it.

CPAs (certified public accountants) usually have to have a college degree, postgrad study in some states, and pass a national exam. They also have to take continuing professional education credits (CPEs) to stay current in their industry. Some tips for choosing an accountant:

• Get recommendations from trusted family, friends, and freelancers.

• Ask candidates for client references, and follow up.

• Find out where they got their tax and accounting training, degrees, and license to practice. In some states, tax preparers need to be licensed or registered. Ask if they're licensed in yours. Some states have tougher licensing requirements than others—which is why you should also check references.

• Ask if they have clients with businesses like yours. You need someone who understands freelancers' tax needs.

• Ask what professional organizations they belong to. Do those organizations offer continuing education? What about having a code of ethics?

• Ask about their availability to answer questions and advise you— obviously especially if the IRS contacts you.

• Ask who would handle the day-to-day and how knowledgeable they are if they're not the senior person.

• See if they can give you a ballpark cost. Keep in mind an experienced accountant, just like a freelancer, might charge more but have valuable experience and get the work done faster. So it's not only about the fee.

• Notice if they ask questions about your business. You want someone interested in your business who can guide you in how the tax laws apply to you.

- Red flags: saying they can help you get bigger refunds than other preparers, calculating their fees as a percentage of the refund, not wanting to sign the return or send you a copy.

- Check out the American Institute of CPAs (aicpa.org).
P.S. Accounting and tax prep fees are deductible!

DOCUMENTING PURCHASE AND PAYMENT

Stephanie loves Apartment Haven, a store that sells space-efficient stuff for apartment dwellers. On one visit, she buys a set of colored stacking boxes and standup files for her home office. She charges them on her credit card. At tax time, she deducts the amount paid to the store as a business expense and uses the store entry on her credit card statement as proof of payment.

But wait. How do we know every item she bought was for business? Maybe she also bought a collapsible drying rack for her delicates. Which is why, for the IRS, proof of payment alone doesn't legitimize a deduction. Stephanie needs to save the store receipt itemizing her purchases, proving they were for business.

Then does she even need the credit card statement? Yes. It proves that she, not someone else, paid for the business items. Otherwise, what's to stop her from submitting the store receipt for her boyfriend's purchases as her own?

There's a symbiosis between proof of purchase (receipt) and proof of payment (such as credit card statement, canceled check, debit card record). You need both as backup when claiming business expenses (scans or photocopies of receipts are OK). For more on record keeping, see Chapter 14.

Q Dear Sara, Can I deduct business expenses before I have clients and actually start freelancing?

A You can deduct up to a certain amount of some start-up costs for your freelance business—assuming you're running a business, not a hobby (the IRS has specifics defining this: See the IRS's "Is Your Hobby a For-Profit Endeavor?"), can justify your costs as necessary business expenses, and have supporting documents as for any business expense. Want to know more? See IRS Publication 535, *Business Expenses,* Chapter 7: Costs You Can Deduct or Capitalize, or talk to your accountant.

TYPICAL TAX DEDUCTIONS

Below is an overview of some business deductions freelancers may typically take. While not exhaustive, it'll get you thinking about the deductions you might be able to take. Every profession and freelancer is unique, so read up on tax issues in your field and consider teaming up with a tax preparer (see Hiring an Accountant) who can help customize the fit between you and the tax code. Also refer to IRS Publication 535, *Business Expenses.* For information on taxes as related to retirement plans, see Chapter 17.

The IRS says a business expense can be deducted only if it's "ordinary and necessary." They define "ordinary" as "common and accepted" in your industry and "necessary" as "helpful and appropriate for your business, trade, or profession."

There's a lot you can deduct, in whole or in part, if it's business-related and not reimbursed by a client or employer. Just take a look at Schedule C. You might even use it to set up your expense records. If you don't see an expense mentioned there, track it anyway, since you may be able to deduct it.

HOME OFFICE

In order to deduct home office expenses, with few exceptions it has to fulfill the IRS's requirement that you use it "exclusively and regularly" as your primary business space, whether a separate room (ideal) or a cordoned-off section (it doesn't have to be a permanent divider); there's no other office where you can work (such as at an employer's workplace or a rented space you're deducting); and it meets the other requirements discussed in Chapter 2. Take a photo of it, so if the IRS comes sniffing and you've moved in the meantime, you've got proof.

If your home office qualifies, you can deduct the percentage of your general (indirect) home expenses correlating to the percentage your home office comprises of your home.

How to figure that? Two common methods are the rooms method or the square footage method, described in Chapter 2.

Examples of indirect expenses you can usually deduct include rent, insurance (excluding health), utilities, your security system, depreciation for the business-use portion of your home if you own it, and certain common repairs, among others.

Some home expenses are deductible, home office or not, such as real estate taxes and mortgage interest. Again, use your home office percentage to calculate the deductible portion for your business. For more info on deducting mortgage interest, see IRS Publication 936, *Home Mortgage Interest Deduction*.

Direct expenses incurred just for the business-use part of your home—say, painting your office—are generally fully deductible. Expenses incurred solely in nonbusiness-use areas—such as painting a room not used for your work—aren't deductible.

If your total business expenses exceed your gross income, deduction of some expenses relating to business use of your home will be more limited. You can carry those to the next tax year, with some restrictions. Visit the IRS website or consult your accountant for details.

If you maintain an office away from home, you can't claim deductions for both. And if you worked at someone's office, you may not be able to claim home office expenses for that time.

Not sure if your home workspace passes the tests, or how to figure out what's deductible? Check the IRS website (for starters, see Selected IRS Tax Resources, page 390) and ask your accountant.

BUSINESS MEALS AND ENTERTAINMENT

You don't have to prove that business income resulted from every business meal or entertainment you have with a contact. But as with the home office, each meal or entertainment expense has to pass some tests to be deductible in the eyes of the IRS:

• It has to be an "ordinary expense" that's "common and accepted" in your profession.

• It has to be a "necessary expense" that's "helpful and appropriate" to your business.
Also, you usually have to be able to show that:
• It was "directly related": It happened in a business space, or the primary goal was to do business and you actually did business or expected a particular business outcome, or

• It was "associated" with your profession and happened immediately before or after a considerable discussion of business.
Plus:
• Any meals or entertainment expenses that you were reimbursed for aren't deductible.

• "Lavish or extravagant" expenses don't qualify. The expense has to be "reasonable" in the course of business.

If they qualify, you can usually deduct 50 percent of the cost of business-related meals and entertainment (for tickets, it's usually 50 percent of face value).

What if you buy dinner for a mixed group of business contacts and friends? You can only deduct your own and the business contacts' expenses. Can't tell who ordered the Caesar salad and who had the porterhouse? Pro-rate the total cost over everyone and deduct just the business head count.

The IRS can take a close look at meals and entertainment deductions, so make sure you can support your claims. Know your business reason (who you were with, their business connection with you, what business you discussed), and the date and location. Write all this on your receipt or in your records. If you aren't sure whether something's deductible, check the IRS website (including IRS Publication 463, *Travel, Entertainment, Gift, and Car Expenses*) and ask your accountant.

GIFTS

Buying a gift for a client could be deductible, to a limit (generally twenty-five dollars per recipient). Check the IRS website (IRS Publication 463, *Travel, Entertainment, Gift, and Car Expenses*). See if any professional organizations you belong to offers discounts on gift items. At this writing, Freelancers Union members can get discounts on flowers, concert tickets, and gift baskets. Deductible or not, stretch those dollars!

OTHER COMMONLY DEDUCTIBLE BUSINESS EXPENSES

If an item or an expense has both business and personal applications, you can deduct the percentage used for business. If you aren't sure what percentage to assign, jot down each time you use it over several weeks and use that as your basis for figuring out your business use percentage over twelve months.

DEPRECIATION DETOUR

Depreciation accounts for the value over time of certain kinds of business property that have a useful life of more than a year. Some examples: your car, computer, camera, cell phone, office fixtures, and furniture.

Whether and how business property is depreciated depends on multiple factors. The IRS has mind-boggling—I mean, meticulous—rules and regulations on all this.

Depreciation requires good record keeping maintained over time—kind of like depreciable items! When you buy equipment, furniture, machinery, or other longer-lasting items, keep proof of purchase and payment in a separate file with your tax-prep materials, with a log where you record when you bought the item, its make, its cost, when you started using it for your business, whether you're deducting it in the first year or depreciating it over X years, and (if you sell it) records of your price and any expenses incurred in the sale. In some circumstances, you may be able to deduct the asset fully in the first year rather than depreciate it—that's called a section 179 deduction. Check the IRS website and consult your accountant.

To learn more, see IRS Publication 946, *How to Depreciate Property*, check out the form where you show your math to the IRS (Internal Revenue Service Form 4562, Depreciation and Amortization) and its instructions, and huddle with your accountant about what's best for you.

Business purchases that last significantly longer than the year you start using them for business might have to be depreciated, i.e., deducted over time.

Office Furniture and Equipment

Office furniture and equipment used just for your business might be deductible. If it does business/personal double duty (like that vintage bureau where you stow art supplies and winter sweaters), just the business-use percentage is potentially deductible.

Technology

Tech is a huge part of most freelancers' business life, so you want to be able to take every deduction or depreciation you're entitled to. Keep purchase/payment records on every item, from your computer and peripherals to any other tech stuff you use for business (backup drives? calculator? digital recorder? audio/video equipment? software?).

Often you can deduct Internet expenses—for example, Internet service; the cost of building, maintaining, and hosting your website; buying your domain name. If you're not the only person using the Internet, come up with a fair percentage for your business use.

Phone

If you only have one phone line (aka a landline) installed at home, you can't deduct the cost of that line, but you *can* deduct long-distance business calls you make on it—they should be broken out on your bill and you should be able to verify each was a business call. Rather than rely on your memory, keep a list of your daily long-distance business calls for the month, match and attach it to your monthly phone statement, and file 'em.

If you add a second line at home just for business use, that line's deductible as a business expense.

At this writing, if you use your cell phone for business only, those costs are deductible. Are personal calls mixed in? You know the drill: Only the business percentage is deductible; the minutes spent on business calls are calculated as a percentage of the total.

Child Care

Depending on your child's age, you may be able to claim a tax credit for child-care expenses if you (and your spouse, if you're married) are both working or actively looking for work and need the child care in order to do work. Special regulations apply around divorce, separation, and custody. For more info see IRS Publication 503, *Child and Dependent Care Expenses* and talk with your accountant.

... and More

Business-related supplies, materials, books, and "professional instruments." These and other items you'd typically use within a year are usually deductible. Items with a longer useful life may have to be depreciated.

Advertising and marketing. From business cards to brochures to print ads to online promotion.

Professional services and permit fees. Examples include business tax prep and "ordinary and necessary" business-related accountants' and attorney's fees.

Professional subscriptions. That online industry newsletter; that trade magazine; that technical journal.

Professional licenses, membership fees, and dues. Usually business or trade license fees are deductible. For memberships and dues, make sure there's a clear business connection. Note: Club membership fees usually aren't deductible.

Fees to maintain or repair your business property. From fixing your laptop to painting your home office.

TRANSPORTATION: YOUR CAR

You can usually deduct expenses for business use of your car. As mentioned in Chapter 14, one of the methods below is normally used to track car expenses. Once you choose, you can't switch for that car. Make sure you check the IRS website or consult your accountant about how your method of depreciating your car affects how you can deduct car expenses. For leased cars, check the IRS website.

1 Standard mileage rate. Every year, the IRS establishes what it calls the "standard mileage rate": a certain amount per mile, based on an assessment of the costs of using a car, which you can use to calculate your business mileage for your car.

2 **Actual car expenses.** With this method, you deduct the business percentage of your actual annual car expenses (including fuel, maintenance, insurance, tolls, and parking fees, to name some).

Which method to use? One way to decide is to keep the records you'd need for both methods during the first year (see Chapter 14 for details). At year's end, do the math to figure which gives you the better deduction.

If your car doesn't need much fixing, actual car expenses might not be as beneficial as the standard mileage rate. For a junker needing lots of TLC in the shop, the actual method might give you a better deduction.

If you've already got enough receipts to keep track of, the standard mileage method doesn't require receipt keeping. For both methods, you do need to track your business miles, dates traveled, and the business purpose.

For more deductible local transportation expenses, read on.

LOCAL TRANSPORTATION

You can also deduct expenses for using other modes of transportation for local business, including mass transit, cabs, rail, even rental car (for travel away from home, see Travel).

While you can deduct transportation costs for going to and from business meetings and for traveling between meetings or workplaces, you can't deduct commuting costs. To find out more about how transportation deductions apply to your particular situation, check IRS Publication 463, *Travel, Entertainment, Gift, and Car Expenses* and consult your accountant.

As with everything else, keep your receipts and track your costs.

TRAVEL

If you travel for business—for example, staying overnight or being away from home significantly beyond a normal workday—you can deduct quite a few of your expenses if the trip's necessary for your work. Have clear, credible records of the when, where, and business reason for your trip. Deductible expenses include transportation, lodging, and usually 50 percent of the cost of (neither-lavish-nor-extravagant!) meals and entertainment—using either the actual costs (keep receipts and records) or the rates that the U.S. General Services Administration (GSA) provides for meals and incidental expenses in cities across the continental United States.

Combining vacation time with business travel? Great—but not on your taxes! It's the by-now-familiar deduction of the percentage applicable to business.

For more information on travel expenses, see IRS Publication 463, *Travel, Entertainment, Gift, and Car Expenses* and "Per Diem Rates" on the GSA Website (gsa.gov).

HEALTH INSURANCE

The health insurance industry is undergoing huge changes, but as of this writing, health insurance premiums are deductible for the self-employed who buy their own health coverage if their business showed a net profit for the year and if they weren't eligible to participate in an employer-subsidized health plan, including through their spouse (if they are in any given month, they can't take the deduction for that period). No can do? If you itemize deductions, look into whether some deduction is possible under medical expenses, elsewhere on your tax form.

There are limits on how much you can deduct for medical expenses. Keep good records of your health expenses and see if you're able to take some deduction. For specifics, check out IRS Publication 502, *Medical and Dental Expenses.*

People with high-deductible health plans may have another option: opening a Health Savings Account, or HSA, out of which they can pay many of their medical expenses tax-free. For details, see Chapter 17 and IRS Publication 969, *Health Savings Accounts and Other Tax-Favored Health Plans.*

TRAINING/EDUCATION

The cost of training or education can be deductible (and possibly travel relating to it), if you can show that it's needed to improve or maintain necessary skills for your business, or that it's mandated by law or other regulations to maintain your license or ability to practice. You can't deduct education costs for meeting your trade's minimum requirements or that make you eligible for a new trade.

If you can't deduct education as a business expense, see if you qualify for a tax credit for education (a tax credit cuts your tax bill, while a tax deduction reduces your taxable income). Talk to your accountant about your plans and check out IRS Publication 970, *Tax Benefits for Education.* For info on tax-advantaged ways to save for education, see Chapter 17.

LOANS

You can deduct credit card and loan interest for purely business-related items. So, suppose you used 60 percent of a loan for business and 40 percent for personal purposes, you can deduct 60 percent of the interest. If the credit card interest is for business and personal items, you can deduct just the interest on the cost of the business purchases.

ESTIMATED TAXES

Remember how we said taxes are a pay-as-you-go proposition? Estimated taxes (federal and state) are the government's way of making sure you pay as your money is made. Below is a summary of how

BARTER SMART

We talked about bartering in Chapter 11, so check there if you're interested in trying it. Even though money doesn't change hands, the value of what you received in a barter has, well, value. So the IRS says you to have to report and pay tax on it. Find out your state's bartering regulations, too, as sales tax and income tax may be due. In a rocky economy, the government's looking for extra dough, just like everyone else. And since assigning value to a barter deal is something of a judgment call, it's apt to attract the notice of our friends in the tax department.

The regulations for reporting bartering depend on the specifics involved. If you barter on any basis, make sure you understand and follow the tax requirements for bartering. Consult your accountant and refer to the IRS website for information. One place to start is its Bartering Tax Center; selected IRS Tax Resources are listed at the end of this chapter.

estimated taxes work. For a full explanation, see IRS Publication 505, *Tax Withholding and Estimated Tax.*

In general, if you anticipate owing one thousand dollars or more on your tax return after subtracting any withholding and refundable credits, you'll need to pay estimated taxes four times a year. Underpay and (no surprise) look for an "underpayment penalty" in the form of an interest charge.

One good thing about paying estimated taxes is that it forces you to budget for taxes by setting aside money from each client payment.

There are two main methods for calculating estimated taxes, over-simplified below:

1 You make quarterly payments of equal amounts, based at minimum on your tax liability of the year before. A minimum percentage gets added if your adjusted gross income for that year

exceeded a certain amount established by the IRS, and you should also revisit your calculations if it looks like your income will be a fair amount higher than the previous year. Depending on how your actual return comes out, you may owe additional tax (generally without penalty if you paid your estimated taxes on time and calculated them properly—see Publication 505 for full details), or you may be owed a refund.

2 You calculate your estimated tax every quarter by figuring your quarterly profit (nutshell: gross income minus deductions and other factors that would affect your net profit). Yes, you or your accountant have to do calculations each quarter, but this method can help you keep your estimated tax payments more aligned with your actual income: less in lean times, more in flush. It also lets you see exactly how your business is doing, which can help you make better Freelance Portfolio decisions.

FORGOT TO PAY YOUR ESTIMATED TAXES?

First, stop forgetting. Put the dates in your calendar: "I put a 'warning date' earlier in my calendar, so I can make sure the funds are in my account to make the payments." If you miss a date, send payment as soon as you discover you missed it. If you don't realize until you're about to make the next payment, add it to the check and the voucher you send.

Expect to pay interest on the late payment. Just to take the government's side here for a minute: If taxes are owed as income is earned, how fair is it to bank the IRS's share, earning interest on it while the IRS can't? And how fair would it be to require employees to pay taxes out of every paycheck via withholding, while you, freelancer, could retain your entire income until tax time? So: You pay estimated taxes, and interest for late payments.

TAX ISSUES WHEN SUBCONTRACTING OR HIRING

We've talked elsewhere about the problems of misclassifying workers. If you're going to engage subcontractors, hire employees, or both, understand the differences between them and be sure you're treating employees as employees and independent contractors as independent contractors; otherwise you may be held liable for employment taxes and penalties. Which is why your bedtime reading should include IRS Publication 15-A, *Employer's Supplemental Tax Guide* and you should have a frank talk with your accountant and attorney if you're considering bringing a few additional hands on deck as independent subcontractors, as employees, or you're not sure of the distinctions.

INDEPENDENT CONTRACTORS

If you engage independent contractors, you usually don't have to withhold or pay taxes on what you pay them, since as self-employed individuals, they have to do the kinds of tax stuff on their own that we've been talking about. Have them promptly fill out and send you Form W-9, Request for Taxpayer Identification Number and Certification (if they're a U.S. citizen or entity or resident alien; if not, check the IRS website and discuss with your accountant), which supplies essential info for your needs.

For each independent contractor to whom you paid a total of $600 or more during the tax year for business-related services, you must file Form 1099-MISC, Miscellaneous Income. You send the form to the contractor and to the IRS (along with Form 1096, Annual Summary and Transmittal of U.S. Information Returns, a top sheet of sorts to use when filing certain paper forms with the IRS—you can batch all the 1099-MISCs under one top sheet). Remember, the IRS likes to match things up—in this case your 1099-MISCs against the indies' reported income. For more information, see the IRS website: General Instructions for Certain Information Returns (Forms 1097, 1098, 1099, 3921, 3922, 5498, and W-2G).

All this, plus invoices from the contractor and proof of payment, will support your tax return claims about making these business payments.

EMPLOYEES

If you hire employees, you'll need to pay employment taxes, including Social Security and Medicare taxes (acronym FICA, as worker benefits received under the Federal Insurance Contributions Act) and Federal Unemployment Tax (acronym FUTA, as this tax comes under the Federal Unemployment Tax Act). You'll also pay SUTA, the state-side version of FUTA. Depending on your state, you might have to have workers' compensation and disability insurance or face tough penalties. And for your bedtime reading: IRS Publication 15 (Circular E), *Employer's Tax Guide*. Check your state tax department for local payroll regulations.

FICA taxes are paid by both you and the employee: You'll withhold an amount from their paychecks and pay a matching amount. Only you, the employer, pay FUTA tax, which is paid to workers if they lose their jobs.

You and each employee need to fill out Form I-9, Employment Eligibility Verification, verifying that the employee can legally work in the United States. Each employee also completes Form W-4, Employee's Withholding Allowance Certificate, which you'll use to calculate how much income tax to withhold.

After the end of the calendar year, you'll file and send employee copies of Form W-2, Wage and Tax Statement, detailing among other things their wages and other compensation for that year, and the tax amounts mentioned above. And, as with filing 1099s with the

SELECTED IRS TAX RESOURCES

Below are some of the many resources you can find on the IRS website (irs.gov). Check these out, surf the site, and keep an eye out for articles on taxes in publications you read. Wade in and get acclimated to tax logic and language. Look up terms you don't know online or ask your accountant when you meet. You'll feel great knowing you're getting a handle on this part of your freelance life. Just type the phrase or number of the publication into your browser.

A–Z Index for Business

Bartering Income

Bartering Tax Center

Child Care Tax Center

General Instructions for Certain Information Returns (Forms 1097, 1098, 1099, 3921, 3922, 5498, and W-2G)

How to Choose a Tax Return Preparer and Avoid Preparer Fraud

Instructions for the Requester of Form W-9

IRS Publication 15 (Circular E), *Employer's Tax Guide*

IRS Publication 15-A, *Employer's Supplemental Tax Guide*

IRS Publication 334, *Tax Guide for Small Business*

IRS Publication 463, *Travel, Entertainment, Gift, and Car Expenses*

IRS Publication 502, *Medical and Dental Expenses*

IRS Publication 503, *Child and Dependent Care Expenses*

IRS Publication 505, *Tax Withholding and Estimated Tax*

IRS Publication 509, *Tax Calendars*

IRS Publication 526, *Charitable Contributions*

IRS Publication 530, *Tax Information for Homeowners*

IRS Publication 535, *Business Expenses*	IRS Publication 970, *Tax Benefits for Education*
IRS Publication 538, *Accounting Periods and Methods*	Recordkeeping Tips for Barter Transactions
IRS Publication 583, *Starting a Business and Keeping Records*	Self-Employed Individuals Tax Center
IRS Publication 587, *Business Use of Your Home*	*Self-Employment Tax (Social Security and Medicare Taxes)*
IRS Publication 936, *Home Mortgage Interest Deduction*	Tax Topics—Topic 420 Bartering Income
IRS Publication 946, *How to Depreciate Property*	Is Your Hobby a For-Profit Endeavor?
IRS Publication 969, *Health Savings Accounts and Other Tax-Favored Health Plans*	

IRS, there's a top sheet you use to file the W-2s called Form W-3SS, Transmittal of Wage and Tax Statements.

Obviously, there are deadlines for all this paperwork and penalties for missing them, so if you're considering hiring, talk to your accountant about what you need to be doing. There are payroll services that can handle payroll paperwork.

Taxes are part of life in this country. Don't be fazed, crazed, or dazed by them. Instead, get to know them. Knowledge is power. Not only because mistakes and missed deadlines will cost you, but because missed opportunities will, too—such as not taking deductions you didn't know about or can't claim because you don't have the necessary documentation. So live and learn, work hard, keep good records, pay your taxes, and take your tax breaks wherever they're rightfully due.

PART 5:
YOUR BUSINESS AND YOUR COMMUNITY

Chapter 16

WORKING, PLAYING, AND STAYING ON TOP OF YOUR GAME

Freelancers should put themselves at the center of their world and the top of their to-do list. Makes sense, right? Without you, nothing happens. Nothing goes out or comes in. Meetings don't start. One freelancer recalls, "My dad took out a big loan to buy his father-in-law's business. He says my grandfather once asked how he could sleep with all the pressure. My dad answered, 'I sleep great. It's you and the bank who ought to be worried, in case something happens to me!' When I feel stressed by my work, I remember that."

Employees get vacation time, sick leave, family leave, bereavement days, and personal days. Those policies exist largely because workers advocated for them. Who advocates for you?

Contented people work harder and longer and have better work relationships. Why ignore something that would make you more successful?

THE INTENTIONAL FREELANCER

Freelancers don't have bosses and the nine-to-five workday to help them set boundaries and priorities. They have to decide what's important day by day, hour by hour.

Sometimes they do it with ambivalence:

"Now and then, my husband will propose we go out to breakfast or lunch. And because I love hanging out with him, it's hard to say no. When I do, I feel guilty, or like someone who was more committed to success wouldn't be doing what I'm doing."

Sometimes they get a wake-up call:

"I ran into a freelancer I know on the street one evening. I hadn't been out all day and was glassy-eyed. He was coming home from a meeting to do more work. He said, 'I thought I was burned out in my company job. Did I even know what burnout was? I'm working harder, earning less—and buying all my own benefits!' We were both laughing—but not because we thought it was funny. We were just kind of hysterical."

And some people have the right perspective:

"I feel that since I live this lifestyle, I have to take advantage of it. I might go to the museum in the afternoon, or to the movies. I know I'm much more productive if I do or see something that's beautiful, makes me happy, and takes me somewhere I haven't been."

By the end of this chapter, I hope you'll know what you intend your work/life policies to be. So when it's tempting to skip breakfast, the gym, sleep, a snuggle with your love, or your kid's plea for "just one more story," you can shrug and say, "Boss's orders." Or "Workers' rights." And then do it, no regrets.

First, let's look at where you are right now.

THE LIFE-QUALITY QUIZ

Knowing yourself is the first step to finding the right work/life fit. Answer each question below by putting a check mark in the column with the response that most closely matches your thoughts or feelings.

	STRONGLY AGREE	SOMEWHAT AGREE	SOMEWHAT DISAGREE	STRONGLY DISAGREE
1: I have enough quality time with my family.				
2: I have enough quality time with my friends.				
3: I have enough quality time just for me.				
4: I have time to learn and do new things outside of work.				
5: I eat healthfully.				
6: I exercise regularly.				
7: My family and I get the medical care we need.				
8: I feel OK with the amount of stress I feel.				
9: I'm happy with the kind of work I do as a freelancer.				

	STRONGLY AGREE	SOMEWHAT AGREE	SOMEWHAT DISAGREE	STRONGLY DISAGREE
10: I'm happy with the kind of clients I have as a freelancer.				
11: I'm happy with the amount of time I spend working.				
12: I'm happy with my day-to-day life as a freelancer.				
13: I have enough money for the things I need (food, shelter, medical care).				
14: I have enough money for the things I want (vacations, going out, clothes, et cetera).				
15: I have or I'm saving money for things that will improve my life or my loved ones' lives in the future (child care, education, retirement, et cetera).				
16: I'm satisfied with how I'm living on my freelance income.				
17: I know what I am and am not willing to give up to live on a freelance income.				
18: I'm not bothered by how others view me as a freelancer.				
19: I'm satisfied with my use of energy, fuel, water, space, and other resources.				
20: I'm satisfied with what I'm doing to help others.				

Scoring

Give the following point values to each answer:

Strongly agree: 4 points

Somewhat agree: 3 points

Somewhat disagree: 2 points

Strongly disagree: 1 point

Add your scores for questions 1–4: _____

Your answers to these questions show your current feelings about Your Personal Life.

Add your scores for questions 5–8: _____

Your answers to these questions show your current feelings about Your Body and Mind.

Add your scores for questions 9–12: _____

Your answers to these questions show your current feelings about Your Work Life.

Add your scores for questions 13–16: _____

Your answers to these questions show your current feelings about Your Financial Life.

Add your scores for questions 17–20: _____

Your answers to these questions show your current feelings about Living in the World.

What Your Scores Mean

If you scored 13–16 points in a category: You feel mostly pretty good about how things are going. Congrats! Keep going!

If you scored 9–12 points in a category: Your satisfaction level might be uneven or so-so across the board. Focus on ratcheting up your satisfaction in lower-scoring areas.

If you scored 5–8 points in a category: Some key issues are causing you concern. Take a step back; review relevant chapters in this book; and talk to friends, family, and your Brain Trust about ways to make changes.

If you scored 4 points in a category: You're likely pretty aware of stressors in your freelance life. Focus on solutions. Read up on the topics

where you want to score higher (financial planning? marketing? health?). Ask for advice. You might find others are having trouble and you can help each other.

HOW TO AVOID OVERWORKING 24/7

Freelancing gives you the freedom to do your life and work your way. But, paradoxically, work isn't always in our control. A project explodes or implodes. A diva client lays waste to your schedule. After a dry spell, it starts raining gigs.

Freelancers with young children often have to work around childcare schedules: "On the days my daughter is home with me, I don't keep regular office hours and can't always turn things around quickly. I compensate by working all hours of the night and constantly checking my smartphone."

Freelancers without kids have different problems but with a similar feel: "Lately I've been realizing I have no balance at all. I *am* my work. If someone asks how I am, I answer based on how my work's going. I think it's mostly because I don't have kids and I work at home—so there's little besides work to think about and little separation (literally!) between home life and work life."

TOP TEN DRUDGE-BUSTERS

Try these ten ways to defeat drudgism.

1: Know Your "Most Productive Day."
"At first I worked all the time, everywhere. Eventually, I realized that was anathema to my cellular structure. I've learned I'm quick and can cover more ground in fewer hours. Now, I wake up and work in bed—my favorite spot—for a few hours. I stop at six at night or so. I don't work after that." (See Chapter 13 for more on productivity.)

2: Have an Availability Policy.

"I don't answer unexpected phone calls when I'm working. Clients sometimes resent that, but you have to ask yourself: Is complete accessibility good for you, your family, and your lifestyle? It's a huge question, especially since we all can be reached 24/7." For tips on developing your policy and sharing it with clients, see Chapter 6.

Then stick to it. "Early in my career, I was practicing martial arts and went away to karate camp for a week. There were only answering machines and services back then, so I left a basic 'away' message. One of my clients got furious that I couldn't be reached and hired someone else for the next project. I had to ask myself if I wanted to work with a client who had that attitude."

Clients who don't like your schedule will get winnowed out over time. It's part of being an intentional freelancer.

> "When do I take time off? Christmas Eve, Christmas. I think that's it. Some years, I work those days, too."

3: Make 'Em Wait.

Being unavailable can make people more determined to work with you (the scarcity draw we talked about in Chapter 4). "I heard about a super-busy freelancer who'd say, politely but firmly, 'I can start your project in X months.' And the best doctors are booked months ahead. I tried it. It's surprising how often people are willing to wait, or we find some small part of the project I can start."

Of course, being able to do this depends on a) the norms in your business, b) being so excellent that clients will wait, and c) having enough financial cushion to afford starting projects on your schedule, not theirs.

4: Forget Faux Free Time.

A short time away—if you're really *away*—can refresh you more than time when you're supposedly "off" but keep checking messages or doing chores. "I almost never take a day where I do neither business work nor housework. Recently, though, I've been having an experience of time passing way too quickly. A friend suggested it might be because we never take a day to do just nothing, relax, and rejuvenate. I've been pondering trying to do that more often." Another freelancer knocks off early on Fridays: "I try to take off Friday afternoons for exercise, meeting friends, or going to the movies."

5: Ease Off the Gas.

Like extra pounds, overwork creeps on gradually. We sneak in message checks here, a half-hour of work there. Stopping short can be hard on your brakes. Try stepping back in the same gradual way you sped up. Ask yourself: "Do I really need to do this now?" Wean yourself off checking your messages. Ratchet back the end of your workday half an hour at a time.

6: Schedule Free Time Blocks.

"I'd sneak work and chores into free time: 'I'll take my laptop to the park!' or 'I'll get exercise by running errands!' Now on Saturdays, my husband cooks us a special breakfast, I work or do chores until three p.m. Then I do a full stop: I leave the house. I get out and do anything but work or chores. Just thinking about that time during the week gives me a mini mental vacation."

7: Subcontract.

Sharing work evens out everyone's workload. These can be some of the best relationships you've ever had. "One thing I love about freelancing is all the wonderful people you meet along the way. I hired an amazing professional copywriter to help me with my copywriting challenges. I would have never had an opportunity to work with him if I hadn't started my own business." It starts with intentional networking.

- Mentor newbies for smaller tasks until they can step up to do more.
- Network with peers for shared projects.
- Network across skill groups to assemble teams for big projects to grow your business.

Before you subcontract or organize a team, make sure you'll get enough income for yourself, not a small fraction of what's usual for you. For information on subcontracting, see Chapters 11 and 15.

8: Little by Little, Build a Financial Cushion.

Working from a place of greater financial security is a powerful drudge-buster: you aren't forced to overbook yourself and pursue every gig, no matter how bad or poorly paid. For tips on taking steps to get there, see Chapter 17.

9: Don't Be Penny-Wise, Pound-Foolish.

Budget for the things that will help you work efficiently: "I sometimes try to save money by not hiring a babysitter when I really should. I need to be better about creating sane blocks of time for work, not stuffing it into spare moments or into hours that should be spent sleeping."

10: Advocate for Unemployment Protection for Independent Workers.

Employees who lose their jobs have unemployment insurance funded by employers to help them meet expenses until they find another job. Freelancers Union is advocating for a fund that would let freelancers contribute pretax dollars to draw on in dry times—lowering their tax burden while weaving a sorely-needed safety net.

QUIZ: THE GOOD-MEDIUM-BAD DAY

In Chapter 13, you filled out a What's Your Ideal Day? chart to compare your ideal day to "what really happens." Here we'll take a deeper dive into "what really happens" to find where your work/life balance goes off-track. Again, there are no right or wrong answers—this is totally for your information. The more detailed you can be, the more insights you'll get, so write them down.

Fill out the chart below explaining what constitutes an "ideal" day, a "good" day, a "medium" day, or a "bad" day.

	GOOD DAY	MEDIUM DAY	BAD DAY
What time do you get up?			
What's your morning prework routine?			
What time do you sit down to work?			
How long do you generally work in one sitting?			
Describe your morning work time.			
When do you usually make calls and answer emails?			
When do you take breaks, and what do you do?			
What's your lunch routine?			
What percentage of time in a typical workday do you devote to: project work, marketing, and administrative work?			
When do you run errands (work or personal)?			
Describe how and when you socialize (with other freelancers, family, friends)—in person or via phone/email.			
When do you have meetings?			
Describe your afternoon work time.			
When do you exercise, and what do you do?			
What happens at dinnertime?			
Describe your evening routine, including work.			
When do you go to bed?			
How do you feel about the day?			

Here's how one freelancer completed her chart:

	GOOD DAY	MEDIUM DAY	BAD DAY
What time do you get up?	7:00 a.m.	8:30 a.m.	9:30 a.m.
What's your morning prework routine?	Healthy breakfast. Shower. Dress. Meditate or stretch 15 minutes before starting work	Breakfast, shower, and dress in sweats. May skip prework meditation or stretch.	Sluggish from late-night work. Carb- and coffee-heavy breakfast. Feel sleepy/jittery. Guilty about late start, so sit down at desk in bathrobe "just to check email."
What time do you sit down to work?	9:30 a.m.	10:00 a.m.	10:45 a.m.
How long do you generally work in one sitting?	Work in 60-minute stretches, setting timer.	Try to keep eye on computer clock and break every hour.	Sit at desk without getting up for hours.
Describe your morning work time.	Project work	Project work, but distracted by administrative tasks and email.	Fitful work, interrupted by email checking, online games, and nonwork social media..
When do you usually make calls and answer emails?	During breaks (about 15 minutes each hour).	Often interrupt tasks to check emails or take/make calls.	Emails and calls all day, interrupting project work time.
When do you take breaks, and what do you do?	Every hour. Check email/make calls or do a home chore or stretch.	Often ignore the hour-break rule, since I feel guilty about frequent interruptions.	No formal breaks, but sit at computer procrastinating with computer games and social media.
What's your lunch routine?	Get off computer. Eat lunch and watch TV or read for pleasure.	Eat at my desk while trying to work on project. OR have lunch date.	Skip lunch, snacking at my desk.
What percentage of time in a typical workday do you devote to: project work, marketing, and administrative work?	60% really focused and productive project work, 30% marketing (including business meals), 10% admin.	90% project work—too much, but I make good headway. 5% marketing, 5% admin to just keep up.	100% project, but little headway. OR 75% administration (left things undone too long), 25% project work and stressed about it.

	GOOD DAY	MEDIUM DAY	BAD DAY
When do you run errands (work or personal)?	Around 3 p.m. go out for an hour to walk, run errands.	Get immersed in work. Run out early evening for quick errands. No time to exercise.	Postpone errands until urgent. OR rush out before stores close.
Describe how and when you socialize (with other freelancers, family, friends)—in person or via phone/email.	Love to network or meet friends for breakfast or coffee	Overlong lunch dates or afternoon meetings that cut into work time.	Cancel dates. Call no one; see no one.
When do you have meetings?	Morning if possible.	Lunch or afternoon meetings.	Prospecting totally off the radar.
Describe your afternoon work time.	Same as morning	Same as morning, but a bit fidgety.	Same as morning, but finally take shower and dress at 4 p.m. to rush through errands.
When do you exercise, and what do you do?	Stretch breaks throughout day. Walk for an hour and/or to exercise class.	Skip stretching, but get to exercise class.	Errands are my exercise. Upset about missing exercise class.
What happens at dinnertime?	Listen to news while making dinner. Eat with husband, watch TV, talk about the day.	Husband works late. Eat dinner alone while watching TV or a movie.	Make and eat a nice dinner, but feel guilty about not enough progress on work and no exercise.
Describe your evening routine, including work.	Exercise class, reading, or watching a movie. Sometimes work	Exercise class followed by work.	Work until bedtime.
When do you go to bed?	11:30 p.m.	12:30 a.m.	1:00–2:00 a.m.
How do you feel about the day?	Creative, in control, energized, happy.	Tired but glad I pushed it if I reached a goal or did good work that day.	Guilty and defeated.

Look at your chart and ask yourself:

1 Where do things start going off-track to turn a good day into a medium or bad day?

2 Are there specific events or behaviors that trigger it?

3 What's one thing I could change in my day that would make a noticeable improvement?

Try changing that one thing and see what happens. Then pick something else and make another little change.

Here's what the freelancer who filled in the sample chart said: "I see that the biggest thing that gets me off-track is how late I stay up. I really need sleep, so if I go to bed late, I sleep late and spend the day racing to catch up. I do marathon work sessions instead of pacing myself. I cancel appointments and skip exercise. Then I stay up late trying to fix everything, and the whole cycle starts again. Just going to bed earlier would make a huge difference in how I feel and work."

SICK DAYS

Employees get paid for sick days and maternity leave. Nobody pays you unless you deliver—and we don't mean the baby. But you could budget so you can afford to take sick days, or some weeks off when the new baby arrives. See Chapter 17 for ideas on budgeting yourself through income ups and downs.

Your subcontracting team can step in, too. You still need to guarantee the quality and oversee the final results. Having a great reputation, doing client Love Banking, and having Blue Chip clients increase your chances of having the kind of client relationships where you can be upfront about what's happening and work out a plan.

If your problems are creating real headaches for them, see what you can do to lighten their load, maybe reducing your price this time, eating rush costs, or squeezing your margins to subcontract it out.

If you're too sick to even monitor subcontractors and the deadline can't be moved, the best save for all might be to negotiate a kill fee and help them find another indie to finish the job.

Take care of your health and if you need medical care, don't delay getting it. Getting affordable health insurance is a major challenge for freelancers. But letting a health issue worsen only gets more expensive.

If you get sick and the opportunity to knock off completely is there, take it. "I was sick recently and since it was a Saturday, I watched TV and did crossword puzzles all day. It was heaven."

BEREAVEMENT HAPPENS TO FREELANCERS, TOO

If someone you love dies (pets, too) your emotions might affect your work. "When my mom died, I kept working. But I felt mentally fogged, was less decisive, and had no patience. I should've taken time off."

Freelancing's flexibility can really help at times like this. Need more sleep? Take it. Want to be with your spiritual community? Do it. Need to empty a house or handle estate matters? Go mobile.

VACATIONS: CAN YOU "TURN IT OFF" AND GO? (CAN YOU AFFORD TO?)

"I take sick days. But I can't honestly say I've ever had a day completely without work."

"Because you can freelance almost anywhere, it gives your life amazing flexibility," Doug says. Which leads to the dark question: If you can work almost anywhere, what's stopping you?

Why is turning it off a struggle for many freelancers? Because "you believe the one time you're away will be when the call comes for a big job!" (and sometimes that actually happens). Because freelancers typically can't afford to let the phone go unanswered. Because with more and more freelancers out there, you're afraid you'll lose ground.

Oh, please.

FIFTEEN WAYS TO TAKE VACATIONS

1: Decide You're Going and Budget for It.
So, another year has passed and you didn't see the Great Wall of China, hike that fourteener, try out that sweet B & B in Maine, or take your kids to visit Uncle Ted's farm before he puts it on the market. Time *will* run out. What will you have done besides work? See Chapter 17 for ways to set aside money for things you want.

2: Don't Succumb to Freelance Superstition.
("When I Leave, the 'Big Call' Will Come.")
That's the lottery ticket approach. If you're prospecting, marketing, and networking, big gigs will come because you've put the odds on your side.

> "I worked from the hospital after my baby was born."

3: Get Off the Gig-Go-Round.
You can't turn off and go if you can't afford to. That means working your Freelance Portfolio, knowing your market value, making sure your skills are worth the price, Love Banking with other freelancers who can refer you for good gigs—and making lifestyle changes so your living costs don't force you to drag projects along over well-deserved holidays.

4: Set a Vacation Policy.

- How often will you take vacations?

- How long will they be? "I take one week in the summer when I put an 'away' message on my email and don't check in."

- Are there slow times in your industry when you can take breaks?

- Will you work at certain times during vacation? Says one freelancer, "I never take work on vacation." Says another: "I often take work on vacation. I put in a couple of hours before anyone's up. Sometimes in the afternoon, my family goes off to do something I'm not that into, and I work another hour or so. Once everyone's in bed, I do another couple of hours. I can pack about six hours of work into a vacation day and still have plenty of downtime."

• Will you check emails and messages? If so, how often? "I might check email or voicemail a couple of times a week, but that's all."

• Will there be times when you don't check emails and messages? If so, when?

5: Block It Out.

Put big X's, colored blocks, or write VACATION in your calendar. Otherwise you might inadvertently make a project commitment and then have to renegotiate, work over vacation, or rush to finish early. No good.

6: Schedule a Staycation.

If travel's not an option, kick back at home. Sleep in, take yourself out for breakfast, catch up on movies, hit the museums, double up your workouts, enroll in a class, or tackle a home project that would make you feel incredibly good to get done.

7: Tack Vacation onto Business Travel.

Add downtime to a business trip, even if it's just taking the scenic route home, stopping to take pictures and eat at a great roadside diner. Just be sure you deduct only your for-real business expenses on your taxes (see Chapter 15).

8: Decide Who Needs to Know You're Going.

This might include your Blue Chips, anyone whose project you're in the middle of (better yet, build it into the schedule from the start: "FYI, I'll be away the week of the fifteenth, but that won't affect delivery"), and anyone you might be in serious discussions with about a future project. Let them know if you'll be reachable while you're gone.

9: Set Up Your "Away" Messages So People Know What to Expect.

Will you check messages daily or every few days? Will you have limited access to voicemail and email? "I was at a campsite where the only cell phone signal was atop a cliff. There'd be people pacing around up there at night, cellphones clamped to ears!" Are you totally unreachable (as in: on a raft, floating down the Amazon)?

Craft your "away" messages to give yourself wiggle room, since you can't totally predict your accessibility, or in case you change your mind: "I often say I have limited access to messages so I can choose whether I want to reply or totally unplug."

> "The handheld has unfortunately changed my vacations. I try to keep it turned off most of the time, but it's a struggle."

10: Book It.

It commits you to the trip, and booking early might get you better rates. But watch out: There may be hefty fees for changes or cancellations, or rules prohibiting them.

11: Go Where They Can't Find You.

Going where there's no cell phone signal, no electricity much less Wi-Fi, and where you're watching the clouds, not uploading to them, takes the entire dilemma out of your hands.

12: Let Technology Help.

The flip side of "Go Where They Can't Find You." Use an online file-sharing service to send or receive files from the road. Stay at hotels with free Wi-Fi. Talk to other freelancers who travel a lot; find out how they plan the tech side of their trips.

13: Don't Trust Technology.

Flip side of "Let Technology Help." Don't expect airport wireless to work, don't expect to find an outlet when you need one, and don't expect reliable Wi-Fi at the hotel or other places that advertise it. Carry a flash drive (secured by password or encryption if needed) that backs up your laptop. Cloud backup is good insurance, too. Speaking of insurance, find out if yours covers theft or damage of your tech equipment during travel. Get good antivirus protection on your computer, and don't trust the security of public equipment.

14: Give Travelmates a Heads-Up.
If you're with other people, make sure they know you'll need to work for specific periods of time. It's part of running your own show.

15: Set Up a Smooth Reentry.
You need time to unpack, wash off the beach sand, make it up to the cat, open the mail, restock the fridge, and—most important—edit your vacation photos: "I set my 'back in the office' date one day after my actual return." Feel like revving up sooner? Your client will be happily surprised to hear: "I'm back early and spent the afternoon working on your project. I'll send some sketches in a couple of days."

THE DAY MY DAUGHTER DIDN'T CRY: PARTNERING, PARENTING, AND ELDER-CARE RESPONSIBILITIES

When Freelancers Union was getting started, I remember being at home on a conference call arguing for a huge grant while my infant daughter played nearby, and just praying she wouldn't cry.

There's been much debate about work/life balance, especially for working parents. Many of us also help our aging parents: "My father's health is fragile. I take him to the doctor and sometimes the hospital, pick up his meds, spend time with him each week, and handle all his finances—a job in itself."

Then there's all the other stuff you have to do to keep modern life going, which can sound like this:

"Cereal for dinner's getting kind of old."

"What do you mean, the cable guy will get here '*sometime* between eight a.m. and eight p.m.'?"

"Omigod. Today is our anniversary."

"How could we already be out of toilet paper?"

Everyone struggles with work/life balance to some degree. But the equation's different for freelancers than for traditional employees.

For traditional employees:

---

geographic distance + inflexible schedules = work/life balance challenges

---

For freelancers, it's the opposite:

---

geographic proximity + flexible schedules = work/life balance challenges

---

Geographic proximity is obviously toughest for home-based free- lancers: "One of the hardest things about working from home is too much intermingling of the business with the personal."

And because freelancers have flexible schedules, it's sometimes assumed they'll run the household if their mate's traditionally employed or has a less-flexible schedule: "My wife's teaching and get- ting her master's degree, so her schedule is nuts. Because I'm home, it makes sense for me to do the housework. I'm mostly OK with it, but three years is a long time. It's hardest when I'm just getting rolling on work and have to stop to deal with a repairperson, run errands, take the dog to the vet, or whatever."

Freelancers with young kids may feel major push-pull between parenting and work: "My kids are in day care two days a week, so those are 'work days' for me. I drop them off, run errands, and head home to get to work by ten, checking email as infrequently as possible. I race out at four forty-five to pick them up. Family time lasts until eight; then I work after bedtime, trying to be in bed by one a.m. On days when my youngest is home, I can work for an hour or two during her nap, but my main work hours are after bedtime. Honestly, I have trouble balancing things. Either I'm focused on my family and home or I'm focused on work (and a little too reliant on TV-as-babysitter)."

For some freelancers, proximity can increase their guilt about not putting in enough family time: "When I had children, I continued to work and hired a sitter, even though I was always home. But if it's hard for many adults to understand that a freelancer working at home is actually *working*, how can children be expected to understand that they 'can't bother Mama' when she's sitting a few feet away? There we were: me on the telephone with clients, my child banging on the door, crying, because he wanted to give me a flower, and the sitter crouched outside, trying to hold him back and secretly wondering, I'm sure, how I could be such a cruel parent."

The stress can get pretty severe: "It's almost impossible to work on anything when the kids are home from school. I still haven't come to a place of comfort where doing housework because it needs to get done instead of doing my work feels OK. I get snarky. I want to know just how many hours I'm supposed to put in daily, but there's no union to negotiate for me."

Even with older kids, there's more of everything: "Now that the kids are in school full time, I have more time for work. I'd like to say I'm back to my old schedule of turning off the phone and shutting out the world, but those days are gone."

MAKING TIME FOR FRIENDS, COMMUNITY, AND ADVOCACY

Mark says: "It's a lot of work to get gigs, but my friends assume I have more free time than they do."

Heather's friends were bolder: "Many of my friends, none of whom worked at home, thought nothing of calling 'to chat' or even dropping by. This was a big problem as I was always on deadline. No matter how often I explained that I couldn't hang out, some people refused to get the message. I'd promise to call when my work was finished for the day, but the damage was done: I was accused of being antisocial, when in truth I was constantly stressed-out trying to keep up with the demands of my projects."

Another adds: "I screen my calls, but it just leaves the ball in my court to call back. I haven't really saved time as much as delayed spending it."

And it's not just friends wanting to chat or hang out. There's all sorts of stuff people think freelancers have time to do: pet-sit, sign for packages, help at the school, run the youth group, coach the team, and on and on.

"People with staff jobs can say, 'I can't do that because I have to work,'" Gina says. "But because freelancers supposedly have more control over their schedules, if they say they 'have' to work, it's viewed more that they 'choose' to work. Which must mean they're putting their priorities ahead of others'. Which must mean they're being selfish." Yet freelancers need their friends: "Truth be told, I'd much rather talk on the phone with my friends than do my work!" They need community with one another, with friends and family, and in organizations of all kinds. We all do, but freelancing can be very lonely without it.

The answer to these work/life-balance questions depends on the situation, who's involved, and your work. Here are some strategic mindsets.

THE FIVE FREELANCE LIFE LAWS

FREELANCE LIFE LAW 1: WORK IS NOT A CHOICE FOR MOST FREELANCERS

When you have to work, *you have to work*. No apologies, no excuses. It's OK to choose to work instead of waiting for the cable guy (or the neighbor's cable guy). Repeat this to yourself until you start believing it. Repeat it to others until they start listening.

FREELANCE LIFE LAW 2: EARNING LESS THAN YOUR MATE DOESN'T MEAN YOU GET STUCK WITH ALL THE GRUNT WORK (UNLESS THAT'S YOUR AGREEMENT)

An agreement being (as you know from Chapter 5) an arrangement as fair as possible for all the parties. And what's fair is a very personal thing. Also, assumptions are not agreements. If you haven't discussed it, it's not an agreement. You might be surprised at the workable solutions that come from a simple conversation.

FREELANCE LIFE LAW 3: BLEND, NOT BOUNDARIES

Work and life have been merging for years. So, let 'em. Because technology finally supports it. Because work today demands it. Because earning a living now often requires it. And because you, freelancer, *can*.

Unlike millions of traditional employees, you *can* work while you wait for the cable guy. You *can* be in and out of the gym before the nine-to-five crew descends at six p.m. You *can* stake out picnic-blanket turf early for the concert in the park and happily work on your laptop and cell phone until your cube-controlled friends arrive. You *can* walk the kids to school, say hi to the teacher, stop for a latte, then hit your desk: "I wake up early with the baby, then doze with him before my daughter wakes up. We eat breakfast together and play until it's time to go to day care. I feel so happy that I can give my children time in the morning, compared to the days I used to scramble for a suitable work outfit, throw lunch together for my daughter, hurry her out the door to day care—and still be late to the office!"

Being in control of their time is a huge reason people love freelancing despite the rocky income: "Being able to create my own schedule has made an enormous difference not only in my work life but in my family life as well. Now that my kids are getting older, I'm even more grateful that as a freelancer I could be more available to my children when they were younger."

FREELANCE LIFE LAW 4: IT STARTS WITH YOU

Believe in your deepest self that your career's worth taking seriously. It's like negotiating price with clients: Waffle too much and they'll question your value. It may mean having some reality check conversations about what you need. Freelancing has a natural elasticity that can help, too.

Make Home/Family Responsibilities Fit Your Schedule, Not Vice Versa.

"I incorporate chores and errands into work breaks so I get them done bit by bit, get some exercise, and can relax later."

Control the Input.

"I have two phone lines: an unlisted 'home' line for family and close friends, and a 'business line' for everyone else. I have a ninety-year-old mother who lives at home with caregivers and two grown sons with children, so if the home line rings, I usually answer. I'm more discriminating with the business line. Caller ID is a godsend. If it's not urgent or I don't recognize the number, I'll let it ring into my voicemail and answer or email at my convenience." Other freelancers I know flip it: They screen personal calls and pick up business ones.

Build In Small Efficiencies.

We talked in Chapter 13 about ways to boost work efficiency. Do it for personal stuff, too. It could be getting your groceries delivered, paying bills online, scheduling and grouping appointments into particular days, starting a carpool or babysitting co-op.

Small efficiencies add up, opening your time, easing your mind, freeing you from the busywork of life so you can engage in the important work of living: comforting a friend ... tending a child ... untangling a parent's finances . . . helping at the fund-raiser . . . training for and completing your first 10K ... fixing up a room to rent out ... planning a surprise party for your mate or best friend.

Expect Things of Others.

One freelancer says: "When I worked in the corporate world, my marriage went down the tubes—I spent all my time at work. It was important to me to have a life when I worked on my own." Marriages do better when there's an agreed-upon division of labor and R & R time built in. "My husband and I go to the gym together in the morning." "My boyfriend's the 'breakfast king'—he gets coffee going, showers, and dresses so the bathroom is free for me when I get up. He'll make an omelette from yesterday's leftovers or start pancake batter, feed the cat, and let me sleep an extra forty-five minutes. I do the menu planning, food shopping, and dinner, and he washes up."

Kids can have responsibilities when they're ready: "My kids are ten and twelve. When they get home from school, they're expected to do their own thing until my work time ends. I think it sets an example of a work ethic. And the kids have a chance to manage their own time."

Look for some reciprocity. Example: Your neighbor asks you to take care of her dog while she's on vacation (or water her plants or whatever). When you take yours, ask her to return the favor. Is she too busy, or does she grudgingly agree, or mess it up somehow? You will, in the future, be "sorry, just too busy" to help her out.

Write a New Job Description.

Company workers can't. You can: "When my kids were young, I shifted to a kind of writing work that didn't require such rigid hours."

Rethink Your Freelancing Goals.

If the push-pull between work and family is a continual stressor and your strategies for managing it just aren't working, maybe it's time to revisit your freelance goals. Can you afford to be a part-time freelancer so you'd have more time for family? How might you economize so you could work less? Can you save money to hire household help? Are you charging enough for your services, so you could conceivably work less but earn more? Can you develop a specialty or passive income streams to help increase your income?

Live It Like You Mean It.

Others will take their cue from you.

- If you're a new grad starting to freelance, do you talk about it in ways that say this is your chosen career path?

- If you're freelancing while you job-hunt, have you made it clear that your freelance work and your job hunt *are* your jobs?

- If you're transitioning into full-time freelancing, do others realize this isn't an in-between thing until you find a company job?

• Keep a schedule (no one needs to know if you change it a lot). Slip it into conversations "... so after work I went to the box office and got tickets." "I finish work at six—I'll give you a call then." "Let's meet after work."

• Look the part. I'm not saying you should sit at your desk in a jacket or heels, but just be aware that people make judgments based on appearance.

When you say no, be polite but don't make excuses: "Unfortunately, I'm busy." Or use an "I can" statement (see Chapter 6): "Sure, I can take care of your dog while you're away, if I can do it before nine a.m. and after five p.m. No? Ah, well, I'm sorry I won't be able to help." Or offer to do something that adds to your work chops: "I won't be able to help at the silent auction, but I could design the poster."

FREELANCE LIFE LAW 5: BE MINDFUL

Think before you commit your precious time, care, skills, and resources. That goes for the gigs you take, the friends you hang with, the money you spend, the causes you join: "My husband and I both do volunteer work. We feel it's very important to do that. He plays guitar and sings for hospital patients, and I teach knitting there one afternoon a week. It gets your mind off yourself, and you realize there's always someone who's worse off than you are."

When you willingly give your best, your all, your awesomeness, everything you touch will shine. And so will you.

NETWORKING WITH FAMILY AND FRIENDS

Family and friends are your biggest fans. They'll brag about you, attend your events and bring their friends, sample your test recipes, hang shelves in your office, watch your kids while you work, and love you enough to tell you that your latest brilliant business idea is in need of adjustment. Don't be afraid to seek help, advice, and work there.

But they're also your family and friends, so know when to knock it off:

TACKY	TACTFUL
Blowing off events or pulling an "eat and run" if there aren't good business contacts there.	At family/friends' events, ask your host if they'd mind introducing you to a couple of people they think might have work interests in common with yours.
Handing out your card with your handshake at a social event.	Circulate and get to know people, and sometime during the event say to several, "I've really enjoyed talking with you. Do you have a card?" [And offer yours].
Using your kid's school friends to get to their influential parents.	Get to know other parents by inviting them to your kid's birthday parties and other events and meeting them through school events.
Joining school and parent groups just to network, without pulling your weight.	Meet people and network by getting involved in your child's school.
Calling only when you need something.	Check in to say hi, how's it going, what's happening, how can I help?

DOING WORK FOR FAMILY AND FRIENDS

Know your policy before you're asked, so if it's a no, you can have an "it's not you, it's me" decline on tap: "It's hard for me to be objective when I work for family and friends—but here are a couple of people I think would do a great job for you."

If you do work for (or with) family and friends, the next question is what (or whether) to charge. Have that conversation before you commit. "I recently did some work for my mom's company and was just waiting for them to request an invoice so I could nobly offer to donate my priceless contribution for the good of the family. They never even brought it up!"

Assume word will get around about your rates, so decide how you'll price family/friends projects: same as any? One-time Love Bank discount followed by usual price? Always a special discount? Maybe swap services (see bartering guidelines in Chapters 11 and 15). Or request something of value for your business: a thanks from the podium; a spot to display your business cards or brochure. Remember people who've never freelanced may not get that you're losing real income for your donated time and skill. Wrap a reminder in a polite suggestion: "I'd love to do that for you and I'm happy to do it free of charge, but would it be possible to . . ."

LOOKING AND FEELING THE PART

As your own boss, how well do you treat yourself? When you can take your lunch break anytime, do you take it at all? When you can work out anytime, do you ever? How do you dress when there's no dress code? Would dozing off at your desk at two a.m. be considered sleeping on the job? And how do you have those all-important water-cooler conversations without a water cooler?

EATING, BREAKS, AND EXERCISE

Freelancing gives you flexibility to do whatever you need to be at your best. Don't miss out on this coolest of perks.

- **Figure out your food/energy balance.** I believe each of us knows, deep down, how to eat to keep our mental and physical energy strong. We know when we feel good and when we don't, and how our eating patterns on a given day contributed to how well we felt and performed. What works for you may not work for the freelancer next door. Experiment. Also make sure you drink enough water—keep a glass by your desk to sip from. All that drinking will then require leaving your post from time to time—which gives your body and brain a break.

> "I sometimes do free work for friends. But it's hard to know where to draw the line."

- **Figure out your work/exercise ratio.** What'll help you stick with exercise? Is it one big workout, or several minis? Is it before work, as a break, or at day's end? Is it solo, with a buddy, or in a group? You have the freedom to mix it up to fit your schedule: midday gym when the machines are available; weights at home on project-heavy days; basketball with friends on weekends.

One freelancer discovered: "Exercise used to feel like something I had to do and I felt guilty if I didn't. In my networking group, someone said she considered exercise time her 'me' time and guarded it jealously. I've latched onto that—that exercise is time for me and worth guarding. Sometimes I still feel guilty if I don't exercise, but now exercise feels a lot more like something I do for myself to help provide that balance between work and home."

Other freelancers feel guilty if they *do* take time out to work out—wouldn't they be more productive if they kept working? That's a mental trap freelancers need to get out of: "Sometimes I have to force myself to stop working and go to the gym. To do it, I remind myself of all the times I've had an epiphany about what to do about a work problem, either en route or after I've finished my workout and feel relaxed and pleasantly tired. Sometimes it's just a tiny passing thought: 'Maybe I could . . .' Or: 'Call . . .' Often it's the thread I can grab onto that starts to untangle the problem. I need to learn to trust that process and let myself have that time."

PERSONAL APPEARANCE

Maeve recalls: "In the market one night, I was surprised to run into an executive recruiter I know who's very connected in my business. I was on deadline and a mess—just running out to buy food for dinner, wearing these faded, frayed, floppy, super-comfy overalls that have a giant rip in the crotch. 'You look like you came from the farm,' he said. I laughed and said something (I hope) witty. Then we talked about other stuff, but for a few seconds there I wished I could have hidden behind the heirloom tomatoes."

There's a stereotype of freelancers in pj's and slippers. If that's you and it makes you happy, go for it. But when you're out and about, take a moment to decide if you'll be comfortable running into a potential work connection. It's not about being someone you're not. It's about being an intentional freelancer, affecting others without saying a word.

A good rule of thumb: Mirror how people dress in the setting you'll be in. "I'm on a committee with a bunch of senior execs," Katie says. "For meetings, I try to dress like the others, who are coming from their offices. At the last meeting, I sat next to a new member from a company I'd love to do projects for. She actually complimented me on my outfit! We talked some; then she said, 'Could I have your card? There's a project we might need some outside help with.' Maybe the discussion would have happened anyway, but her opening comment showed that her first impression was about how I looked. It helped make a bond."

SLEEP: NATURE'S POWER-SAVE

Sleep is as important as anything else you do for your health, but it's something most of us skimp on.

Our sleep needs change over time, and some of us need more than others, but we should all buck the tide of "progress" that has shortened our sleep time over the last 100 years. We just aren't built for it.

You need the benefits to your blood pressure, hormonal system, kidneys, brain (including memory integration), and other functions that happen in the quiet of the night. "Sleep helps the creative work I did that day 'cool off.' " Geoff says. "My unconscious works while I sleep. I'll often awaken with an insight, a solution to a problem, or a new way to look at my work."

Some tips for good sleep:

- Try to be consistent about your bedtime and when you get up.

- Stay away from caffeine (chocolate, too!) and alcohol before bed.

- Finish workouts three hours or more before bed.

- Have a calming routine before bed.

> "I don't keep candy or cookies in the house. It's too easy to grab handfuls all day."

To learn more about sleep, one useful resource is the National Sleep Foundation website (sleepfoundation.org).

HANDLING STRESS

Based on Freelancers Union surveys and years of talking with freelancers, here are their top stressors:

1 **The stress of episodic income.** "As a freelancer you truly don't know where the next dollar is coming from or what you're going to earn in a calendar year. Not everyone can handle that kind of insecurity and yes, it is stressful." Former staffers might especially feel the pain: "I never used to worry about money. Now I worry all the time."

2 **The stress of work/life balance.** "I try to get to the gym and not work on weekends. Sometimes that's possible, sometimes it isn't."

3 **The stress of isolation.** "It's kind of scary how much I talk to myself."

4 The stress of identity. "It's annoying to have to explain and sometimes justify my freelancing. People don't really understand what I do."

Stress can have consequences ranging from headaches to back-aches; stomach problems to sleep problems; panic attacks to problems

DEPRESSION

"The biggest challenge for me is to remain positive when I don't have any work and it seems no one will ever hire me again. I know that's not true, but downtime can play tricks on your brain."

Your emotions can affect your productivity and well-being. It's one thing to feel a little down for several days, but depression can drain you for much longer and needs to be treated.

The signs of depression vary, but below are some symptoms from the National Institute of Mental Health:

- Feeling sad or "empty"

- Feeling hopeless, irritable, anxious, or guilty

- Loss of interest in favorite activities

- Feeling exhausted

- Not being able to concentrate or remember details

- Not being able to sleep, or sleeping too much

- Overeating, or not wanting to eat at all

- Thoughts of suicide, suicide attempts

- Aches or pains, headaches, cramps, or digestive problems.

Depression isn't something to be ashamed of or try to tough out. Consult your doctor about any symptoms that concern you.

Reprinted from The National Institute of Mental Health (NIMH) (nimh.nih.gov) with decision making or concentrating, to name some. Coworkers can cover for stressed-out staffers, but freelancers can't afford the drag. If stress is getting you down, consult your doctor.

Seven Stress Busters

1 **Portfolio, portfolio, portfolio.** The more you take control of your Freelance Portfolio, the better you can ride the waves of freelancing.

2 **Be excellent.** Improving your skills and developing sought-after specialties will make you a freelancer who can command top dollar and top gigs.

3 **Seek financial balance.** The more you can reduce your living costs, pay down debt, start saving, and track your income and spending, the less frazzled you'll feel about money. For more on money, health insurance, and safety nets for freelancers, see Chapter 17.

4 **Find your work rhythm.** As a freelancer, you're free to work the way *you* work most productively, healthfully, and happily. Find out what that is (for more on work habits, see Chapter 13): "What I learned after years of stress and breakups is that I have to respect the rhythms of my body and mind."

5 **Get a life.** "It isn't work habits I'd like to improve—it's life habits. I need to do other things so I don't work all week and all weekend, which is what I do now."

6 **Pad the schedule.** But never tell.

7 **Don't go it alone.** Confide in your Brain Trust. Help and hang out with family and friends. Network with other freelancers as potential subcontractors, project partners, and problem solvers (see De-Isolate!).

DE-ISOLATE!

Freelancing can put the "sole" in sole proprietor. Even if your work connects you with lots of people, you might feel the loneliness of being on the hook for every decision: "One of the most challenging things is not having anyone to bounce ideas off of."

Extroverts can find the silence deafening: "So much is done by email, the phone hardly ever rings. It has led to hours of silence in my life. Last week, a client actually *called* me. I was so glad to hear her voice; it was nuts."

Introverts might relish the silence but might not get out there to network: "I make my priorities and don't let clients make them for me. I'm very protective of this benefit of working for myself. But my best work habit is also the worst thing I can do for my business: I isolate myself."

"As a freelance TV writer, I spent up to eight hours a day on story conference calls, never leaving the house. I think of these as my pajama years."

If you're thinking about freelancing or starting out, ask yourself how you do with alone time, and how you plan to scratch your social itch.

Savor the flip side of solopreneurship: the freedom to come and go as you please in your own professional life: "I love that I don't have to commute to an office during rush hour. I love being able to take a class in the afternoon or an extra long walk with my dog on a nice day."

Set up a structure for connecting with people, places, and activities. One freelancer says, "A friend had a summer-evening tradition called Thursdays in the Park with Jane. Open invite, always the same time and location on a beautiful slope near a fountain. She'd get there first with her picnic blanket. People brought their own food and stuff to share. We'd eat, laugh, and play Frisbee until it was dark. Perfect early start to the weekend."

For more on building community, see Chapter 12.

CONFRONTING THE F-WORD

How do people react to you as a freelancer?

Even though freelancers form a huge sector of the workforce, society doesn't always know what to "do" with them.

Some still think freelancing equals slacking: "There's this perception that if you're not working in an office, you're not really working. What it really means is that you're working all the time."

Others have idealized visions of freelancing. While their enthusiasm is genuine, they may not offer the kind of understanding you really need: "A lot of people were excited about this 'new chapter' in my life and were sure everything would somehow just work out. I appreciated their optimism, but it's better to be realistic. There are a lot of ups and downs in the freelance world, and you have to be prepared."

Bottom line: They don't get it. But how could they, unless they've been there?

Freelancers are blazing a trail for a model of work that's been around forever, but was eclipsed for generations by the centralized, mass-production industrial model. Now, technology, a changeable economy, and the shift toward decentralized work have made freelancing mainstream. The world is still catching up to that reality.

"In my staff job, my calendar was crammed with meetings. This week my calendar says 'Pilates' on Tuesday and Thursday, 'Haircut' on Wednesday. That's it."

Your image starts with you. If you want to be taken seriously as a freelancer, you have to address these three key elements of stability in your own mind and life:

- Identity (who am I?)

- Society (where do I fit?)

- Economy (do I have enough?)

I hope this book has helped you discover that you can address these core questions. It goes like this:

TEN POINTS OF FREELANCE PRIDE

> "How am I perceived by people with company jobs? They're envious."

1 Know and grow your skills.

2 Pursue work you love.

3 Be excellent at it.

4 Attract the best clients possible.

5 Get your elevator speech down for the "what do you do?" question.

6 Be businesslike in how you walk and talk about your work.

7 Be a hub and a hive: connected, active, and giving.

8 Have some money in the bank (see Chapter 17).

9 Take the best care of yourself that you can.

10 Thoroughly enjoy your life.

We talked in other chapters about being there for your clients. Be there for yourself, too. It starts with the day-to-day: good sleep, the right food, a productive routine, and ways to destress, take time off, and connect with others. It deepens into a strong, clear way of seeing yourself and being in the world:

"Gigs are great; they teach me and help me get the next gig. But they are not me. *I* tie all the pieces of my career together. That's a powerful feeling."

"When I went from being a manager to being 'just me,' it was amazing how fast my phone stopped ringing and emails stopped arriving. I realized that no matter how good I was as an employee, I was just a gateway to the larger company. That was a good reality check. Now I don't buy into anyone's hype. We're all just trying to make it, inside a company or out."

"Most people think what I do is really, really cool and many seem to envy my courage at setting out to do it and succeeding. I like how brave and confident they think I am, but the truth is that it'd be much, much more difficult for me to work at a staff job than it is to do what I do. I'd be miserable. So it's a very easy choice to be a freelancer, and one that doesn't really require any bravery at all."

YOUR SAFETY NETS

Like everyone else, you need money to keep a roof over your head, pay your taxes, tide you through emergencies, get medical care, send your kids to college, kick back in retirement—and help some of your dreams come true.

But freelancers lack the economic protections millions rely on: unemployment insurance, group health insurance, company-matched retirement savings, as well as access to credit.

Let's get you started on weaving your safety net. These are big subjects that fluctuate with changing laws and policies. Your needs, too, are unique and may change over time. So see this chapter as just the beginning of your explorations, ideally lessening some of the scary unknowns and prepping you for a deeper dive.

HEALTH INSURANCE

As medicine advanced in the early twentieth century, so did medical costs. The solution? Share the burden: Healthy people could regularly pay a certain amount, or premium, to help defray costs for the sick, ensuring the same for themselves when they needed care. This distributed costs over a large group, or risk pool, to help the subgroup needing the care.

ADVOCACY
ALERT

WE NEED A *NEW* NEW DEAL When America moved from agriculture to industry in the mid-nineteenth century, work hours were limitless and conditions appalling. Eventually workers organized and by the 1930s leveraged change via President Franklin Delano Roosevelt's New Deal. These laws linked the fortunes of worker and employer and spawned many worker safety nets, from minimum pay and work hours to antidiscrimination, unemployment protection, and Social Security.

But work has changed. Work relationships are fluid, not fixed. Businesses expand and contract as markets fluctuate. Workers move from job to job or gig to gig. With independent workers now some 42 million strong, we need safety nets for the new, fluid workforce. They need to be *portable* with the worker and *affordable* to the worker. Otherwise this huge and growing economic sector won't be self-sustaining—a disaster for them and the economy.

Businesses eventually bought into these plans to attract workers. Thus were born the private health insurance industry and the employer health benefit system.

The two keys here: a large enough risk pool to keep premiums affordable, and employers helping absorb costs. You can see how the system becomes strained as people live longer, requiring more medical care; costs for treating chronic illnesses and for preventive care are added; the healthy stop buying coverage when job loss or rising premiums make it unaffordable; and the risk pool shrinks, driving prices even higher. Insurers handled these pressures by reducing coverage for preventive care, raising premiums and deductibles (the amount you pay before insurance kicks in), restricting choices, and raising prices or denying coverage for the sick (preexisting conditions).

The result was high-deductible "catastrophic care" insurance mainly covering only major medical issues, exorbitant plans for those with preexisting conditions, mazes of exceptions and limitations, and lots of people with inadequate, unaffordable, or no coverage.

Independent, temp, and part-time workers have had to navigate this maze alone and have generally paid much higher premiums than employees, whose costs (even if rising) are shared by their employers. Unless you live in a state with lower premiums or have a partner with employer-sponsored coverage, you're on your own. Many have rolled the dice and gone without.

Few disagree that we need an affordable model that better covers routine care *and* major medical problems. But that's where consensus ends. Here is a snapshot of where things are today, the changes afoot, and the imperfect choices facing freelancers. *Note:* The system is undergoing major changes, so keep abreast of the news and *verify* when you research plans. And check the Appendix for some useful insurance resources to help you along.

"NOTHING ENDURES BUT CHANGE"

Heraclitus was one wise old Greek, but even he probably couldn't have imagined how well his words would describe our health insurance situation. When the Patient Protection and Affordable Care Act (PPACA), aka the Affordable Care Act (ACA) became law in March 2010, this huge, heatedly debated piece of legislation mandated phased-in changes over a four-year period aimed at overhauling the mammoth U.S. health insurance system.

The law's too big to detail fully here, but significant features include greater oversight of insurance rate increases; start-up loans to fund nonprofit, "consumer operated and oriented plans" called CO-OPs (Freelancers Union received funding to set up CO-OPs in New York, New Jersey, and Oregon); the creation of health insurance exchanges where consumers can comparison shop for plans, encouraging competition among insurers (each state will have an exchange, so look up yours and check to see if your state has a CO-OP); prohibition against insurers denying coverage to those with preexisting conditions; tax credits for small business and individuals to encourage coverage; and, in 2014, mandatory health insurance for all.

Although debate continues about the Affordable Care Act and its final form is uncertain, the phase-in has begun, and some say those effects are irreversible.

For complete information about the Affordable Care Act and much else on health insurance (including options for the self-employed), log onto HealthCare.gov (healthcare.gov), a federal government website managed by the U.S. Department of Health and Human Services.

GET SMART ABOUT HEALTH INSURANCE AND MEDICAL EXPENSES

New law or no, here are some ways to think about your health insurance needs and handle costs.

Talk their talk. Check these glossaries: one via the Bureau of Labor Statistics: Definitions of Health Insurance Terms (bls .gov) and a Health Insurance Glossary from the Health Insurance Resource Center (healthinsurance.org).

Get specific about your health and medical needs. Some examples:

List the medical care you've received in recent years: what, how often, and the cost.

List your doctors. How important is it to you to have free choice of docs and/or keep the ones you have?

Are you hoping to have kids in the not-too-distant future? You'll need a plan with maternity coverage.

Already have a family or getting on in midlife? You may want good prescription coverage.

Consider your location. Living costs and risk factors from state to state affect premium costs. Thinking about moving? Check out health insurance alongside real estate listings. One place to research health insurance info state by state is on the Health Insurance Resource Center website: State-specific Health Insurance Resources (healthinsurance.org).

Consider your finances. High-deductible insurance with lower monthly premiums shifts more of the everyday medical expenses to you while covering more of the costs for medical events that can devastate your finances. You might consider a high-deductible plan if you don't need to see doctors much and mainly want to ensure coverage for major medical situations. While you don't want to undershoot your coverage, you don't want to pay for coverage you won't be using.

Comparison shop. That's easier than it used to be, thanks to websites—eHealthInsurance (ehealthinsurance.com), GoHealth (gohealthinsurance.com), or InsureMonkey (insuremonkey .com), for example—that can help you start looking at your options. Absolutely read the fine print. If you use an insurance broker, find someone you trust—ask close friends and family for recommendations.

Take your tax breaks. See Chapter 15 for details, talk to your accountant, and see Health Savings Accounts (HSAs): Pay Your Medical Bills and Save on Taxes, below.

Haggle some; check their math. Let your docs know you're open to discussing ways to save. Research costs (obviously price isn't the only factor). If you're hit with a charge you have reason to think is high, talk it through, and/or see if they're open to a payment arrangement.

Do an annual insurance checkup. Have your health status or medical needs changed? Are better plans available?

HEALTH SAVINGS ACCOUNTS (HSAS): PAY YOUR MEDICAL BILLS AND SAVE ON TAXES

If you have a high-deductible health plan, you may qualify to open an HSA, which can help you save in two expensive areas of freelance life. Briefly:

You set up the account with a bank, insurance company, or brokerage firm offering HSAs. You fund it with money you use purely for paying medical expenses (not your plan deductible). That money is tax-deductible and its earnings tax-free. Any leftover balance carries over to the next year(s).

There are caps on contributions (and penalties if you break any of the rules). Check out offerings, compare fees, and talk to your accountant and to people who have HSAs. For important information about HSAs and more, see IRS Publication 969, *Health Savings Accounts and Other Tax-Favored Health Plans.*

THE MAJOR TYPES OF PRIVATE HEALTH INSURANCE

Large Employer Group Insurance

Since they bring a large risk group under one plan, large employers have leverage to get competitive costs and choices. They foot a big chunk of the costs, too. Group plans require that everyone be covered at the same cost, including those with preexisting conditions. Employees might also have access to dental, disability, and life insurance.

Small Employer Group Insurance

The difference between small employer group insurance and large employer group insurance is the difference between small and large risk pools. The smaller the group, the more costly the entire plan becomes, should there be significant illness in the group. Result: possibly fewer plan options and higher overall costs.

Insurance Through Associations or Other Entities

Some professional and other groups (alumni groups, unions, et cetera) offer health insurance to members through an insurer. These can include what some call affinity plans. Rates may or may not be lower and choices may be narrower, so research the insurer, do your comparison shopping, and weigh the fit with your needs.

Also check whether your local chamber of commerce or other local nonprofits offer plans.

Individual Insurance

If you, private citizen, buy health insurance on the open market, as a tiny risk pool of one, you'll generally pay higher premiums, have more limited choices, and you may have a harder time being accepted.

You may be able to qualify as a small employer (or "group-of-one") in some states. Check your state department of insurance. To find yours, try the state web map on the National Association of Insurance Commissioners (NAIC) State Web Map (naic.org). Or check the Kaiser Family Foundation's State Health Facts website (statehealthfacts .org; search term: Small Group Health Insurance Market Guaranteed Issue).

FINANCES FOR FREELANCERS

If finances stress you out, join the crowd. Lots of us aren't great with money—and maybe less rational than we think.

In his book *Predictably Irrational*, behavioral economist Dan Ariely tells how he and two colleagues asked people to choose between a delectable Lindt chocolate truffle for fifteen cents or a tasty but more commonplace Hershey's Kiss for one cent. Approximately 73 percent chose the truffle, correctly surmising an excellent value for the price. Around 27 percent chose the Hershey's Kiss.

> "Money can get very tight or you can be rolling in it."

Then the researchers lowered each price by one cent: truffle for fourteen cents; Kiss for free. And logic promptly fled: The 27 percent choosing the Kiss ballooned to around 69 percent, while the truffle's popularity plummeted to 31 percent. These results may not surprise you if you've ever shopped Black Friday and know first-hand how quickly humans can ditch rational thought about money.

Don't know much about personal finance? Join the crowd again. Most of us are self-taught. Yet we all need financial stability—especially

FREELANCERS INSURANCE COMPANY

ANOTHER GROUP OPTION

Offering affordable health insurance to freelancers was one of the Freelancers Union's first goals. Today, we're proud to offer health insurance to Freelancers Union members in New York state through our own social-purpose insurance company called Freelancers Insurance Company (FIC). We also are starting the first "medical home" for freelancers, slated to open in January 2013. This new model emphasizes primary care, in which your doctor, nurse practitioner, or health coach work as a team to keep you healthy. In addition, they will reach out to any specialist you might see to help coordinate your care and medications.

Our risk pool size lets us offer competitive rates and options to low- and high-risk participants, similar to large employers. (We also offer dental and disability insurance, which you generally can't get on the open market without significant added expense.) Because the risk pool is a specific group— freelancers—we also work to tailor the program to their needs.

We aim to combine the lower costs and greater choice of large-employer plans with the member-focused aspects of association models. And since FIC has no private shareholders, it's answerable only to the nonprofit Freelancers Union, its members, and the funders who hold it accountable for fulfilling specific principles of social entrepreneurship. While it's not perfect, it's an impressively large working model of a community-based, privately funded system of health insurance delivery that's more responsive to members' needs, more comprehensive and affordable than they'd find elsewhere, and portable with the worker.

This year Freelancers Union was chosen to receive loans to establish nonprofit health insurance companies called CO-OPs (consumer operated and oriented plans) in New York, New Jersey, and Oregon. We're excited to offer health care to even more consumers—freelancers and nonfreelancers alike.

freelancers working without a net—and especially if you want the things financial health can buy, such as a home mortgage or a business loan (both harder for freelancers to get with their irregular income).

The financial health equation is the inverse of the (only slightly more dreaded) weight loss equation:

---

less input (eat fewer calories) + more output (get more exercise) = weight loss

---

more input (earn and save more) + less output (spend less) = financial gain

---

Financial decisions are hugely personal and depend on multiple factors, but we'll unpack some key financial stability principles that can help make the peaks and valleys of freelancing less frequent and steep. You'll also find selected finance resources in the Appendix. It's just the tip of the iceberg, so take things step by step and know you can find whatever you need to know.

To take better control of your finances and make money decisions from a calm, clear place, try keeping accounts at one bank to stream-line tracking and transferring funds. Or have a physical-bank checking account and several online-bank accounts. Compare services and interest rates. Some people find that using an online budget site such as Mint (mint.com) that aggregates their account info in one place really helps them oversee things.

Personal finance software and online budgeting services and tools can also help eliminate guesswork and calculations. Read reviews and ask other freelancers what they use. Often you can just plug in numbers without personal info, but in cases where you do need to share more info, make sure you feel comfortable providing any account data an online service may require, vet its reputation and security record, and understand its security and privacy policies and practices (remember, these can change). Speaking of security, don't instruct your personal computer to remember passwords for financial accounts, and keep your computer security software current.

Also, set aside a little time each week to deal with money issues. Do your bookkeeping, and then a little more: Read something about money or check out some financial tools online. You'll learn a lot over time.

GETTING A HANDLE ON THE OUTPUT AND THE INPUT

Your budget will tell you exactly how much you need to meet your expenses and how much you can green-light for treats. It's key to managing money stress. What follows is one approach.

FIRST, KNOW WHAT YOU SPEND

This is the output part. The My Budget chart below will help you chart where your money goes. Customize it with your own categories or do a couples version. Look at examples of budgets online. You can work pencil-to-paper or use digital budgeting tools (type "budgeting software" or "online budget tools" into your browser for some options).

"Make a budget. I'm suggesting this but never did it."

Expenses fall in two big buckets:

1 fixed expenses, where the amounts don't change (example: mortgage or rent payment); and

2 variable expenses (example: food bill), which do.

Many expenses are paid monthly. Some, such as estimated taxes or tuition, might be paid quarterly, semiannually, or annually. Some, such as child care, may be paid weekly.

For longer-cycle payments, calculate a monthly amount. For weekly fixed expenses, multiply by four for a monthly total.

For variable expenses, average several weeks' or months' worth of bills or receipts.

Finally, there are "sometimes" expenses: They don't happen regularly, but they happen! A few examples: haircuts (yours; the dog's), travel, medical bills (yours; the dog's), gifts, eating out. Look at half a year's worth or more of your bank and credit card records. Make a list. Calculate an average for each.

Fill in your chart.

Total everything up.

Uncover your eyes.

This is the minimum amount (assuming no changes in your spending habits and no unanticipated expenses . . . *right*) you need each month to meet your living expenses.

NEXT, KNOW YOUR INCOME

"The right amount to save? I wish I knew so I wouldn't feel so worried about spending."

Now for the input part. Do you know what you've earned so far this year? With your budget, you can stay on top of your income.

Want an estimated version? Average your earnings over the past several months or pull last year's tax return and figure a monthly average.

Want a real-time version? Enter your income so far this month. For a family budget, include your mate's income, too.

If you keep a running tab of your income over the month, you'll spot any looming shortfall between your income and your expenses. Does that happen a lot? Good to know. Maybe you need to:

• Reduce expenses

• Raise rates

• Increase client volume

• Negotiate more frequent payments

MY BUDGET

MONTHLY INCOME	MONTHLY EXPENSES
Client payments: $	**Fixed Expenses**
Wages/salary: $	Rent or mortgage: $
Tips: $	Property tax: $
Alimony/Child support [or list as an expense, as applicable]: $	Health insurance: $
Social Security: $	Other insurance: $
Other monthly income (list): $	College/other loans (list): $
TOTAL MONTHLY INCOME: $	Car payment: $
Any nonmonthly income (list, calculated monthly): $	Car insurance: $
	Child care: $
	Cable: $
	Internet: $
	Other (list): $
	TOTAL MONTHLY FIXED EXPENSES: $
	Variable Expenses
	Utilities: $
	Phone: $
	Food: $
	Car (gas, maintenance, parking, tolls) / Transportation: $
	Personal (list, including "sometimes" expenses): $
	Other (list, including "sometimes" expenses): $
	TOTAL MONTHLY VARIABLE EXPENSES: $
	Nonmonthly Expenses (estimated taxes, tuition, etc., calculated monthly - list): $
	TOTAL NONMONTHLY EXPENSES: $
TOTAL MONTHLY INCOME: $	**Total Monthly Expenses** [Fixed + Variable + Nonmonthly]: $

- Push the slow payers
- Prospect for Blue Chips
- Develop a higher-paying specialty or
- All of the above

Keeping a monthly budget lets you see how your career is going. You can compare by month or year (trending up? down? busy season better or worse?). You can even forecast income/saving needs (how much money will I need per month to hire a babysitter three afternoons a week . . . or what about taking scuba lessons?). Need some help getting a handle on things? Maybe a professional bookkeeper can help you get your budgeting and record keeping system up and rolling, and work with you on how to monitor it.

I hear you saying, "A monthly budget won't work for me, because my freelance income is so inconsistent from month to month." Sit tight. We're getting to that.

FINANCIAL FREEDOM FOR FREELANCERS

OK, so somehow with your episodic income, you need to pay your monthly bills, save for taxes, build a safety net for dry time and emergencies, save for your retirement—oh, and have some fun.

MONEY ALERT

YOUR WEEKLY ALLOWANCE In your monthly budget, you calculated personal and "sometimes" expenses. These include necessities like toothpaste—and niceties like clothes, going out, ordering in, and gifts. You've also budgeted for groceries. If your numbers are based in reality, you should be able to figure a weekly spending budget and keep to it. Obviously, charged and debited purchases count against it, too.

And don't thank the banks for putting ATMs on every corner. They profit from your spending. "I hate paying ATM fees, so I walk to a branch where I can use the ATM for free. Just going that extra distance makes me more cautious about spending."

If you've already got a method that's working for you, great! The approach below is one way to organize your finances so you're paying your expenses *and* saving for your future. To explore others, check out personal finance books and resources, or assign a few among your freelancers group and have folks report on them.

> "Saving for taxes? I can't even talk about it because I don't want to be confronted by how lousy I am at it."

To achieve financial stability, you need to continually fund these four accounts:

1 Expenses

2 Taxes

3 Emergencies

4 Retirement

Divide Up Those Checks!

When a payment comes in, deposit a percentage into each account. You might keep your expenses account at a physical bank for check writing and ATM access. Depending on that bank's minimums, fees, and interest rates and your comfort level with having accounts online, you might decide to make others online bank accounts that you transfer money into (the retirement money will eventually be parked in retirement investments—see Retirement, below).

The percentages you choose are up to you and might change. But taxes are a certainty, so get that percentage nailed down. Absolutely, positively attend to funding your tax account. The last thing you want after working hard to earn your income is to be in debt to the IRS. They tend to keep track of these things, meaning that the interest and penalties will just accrue ... and accrue ... as will what you'll pay an accountant to untangle the mess. So find out your tax bracket from your accountant. He or she might approximate this based on your tax returns of the past several years and your anticipated income. You could even fine-tune it quarterly, as you pay your estimated taxes.

> "If you're going to freelance, you need a cushion. You must have a cushion."

If your expenses include debt to pay down, that takes precedence and will affect your allocations. Still, *really* try to put some amount, however small, into your emergencies and retirement accounts. Those two accounts are your future debt fighters.

Initially, you might focus on building your expenses and emergencies accounts, with a smaller amount for retirement; then change the mix as the accounts grow or reach goal amounts.

Goal amounts depend on your situation. Your emergencies account goal might depend on the economy, your worst-case dry-time scenario, your industry's payment schedules, and your personal needs. Opinions vary, but imagine how amazing you'd feel to have at least six to nine months' worth of expenses on tap for emergencies.

For your retirement account, your goals may depend on which retirement options you choose and your age, among other factors.

If your income is very episodic and you get a fat check that'll cover your monthly expenses, you might deposit the necessary amount in your expenses account, fund your taxes account, and divvy up the remainder over the other two. This can be a great peace-of-mind strategy.

If you're waiting for a big payment, you can anticipate and bridge the income gap by changing your percentages ahead of time, shifting more paycheck income to your expenses account.

Things might still be touch and go while you build your accounts, but in time you'll have enough in your expenses account to pay your bills even if the actual checks received in a given month don't actually do that. If really lean times or a major unanticipated expense hit, your emergencies account can cushion you temporarily (which you then replenish!).

The more flush you feel in good times, the more you should stick with your plan for funding your accounts. That's your prime time for building the safety net that'll carry you through dry time. You can even set up additional accounts to fund other goals (new computer? honeymoon?).

With this approach, you're building the economic freedom and security essential to freelance success and well-being.

- You're saving money, not just making ends meet.

- You'll know when you've met your monthly expenses and can save extra dough or have a splurge.

- You're building a financial safety net that empowers you to turn down crappy gigs and crazy clients, and walk away from a negotiation where you're getting screwed.

- You'll be better able to bounce back from a deadbeat client versus suffering deprivation, stress, and credit score harm if you can't pay your bills.

UNEMPLOYMENT FUND FOR FREELANCERS? While employees have unemployment insurance to help tide them over between jobs, there's no comparable safety net to help freelancers weather a dry spell of not enough or no work—which happened to 79 percent of freelancers in our 2011 survey. Why not set up tax-advantaged unemployment savings plans through professional associations that freelancers could contribute to, lowering their tax burden while building savings they could draw on in dry time?

ADVOCACY
ALERT

BETTER TO EARN INTEREST THAN PAY IT: DEBT DEFENSE

Avoiding credit card debt is easier said than done, and paying down debt takes patience and perseverance. Although debt issues are complex and debt recovery is a subject unto itself, here are some strategies to help you prevent debt problems or take steps to prevail.

Dump the bad old spending habits. It's your ultimate long-term stealth move to defend against or defray debt. If you've got a credit card balance, quit using your credit cards. Debit cards, too. Return to a simpler, more direct relationship with your money.

Be choosy. Compare credit card services and terms (including looking for a card with no annual fee or one with a permanent lower interest rate). Visit a website that lets you compare cards, such as Bankrate (bankrate.com) or CardTrak (cardtrak.com).

Try negotiating a lower interest rate. If you've incurred some interest charges but have a good credit history and payment record, try negotiating a better interest rate as a valued client.

Call. If you realize you've missed a bill payment deadline, send payment ASAP, call to let them know, and ask if they'll waive any late charges. If you've been a reliable paying client, they might.

Shun store credit cards. They tend to have high interest rates.

Go to cash. You'll get up close and personal with how often you throw down the plastic when you're not throwing it down anymore.

Calculate your rate. To calculate various debt repayment scenarios—such as how long it would take to pay off X amount in credit card debt, at Y interest rate, if you pay Z amount per month, and how much would be paid in interest—plug numbers into an online debt calculator. Bankrate.com and CNNMoney.com have good ones.

Try Triple-A troubleshooting. Debt is a tough customer, so try Chapter 7's tactic for handling tough clients:

1 *Acknowledge* the problem, laying out all the facts.

2 *Analyze* your situation.

3 *Act* to formulate a plan to pay down the debt, budget yourself through the crisis, and repair your credit over time.

CREDIT ... *DREAD IT?*

Think of your credit report as your financial report card and your credit score as your grade. Your credit report documents your bill-paying reliability, among other aspects of your credit history. Your credit score, called a FICO score after its originator, the Fair Isaac Corporation, is a calculation of your credit risk based on multiple elements, including how much debt you're carrying and how you've paid past debts. The score tops out at 850. These days, you're wise to shoot for a score of more than 750.

While getting your credit score entails paying a fee, the Fair Credit Reporting Act (FCRA) mandates that you be allowed to obtain a free copy of your credit report from each of the three nationwide credit reporting companies (Equifax, Experian, and TransUnion) once every twelve months. You can get all three at once (it can be useful to compare them) or order one at a time, over time (useful for tracking changes)—your call. The companies have centralized this process:

Online: Visit AnnualCreditReport.com (annualcreditreport .com) and follow the instructions to complete and submit the request form.

By phone: Call (toll-free) 877-322-8228

By mail: Complete the Annual Credit Report Request Form and mail to:

Annual Credit Report Request Service
P.O. Box 105281
Atlanta, GA 30348-5281

If you need another copy within a twelve-month period, you can buy one by contacting:

Equifax 800-685-1111 (equifax.com)

Experian 888-397-3742 (experian.com)

TransUnion 800-888-4213 (transunion.com)

There are other circumstances when you can get a free report, including if you're denied credit or insurance because of material in the report. For details, see the Federal Trade Commission website ("Facts for Consumers: How to Dispute Credit Report Errors"; ftc.gov).

Note: Getting your report too often can actually lower your score. *Tip:* If you're getting a loan or refinancing, see if you can get a copy of your report from the lender (since they'll have one), rather than requesting your own.

If the report contains negative-but-true material, the unfortunate reality is that much of it can stay on the report for around seven years (some items longer, or with no time limit).

If there's information in a credit report that's inaccurate or incomplete, the FCRA says the credit reporting company and the entity that provided the information are responsible for correcting it. For basic guidelines on how to proceed, visit the Federal Trade Commission website: "Facts for Consumers: How to Dispute Credit Report Errors." (ftc.gov/bcp/edu/pubs/consumer/credit/cre21.shtm). Since this process can take time, it's a good idea to review your reports well ahead of any activity that would involve a credit check (for example, applying for a loan or buying insurance).

Bottom line, this is the report lenders will see, whether or not you agree with it. So handle any issues you find and do what you can to improve your score.

If you're denied credit or offered less favorable terms on the basis of your credit history, you should receive written notification, including of your right to receive a free credit report and your credit score if it was a factor in the evaluation.

For additional resources, see the Appendix.

RETIREMENT

Whether you never want to retire, fear you can't afford to, or retirement's still decades away, there's a four-letter word for it: *save*. According to findings from the 2011 Freelancers Union Annual Independent Worker Survey of more than 2,500 independent workers from each of the fifty states, 27 percent said they had not saved anything for retirement, citing these as some of the reasons:

- 78 percent didn't make enough money.

- 39 percent were not paid regularly.

- 19 percent didn't understand retirement account options or how to choose one.

- 15 percent didn't know how to choose a financial services company/provider.

You can see how pay scale and erratic payment schedules are strong factors in freelancers' retirement savings challenges. That's why it's important to do your market research and skill upgrades so you can land the best clients and charge as much as possible, why we need to stop late-paying and deadbeat clients, and why budgeting to set aside some portion of your payments for retirement, even if your income is small, is an essential habit to cultivate.

"A financial planner I know described retirement as 'a time when you only do work you want to do, not work you have to do.' I love that idea."

THE TWO BIGGEST MYTHS ABOUT RETIREMENT SAVING

Myth 1: I can't save enough to make a difference. **Truth:** Wrong approach. Every deposit makes a difference, because earnings on invested income compound over time. If you're young and have debts, saving might feel overwhelming, but time is on your side and small amounts add up.

Myth 2: It's too late to save. **Truth:** Not true. Anything trumps nothing. And anything, invested and earning dividends or interest, amounts to something. Just start. Now. Adjust your retirement time line if necessary (how many people actually retire at sixty-five anymore, anyway—or even want to, if they're doing what they love?). When I worked on a kibbutz, it was inspiring to see people joyfully working far into their late years. Freelancers, able to live and work holistically, can do that. Saving puts you in control of your future work and can mean the difference between having to work full-out forever and being able to be selective about your projects or work only as much as you want.

To play with savings scenarios, try plugging numbers into a compound interest calculator like those from Moneychimp (moneychimp .com) or Bankrate (bankrate.com).

WHY RETIREMENT SAVING IS ESPECIALLY IMPORTANT FOR FREELANCERS

Many employees can enroll in employer retirement funds that make money while they work. Sign a form or two, and the account is set up and contributions are carved from their paychecks before they can spend that money, executing a flawless, perfectly legal end run around the Tax Man, too. Sometimes the employer matches some portion of the contribution. If all goes well, those employees wake up at age 59½ (when they can withdraw the money without penalty) to a tidy nest egg.

Obviously, it's not quite that simple, but it's pretty sweet. As your own boss, you have to pull that money out of your paychecks, set up the investment accounts, and monitor them. The good news is, you have access to the same investments employers do, and, depending on your income, you might be able to save more in your tax-deferred accounts than the W-2 crowd can in their retirement plans.

RETIREMENT SAVINGS PLANS AT A GLANCE

Let's assume you've started dividing up your checks and steadily depositing a percentage for retirement. There is a lot more you can do besides let it sit there earning the bank's low interest rate. And, just like the employer who whisks that dough into a retirement instrument, you want to get it off-limits for spending.

Retirement plans motivate retirement saving by offering a tax advantage for setting aside money in a special account that's invested and accrues to become your nest egg. Generally, you contribute money from your income without paying income tax on some or all of it. Generally, it stays in that account until it's distributed to you in your later years—presumably when needed in retirement—when you pay taxes on your pretax contributions and the earnings. This reduces your taxable income in your peak earning years, deferring the tax to your later years, the assumption being that you'll be earning less then, so your overall tax burden will be lower.

Some retirement contributions can be made after-tax, with no tax paid on the income or earnings when the money is later distributed.

With certain important exceptions, if you withdraw monies early, there are penalties atop any taxes owed.

You may have more than one retirement account so you can make more contributions. While this may restrict your ability to make some contributions or might affect their deductibility, it can give you options and flexibility in your financial planning. Some accounts allow you to take loans or early distributions for very specific reasons.

Which accounts are best for you, and how much to contribute, depends on your unique situation and how much you're able to set aside per year (some retirement accounts let you save more; some less). There are numerous retirement plan options, but really a handful that are meaningful for most of us, and for freelancers. A selective overview follows. Use it as a jumping-off point for your own research and discussions with your accountant about your needs. See the Appendix for some useful resources.

Note: These plans are detailed, so the encapsulations below are just that. Also, the terms of these plans can and do change, so be sure to verify all terms before proceeding.

Traditional IRA (Individual Retirement Arrangement) at a Glance

Maximum contribution per year: $5,000, plus $1,000 if you're fifty or older.

Tax highlights: Contributions may be completely or partially tax-deductible. You pay tax on the earnings upon distribution, and on any part of the contribution that was deductible.

Withdrawal age: 59½, with a 10 percent penalty tax for early withdrawal, atop any income tax owed, with some exceptions.

Note: The IRA is essentially the government's way of offering a retirement savings instrument to people who don't have access to a 401(k) through employment. If your spouse (or you) has or is eligible for a 401(k) through employment, there may be limits on the deductibility of your contributions to an IRA. If you make any nondeductible contributions, talk to your accountant about the proper documentation and keep track of it, since you'll need it later to prove that income tax isn't due on those amounts when you withdraw them.

SIMPLE (Savings Incentive Match Plan for Employees) IRA at a Glance

Maximum contribution per year: Generally $11,500, plus $2,500 if you're fifty or older.

Matching contributions: Employer matches up to 3 percent. (See Note.)

Tax highlights: Taxes are paid when the monies are withdrawn.

Withdrawal age: 59½ with a 10 percent additional tax on early withdrawals (with some exceptions), which rises to 25 percent if done within the first two years.

Note: You can set up a SIMPLE IRA for yourself and your employees if you have 100 employees or fewer.

SEP (Simplified Employee Pension Plan) IRA

Maximum contribution per year: Up to 25 percent of your compensation (if a salary), or calculate your allowable contribution from your self-employment income by referring to the rate tables or worksheets in IRS Publication 560, *Retirement Plans for Small Business,* or discussing with your accountant. Total maximum contribution: $50,000.

Tax highlights: Your contributions are tax-deductible. Taxes are paid when the monies are withdrawn.

Withdrawal age: 59½, with a 10 percent penalty tax for early withdrawal, atop any income tax owed, with some exceptions.

Note: While there are limits if you have another defined contribution plan, in general, this plan allows you to save a sizable amount of money, so give it a close look. Setup is easy. Note that if you have employees and contribute to your own SEP IRA, you have to contribute a proportional amount for them.

Roth IRA

Maximum contribution per year: $5,000, plus $1,000 if you're fifty or older, though how much you can contribute is reduced or eliminated at higher levels of income and can also depend on whether traditional IRA contributions were also made.

Tax highlights: Unlike a traditional IRA, Roth IRA contributions are after-tax contributions, i.e., not tax-deductible. But distributions (earnings included) from a Roth IRA are not taxed, whereas traditional IRA distributions may be taxed.

Withdrawal age: 59½ *if* you reach that age at least five years from the start of the year you first contributed to a Roth IRA. There are some other instances where distribution before 59½ is penalty-free, assuming the same time frame from first contribution.

Note: While you can't contribute as much to a Roth as to a SEP IRA and you have to pay taxes on your Roth contributions, that might be OK with you depending on your income, your ability to take other deductions, and your tax bracket—plus, you can happily anticipate tax-free distribution on the back end. Want to really boost your after-tax advantage? Have both a Roth and a SEP. Talk with your accountant.

401(k) at a Glance

Maximum contribution per year: In general, $17,000, plus $5,500 if you're fifty or older (for 2012).

Tax highlights: You pay Social Security, but not income tax, when you make the contribution. Taxes are deferred until you begin withdrawing the money, when you're taxed on both your contributions and your earnings.

Withdrawal age: 59½ with a 10 percent penalty tax for early withdrawal, atop any income tax owed, with some exceptions.

Note: Since these accounts are fairly complex and expensive to establish and maintain, they're mainly intended for companies. If you have a

401(k) as an employee, the company may or may not match some portion of your contribution. When you leave the company, you can take your own contributions with you, but you may or may not be able to take the employer's contributions. How much you can take, and when (called vesting), is based on the plan's vesting schedule.

Solo 401k (aka Individual 401(k), Solo-k, Uni-k, or One-Participant k)

Maximum contribution per year: $17,000, plus $5,500 "catch-up contribution" if you're fifty or older, plus up to 25 percent of your compensation (if a salary), or calculate your allowable contribution from your self-employment income by referring to the rate tables or worksheets in IRS Publication 560, *Retirement Plans for Small Business,* or discussing with your accountant. Total maximum contribution: $50,000, excluding the catch-up contribution.

Tax highlights: Contributions are made pretax.

Withdrawal age: 59½, with a probable 10 percent penalty tax for early withdrawal, atop any income tax owed.

Note: This 401(k) can cover a business owner who has no employees (such as a sole proprietor) or a business owner and spouse and lets you contribute as both boss and employee. Although it can allow you to save a large amount, there's some complexity and expense involved in managing it.

Keogh

Maximum contribution per year: There's more than one type of plan. In general, for someone who's self-employed and has only the Keogh plan: 25 percent of your allowable income, up to $50,000. Contributions to a defined-benefit Keogh plan can go much higher.

FREELANCERS RETIREMENT PLAN

Freelancers Union developed a riff on the employer 401(k) that offers members the easy administration, professionally selected offerings, and contribution levels that employees enjoy—plus special freelance-friendly features.

Maximum contribution per year: $17,000, plus a $5,500 "catch-up contribution" if you're fifty or older, plus "profit-sharing contributions" of up to 25 percent of your earned income, less your contributions, capping at $50,000 (not including the catch-up contribution).

Tax highlights: Unless they're Roth contributions (see Roth IRA), contributions are tax-deductible and taxes are deferred until you start withdrawing the money, when you're taxed on the contributions and earnings. Some enrollment and contribution limitations apply.

Withdrawal age: 59½, with a possible 10 percent penalty tax for early withdrawal, atop any income tax owed, with some exceptions. Earnings from any Roth contributions are taxable unless you've been participating in Roth contributions for five years minimum.

Notes: Members can't contribute to this plan and a SEP plan in the same calendar year. The plan's designed as a retirement savings vehicle for the 1099 earnings of the self-employed. Freelancers Union handles administration and filing of certain forms. You have access to expert-monitored investments, and there are no minimums. You can choose to make monthly automated contributions—but you can easily change or stop them if your income fluctuates.

All of this is made financially possible through the members' contributions, which are paid into a trust fund just for them, and through the trust fund's earnings. It's an example of how a group can independently set up viable systems that provide the positives of traditional models, offer better choices than group members could get on their own, but meet the individual's needs.

To learn more, visit the Freelancers Union website (freelancersunion.org).

Tax highlights: Contributions are tax-deductible. Taxes are deferred until you start withdrawing the money, when you're taxed on the contributions and earnings.

Withdrawal age: 59½, with a 10 percent penalty tax, atop any income tax owed, with some exceptions.

Note: While Keoghs let you put away a good amount of money, they aren't as common since the more user-friendly SEP IRA has come along. The defined-benefit version is especially complex. Talk with your accountant about whether a Keogh makes sense for you.

TEN STEPS TO RETIREMENT INVESTING

If you're overseeing your own retirement saving and investing, here are some consumer-awares:

1 **Start saving.** Any amount. Use the system in this chapter or whatever works for you.

2 **Start learning.** Employees' retirement plan investments are reviewed by financial professionals, but freelancers have to mentor themselves—and no matter where your money's invested, you need to oversee it and at least once a year do a full performance evaluation. So read up on money, investing, retirement investing, and mutual funds. Get mutual fund recommendations from knowledgeable family and friends; pay a financial consultant for some sessions. Learn how investors weigh investment risk and reduce it by diversifying investments across a mix of lower-to-higher-risk investments. Understand how the mix commonly changes as you near retirement age, and discover your own risk tolerance level. P.S. If this diversification stuff sounds familiar, it's because you're applying the same logic to balancing your Freelance Portfolio. You've been investing in yourself all along.

3 Calculate how much you need to save for retirement. There are multiple variables to consider, from your age to your health and more. Online retirement calculators may help give you a general idea but can't integrate the complexities of your situation. Ideally, a financial planning professional can work with you to customize a plan. While you figure things out, get started with Steps 1 and 2.

4 Decide where you want to set up your retirement investments. Track performance; compare the minimum contribution requirements and administrative costs and fees; look for a low expense ratio (individual investors, alas, can't get the same cost breaks that employees, thanks to the size of the assets being invested, can). If all the decisions seem a little overwhelming, especially at first, one mutual fund company to consider is Vanguard (vanguard.com), which currently is the biggest and least expensive such company in the United States.

5 If you have a significant amount to invest, you might work with a broker or financial adviser. This is a service you pay for, so assess the quality of the service and amount of attention you'll get. Ask about the adviser's fees (which are charged atop any mutual fund fees). Ask how he or she will monitor your accounts, make decisions, assess performance, and communicate with you. Make sure you're comfortable with the adviser's investing philosophy and risk tolerance—and that he or she knows yours.

6 Consolidate. If you have retirement accounts from previous employers or in other places, pulling them all under one investment firm's roof can make your retirement saving easier to monitor and manage, and less likely that an account might get lost (it happens).

7 Get involved. Suggest that your professional association invite a financial professional to give a retirement planning talk (we have them at Freelancers Union). Raise awareness about making retirement programs available through industry organizations and community groups. We need more ways to provide individual investors with the efficiencies, economies, and investment opportunities of large employer-type models.

8 Have a financial routine and streamline it where you can. Habitually divide up those checks to put a percentage in your retirement savings account. Bookmark financial websites you visit frequently.

9 Reassess. Do an annual performance review of your retirement strategy. Are your lifestyle and finance goals still the same? If not, how does that affect your strategy?

10 Make a will. A major step in protecting your assets is deciding what happens to everything you've carefully built for the loved ones you leave behind. If you don't determine how you want your assets apportioned after you leave this world, Uncle Sam will. Think it through and take care of it.

SAVING FOR EDUCATION

For decades, college tuition has been rising at double or triple the inflation rate annually. Below are some tax-advantaged ways you can save for education.

For federal student aid options, visit the U.S. Department of Education website ED.gov (ed.gov).

If you have student loans you're having trouble paying, the Consumer Financial Protection Bureau "Student Debt Repayment Assistant" (consumerfinance.gov) may help you understand various repayment possibilities.

If you're considering professional training or education, see the tax info on this in Chapter 15.

Note: As with retirement savings options, these instruments are subject to change. Also, their rules or tax advantages may change if used in conjunction with other education-related instruments, tax credits, or tax-free assistance. Talk with your accountant about coordinating your education financial strategy and verify all terms. See the Appendix for selected education resources.

ESA (COVERDELL EDUCATION SAVINGS ACCOUNT)

For kids under eighteen, you can use ESAs to save on taxes and on certain expenses for college and (currently) elementary and secondary school at eligible institutions, from kindergarten through twelfth grade. You can find out from the school if it's eligible.

ESA contributions are made after taxes but grow tax-free (with some contribution limits, depending on income). The child's the beneficiary. Allowable expenses may include tuition, fees, books, supplies, tutoring, uniforms, and more. When money's withdrawn, some tax may be due. Tax and penalty may be due if money's withdrawn for unallowable expenses.

Multiple ESAs can be set up for a child (for example: by you, a grandparent, and an aunt or uncle), but the total maximum annual contribution to all ESAs combined for that child is $2,000. You may pay an excise tax on any excess, so make sure everyone communicates about who's contributing how much.

If the child doesn't go to college, you may be able to change the beneficiary to certain other family members under thirty. Any monies left in the account go to the beneficiary once he or she turns thirty—and tax and with some exceptions penalty tax will be due, so check with your accountant about the rules. Also, find out how any account fees might affect performance.

529 PLAN (AKA QUALIFIED TUITION PROGRAM OR QTP)

Again, thank the tax code for the sexy name. These savings plans, origi-nally incubated at the state level, are a tax-advantaged alternative to college loans. As with the ESA, there's a beneficiary—often your child or a grandchild, but it could be almost anyone, including you. You can put money into a 529 plan to prepay or contribute toward certain "postsecondary" expenses such as tuition, fees, books and supplies, a certain amount of room and board, and more. If you use a distribution for an unallowable expense, federal, state, and penalty tax may apply. Special rules apply if the beneficiary gets a scholarship or other tax-free educational assistance.

While the money you put in isn't deductible on your federal taxes, you generally don't pay federal tax on the earnings when the money's distributed. Your state may do the same, and may offer certain extra inducements to open a plan there rather than in another state. (States administer these plans.) Using your state's plan also means you won't pay state taxes when the money's withdrawn.

The maximum contribution per year free of gift tax is $13,000 for an individual or $26,000 if you're a married couple filing jointly, if you make no other gifts to the child that year. Unused funds can be refunded to you or designated for another beneficiary, according to the plan's rules.

529 plans have underlying investments that differ across firms and states, and the ones that advisers sell usually have a sales charge (aka a load) up-front. To learn more about specific plans' rules, con-tact the state agency administering the plan, and ask the educational institution(s) you're interested in whether they participate in a plan. An excellent resource on 529 plans and other tools and info on pay-ing for college is savingforcollege.com. For this and other resources, see the Appendix.

You get a hero's welcome for making it through this chapter! This part of freelancing—the off-the-grid, out-on-a-limb, without-a-net part—isn't easy. But it's the part we all have to face if we want a better life for freelancers now and in the future.

New Mutualism—people helping people in the new economy—starts with being an intentional freelancer, making clear decisions to help yourself live a long and sustainable life as a freelancer. They might be tough decisions. But freelancers *are* tough. And because the work-to-income relationship is so direct for them, they quickly know when economic truths must be faced:

"I can get as much work as I want, but it's paying less and less."

"I spend a lot of time finding work and less time doing it."

"One good year doesn't predict another one."

"You have to be disciplined enough to sense when you have to adjust your business."

So, ask yourself: "What did I do today for my future? For my safety nets?" Maybe you read an article about money, set up your accounts so you can start dividing up your checks, resisted buying something that wasn't in your budget, researched a new insurance plan. Start wherever you are to take control of your freelance life for your own peace of mind.

Peace of mind is also knowing you can afford the life you're living, in good years and in lean. It's knowing how to budget, save, invest, and work your Freelance Portfolio so you can make a plan and track your progress. Or change the plan when your goals change—for example, when you want to move, travel, have a baby, retire.

I believe freelancers, who've always had to do for themselves, can help themselves and one another learn, adapt, and grow through anything. So make your freelance life choices consciously. Proudly. Be an intentional freelancer. You deserve no less.

Conclusion

THE FUTURE IS NOW . . . AND IT'S US

I live near a place where history was made. Beginning on September 17, 2011, a large crowd gathered in a public park in the heart of Wall Street, the nation's financial capital. Their numbers were hard to count but growing, pouring in from both sides of the political divide, with similar groups springing up across the country. Their name, Occupy Wall Street, spoke volumes to power: "We the people live here, too." Their message, though disjointed, was clear: What brought us this far could not carry us forward.

These protestors were giving voice to long-standing economic and social imbalances that finally erupted in a frightening, roiling world economy as we entered the twenty-first century. Our times seem to defy explanation and prediction.

In that way, they aren't so different from when we transitioned from agriculture to industry some 100 years ago. Then, too, unprecedented advances supposed to help us prosper expanded the wealth of too few at too high a human price. Workers toiled for limitless hours in unsafe conditions for subsistence wages, unable to afford proper medical care. Corruption was rampant, and the divide between the extremely wealthy and everyone else was vast and growing.

Then, too, it took a while for people to mobilize for change, and to know what change was needed. But eventually their outcry resulted in the New Deal laws that helped frame the new worker/employer relationship and that protect company workers today. It was a giant achievement. But what worked then doesn't fit how we live and work now. In our grandparents' generation and before, the norm was one job for life. In our parents' generation, that changed to having four or five jobs over your career. The new reality? You'll likely have four or five jobs at once.

Businesses have radically trimmed staff in order to survive in an economy where consumer demand shifts overnight. The self-employed population has exploded. It's a type of work virtually unprotected by law, though taxed more. And, as their own bosses, freelancers have to buy their own health insurance, tide themselves through unemployment, and fully fund their own retirement.

Doing this successfully as an individual in the open market is a tall order even in a good economy. Fortunately, freelancers' numbers are large enough now that they've become a force to be recognized and reckoned with. Technology is helping them work more efficiently, find new clients, and find and help one another. And while they've always had a lot to offer the economy, I believe the new economy and work world will have a lot to offer them.

The future economy will likely depend on independent workers:

- As the workforce is rebuilt post-recession, it's estimated half will be independent or contingent workers.

- The temp workforce will grow at twice the pace of overall employment between now and 2018.

HOW WILL WORK BE ORGANIZED?

Maybe the real question is: How will work be disorganized?

I love business visionary Dee Hock's view of the "chaordic" system—a dynamic fusion of order and chaos—as a way to think about the new world of work. If you can handle messy, scary, and wild, it'll give you flashes of wonder. Here are some of the changes I think hold opportunity for freelancers.

THE (OLD) CENTER WON'T HOLD

What's happening: There'll still be company headquarters, divisions, and branches, but technology has made location largely irrelevant. Just as the life force of a tree can't be found in any one part, so the life force of the organization won't be found in headquarters but in all of its branches, down to the individuals doing the work. Growth will happen wherever there's fertile soil (new markets and skilled workers). Management won't be top-down so much as grassroots-up. The role of company leaders will be to tap into and support the intelligence and skills of this far-flung group.

What it means for freelancers: Companies are already decentralizing operations, engaging freelancers to do what staffers once did. The same technology that frees companies to be anywhere goes for freelancers, too. Increasingly, you can work from anywhere, live where you want (where the skiing's great . . . where your family is . . . where there are no state taxes . . . where the health insurance is affordable), and structure your time, career, and life your way: "What I like best about freelancing is having the freedom to work where I want, when I want—with minimal meetings."

NIMBLENESS WILL BE REWARDED

What's happening: The blistering pace of innovation, competition, and change rewards the nimble. Corporate giants stumble and crash while upstarts catch fire, with affordable technologies helping them control costs while they grow. Technology also lets businesses sense market changes minute-to-minute and quickly develop the means to meet demand. Companies with low overhead, little investment in protecting the establishment, and the ability to turn on a dime to anticipate and lead the new, will win.

What it means for freelancers: As a freelancer, you're a master of nimbleness. You need it to survive. The good news: Now the rest of the business world also needs what you have. Companies are engaging teams of freelancers to leap in and do what's needed, when needed. Building those relationships—with the businesses that need the teams and with freelancers who can be your teammates—will help you land Blue Chip clients and stabilize your income without the risk of tying your fortune to a single employer.

But solopreneurs today can also use technology and freelance teams to develop and launch their own new ventures. As you read this, the next Big Idea might be hatching in the mind of a solitary freelancer tapping away in a café or a coworking space. Now, more than ever, that idea has the potential to be more than just a dream.

CONNECTION IS POWER

What's happening: We're moving from the age of information to the age of influence. Businesses that genuinely connect with consumers get the buy. There's a wish to know and trust the person behind the product. And with the proliferation of review sites and product discussion boards, there's no place to hide from a gaffe or a flop.

What it means for freelancers: Even though it's unlikely you'll ever run an ad during the Super Bowl, thanks to the Internet, the world can be your customer. You can use it to build trust and a following for your information, products, and services. You can use it to crowd-source feedback for business ideas and even raise money instead of waiting for banks to become freelance-friendly lenders. And speaking of gaffes and flops, at Freelancers Union, technology helped us develop a grass-roots movement to expose bad clients and praise good ones, in the form of the Client Scorecard.

The best freelancers are masters of connection. They've honed their ability to find mutually profitable connections with people and projects. They've got a smooth interface going between work and home life, where each benefits and builds the other. They've got their Brain Trust on tap for advice and support. Freelancers' connection-driven lifestyle and habits position them to succeed in the age of influence.

FROM COMPETITION TO COOPERATION: THE MUTUALIST ECONOMY

What's happening: Instead of competing, businesses will forge relationships in order to leave no profit unturned. The large, well-capitalized, and well-infrastructured will affiliate with the small, clued in, and inventive in cooperative ventures for mutual benefit. Alongside the old "win-lose" model will grow a mutualist "win-win" model.

What it means for freelancers: Freelancers can form partnerships to develop and launch their ideas. They can also build their own marketplaces such as Etsy (etsy.com), and collaborate on solutions to widespread professional problems. Our Freelancers Union Contract Creator is a shining example of a crowd-sourced solution to the common problem of unfair or nonexistent freelance contracts. And they can unite across professions to increase their bargaining power for freelance-friendly policies.

ADVOCACY ALERT

WHERE WILL YOU GET BENEFITS IN THE FUTURE? Mutualist models hold promise for building portable, affordable safety nets for the new workforce that don't rely on government programs or subsidies and don't answer to profit-seeking investors.

Freelancers Union's retirement plan and insurance company show how individuals can pool their numbers and dollars to build self-sustaining systems offering competitive benefits and retirement savings instruments. Systems like these could come together into larger federations to offer even greater economies of scale, services, and pricing.

The new independent middle class needs clout to bargain for better prices and better policies on safety net issues. Forming cooperative groups can help them exert leverage together that individuals lack on their own.

As for funding new ventures, our nation can't afford to miss any opportunity to build profit in the new economy. Banks need to look at microloan models for incubating seedling ideas and microbusinesses. Independent workers should be judged by the quality of their ideas, not the consistency of their cash flow. Whether it's a super-niche venture that deeply penetrates a market or a Big Idea that needs space and time to grow, no viable venture should be left behind.

THE AGE OF I, THE AGE OF US

> "You have to create your own life and business in this world. I say go for it."

As the economic infrastructure we've relied on for decades has crumbled, a paradox of opportunity and risk has opened up for all workers. Thrown back on their own resources, they're creating nontraditional career paths, getting gigs, developing their own profit-making products and projects, and finding their own way. Independent workers, never adequately served by the existing systems and well acquainted with the risks of living off the work grid, understand the dynamics of this multifaceted way of living and working. They can benefit from the changes. And they can lead them.

Freelancers' growing numbers concentrate their power in a new collective "I": a large, diverse-yet-committed community seeking fair wages for honest work and a fair opportunity to make it on their own, doing what they love. By joining hands, they're building the new scaffold for success in the twenty-first century, and asserting their rights as they do.

THE FREELANCER BILL OF RIGHTS

We freelancers, as fully contributing members of the workforce, do affirm the following rights:

1 The right to recognition for our economic contributions

2 The right to a fair wage for a fair day's work

3 The right to fair taxation

4 The right to unemployment protection

5 The right to affordable health care

6 The right to have access to capital for professional innovation

7 The right to training for professional growth

8 The right to a hive that thrives: individuals working alone

and together for the common good of the independent worker community

9 The right to a government that will partner and protect

10 The right to security sufficient to help us to launch future generations and sustain us in old age.

In the Introduction, I mentioned that my goal in writing this book was to help you have many good days as a freelancer. I hope you've discovered lots of ways to do that, and know that there are always places and people you can turn to for information and support—most especially your fellow freelancers. As a freelancer, you're a master of new beginnings. There's a long tradition of that in this country. So work fearlessly and with joy, and help others do the same. Together, we can make work life more successful and secure for all, and make the Freelancer Bill of Rights a reality for every independent worker, now and in the future.

SELECTED SOURCES & OTHER HELPFUL RESOURCES

BARTERING

GOVERNMENT RESOURCES

Internal Revenue Service (IRS)
(irs.gov):

Barter Exchanges

Bartering Income

Bartering Tax Center

Recordkeeping Tips for Barter
Transactions

"Tax Topics—Topic 420 Bartering
Income"

WEBSITES

BerkShares, Inc (berkshares.org)

Calgary Dollars (calgarydollars.ca)

Ithaca Hours—Local Currency—
Ithaca, New York
(ithacahours.org)

Ithaca Hours Online
(ithacahours.com)

Time Banks USA (timebanks.org)

ORGANIZATIONS

IRTA (International Reciprocal
Trade Association) (irta.com)

National Association of Trade
Exchanges (natebarter.com)

EDUCATION

GOVERNMENT RESOURCES

Consumer Financial Protection
Bureau. "Student Debt
Repayment Assistant."
(consumerfinance.gov)

IRS Publication 970, *Tax Benefits
for Education*. (irs.gov)

WEBSITES

College Savings Plans Network
(CSPN) (collegesavings.org)

Savingforcollege.com
(savingforcollege.com)

ORGANIZATIONS

FAFSA (Free Application for
Federal Student Aid) on the
Web—Federal Student Aid
(fafsa.ed.gov)

Project on Student Debt:
The Institute for College
Access & Success
(projectonstudentdebt.org)

U.S. Department of Education
(ED.gov)

FINANCE

BOOKS & SHORT PUBLICATIONS

Benun, Ilise. *The Creative
Professional's Guide to Money.*

D'Agnese, Joseph and Denise
Kiernan. *The Money Book for
Freelancers, Part-Timers, and
the Self-Employed.*

Gichon, Galia. *My Money Matters
Kit.*

ARTICLES & WEB PAGES

BizFilings Business Owner's Toolkit
(bizfilings.com)

"Family Monthly Budget Sheet"

Family Works

Freelance Switch and Errumm
Web Consulting. "Freelance
Switch Hourly Rate Calculator."
(freelanceswitch.com/rates)

GOVERNMENT RESOURCES

Board of Governors of the Federal
Reserve System. "Consumer's
Guide to Credit Cards."
(federalreserve.gov)

Federal Deposit Insurance
Corporation (FDIC) (fdic.gov):

Money Smart—A Financial
Education Program

Money Smart Information Booth

Federal Trade Commission (FTC)
(ftc.gov):

Credit & Loans

Credit Card Repayment Calculator

Facts for Consumers: Credit
Repair: How to Help Yourself

Facts for Consumers: How to
Dispute Credit Report Errors

Fair Debt Collection Practices
Act Links

Free Annual Credit Reports

Money Matters

Internal Revenue Service (IRS)
(irs.gov):

IRS Publication 560, *Retirement
Plans for Small Business*

IRS Publication 590, *Individual
Retirement Arrangements
(IRAs)*

IRS Retirement Plans Navigator

Retirement Plans for Self-
Employed People

Tax Information for Plan Sponsor/
Employer

Types of Retirement Plans

U.S. Department of Labor,
Employee Benefits Security
Administration (EBSA). *Taking
the Mystery Out of Retirement
Planning.* (dol.gov)

U.S. Social Security Administration.
"Retirement Estimator."
(socialsecurity.gov or ssa.gov)

WEBSITES

AnnualCreditReport.com
(annualcreditreport.com)

Bankrate (bankrate.com)

CardTrak (cardtrak.com)

CNNMoney (money.cnn.com)

Down-to-Earth Finance
(downtoearthfinance.com)

Equifax (equifax.com)

Experian (experian.com)

Feed the Pig (feedthepig.org)

FICO (Fair Isaac Corporation)
(fico.com)

Investopedia (investopedia.com)

Kiplinger (kiplinger.com)

Lending Club (lendingclub.com)

Mint.com (mint.com)

Moneychimp (moneychimp.com)

Morningstar (morningstar.com)

Mutual Fund Education Alliance
(mfea.com)

Prosper Marketplace, Inc
(prosper.com)

"ScoreInfo" (scoreinfo.org)

SmartMoney (smartmoney.com)

360 Degrees of Financial
Literacy [Provided by
the American Institute of
Certified Public Accountants]
(360financialliteracy.org)

TransUnion (transunion.com)

Vanguard (vanguard.com)

ORGANIZATIONS

Choose to Save or ASEC
Programs [Employee Benefit
Research Institute (EBRI)]
(choosetosave.org)

FDIC Money Smart Information
Booth (69.0.254.19/wwMS/
english/InfoBooth/)

MyMoney.gov (mymoney.gov)

National Credit Union
Administration (NCUA)
(ncua.gov)

National Foundation for Credit
Counseling (nfcc.org)

GENERAL INTEREST

BOOKS & SHORT PUBLICATIONS

Ariely, Dan. *Predictably Irrational.*

Botsman, Rachel, and Roo Rogers.
What's Mine Is Yours.

Leadbeater, Charles. *We-Think.*

Lesonsky, Rieva, and the Staff
of *Entrepreneur* Magazine.
*Entrepreneur Magazine's Start
Your Own Business.*

Pink, Daniel H. *Free Agent Nation.*

Putnam, Robert D. *Bowling Alone.*

Riesman, David, with Nathan Glazer
and Reuel Denney. *The Lonely
Crowd.*

Rushkoff, Douglas. *Program or Be
Programmed.*

Shirky, Clay. *Here Comes Everybody.*

Stim, Richard, and Lisa Guerin.
Whoops! I'm in Business.

ARTICLES & WEB PAGES

Horowitz, Sara, Althea Erickson, and Gabrielle Wuolo. *Independent, Innovative, and Unprotected: How the Old Safety Net Is Failing America's New Workforce.* (fu-res.org)

Horowitz, Sara, Hollis Calhoun, Althea Erickson, and Gabrielle Wuolo. "America's Uncounted Independent Workforce." (fu-res.org)

Intuit. *Intuit 2020 Report: Twenty Trends That Will Shape the Next Decade.* (intuit.com)

WEBSITES

Escape from Cubicle Nation (escapefromcubiclenation.com)

Freelance Folder (freelancefolder.com)

Freelancers Union (freelancersunion.org)

FreelanceSwitch (freelanceswitch.com)

Harvard Business Review Magazine (hbr.org)

StevePavlina.com (stevepavlina.com)

TechCrunch (techcrunch.com)

The Solopreneur Life (thesolopreneurlife.com)

HEALTH

GOVERNMENT RESOURCES

National Institute of Mental Health (NIMH). "Depression." (nimh.nih.gov)

ORGANIZATIONS

MedlinePlus [A Service of the U.S. National Library of Medicine, National Institutes of Health (NIH)] (nlm.nih.gov/medlineplus)

National Health Information Center (NHIC) (health.gov/nhic)

National Institutes of Health (NIH) (nih.gov)

National Sleep Foundation (sleepfoundation.org)

U.S. Department of Health and Human Services (hhs.gov)

U.S. National Library of Medicine (nlm.nih.gov)

INSURANCE

ARTICLES & WEB PAGES

The Actors Fund. "Healthcare and Health Insurance." (actorsfund.org)

The AHIRC Directory [The Artists' Health Insurance Resource Center (created by the Actors Fund)] (ahirc.org)

Consumer Reports. "Insurance." (consumerreports.org):

Freelancers Union. "Insurance and Benefits." (freelancersunion.org)

Freelancers Union. *Independent Workforce Issue Brief: Unemployment Insurance.* (fu-res.org)

Health Insurance Resource Center. "Health Insurance Glossary." (healthinsurance.org)

GOVERNMENT RESOURCES

Bureau of Labor Statistics "Definitions of Health Insurance Terms." (bls.gov)

WEBSITES

The Center for Consumer Information & Insurance Oversight (CCIIO) [Centers for Medicare and Medicaid Services (CMS)] (cciio.cms.gov)

eHealthInsurance (ehealthinsurance.com)

eHealthInsurance (ehealthinsurance.org)

The Entertainment Industry Group Insurance Trust (TEIGIT) (teigit.com)

GoHealth (gohealthinsurance.com)

Healthcare Blue Book (healthcarebluebook.com)

Health Insurance Resource Center (healthinsurance.org)

Health Plan One (healthplanone.com)

Insure.com (insure.com)

InsureMonkey (insuremonkey.com)

Kaiser Family Foundation State Health Facts (statehealthfacts.org)

MyHealthCafe.com (myhealthcafe.com)

ORGANIZATIONS

Insurance Information Institute (I.I.I.) (iii.org)

Centers for Medicare and Medicaid Services (CMS), Department of Health and Human Services (HHS) (cms.gov)

HealthCare.gov (healthcare.gov)

National Association of Health Underwriters (NAHU) (nahu.org)

National Association of Insurance Commissioners (NAIC). Map of NAIC States and Jurisdictions (state insurance departments). (naic.org)

INTERPERSONAL

BOOKS & SHORT PUBLICATIONS

Cialdini, Robert B. *Influence.*

Navarro, Joe, with Toni Sciarra Poynter. *Louder Than Words.*

Post, Peggy, and Anna Post, Lizzie Post, and Daniel Post Senning. *Emily Post's Etiquette.*

Post, Peggy, and Peter Post. *Emily Post's The Etiquette Advantage in Business.*

Tannen, Deborah. *You Just Don't Understand.*

WEBSITES

The Emily Post Institute (emilypost.com)

Meetups (meetup.com) (freelance.meetup.com)

ORGANIZATIONS

American Staffing Association (ASA) (americanstaffing.net)

LEGAL

BOOKS & SHORT PUBLICATIONS

Ackerman, J. S., and Katherine Colgan. *Freelancers Copyright Guide.* National Writers Union [free download] (nwu.org)

Graphic Artists Guild. *Graphic Artists Guild Handbook of Pricing and Ethical Guidelines.*

Warner, Ralph. *Everybody's Guide to Small Claims Court.*

ARTICLES & WEB PAGES

AIGA (American Institute of Graphic Arts). "Standard Form of Agreement for Design Services." (aiga.org)

American Arbitration Association. "Arbitration." (adr.org)

American Bar Association. "Consumers' Guide to Legal Help." (www.americanbar.org)

Editorial Freelancers Association (the-efa.org):

"Resources: Common Rates," Editorial Rates

"Resources: Letter of Agreement"

Edwards, Paul, and Sarah Edwards, in *Entrepreneur* (entrepreneur.com):

"Setting Up a Homebased Business Legally"

"Your Homebased Business' Structure"

Freelancers Union. "Contract Creator." (freelancersunion.org)

Graphic Artists Guild. "Contract Monitor." (graphicartistsguild.org)

Ruckelshaus, Catherine K. "Leveling the Playing Field: Protecting Workers and Businesses Affected by Misclassification: Testimony of Catherine K. Ruckelshaus, National Employment Law Project, Hearing Before the United States Congress Senate Committee on Health, Education, Labor & Pensions." National Employment Law Project, June 17, 2010 (nelp.org)

GOVERNMENT RESOURCES

Harris, Seth D. "Statement of Seth D. Harris, Deputy Secretary, U.S. Department of Labor, Before the Committee on Health, Education, Labor, and Pensions, U.S. Senate, June 17, 2010." U.S. Department of Labor Newsletter, June 3, 2010. (dol.gov)

Internal Revenue Service (IRS). "Independent Contractor (Self-Employed) or Employee?" (irs.gov)

U.S. Copyright Office. "Copyright Basics." (copyright.gov)

U.S. Department of Labor, Employment and Training Administration CareerOneStop. "Licensed Occupations." (acinet.org)

U.S. Government Accountability Office (GAO). *Report to Congressional Requesters: Employee Misclassification: Improved Coordination, Outreach, and Targeting Could Better Ensure Detection and Prevention.* August 2009. [GAO-09-717] (gao.gov)

U.S. Small Business Administration (SBA). "Search for Business Licenses and Permits." (sba.gov)

WEBSITES

Furnari Scher (furnarischer.com)

National Arbitration Forum (arb-forum.com)

The New Ultimates (newultimates.com)

Nolo (nolo.com)

Switchboard (switchboard.com)

Trademarks, Etc. (trademarksetc.com)

ORGANIZATIONS

American Arbitration Association (adr.org)

American Bar Association (americanbar.org)

Bureau of Consumer Protection (BCP) Business Center [Federal Trade Commission (FTC)] (business.ftc.gov)

WEBSITES

BizFilings Business Owner's Toolkit
(bizfilings.com)

Entrepreneur magazine
(entrepreneur.com)

Mashable.com (mashable.com)

ORGANIZATIONS

National Association for the Self-
Employed (NASE) (nase.org)

National Small Business Association
(NSBA) (nsba.biz)

SCORE (Service Corps of Retired
Executives) (score.org)

U.S. Small Business Administration
(SBA) (sba.gov)

TAXES, ACCOUNTING, BOOKKEEPING

BOOKS & SHORT PUBLICATIONS

Thompson, Brigitte A. *Bookkeeping
Basics for Freelance Writers.*

ARTICLES & WEB PAGES

Freelancers Union. "Independent
Workforce Issue Brief: Tax
Challenges." (fu-res.org)

GOVERNMENT RESOURCES

Internal Revenue Service (IRS)
(irs.gov):

A–Z Index for Business

Barter Exchanges

Bartering Income

Bartering Tax Center

Child Care Tax Center

General Instructions for Certain
Information Returns (Forms
1097, 1098, 1099, 3921, 3922,
5498, and W-2G)

How to Choose a Tax Return
Preparer and Avoid Preparer
Fraud

Instructions for the Requester of
Form W-9

IRS Publication 15 (Circular E),
Employer's Tax Guide

IRS Publication 15-A, *Employer's
Supplemental Tax Guide*

IRS Publication 334, *Tax Guide for
Small Businesses*

IRS Publication 463, *Travel,
Entertainment, Gift, and Car
Expenses*

IRS Publication 502, *Medical and
Dental Expenses*

IRS Publication 503, *Child and
Dependent Care Expenses*

IRS Publication 505, *Tax
Withholding and Estimated Tax*

IRS Publication 509, *Tax
Calendars*

IRS Publication 526, *Charitable
Contributions*

IRS Publication 530, *Tax
Information for Homeowners*

IRS Publication 535, *Business
Expenses*

IRS Publication 538, *Accounting
Periods and Methods*

IRS Publication 583, *Starting a
Business and Keeping Records*

IRS Publication 587, *Business Use
of Your Home*

IRS Publication 936, *Home
Mortgage Interest Deduction*

IRS Publication 946, *How to
Depreciate Property*

IRS Publication 969, *Health
Savings Accounts and Other
Tax-Favored Health Plans*

IRS Publication 970, *Tax Benefits
for Education*

Is Your Hobby a For-Profit
Endeavor?

Recordkeeping Tips for Barter
Transactions

Self-Employed Individuals Tax
Center

Self-Employment Tax (Social
Security and Medicare Taxes)

"Tax Topics—Topic 420 Bartering
Income"

"Tax Topics—Topic 509 Business
Use of Home"

"Tax Topics—Topic 704
Depreciation"

U.S. General Services
Administration (gsa.gov)
"Per Diem Rates"

WEBSITES

Datamaster Accounting Services
(datamasteraccounting.com)

ORGANIZATIONS

American Institute of Certified
Public Accountants
(aicpa.org)

INDEX

T

tax deductions, 376–385
  see also income tax
teamwork. *See* subcontracting and
  teamwork
technology, 260, 335, 469–470
  communal office spaces, 57
  computer screens, 61, 65, 346
  office setup, 64–66
  password protection, 56, 171, 443
  tax benefits, 381
  tech support, 40, 57, 237, 304
  wireless networks, 64, 332
  see also email and text messages;
  websites
temporary employment, 84, 88, 95,
  296–297, 469
  defined, 6, 7
  permatemps, 167, 168
testimonials, 160, 303
text messages. *See* email and text
  messages
time management, 324–346
trade secrets, 132, 138, 244
Transient Workers Union, 13, 163,
  299
troubleshooting problems, 173–202
  blame and responsibility, 179
  computer problems, 64
  late-paying clients. *See* deadbeat
  clients
written agreements, 174, 179
Twitter. *See* social media

U

UL (Underwriters' Laboratory)
  safety requirements, 56
undercharging, 34, 40
  see also fee structures
unemployment protection, 95, 164,
  403, 449
unions
  Freelancers Union, 1, 14, 16, 17, 47,
  84, 168, 170
  insurance through, 439
  Transient Workers Union, 13,
  163, 299
unpaid wages, 193–202, 316

V

vacation time, 408–412
virtual assistant (VA), 171
virtual business cards, 49
volunteer and pro bono work, 94,
  97, 309, 420

W

W-2 form, Internal Revenue Service
  reporting, 162, 163, 168, 314,
  370, 389–391

webinars for extra revenue,
  277–278
websites, 233–238
  affiliate marketing, 280
  domain names, 235
  included on business cards, 49
  tax benefits, 381
  see also online marketing
wireless networks, 64, 332
word of mouth networking, 82, 96,
  102, 206, 247, 251
work habits, 324–346
workers' compensation benefits,
  164
works for hire, 131, 138
workspace
  coffee shops and libraries, 54,
  327, 332
  coworking, 57, 66, 144, 310–313,
  319, 327, 470, 479
  home offices, 51–56
  on-site projects, 162
  see also office setup

X

X-factor, explained, 102

ABOUT SARA HOROWITZ

As founder and executive director of Freelancers Union and CEO of the union's Freelancers Insurance Company, Sara Horowitz has been helping workers solve their problems for nearly two decades.

A MacArthur Foundation "Genius" fellow, Sara has long been a leading voice for the emerging economy. She recognized early on the vital role independent workers would play in our networked, interconnected world.

Sara founded Freelancers Union in 1995 on the belief that all workers should have the freedom to build meaningful, connected, and independent lives—backed by a system of mutual and public support. With nearly 200,000 members nationwide, Freelancers Union helps this growing independent sector build creative, cooperative, market-based solutions to today's pressing social challenges.

Sara saw that one of the biggest challenges facing independent workers is the lack of access to affordable health insurance. Rather than wait for the government or the private sector to solve this problem, in 2008 Sara launched Freelancers Insurance Company (FIC), a social-purpose business owned by Freelancers Union. Its mission is to provide independent workers with high-quality, affordable, and portable health insurance. With revenues approaching $100 million, FIC now insures more than 25,000 New Yorkers .

Sara is the daughter of a labor lawyer and granddaughter of a vice president of the International Ladies' Garment Workers' Union. After studying at Cornell University's School of Industrial and Labor Relations, she earned a law degree from SUNY Buffalo Law School and a master's degree from Harvard's John F. Kennedy School of Government. She is a life-long resident of Brooklyn, New York.

Recognized as a leading social entrepreneur, Sara was named one of *Forbes*'s Top 30 Social Entrepreneurs, *Businessweek*'s Top 25 Most Promising Social Entrepreneurs, and *Crain's New York Business*'s 25 People to Watch.